MyEngineeringLab™

Right now, in your course, there are young men and women whose engineering achievements could revolutionize, improve, and sustain future generations.

Don't Let Them Get Away.

Thinking Like an Engineer, Third Edition, together with MyEngineeringLab, is a complete solution for providing an engaging in-class experience that will inspire your students to stay in engineering, while also giving them the practice and scaffolding they need to keep up and be successful in the course.

Learn more at **www.myengineeringlab.com**

Elizabeth A. Stephan • David R. Bowman • William J. Park
Benjamin L. Sill • Matthew W. Ohland

Thinking Like an Engineer

An Active Learning Approach
ENGR 1050, 1060

Fourth Custom Edition for Clemson University

Taken from:
Thinking Like an Engineer: An Active Learning Approach,
Third Edition
by Elizabeth A. Stephan, David R. Bowman, William J. Park,
Benjamin L. Sill, and Matthew W. Ohland

Cover Art: Blue guitar/Evgeny Guityaev/Shutterstock
X-ray of guitar/Gustoimages/Scienc Photo Library

Taken from:

Thinking Like an Engineer: An Active Learning Approach, Third Edition
by Elizabeth A. Stephan, David R. Bowman, William J. Park, Benjamin L. Sill, and
Matthew W. Ohland
Copyright © 2015, 2013, 2011 by Pearson Education, Inc.
Upper Saddle River, New Jersey 07458

This special edition published in cooperation with Pearson Learning Solutions.

Pearson Learning Solutions, 501 Boylston Street, Suite 900, Boston, MA 02116
A Pearson Education Company
www.pearsoned.com

Printed in the United States of America

000200010271898504

CN

7 16

ISBN 10: 1-269-91096-5
ISBN 13: 978-1-269-91096-5

CONTENTS

PREFACE

At our university, all students who wish to major in engineering begin in the General Engineering Program, and after completing a core set of classes, they can declare a specific engineering major. Within this core set of classes, students are required to take math, physics, chemistry, and a two-semester engineering sequence. Our courses have evolved to address not only the changing qualities of our students, but also the changing needs of our customers. The material taught in our courses is the foundation upon which the upper level courses depend for the skills necessary to master more advanced material. It was for these freshman courses that this text was created.

We didn't set out to write a textbook: we simply set out to find a better way to teach our students. Our philosophy was to help students move from a mode of learning, where everything was neatly presented as lecture and handouts where the instructor was looking for the "right" answer, to a mode of learning driven by self-guided inquiry. We wanted students to advance beyond "plug-and-chug" and memorization of problem-solving methods—to ask themselves if their approaches and answers make sense in the physical world. We couldn't settle on any textbooks we liked without patching materials together—one chapter from this text, four chapters from another—so we wrote our own notes. Through them, we tried to convey that engineering isn't always about having the answer—sometimes it's about asking the right questions, and we want students to learn how to ask those sorts of questions. Real-world problems rarely come with all of the information required for their solutions. Problems presented to engineers typically can't be solved by looking at how someone else solved the exact same problem. Part of the fun of engineering is that every problem presents a unique challenge and requires a unique solution. Engineering is also about arriving at an answer and being able to justify the "why" behind your choice, and equally important, the "why not" of the other choices.

We realized quickly, however, that some students are not able to learn without sufficient scaffolding. Structure and flexibility must be managed carefully. Too much structure results in rigidity and unnecessary uniformity of solutions. On the other hand, too much flexibility provides insufficient guidance, and students flounder down many blind alleys, thus making it more difficult to acquire new knowledge. The tension between these two must be managed constantly. We are a large public institution, and our student body is very diverse. Our hope is to provide each student with the amount of scaffolding they need to be successful. Some students will require more background work than others. Some students will need to work five problems, and others may need to work 50. We talk a great deal to our students about how each learner is unique. Some students need to listen to a lecture; some need to read the text over three times, and others just need to try a skill and make mistakes to discover what they still don't understand. We have tried to provide enough variety for each type of learner throughout.

Over the years, we have made difficult decisions on exactly what topics, and how much of each topic, to teach. We have refined our current text to focus on mastering four areas, each of which is introduced below.

PART 1: ENGINEERING ESSENTIALS

There are three threads that bind the first six chapters in Engineering Essentials together. The first is expressed in the part title: all are essential for a successful career in engineering. The second is communications. Part 1 concludes with an introduction to a problem-solving methodology.

First, as an aspiring engineer, it is important that students attempt to verify that engineering is not only a career that suits their abilities but also one in which they will find personal reward and satisfaction.

Second, practicing engineers often make decisions that will affect not only the lives of people but also the viability of the planetary ecosystem that affects all life on Earth. Without a firm grounding in making decisions based on ethical principles, there is an increased probability that undesirable or even disastrous consequences may occur.

Third, most engineering projects are too large for one individual to accomplish alone; thus, practicing engineers must learn to function effectively as a team, putting aside their personal differences and combining their unique talents, perspectives, and ideas to achieve the goal.

Finally, communications bind it all together. Communication, whether written, graphical, or spoken, is essential to success in engineering.

This part ends off where all good problem solving should begin—with estimation and a methodology. It's always best to have a good guess at any problem before trying to solve it more precisely. SOLVEM provides a framework for solving problems that encourages creative observation as well as methodological rigor.

PART 2: UBIQUITOUS UNITS

The world can be described using relatively few dimensions. We need to know what these are and how to use them to analyze engineering situations. Dimensions, however, are worthless in allowing engineers to find the numeric solution to a problem. Understanding units is essential to determine the correct numeric answers to problems. Different disciplines use different units to describe phenomena (particularly with respect to the properties of materials such as viscosity, thermal conductivity, density and so on). Engineers must know how to convert from one unit system to another. Knowledge of dimensions allows engineers to improve their problem-solving abilities by revealing the interplay of various parameters.

PART 3: SCRUPULOUS WORKSHEETS

When choosing an analysis tool to teach students, our first pick is Excel™. Students enter college with varying levels of experience with Excel. To allow students who are novice users to learn the basics without hindering more advanced users, we have placed the basics of Excel in the Appendix material, which is available online. To help students determine if they need to review the Appendix material, an activity has been included in the introductions to Chapter 10 (Worksheets), Chapter 11 (Graphing), and Chapter 12 (Trendlines) to direct students to Appendices B, C, and D, respectively.

Once students have mastered the basics, each chapter in this part provides a deeper usage of Excel in each category. Some of this material extends beyond a simple introduction to Excel, and often, we teach the material in this unit by jumping around, covering half of each chapter in the first semester, and the rest of the material in the second semester course.

Chapter 12 introduces students to the idea of similarities among the disciplines, and how understanding a theory in one application can often aid in understanding a similar theory in a different application. We also emphasize the understanding of models (trendlines) as possessing physical meaning. Chapter 13 discusses a process for determining a mathematical model when presented with experimental data and some advanced material on dealing with limitations of Excel.

Univariate statistics and statistical process control wrap up this part of the book by providing a way for engineering students to describe both distributions and trends.

PART 4: PUNCTILIOUS PROGRAMMING

Part 4 (Punctilious Programming) covers a variety of topics common to any introductory programming textbook. In contrast to a traditional programming textbook, this part approaches each topic from the perspective of how each can be used in unison with the others as a powerful engineering problem-solving tool. The topics presented in Part 4 are introduced as if the student has no prior programming ability and are continually reiterated throughout the remaining chapters.

For this textbook we chose MATLAB™ as the programming language because it is commonly used in many engineering curricula. The topics covered provide a solid foundation of how computers can be used as a tool for problem solving and provide enough scaffolding for transfer of programming knowledge into other languages commonly used by engineers (such as C/C++/Java).

THE "OTHER" STUFF WE'VE INCLUDED...

Throughout the book, we have included sections on surviving engineering, time management, goal setting, and study skills. We did not group them into a single chapter, but have scattered them throughout the part introductions to assist students on a topic when they are most likely to need it. For example, we find students are much more open to discuss time management in the middle of the semester rather than the beginning.

In addition, we have called upon many practicing and aspiring engineers to help us explain the "why" and "what" behind engineering. They offer their "Wise Words" throughout this text. We have included our own set of "Wise Words" as the introduction to each topic here as a glimpse of what inspired us to include certain topics.

NEW TO THIS EDITION

The third edition of *Thinking Like an Engineer: An Active Learning Approach* (TLAE) contains new material and revisions based off of the comments from faculty teaching with our textbook, the recommendations of the reviewers of our textbook, and most importantly, the feedback from our students. We continue to strive to include the latest software releases; in this edition, we have upgraded to Microsoft Office (Excel) 2013 and MATLAB 2013. We have added approximately 30% new questions. In addition, we have added new material that reflects the constant changing face of engineering education because many of our upperclassman teaching assistants frequently comment to us "I wish I had ___ when I took this class."

New to this edition, by chapter:

- Chapter 1: Everyday Engineering

  - New section on the field of Engineering Technology.

- Chapter 3: Design and Teamwork

  - New sequence of topics, to allow expanded discussion on defining the problem, determining criteria, brainstorming, making decisions and testing solutions.

- Chapter 8: Universal Units

  - New section on Electrical Concepts.

- Chapter 14: Statistics

  - Combined material from Chapters 14 (Excel) and 18 (MATLAB) in TLAE 2e to make a single unified chapter on Statistics.

- Chapter 16: Variables and Data Types

  - New material on the various ways MATLAB stores and processes data.
  - Selected material from TLAE 2e has been moved to this chapter, including cell arrays.

- Chapter 18: Input/Output in MATLAB

  - Combined material from Chapter 20 in TLAE 2e on using Microsoft Excel to input data to and output data from MATLAB.

- Chapter 19: Logic and Conditionals

  - New sections on Switch Statements and using Errors and Warnings.

- Online Appendix Materials

  - Umbrella Projects have all been moved online to allow for easier customizing of the project for each class.

HOW TO USE

As we have alluded to previously, this text contains many different types of instruction to address different types of learners. There are two main components to this text: hard copy and online.

In the hardcopy, the text is presented topically rather than sequentially, but hopefully with enough autonomy for each piece to stand alone. For example, we routinely discuss only part of the Excel material in our first semester course, and leave the rest to the second semester. We hope this will give you the flexibility to choose how deeply into any given topic you wish to dive, depending on the time you have, the starting abilities of your students, and the outcomes of your course. More information about topic sequence options can be found in the instructor's manual.

Within the text, there are several checkpoints for students to see if they understand the material. Within the reading are **Comprehension Checks**, with the answers provided in the back of the book. Our motivation for including Comprehension Checks within the text rather than include them as end of part questions is to maintain the active spirit of the classroom within the reading, allowing the students to self-evaluate their understanding of the material in preparation for class—to enable students to be self-directed learners, we must encourage them to self-evaluate regularly. At the end of each chapter, **In-Class Activities** are given to reinforce the material in each chapter. In-Class Activities exist to stimulate active conversation within pairs and groups of students working through the material. We generally keep the focus on student effort, and ask them to keep working the problem until they arrive at the right answer. This provides them with a set of worked out problems, using their own logic, before they are asked to tackle more difficult problems. The **Review** sections provide additional questions, often combining skills in the current chapter with previous concepts to help students climb to the next level of understanding. By providing these three types of practice, students are encouraged to reflect on their understanding in preparing for class, during class, and at the end of each chapter as they prepare to transfer their knowledge to other areas. Finally we have provided a series of **Umbrella Projects** to allow students to apply skills that they have mastered to larger-scope problems. We have found the use of these problems extremely helpful in providing context for the skills that they learn throughout a unit.

Understanding that every student learns differently, we have included several media components in addition to traditional text. Each section within each chapter has an accompanying set of **video lecture slides** ▶. Within these slides, the examples presented are unique from those in the text to provide another set of sample solutions. The slides are presented with **voiceover**, which has allowed us to move away from traditional in-class lecture. We expect the students to listen to the slides outside of class, and then in class we typically spend time working problems, reviewing assigned problems, and providing **"wrap-up" lectures**, which are mini-versions of the full lectures to summarize what they should have gotten from the assignment. We expect the students to come to class with questions from the reading and lecture that we can then help clarify. We find with this method, the students pay more attention, as the terms and problems are already familiar to them, and they are more able to verbalize what they don't know. Furthermore, they can always go back and listen to the lectures again to reinforce their knowledge as many times as they need.

Some sections of this text are difficult to lecture, and students will learn this material best by **working through examples**. This is especially true with Excel and MATLAB, so you will notice that many of the lectures in these sections are shorter than previous material. The examples are scripted the first time a skill is presented, and students are expected to have their laptop open and work through the examples (not just read them). When students ask us questions in this section, we often start the answer by asking them to "show us your work from Chapter XX." If the student has not actually worked the examples in that chapter, we tell them to do so first; often, this will answer their questions.

After the first few basic problems, in many cases where we are discussing more advanced skills than data entry, we have **provided starting worksheets and code** in the online version by "hanging" the worksheets within the online text. Students can access the starting data through the online copy of the book. In some cases, though, it is difficult to explain a skill on paper, or even with slides, so for these instances we have included **videos**.

Finally, for the communication section, we have provided **templates** for several types of reports and presentations. These can also be accessed in the Pearson eText version, available with adoption of MyEngineeringLab™. Visit www.pearsonhighered.com/TLAE for more information.

MyEngineeringLab™

Thinking Like an Engineer, Third Edition, together with MyEngineeringLab provides an engaging in-class experience that will inspire your students to stay in engineering, while also giving them the practice and scaffolding they need to keep up and be successful in the course. It's a complete digital solution featuring:

- A customized study plan for each student with remediation activities provides an opportunity for self paced learning for students at all different levels of preparedness.
- Automatically graded homework review problems from the book and self study quizzes give immediate feedback to the student and provide comprehensive gradebook tracking for instructors.
- Interactive tutorials with additional algorithmically generated exercises provide opportunity for point-of-use help and for more practice.
- "Show My Work" feature allows instructors to see the entire solution, not only the graded answer.
- Learning objectives mapped to ABET outcomes provide comprehensive reporting tools.
- Selected spreadsheet exercises are provided in a simulated Excel environment; these exercises are automatically graded and reported back to the gradebook.
- Pre-built writing assignments provide a single place to create, track, and grade writing assignments, provide writing resources, and exchange meaningful, personalized feedback to students.
- Available with or without the full eText.

If adopted, access to MyEngineeringLab can be bundled with the book or purchased separately. For a fully digital offering, learn more at www.myengineeringlab.com or www.pearsonhighered.com/TLAE.

ADDITIONAL RESOURCES FOR INSTRUCTORS

Instructor's Manual—Available to all adopters, this provides a complete set of solutions for all activities and review exercises. For the In-Class Activities, suggested guided inquiry questions along with time frame guidelines are included. Suggested content sequencing and descriptions of how to couple assignments to the Umbrella Projects are also provided.

PowerPoints—A complete set of lecture PowerPoint slides make course planning as easy as possible.

Sample Exams—Available to all adopters, these will assist in creating tests and quizzes for student assessment.

MyEngineeringLab—Provides web-based assessment, tutorial, homework and course management. www.myengineeringlab.com

All requests for instructor resources are verified against our customer database and/or through contacting the requestor's institution. Contact your local Pearson/Prentice Hall representative for additional information.

WHAT DOES THINKING LIKE AN ENGINEER MEAN?

We are often asked about the title of the book. We thought we'd take a minute and explain what this means, to each of us. Our responses are included in alphabetical order.

For me, thinking like an engineer is about creatively finding a solution to some problem. In my pre-college days, I was very excited about music. I began my musical pursuits by learning the fundamentals of music theory by playing in middle school band and eventually worked my way into different bands in high school (orchestra, marching and, jazz band) and branching off into teaching myself how to play guitar. I love playing and listening to music because it gives me an outlet to create and discover art. I pursued engineering for the same reason; as an engineer, you work in a field that creates or improves designs or processes. For me, thinking like an engineer is exactly like thinking like a musician—through my fundamentals, I'm able to be creative, yet methodical, in my solutions to problems.

D. Bowman, Computer Engineer

Thinking like an engineer is about solving problems with whatever resources are most available—or fixing something that has broken with materials that are just lying around. Sometimes, it's about thinking ahead and realizing what's going to happen before something breaks or someone gets hurt—particularly in thinking about what it means to fail safe—to design how something will fail when it fails. Thinking like an engineer is figuring out how to communicate technical issues in a way that anyone can understand. It's about developing an instinct to protect the public trust—an integrity that emerges automatically.

M. Ohland, Civil Engineer

To me, understanding the way things work is the foundation on which all engineering is based. Although most engineers focus on technical topics related to their specific discipline, this understanding is not restricted to any specific field, but applies to everything! One never knows when some seemingly random bit of knowledge, or some pattern discerned in a completely disparate field of inquiry, may prove critical in solving an engineering problem. Whether the field of investigation is Fourier analysis, orbital mechanics, Hebert boxes, personality types, the Chinese language, the life cycle of mycetozoans, or the evolution of the music of Western civilization, the more you understand about things, the more effective an engineer you can be. Thus, for me, thinking like an engineer is intimately, inextricably, and inexorably intertwined with the Quest for Knowledge. Besides, the world is a truly fascinating place if one bothers to take the time to investigate it.

W. Park, Electrical Engineer

Engineering is a bit like the game of golf. No two shots are ever exactly the same. In engineering, no two problems or designs are ever exactly the same. To be successful, engineers need a bag of clubs (math, chemistry, physics, English, social studies) and then need to have the training to be able to select the right combination of clubs to move from the tee to the green and make a par (or if we are lucky, a birdie). In short, engineers need to be taught to THINK.

B. Sill, Aerospace Engineer

I like to refer to engineering as the color grey. Many students enter engineering because they are "good at math and science." I like to refer to these disciplines as black and white—there is one way to integrate an equation and one way to balance a chemical reaction. Engineering is grey, a blend of math and science that does not necessarily have one clear answer. The answer can change depending on the criteria of the problem. Thinking like an engineer is about training your mind to conduct the methodical process of problem solving. It is examining a problem from many different angles, considering the good, the bad and the ugly in every process or product. It is thinking creatively to discover ways of solving problems, or preventing issues from becoming problems. It's about finding a solution in the grey and presenting it in black and white.

E. Stephan, Chemical Engineer

Lead author note: When writing this preface, I asked each of my co-authors to answer this question. As usual, I got a wide variety of interpretations and answers. This is typical of the way we approach everything we do, except that I usually try and mesh the responses into one voice. In this instance, I let each response remain unique. As you progress throughout this text, you will (hopefully) see glimpses of each of us interwoven with the one voice. We hope that through our uniqueness, we can each reach a different group of students and present a balanced approach to problem solving, and, hopefully, every student can identify with at least one of us.

—Beth Stephan
Clemson University
Clemson, SC

ACKNOWLEDGMENTS

When we set out to formalize our instructional work, we wanted to portray engineering as a reality, not the typical flashy fantasy portrayed by most media forums. We called on many of our professional and personal relationships to help us present engineering in everyday terms. During a lecture to our freshman, Dr. Ed Sutt [PopSci's 2006 Inventor of the Year for the HurriQuake Nail] gave the following advice: *A good engineer can reach an answer in two calls: the first, to find out who the expert is; the second, to talk to the expert.* Realizing we are not experts, we have called on many folks to contribute articles. To our experts who contributed articles for this text, we thank: Dr. Lisa Benson, Dr. Neil Burton, Jan Comfort, Jessica (Pelfrey) Creel, Jason Huggins, Leidy Klotz, and Troy Nunmaker.

To Dr. Lisa Benson, thank you for allowing us to use "Science as Art" for the basis of many photos that we have chosen for this text. To explain "Science as Art": *Sometimes, science and art meet in the middle. For example, when a visual representation of science or technology has an unexpected aesthetic appeal, it becomes a connection for scientists, artists and the general public. In celebration of this connection, Clemson University faculty and students are challenged to share powerful and inspiring visual images produced in laboratories and workspaces for the "Science as Art" exhibit.* For more information, please visit www.scienceasart.org. To the creators of the art, thank you for letting us showcase your work in this text: Martin Beagley, Dr. Caye Drapcho, Eric Fenimore, Dr. Scott Husson, Dr. Jaishankar Kutty, Dr. Kathleen Richardson, and Dr. Ken Webb. A special thanks Russ Werneth for getting us the great Hubble teamwork photo.

To the Rutland Institute for Ethics at Clemson University: The four-step procedure outlined in Chapter 2 on Ethics is based on the toolbox approach presented in the Ethics Across the Curriculum Seminar. Our thanks to Dr. Daniel Wueste, Director, and the other Rutlanders (Kelly Smith, Stephen Satris and Charlie Starkey) for their input into this chapter.

To Jonathan Feinberg and all the contributors to the Wordle (http://www.wordle.net) project, thank you for the tools to create for the Wordle images in the introduction sections. We hope our readers enjoy this unique way of presenting information, and are inspired to create their own Wordle!

To our friends and former students who contributed their Wise Words: Tyler Andrews, Corey Balon, Ed Basta, Sergey Belous, Brittany Brubaker, Tim Burns, Ashley Childers, Jeremy Comardelle, Matt Cuica, Jeff Dabling, Christina Darling, Ed D'Avignon, Brian Dieringer, Lauren Edwards, Andrew Flowerday, Stacey Forkner, Victor Gallas Cervo, Lisa Gascoigne, Khadijah Glast, Tad Hardy, Colleen Hill, Tom Hill, Becky Holcomb, Beth Holloway, Selden Houghton, Allison Hu, Ryan Izard, Lindy Johnson, Darryl Jones, Maria Koon, Rob Kriener, Jim Kronberg, Rachel Lanoie, Mai Lauer, Jack Meena, Alan Passman, Mike Peterson, Candace Pringle, Derek Rollend,

Eric Roper, Jake Sadie, Janna Sandel, Ellen Styles, Adam Thompson, Kaycie (Smith) Timmons, Devin Walford, Russ Werneth, and Aynsley Zollinger.

To our fellow faculty members, for providing inspiration, ideas, and helping us find countless mistakes: Dr. Steve Brandon, Dr. Ashley Childers, Andrew Clarke, Dr. David Ewing, Dr. Sarah Grigg, Dr. Richard Groff, Dr. Apoorva Kapadia, Dr. Sabrina Lau, Dr. Jonathan Maier, Dr. William Martin, Jessica Merino, and John Minor. You guys are the other half of this team that makes this the best place on earth to work! We could not have done this without you.

To the staff of the GE program, we thank you for your support of us and our students: Kelli Blankenship, Lib Crockett, Chris Porter, and all of our terrific advising staff both past and present. To the administration at Clemson, we thank you for your continued support of our program: Associate Dean Dr. Randy Collins, Interim Director Dr. Don Beasley, Dean Dr. Anand Gramopadhye, Provost Nadim Aziz. Special thanks to President Jim Barker for his inspirational leadership of staying the course and giving meaning to "One Clemson." We wish him all the best as he retired from the Presidency this December.

To the thousands of students who used this text in various forms over the years—thanks for your patience, your suggestions, and your criticism. You have each contributed not only to the book, but to our personal inspirations to keep doing what we do.

To all the reviewers who provided such valuable feedback to help us improve. We appreciate the time and energy needed to review this material, and your thoughtful comments have helped push us to become better.

To the great folks at Prentice Hall—this project would not be a reality without all your hard work. To Eric Hakanson, without that chance meeting this project would not have begun! Thanks to Holly Stark for her belief in this project and in us! Thanks to Scott Disanno for keeping us on track and having such a great vision to display our hard work. You have put in countless hours on this edition—thanks for making us look great! Thanks to Tim Galligan and the fabulous Pearson sales team all over the country for promoting our book to other schools and helping us allow so many students to start "Thinking Like Engineers"! We would not have made it through this without all of the Pearson team efforts and encouragement!

FINALLY, ON A PERSONAL NOTE

DRB: Thanks to my parents and sister for supporting my creative endeavors with nothing but encouragement and enthusiasm. To my grandparents, who value science, engineering, and education to be the most important fields of study. To my co-authors, who continue to teach me to think like an engineer. To Dana, you are the glue that keeps me from falling to pieces. Thank you for your support, love, laughter, inspiration, and determination, among many other things. You are entirely too rad. I love you.

MWO: My wife Emily has my love, admiration, and gratitude for all she does, including holding the family together. For my children, who share me with my students—Charlotte, whose "old soul" touches all who take the time to know her; Carson, who is quietly inspiring; and Anders, whose love of life and people endears him to all. I acknowledge my father Theodor, who inspired me to be an educator; my mother Nancy, who helped me understand people; my sister Karen, who lit a pathway in engineering; my brother Erik, who showed me that one doesn't need to be loud to be a leader; and my mother-in-law Nancy Winfrey, who shared the wisdom of a long career. I recognize those who helped me create an engineering education career path: Fred Orthlieb, Civil and Coastal

Engineering at the University of Florida, Marc Hoit, Duane Ellifritt, Cliff Hays, Mary Grace Kantowski, and John Lybas, the NSF's SUCCEED Coalition, Tim Anderson, Clemson's College of Engineering and Science and General Engineering, Steve Melsheimer, Ben Sill, and Purdue's School of Engineering Education.

WJP: Choosing only a few folks to include in an acknowledgment is a seriously difficult task, but I have managed to reduce it to five. First, Beth Stephan has been the guiding force behind this project, without whom it would never have come to fruition. In addition, she has shown amazing patience in putting up with my shenanigans and my weird perspectives. Next, although we exist in totally different realities, my parents have always supported me, particularly when I was a newly married, destitute graduate student fresh off the farm. Third, my son Isaac, who has the admirable quality of being willing to confront me with the truth when I am behaving badly, and for this I am grateful. Finally, and certainly most importantly, to Lila, my partner of more than one-third century, I owe a debt beyond anything I could put into words. Although life with her has seldom been easy, her influence has made me a dramatically better person.

BLS: To my amazing family, who always picked up the slack when I was off doing "creative" things, goes all my gratitude. To Anna and Allison, you are wonderful daughters who both endured and "experienced" the development of many "in class, hands on" activities—know that I love you and thank you. To Lois who has always been there with her support and without whining for over 40 years, all my love. Finally, to my co-authors who have tolerated my eccentricities and occasional tardiness with only minimum grumbling, you make great teammates.

EAS: To my co-authors, for tolerating all my strange demands, my sleep-deprived ravings and the occasional "I need this now" hysteria—and it has gotten worse with the third edition—you guys are the best! To my mom, Kay and Denny—thanks for your love and support. To Khadijah & Steven, wishes for you to continue to conquer the world! To Brock and Katie, I love you both a bushel and a peck. You are the best kids in the world, and the older you get the more you inspire me to be great at my job. Thank you for putting up with all the late nights, the lack of home-cooked meals, and the mature-beyond-your-years requirements I've asked of you. Finally, to Sean . . . last time I swore the rough parts were done, but man this edition was tough to finish up! I love you more than I can say—and know that even when I forget to say it, I still believe in us. "Show a little faith, there's magic in the night . . ."

Part 2

UBIQUITOUS UNITS

You may not be sure what the word "ubiquitous" means ... we suggest you look it up!

Ubiquitous: **yoo·bik·we·teous** ~ adjective;

   definition _____

LEARNING OBJECTIVES

The overall learning objectives for this unit include:
Chapter 7:

- Identify basic and derived dimensions and units.
- Express observations in appropriate units and perform conversions when necessary. Apply the laws governing equation development to aid in problem solutions.

Chapter 8:

- Apply basic principles from mathematical and physical sciences, such as the conservation of energy and the ideal gas law, to analyze engineering problems.
- Convert units for physical and chemical parameters such as density, energy, pressure, and power as required for different systems of units.
- Use dimensions and units to aid in the solution of complex problems.

Chapter 9:

- Identify when a quantity is dimensionless.
- Using a graph of dimensionless groups, extract information from the plot about the physical system.
- Given a set of parameters, determine appropriate dimensionless groups using Rayleigh's Method.
- Determine the Reynolds Number; interpret the Reynolds Number for fluid flow in a pipe.

Engraving from Mechanics Magazine published in London in 1824

Imagine you are in a small boat with a large stone in the bottom of the boat. The boat is floating in the swimming pool in the campus recreation center. What happens to the level of water in the pool if you throw the stone overboard? Assume no water splashes out of the pool or into the boat.

Archimedes was a Greek scientist and mathematician. Most people know Archimedes for his discovery of buoyancy. According to legend, the king asked Archimedes to determine if his new crown was made of pure gold. Before this, no method had been developed for measuring the density of irregularly shaped objects. While taking a bath, Archimedes noted that the water rose in proportion to the amount of his body in the tub. He shouted "Eureka (I have found it)!" and ran though the streets naked because he was so excited he forgot to get dressed. While Archimedes never recounts this tale himself, he does outline Archimedes' principle in his treatise *On Floating Bodies:* **A body immersed in a fluid is buoyed up by a force equal to the weight of the displaced fluid**. Before we can begin to answer the question of the boat and the stone (the answer is found on the final page of Chapter 8), we need to understand the principles of dimensions and units

NOTE

"Give me a place to stand on, and I will move the Earth."
—*Archimedes*

In addition to buoyancy, Archimedes made many contributions to science, including the explanation of the lever, and is considered one of the greatest mathematicians.

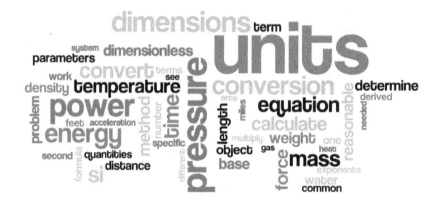

CHAPTER 7
FUNDAMENTAL DIMENSIONS AND BASE UNITS

As aspiring engineers you must learn to distinguish among many terms that laymen tend to use interchangeably. You must also understand the technical meaning of terms that are misunderstood by those untrained in science or engineering. One term that is often misunderstood is "dimension." To most people, a dimension refers to a straight line (length, one dimension), a flat surface (area, two dimensions), or a solid object (volume, three dimensions). Some slightly more educated folks might include time as a fourth dimension. The number of concepts classified as dimensions is far broader.

A **dimension** is a measurable physical idea; it generally consists solely of a word description with no numbers. A **unit** allows us to quantify a dimension—to state a number describing how much of that dimension exists in a specific situation. Units are defined by convention and related to an accepted standard.

- Length is a dimension. There are many units for length, such as mile, foot, meter, light-year, and fathom.
- Time is a dimension. There are many units for time, such as second, minute, hour, day, fortnight, year, and century.
- Temperature is a dimension. There are many units for temperature, such as Celsius, Fahrenheit, and kelvin.

The dimensions of length, time, and temperature are familiar to us, but in reality, we do not often use these words since they are fairly vague.

We do not say . . .	We do say . . .
It is really a long **length** to Lumberton.	Lumberton is about 175 **miles** away.
Bake the cake for a **time**.	Bake the cake for 35 **minutes**.
Set the oven to a high **temperature**.	Set the oven to 450 **degrees Fahrenheit**.

The difference between the left and the right columns is that the statements on the left refer to dimensions and those on the right refer to established standards or units.

7.1 THE METRIC SYSTEM

LEARN TO: List the seven fundamental dimensions and their symbol

List the seven base SI units, their symbol, and the matching fundamental dimensions

Express units using the official SI rules

NOTE

Within this text, dimensions are shown in braces { } and units in brackets [ ].

The SI system (Le Système International d'Unités), commonly known as the metric system, is the standard set of units for most of the world. Originally developed by French scientists under King Louis XVI, the SI system was finalized by the international scientific community as the standard unit system in 1971. This system defines seven base units, from which all others are derived. Table 7-1 shows the seven base units and their corresponding fundamental dimensions.

Table 7-1 Fundamental dimensions and base units

Dimension	Symbol	Unit	Symbol
Length	L	meter	m
Mass	M	kilogram	kg
Time	T	second	s
Temperature	Θ	kelvin	K
Amount of substance	N	mole	mol
Light intensity	J	candela	cd
Electric current	I	ampere	A

SI Prefixes

The SI system is based upon multiples of 10. By using an **SI prefix** when reporting numbers, we avoid scientific notation or long strings of zeros. For example, instead of saying, "The distance to Atlanta is 198,000 meters," we would say, "The distance to Atlanta is 198 kilometers."

For a list of SI prefixes, refer to the inside cover of this book or to Table 7-2. Note that the abbreviations for all SI prefixes from kilo- down to yocto- are lowercase, whereas from Mega- up to Yotta- are uppercase.

Determining the appropriate SI prefix to use becomes simple when the number is placed in engineering notation: just examine the exponent.

As a reminder, scientific and engineering notation are defined as follows:

Scientific notation is typically expressed in the form $\#.\#\#\# \times 10^N$, where the digit to the left of the decimal point is the most significant nonzero digit of the value being represented. Sometimes, the digit to the right of the decimal point is the most significant digit instead. The number of decimal places can vary, but is usually two to four. N is an integer, and multiplying by 10^N serves to locate the true position of the decimal point.

Engineering notation is expressed in the form $\#\#\#.\#\#\# \times 10^M$, where M is an integer multiple of 3, and the number of digits to the left of the decimal point is 1, 2, or 3 as needed to yield a power of 10 that is indeed a multiple of 3. The number of digits to the right of the decimal point is typically between two and four.

Table 7-2 SI prefixes (example: 1 millimeter [mm] = 1 × 10⁻³ meters [m])

Numbers Less than One			Numbers Greater than One		
Power of 10	Prefix	Abbreviation	Power of 10	Prefix	Abbreviation
10^{-1}	deci-	d	10^{1}	deca-	da
10^{-2}	centi-	c	10^{2}	hecto-	h
10^{-3}	milli-	m	10^{3}	kilo-	k
10^{-6}	micro-	μ	10^{6}	Mega-	M
10^{-9}	nano-	n	10^{9}	Giga-	G
10^{-12}	pico-	p	10^{12}	Tera-	T
10^{-15}	femto-	f	10^{15}	Peta-	P
10^{-18}	atto-	a	10^{18}	Exa-	E
10^{-21}	zepto-	z	10^{21}	Zetta-	Z
10^{-24}	yocto-	y	10^{24}	Yotta-	Y

● **EXAMPLE 7-1**

Express the following values using scientific notation, engineering notation, and using the correct SI prefix.

Standard	Scientific	Engineering	With Prefix
(a) 43,480,000 m	4.348×10^{7} m	43.48×10^{6} m	43.48 Mm
(b) 0.0000003060 V	3.060×10^{-7} V	306.0×10^{-9} V	306.0 nV
(c) 9,860,000,000 J	9.86×10^{9} J	9.86×10^{9} J	9.86 GJ
(d) 0.0351 s	3.51×10^{-2} s	35.1×10^{-3} s	35.1 ms

Note that the numeric values of the mantissa are the same in the last two columns, and the exponent in engineering notation specifies the metric prefix.

COMPREHENSION CHECK 7–1

Express the following values using scientific notation, engineering notation, and using the correct SI prefix.

Standard	Scientific	Engineering	With Prefix
(a) 3,100 J			
(b) 26,510,000 W			
(c) 459,000 s			
(d) 0.00000032 g			

Official SI Rules

When reporting units using the SI system, follow these official rules.

- **If a unit abbreviation appears as a capital letter, it has been named after a person; all other abbreviations appear as lowercase letters.** For example, the abbreviation "N" stands for "newton," the SI unit of force named after Isaac Newton.

  Correct: The book weighs 5 N.   Incorrect: The book weighs 5 n.
  Correct: The rod is 5 m long.   Incorrect: The rod is 5 M long.

  The one exception to this rule is the volumetric unit of liter. The abbreviation is shown as L, since a lowercase l can be confused with both the number 1 and the uppercase letter I.

- **Symbols of units are not shown as plural.**

  Correct: 10 centimeters = 10 cm   Incorrect: 10 centimeters ≠ 10 cms

- **Symbols are not shown with a period unless they appear at the end of a sentence.**

  Correct: The rod is 5 mm long.   Incorrect: The rod is 5 mm. long.

- **Symbols are written in upright Roman type (m, k, L) to distinguish them from mathematical variables (m, k, l), which are indicated by italics.**

- **One space separates the number and symbol, except with the degree symbol referring to an angle.**

  Correct: 5 mm or 5°   Incorrect: 5mm or 5 °

- **Spaces or commas may be used to group digits by threes.**

  Correct: 1 000 000 or 1,000,000

- **Symbols for derived units formed by multiple units are joined by a space or interpunct (the center dot). Care must be taken to avoid confusing SI prefixes with units.**

  Correct: kg m or kg · m   Incorrect: kgm or mkg

  This is particularly important when confusion might arise. For example, "ms" stands for millisecond, but "m s" stands for meter second. In cases like this, using a center dot is preferable since it is less likely to be misunderstood.

- **Symbols for derived units formed by dividing units are joined by a virgule (the "slash" /) or shown with a negative exponent. Care must be taken to appropriately display the entire denominator.**

  Correct: $N/(m\ s^2)$ or $N\ m^{-1}\ s^{-2}$ Incorrect: $N/m\ s^2$

- **Do not combine prefixes to form compound prefixes. Use the single correct prefix.**

  Correct: picojoules (pJ)   Incorrect: millinanojoules (mnJ)
  Correct: Gigaseconds (Gs)   Incorrect: kiloMegaseconds (kMs)

COMPREHENSION CHECK 7-2

Indicate if the following units are correctly expressed according to the official SI rules. If the unit is incorrectly displayed, show the correction.

(a) Reading this sentence took 5 Secs.
(b) The average person's pupils are 60mms. apart.
(c) One gallon is the same as 380 microkiloliters.

7.2 OTHER UNIT SYSTEMS

Prior to the adoption of the SI unit system by the scientific community, several other systems of units were used and are still used today, particularly in the United States. The other countries that use non-SI units are Liberia and Myanmar. Great Britain officially converted to metric in 1965, but it is still common there to see nonmetric units used in communications for the general public.

It is important to know how to convert between all unit systems. Table 7-3 compares several systems. The system listed as AES (American Engineering System) is in common use by the general public in the United States. The USCS (United States Customary System) is commonly called "English" units.

Table 7-3 Comparison of unit system, with corresponding abbreviations

Dimension	SI (MKS)	AES	USCS
Length {L}	meter [m]	foot [ft]	foot [ft]
Mass {M}	kilogram [kg]	pound-mass [lb$_m$]	slug
Time {T}	second [s]	second [s]	second [s]
Relative temperature {Θ}	Celsius [°C]	Fahrenheit [°F]	Fahrenheit [°F]
Absolute temperature {Θ}	kelvin [K]	Rankine [°R]	Rankine [°R]

Accepted Non-SI Units

The units in Table 7-4 are not technically in the SI system, but due to their common usage, are acceptable for use in combination with the base SI units.

Table 7-4 Acceptable non-SI units

Unit	Equivalent SI	Unit	Equivalent SI
Astronomical unit [AU]	1 AU = 1.4959787×10^{11} m	day [d]	1 d = 86,400 s
Atomic mass unit [amu]	1 amu = $1.6605402 \times 10^{-24}$ g	hour [h]	1 h = 3,600 s
Electronvolt [eV]	1 eV = $1.6021773 \times 10^{-19}$ J	minute [min]	1 min = 60 s
Liter [L]	1 L = 0.001 m^3	year [yr]	1 yr = 3.16×10^7 s
		degree [°]	1° = 0.0175 rad or 1 rad = 57.3°

NOTE

1 liter does not equal 1 cubic meter!

7.3 CONVERSION PROCEDURE FOR UNITS

LEARN TO: Follow the 5-step conversion procedure to convert from one unit to a different unit within a fundamental dimension

LENGTH

1 m = 3.28 ft

1 km = 0.621 mi

1 ft = 12 in

1 in = 2.54 cm

1 mi = 5,280 ft

1 yd = 3 ft

We use conversion factors to translate from one set of units to another. This must be done correctly and consistently to obtain the right answers. Some common conversion factors can be found inside the cover of this book, categorized by dimension. Although many more conversions are available, all the work for a typical engineering class can be accomplished using the conversions found in this table.

Let us examine the conversions found for the dimension of length, as shown in the box, beginning with the conversion: 1 meter [m] = 3.28 feet [ft]. By dividing both sides of this equation by 3.28 feet, we obtain

$$\frac{1\ m}{3.28\ ft} = 1$$

or in other words, "There is 1 meter per 3.28 feet." If we divide both sides of the original expression by 1 meter, we obtain

$$1 = \frac{3.28\ ft}{1\ m}$$

or in other words, "In every 3.28 feet there is 1 meter."

The number 1 is dimensionless, a pure number. *We can multiply any expression by 1 without changing the expression.* We do this so as to change the units to the standard we desire.

For example, on a trip we note that the distance to Atlanta is 123 miles [mi]. How many kilometers [km] is it to Atlanta? From the conversion table, we can find that 1 kilometer [km] = 0.621 miles [mi], or

$$1 = \frac{1\ km}{0.621\ mi}$$

By multiplying the original quantity of 123 miles by 1, we can say

$$(123\ mi)(1) = (123\ mi)\left(\frac{1\ km}{0.621\ mi}\right) = 198\ km$$

Note that we could have multiplied by the following relationship:

$$1 = \frac{0.621\ mi}{1\ km}$$

We would still have multiplied the original answer by 1, but the units would not cancel and we would be left with an awkward, meaningless answer.

$$(123\ mi)(1) = (123\ mi)\left(\frac{0.621\ mi}{1\ km}\right) = 76\ \frac{mi^2}{km}$$

As a second example, we are designing a reactor system using 2-inch [in] diameter plastic pipe. The design office in Germany would like the pipe specifications in units of centimeters [cm]. From the conversion table, we find that 1 inch [in] = 2.54 centimeters [cm], or

$$1 = \frac{1 \text{ in}}{2.54 \text{ cm}}$$

By multiplying the original quantity of 2 inches by 1, we can say

$$(2 \text{ in})(1) = (2 \text{ in})\left(\frac{2.54 \text{ cm}}{1 \text{ in}}\right) = 5 \text{ cm}$$

In a final example, suppose a car travels at 40 miles per hour (abbreviated mph). Stated in words, "a car traveling at a rate of 40 mph will take 1 hour to travel 40 miles if the velocity remains constant." By simple arithmetic this means that the car will travel 80 miles in 2 hours or 120 miles in 3 hours. In general,

$$\text{Distance} = (\text{velocity})(\text{time elapsed at that velocity})$$

Suppose the car is traveling at 40 mph for 6 minutes. How far does the car travel? Simple calculation shows

$$\text{Distance} = (40)(6) = 240$$

Without considering units, the preceding example implies that if we drive our car at 40 mph, we can cover the distance from Charlotte, North Carolina, to Atlanta, Georgia, in 6 minutes! What is wrong? Note that the velocity is given in miles per hour, and the time is given in minutes. We need to apply the conversion factor that 1 hour = 60 minutes. If the equation is written with consistent units attached, we get

$$\text{Distance} = \left(\frac{40 \text{ mi}}{\text{h}}\right)\left(\frac{6 \text{ min}}{}\left|\frac{1 \text{ h}}{60 \text{ min}}\right.\right) = 4 \text{ mi}$$

IMPORTANT CONCEPT

Be sure to *always* include units in your calculations *and* your final answer!

It seems more reasonable to say "traveling at a rate of 40 miles per hour for a time period of 6 minutes will allow us to go 4 miles."

To convert between any set of units, the following method demonstrated in Examples 7-2 to 7-9 is very helpful. This procedure is easy to use, but take care to avoid mistakes. If you use one of the conversion factors incorrectly, say, with 3 in the numerator instead of the denominator, your answer will be in error by a factor of 9.

Unit Conversion Procedure

1. Write the value and unit to be converted.
2. Write the conversion formula between the given unit and the desired unit.
3. Make a fraction, equal to 1, of the conversion formula in Step 2, such that the original unit in Step 1 is located either in the denominator or in the numerator, depending on where it must reside so that the original unit will cancel.
4. Multiply the term from Step 1 by the fraction developed in Step 3.
5. Cancel units, perform mathematical calculations, and express the answer in "reasonable" terms (i.e., not too many decimal places).

● **EXAMPLE 7-2**   Convert the length 40 yards [yd] into units of feet [ft].

Method	Steps
(1) Term to be converted	40 yd
(2) Conversion formula	1 yd = 3 ft
(3) Make a fraction (equal to one)	$\dfrac{3 \text{ ft}}{1 \text{ yd}}$
(4) Multiply	$\dfrac{40 \text{ yd}}{} \bigg| \dfrac{3 \text{ ft}}{1 \text{ yd}}$
(5) Cancel, calculate, be reasonable	120 ft

● **EXAMPLE 7-3**   Convert the time 456,200 seconds [s] into units of minutes [min].

Method	Steps
(1) Term to be converted	456,000 s
(2) Conversion formula	1 min = 60 s
(3) Make a fraction (equal to one)	$\dfrac{1 \text{ min}}{60 \text{ s}}$
(4) Multiply	$\dfrac{456,000 \text{ s}}{} \bigg| \dfrac{1 \text{ min}}{60 \text{ s}}$
(5) Cancel, calculate, be reasonable	7,600 min

COMPREHENSION CHECK 7-3

The highest mountain in the world is Mount Everest in Nepal. The peak of Mount Everest is 29,029 feet above sea level. Convert the height from feet [ft] to miles [mi].

COMPREHENSION CHECK 7-4

To be considered a full time employee, companies in the United States required you work more than 30 hours in a week. Convert the time 30 hours [h] into units of minutes [min].

7.4 CONVERSIONS INVOLVING MULTIPLE STEPS

LEARN TO: Follow the 5-step conversion procedure to convert units when multiple steps are required

Sometimes, more than one conversion factor is needed. We can multiply by several conversion factors, each one of which is the same as multiplying by 1, as many times as needed to reach the desired result. For example, suppose we determined that the distance to Atlanta is 123 miles [mi]. How many yards [yd] is it to Atlanta? From the conversion table, we do not have a direct conversion between miles and yards, but we see that both can be related to feet. We can find that 1 mile [mi] = 5,280 feet [ft], or

$$1 = \frac{5{,}280 \text{ ft}}{1 \text{ mi}}$$

We can also find that 1 yard [yd] = 3 feet [ft], or

$$1 = \frac{1 \text{ yd}}{3 \text{ ft}}$$

By multiplying the original quantity of 123 miles by 1 using the first set of conversion factors, we can say:

$$(123 \text{ mi})(1) = (123 \text{ mi})\left(\frac{5{,}280 \text{ ft}}{1 \text{ mi}}\right) = 649{,}440 \text{ ft}$$

If we multiply by 1 again, using the second set of conversion factors and applying reasonableness:

$$(649{,}440 \text{ ft})(1) = (649{,}440 \text{ ft})\left(\frac{1 \text{ yd}}{3 \text{ ft}}\right) = 216{,}000 \text{ yd}$$

This is usually shown as a single step:

$$(123 \text{ mi})\left(\frac{5{,}280 \text{ ft}}{1 \text{ mi}}\right)\left(\frac{1 \text{ yd}}{3 \text{ ft}}\right) = 216{,}000 \text{ yd}$$

● **EXAMPLE 7-4**   Convert the power of 3,780,000 kilowatts [kW] into units of Gigawatts [GW].

Method	Steps
(1) Term to be converted	3,780,000 kW
(2) Conversion formula	$1 \text{ kW} = 1 \times 10^3 \text{ W}$ $1 \text{ GW} = 1 \times 10^9 \text{ W}$
(3) Make a fraction (equal to one)	$\dfrac{1 \times 10^3 \text{ W}}{1 \text{ kW}} \quad \dfrac{1 \text{ GW}}{1 \times 10^9 \text{ W}}$
(4) Multiply	$\dfrac{3{,}780{,}000 \text{ kW}}{} \left\vert \dfrac{1 \times 10^3 \text{ W}}{1 \text{ kW}} \right\vert \dfrac{1 \text{ GW}}{1 \times 10^9 \text{ W}}$
(5) Cancel, calculate, be reasonable	3.78 GW

● EXAMPLE 7-5

Convert the length 40 yards [yd] into units of millimeters [mm].

Method	Steps
(1) Term to be converted	40 yd
(2) Conversion formula	1 yd = 3 ft 1 ft = 12 in 1 in = 2.54 cm 1 cm = 10 mm
(3) Make fractions (equal to one)	$\dfrac{3\text{ ft}}{1\text{ yd}} \quad \dfrac{12\text{ in}}{1\text{ ft}} \quad \dfrac{2.54\text{ cm}}{1\text{ in}} \quad \dfrac{10\text{ mm}}{1\text{ cm}}$
(4) Multiply	$\dfrac{40\text{ yd}}{}\left\lvert\dfrac{3\text{ ft}}{1\text{ yd}}\right\rvert\left\lvert\dfrac{12\text{ in}}{1\text{ ft}}\right\rvert\left\lvert\dfrac{2.54\text{ cm}}{1\text{ in}}\right\rvert\left\lvert\dfrac{10\text{ mm}}{1\text{ cm}}\right.$
(5) Cancel, calculate, be reasonable	37,000 mm

● EXAMPLE 7-6

Convert 55 miles per hour [mph] to units of meters per second [m/s].

Note that we have two units to convert here, miles to meters, and hours to seconds.

Method	Steps
(1) Term to be converted	55 mph
(2) Conversion formula	1 km = 0.621 mi 1 km = 1,000 m 1 h = 60 min 1 min = 60 s
(3) Make fractions (equal to one) (4) Multiply	$\dfrac{55\text{ mi}}{h}\left\lvert\dfrac{1\text{ km}}{0.621\text{ mi}}\right\rvert\left\lvert\dfrac{1,000\text{ m}}{1\text{ km}}\right\rvert\left\lvert\dfrac{1\text{ h}}{60\text{ min}}\right\rvert\left\lvert\dfrac{1\text{ min}}{60\text{ s}}\right.$
(5) Cancel, calculate, be reasonable	24.6 m/s

● EXAMPLE 7-7

Convert the volume of 40 gallons [gal] into units of cubic feet [ft³].

By examining the "Volume" box in the conversion table, we see that the following facts are available for use:

$$1\text{ L} = 0.264\text{ gal} \quad \text{and} \quad 1\text{ L} = 0.0353\text{ ft}^3$$

By the transitive property, if a = b and a = c, then b = c. Therefore, we can directly write

$$0.264\text{ gal} = 0.0353\text{ ft}^3$$

VOLUME
1 L = 0.264 gal
1 L = 0.0353 ft³
1 L = 33.8 fl oz
1 mL = 1 cm³

Method	Steps
(1) Term to be converted	40 gal
(2) Conversion formula	$0.264\text{ gal} = 0.0353\text{ ft}^3$
(3) Make a fraction (equal to one)	$\dfrac{0.0353\text{ ft}^3}{0.264\text{ gal}}$
(4) Multiply	$\dfrac{40\text{ gal}}{}\left\lvert\dfrac{0.0353\text{ ft}^3}{0.264\text{ gal}}\right.$
(5) Cancel, calculate, be reasonable	5.3 ft³

This picture shows 5-gallon water bottles made from polycarbonate. Millions of these bottles are made each year around the world to transport clean water to remote locations.

The use of polycarbonate to contain products for consumption has raised safety concerns because bisphenol A is leached from the plastic into the stored liquid. In July 2012, the US Food and Drug Administration banned the use of BPA in bottles and cups used by infants and small children.

Photo courtesy of E. Stephan

One frequently needs to convert a value that has some unit or units raised to a power, for example, converting a volume given in cubic feet to cubic meters. It is critical in this case that the power involved be applied to the *entire* conversion factor, both the numerical values and the units.

● **EXAMPLE 7-8**

Convert 35 cubic inches [in^3] to cubic centimeters [cm^3 or cc].

NOTE

When raising a quantity to a power, be sure to apply the power to both the value and the units.

Method	Steps
(1) Term to be converted	$35\ in^3$
(2) Conversion formula	$1\ in = 2.54\ cm$
(3) Make fractions (equal to one)	$\dfrac{(2.54\ cm)^3}{(1\ in)^3}$
(4) Multiply	$\dfrac{35\ in^3}{}\left\lvert\dfrac{(2.54)^3\ cm^3}{1\ in^3}\right.$
(5) Cancel, calculate, be reasonable	$574\ cm^3$

Note that in some cases, a unit that is raised to a power is being converted to another unit that has been defined to have the same dimension as the one raised to a power. This is difficult to say in words, but a couple of examples should clarify it.

If one is converting square meters [m^2] to acres, the conversion factor is *not* squared, since the conversion provided is already in terms of length squared: 1 acre = 4,047 m^2.

If one is converting cubic feet [ft^3] to liters [L], the conversion factor is *not* cubed, since the conversion provided is already in terms of length cubed: 1 L = 0.0353 ft^3.

COMPREHENSION CHECK 7–5

In January 2008, *Scientific American* reported that physicists Peter Sutter and Eli Sutter of Brookhaven National Laboratories made a pipette to measure droplets in units of a zeptoliter. Previously, the smallest unit of measure in a pipette was an attoliter. Convert the measurement of 5 zeptoliters into units of picoliters.

COMPREHENSION CHECK 7-6

Officially, a hurricane is a tropical storm with sustained winds of at least 74 miles per hour. Convert this speed into units of kilometers per minute.

COMPREHENSION CHECK 7-7

Many toilets in commercial establishments have a value printed on them stating the amount of water consumed per flush. For example, a label of 2 Lpf indicates the consumption of 2 liters per flush. If a toilet is rated at 3 Lpf, how many flushes are required to consume 20 gallons of water?

RULES OF THUMB

1 quart ≈ 1 liter	1 cubic foot ≈ 7.5 gallons
1 cubic meter ≈ 250 gallons	1 cubic meter ≈ 5, 55-gallon drums
1 cup ≈ 250 milliliters	1 golf ball ≈ 1 cubic inch

LESSONS OF THE MARS CLIMATE ORBITER

Some of you may have heard that the loss of the Mars Climate Orbiter (MCO) spacecraft in 1999 was due to a unit conversion error. The complete story is rather more complicated and illustrates a valuable lesson in engineering design. Most engineering failures are not due to a single mistake, since built-in redundancies and anticipation of failure modes make this unlikely. Three primary factors (plus bad luck) conspired to send the MCO off course.

First, the spacecraft was asymmetrical, with the body of the spacecraft on one side and a large solar panel on the other. You might think shape is not an issue in the vacuum of space, but in fact it is, and the NASA engineers were

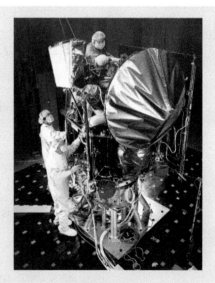

(continued)

well aware of the potential problems. The panel acted like a sail, causing the craft to slowly change its orientation and requiring the MCO to make occasional small corrections by firing thrusters onboard the craft. This was a perfectly manageable "problem."

Second, the software on the spacecraft expected thruster data in SI units, requiring the force expressed in newtons. On the Earth, a separate system calculated and sent instructions to the MCO concerning when and how long to fire its thrusters. The Earth-based system relied on software from an earlier Mars mission, and the thruster equations had to be modified to correct for the thrusters used on the new spacecraft. The original software had been written correctly, with the conversion factor from pound-force to newtons included. However, this conversion was neither documented nor obvious from the code, being buried in the equations. When the equations were rewritten, the programmers were unaware of the conversion factor and it was left out of the new code. This sent incorrect thruster-firing data to the MCO, specifically being too small by a factor of 4.45. This problem alone was manageable by comparing the calculated trajectory with tracking data.

Finally, after the third trajectory correction, the MCO entered "safe mode" while adjusting the solar panel, indicating a fault on the craft. At about the same time, the preliminary indications that the spacecraft trajectory was flawed began to come in. Unfortunately, the engineers spent the next several weeks trying to determine what caused the craft to enter safe mode, falsely assuming the preliminary trajectory data was in error and waiting for longer-term tracking to give a better estimate. In the end, the spacecraft arrived at Mars about 100 kilometers off course.

Here is where the bad luck comes in. Other configurations of the craft or trajectory might have caused the 100 kilometer error to be away from Mars or parallel to the surface, in which case the trajectory could have been corrected later. Unfortunately, the trajectory was 100 kilometers lower than expected, and the MCO was probably destroyed by heating and stresses as it plunged through the Martian atmosphere. Cost: well over $100 million.

7.5 CONVERSIONS INVOLVING "NEW" UNITS

LEARN TO: Apply the 5-step conversion procedure to any units

In the past, many units were derived from common physical objects. The "inch" was the width of man's thumb, and the "foot" was the heel-to-toe length of a king's shoe. Obviously, when one king died or was deposed and another took over, the unit of "foot" changed, too. Over time, these units were standardized and have become common terminology.

New units are added as technology evolves; for example, in 1999 the unit of katal was added as an SI derived unit of catalytic activity used in biochemistry. As you proceed in your engineering field, you will be introduced to many "new" units. The procedures discussed here apply to *any* unit in *any* engineering field.

● **EXAMPLE 7-9**

According to the U.S. Food and Drug Administration (21CFR101.9), the following definition applies for nutritional labeling:

1 fluid ounce means 30 milliliters

Using this definition, how many fluid ounces [fl oz] are in a "U.S. standard" beverage can of 355 milliliters [mL]?

Method	Steps
(1) Term to be converted	355 mL
(2) Conversion formula	1 fl oz = 30 mL
(3) Make a fraction (equal to one) (4) Multiply	$\dfrac{355 \text{ mL}}{} \left\| \dfrac{1 \text{ fl oz}}{30 \text{ mL}} \right.$
(5) Cancel, calculate, be reasonable	11.8 fl oz

● **EXAMPLE 7-10**

The volume of water in a reservoir or aquifer is often expressed using the unit of acre-foot. A volume of 1 acre-foot is the amount of water covering an area of 1 acre to a depth of 1 foot.

Lake Mead, located 30 miles southeast of Las Vegas, Nevada, is the largest man-made lake in the United States. It holds approximately 28.5 million acre-feet of water behind the Hoover Dam. Convert this volume to units of gallons.

Method	Steps
(1) Term to be converted	28.5×10^6 acre feet
(2) Conversion formula	1 acre = 4,047 m^2 1 m = 3.28 ft 1 m^3 = 1,000 L 1 L = 0.264 gal
(3) Make a fraction (4) Multiply	$\dfrac{28.5 \times 10^6 \text{ acre ft}}{} \left\| \dfrac{4,047 \text{ m}^2}{1 \text{ acre}} \right\| \dfrac{1 \text{ m}}{3.28 \text{ ft}} \left\| \dfrac{1,000 \text{ L}}{1 \text{ m}^3} \right\| \dfrac{0.264 \text{ gal}}{1 \text{ L}}$
(5) Cancel, calculate, be reasonable	9.3×10^{12} gal

COMPREHENSION CHECK 7-8

A hogshead is a unit of volume describing a large barrel of liquid. Convert 10 hogsheads into units of cubic feet. Conversion factor: 1 hogshead = 63 gallons.

COMPREHENSION CHECK 7-9

In NCAA basketball, a "three-point shot" is defined by an arc radius of 20 feet, 9 inches. Convert this length to units of cubits. Conversion factor: 1 cubit = 0.45 meters.

COMPREHENSION CHECK 7-10   A boat is traveling at 20 knots. Convert this speed to units of meters per second. Conversion factor: 1 knot = 1 nautical mile per hour; 1 nautical mile = 6,076 feet.

7.6 DERIVED DIMENSIONS AND UNITS

LEARN TO: Identify a quantity as a fundamental or derived dimension and express the fundamental dimensions of the quantity using fractional or exponential notation
Given the units of a quantity, determine the fundamental dimensions
Given the fundamental dimensions of a quantity, determine the base SI units

With only the seven base dimensions in the metric system, all measurable things in the known universe can be expressed by various combinations of these concepts. These are called **derived dimensions**. As simple examples, area is length squared, volume is length cubed, and velocity is length divided by time.

As we explore more complex parameters, the dimensions become more complex. For example, the concept of force is derived from Newton's second law, which states that force is equal to mass times acceleration. Force is then used to define more complex dimensions such as pressure, which is force acting over an area, or work, which is force acting over a distance. As we introduce new concepts, we introduce the dimensions and units for each parameter.

Sometimes, the derived dimensions become quite complicated. For example, electrical resistance is mass times length squared divided by both time cubed and current squared. Particularly in the more complicated cases like this, a **derived unit** is defined to avoid having to say things like "The resistance is 15 kilogram-meters squared divided by second cubed ampere squared." It is much easier to say "The resistance is 15 ohms," where the derived unit "ohm" equals one $(kg\ m^2)/(s^3\ A^2)$.

Within this text, dimensions are presented in exponential notation rather than fractional notation.

Quantity	Fractional Notation	Exponential Notation
Velocity	$\dfrac{L}{T}$	$L^1\ T^{-1}$
Acceleration	$\dfrac{L}{T^2}$	$L^1\ T^{-2}$

One way to determine the dimensions of a quantity, such as volume, is to examine the common units used to express the quantity. While volume can be expressed in gallons, it can also be expressed as cubic feet or cubic meters. The units of cubic meters express volume in a manner easily transferred to dimensions. Remember, the boxes on the inside front cover of the textbook show units that have equivalent dimensions. The units of gallons and of cubic feet and of cubic meters are dimensionally equal to length cubed.

Quantity	Units	Equivalent Units	M	L	T	Θ	N	J	I
						Dimensions			
Volume	gal	m³	0	3	0	0	0	0	0

● **EXAMPLE 7-11**   Determine the fundamental dimensions of the following quantities.

Quantity	Units	Equivalent Units	M	L	T	Θ	N	J	I
						Dimensions			
area	acres	m²	0	2	0	0	0	0	0
distance	yd	m	0	1	0	0	0	0	0
mass	slug	kg	1	0	0	0	0	0	0
temperature	°C	K	0	0	0	1	0	0	0
time	h	s	0	0	1	0	0	0	0

Currently, there are officially 22 named derived units in the SI system. All are named after famous scientists or engineers who are deceased. Five of the most common derived units can be found in Table 7-5 and on the back cover of the textbook. It is worth noting that numerous common derived dimensions do not have a corresponding named derived SI unit. For example, there is no named derived SI unit for the derived dimension velocity as there is for force (newton) or electrical resistance (ohm).

Table 7-5 Common derived units in the SI system

Dimension	SI Unit	Base SI Units	Derived from
Force (F)	newton [N]	$1\,N = 1\dfrac{kg\,m}{s^2}$	$F = ma$ Force = mass times acceleration
Energy (E)	joule [J]	$1\,J = 1\,N\,m = 1\dfrac{kg\,m^2}{s^2}$	$E = Fd$ Energy = force times distance
Power (P)	watt [W]	$1\,W = 1\dfrac{J}{s} = 1\dfrac{kg\,m^2}{s^3}$	$P = E/t$ Power = energy per time
Pressure (P)	pascal [Pa]	$1\,Pa = 1\dfrac{N}{m^2} = 1\dfrac{kg}{m\,s^2}$	$P = F/A$ Pressure = force per area
Voltage (V)	volt [V]	$1\,V = 1\dfrac{W}{A} = 1\dfrac{kg\,m^2}{s^3\,A}$	$V = P/I$ Voltage = power per current

■ A note of caution: One letter can represent several quantities in various engineering disciplines. For example, the letter "P" can indicate pressure, power, or vertical load

on a beam. It is important to examine and determine the nomenclature in terms of the context of the problem presented.
- Always remember to include the units in calculations.

Similar to breaking down volume to be expressed as cubic meters, the named SI derived dimensions can be expressed in base SI unit. Using the base SI units allows for the dimensions to be easily determined.

● EXAMPLE 7-12

Determine the fundamental dimensions of the following quantity.

Quantity	Units	Equivalent Units	Dimensions						
			M	**L**	**T**	**Θ**	**N**	**J**	**I**
Force	newton	$\dfrac{kg\,m}{s^2}$	1	1	−2	0	0	0	0

By understanding that a newton is the name given to the unit set of $\dfrac{kg\,m}{s^2}$, the fundamental dimensions become simple to determine. The five common derived units in Table 7-5 occur so frequently in engineering calculations you will want to memorize each dimension and the equivalent base SI units.

COMPREHENSION CHECK 7-11

Determine the fundamental dimensions of the following quantities.

Quantity	Units	Dimensions						
		M	**L**	**T**	**Θ**	**N**	**J**	**I**
Density	lb_m/ft^3							
Evaporation	slug/h							
Flowrate	gal/min							

COMPREHENSION CHECK 7-12

Determine the fundamental dimensions of the following quantities.

Quantity	Units	Dimensions						
		M	**L**	**T**	**Θ**	**N**	**J**	**I**
Energy	calories							
Power	horsepower							
Pressure	atmospheres							
Voltage	volts							

Dimensions can help us identify combinations of variables as a familiar quantity by examining their base SI units and fundamental dimensions.

● EXAMPLE 7-13

Identify the quantity through the use of fundamental dimensions. Choose from the following quantities:

(A) Acceleration   **(B)** Energy   **(C)** Force

(D) Power   **(E)** Pressure   **(F)** Velocity

$$A\rho v^3$$

where:

A = area [acres]
ρ = density [kg/m^3]
v = velocity [m/s]

First, we can express each quantity individually in terms of fundamental dimensions:

$A \; [=] \; \text{acres} \; [=] \; m^2 \; \{=\} \; L^2$
$\rho \; \{=\} \; M/L^3$
$v \; \{=\} \; L/T$

Combining these quantities together in the given expression:

$$A\rho v^3 \; \{=\} \; \frac{L^2}{} \left| \frac{M}{L^3} \right| \left(\frac{L}{T} \right)^3$$

Note that since velocity is cubed in the original expression, the dimensions of velocity must be cubed.

This will simplify to:

$$\frac{M \, L^2}{T^3}$$

This is equivalent to the dimensions of Choice D, Power.

COMPREHENSION CHECK 7-13

Identify the quantity through the use of fundamental dimensions. Choose from the following:

(A) Acceleration   **(B)** Energy   **(C)** Force

(D) Power   **(E)** Pressure   **(F)** Velocity

$$nRT$$

where:

n = amount [mol]
R = ideal gas constant [atm L/(mol K)]
T = temperature [K]

Special Unit: Radian

The derived unit of **radian** is defined as the angle at the center of a circle formed by an arc (S) equal in length to the radius (r) of that circle. In a complete circle there are 2π radians. Since by definition a radian is a length (S) divided by a length (r), it is a dimensionless ratio.

$$1 \text{ radian } [\text{rad}] = S/r$$

Thus, an angle has units, but is dimensionless! In addition to radians, another common unit used for angle is the degree [°]. There are 360° in a complete circle.

$$360° = 2\pi \text{ radians}$$

7.7 EQUATION LAWS

LEARN TO: Determine if an expression is a valid using plus law, unit law, and per law
Use the plus law, unit law, or per law, to determine dimensions/units of a quantity
Recognize that in equations, units must be consistent in order for resulting calculations to be valid

Equations are mathematical "sentences" composed of "words" (terms) that are strung together with "punctuation marks" (mathematical symbols, such as +, −, ×, ÷, and =). Just as there are rules in the English language that govern how a sentence is structured, there exists a set of "rules" for equations.

Addition and Subtraction

Suppose we are interested in the manufacture and use of sandpaper for furniture construction. We think for a while and then develop a list of the important quantities that affect the final product, along with their respective units and dimensions:

W	Wood removed	[in]	L
R	Roughness diameter	[mm]	L
D	Density of grains	[kg/m³]	$\frac{M}{L^3}$
A	Adhesive thickness	[mm]	L
H	How heavy the paper is	[N]	$\frac{ML}{T^2}$
O	Operation stroke length	[cm]	L
K	Kernel (grain) spacing	[mm]	L

Let us propose a simple equation with only plus and minus signs that could possibly relate several of these parameters. If we are interested in how heavy the product would be, we might assume this would depend on the thickness of the adhesive, the diameter of the roughness, and the grain density. We will try

$$H = A + R + D$$

Each of these terms represents something "real," and consequently we expect that each term can be expressed in terms of fundamental dimensions. Writing the equation in terms of dimensions given:

$$\frac{M\,L}{T^2} = L + L + \frac{M}{L^3}$$

IMPORTANT CONCEPT:
PLUS LAW

Every term being added or subtracted in an equation must have the same dimension.

It is obvious that this is just terrible! We cannot add length and mass or time; as the adage goes, "You can't add apples and oranges!" The same holds true for dimensions. As a result of this observation, we see that this cannot possibly be a valid equation. This gives one important "law" governing equations, the **Plus law**.

Let us try this again with another equation to see if we can determine how effective the sandpaper will be, or how much wood will be removed after each stroke. We might assume this depends on the operation stroke length, the roughness diameter, and the spacing of the grains.

$$W = O + R + K$$

Substituting dimensions,

$$L = L + L + L$$

We see that at least dimensionally, this can be a valid equation, based on the Plus law. Next, units can be inserted to give

$$\text{inches} = \text{centimeters} + \text{millimeters} + \text{millimeters}$$

IMPORTANT CONCEPT:
UNIT LAW

Every term in an equation must have the same units so that the arithmetic operations of addition and subtraction can be carried out.

COROLLARY TO
UNIT LAW

A dimensionally consistent and unit consistent equation is not necessarily a valid equation in terms of physical meaning.

Dimensionally, this equation is fine, but from the perspective of units, we cannot carry out the arithmetic above without first converting all the length dimensions into the same units, such as millimeters. We can state an important result from this observation as well, forming the **Unit law**.

It is important to state a corollary to this observation. If two parameters have the same dimensions and units, it is not always meaningful to add or subtract them.

Two examples show this.

1. If Student A has a mass m_A [kilograms] and Student B a mass m_B [kilograms], then the total mass of both students [kilograms] is the sum of the two masses. This is correct and meaningful in both dimensions and units.
2. Suppose we assume that an equation to predict the mass of a car is this: mass of the car in kilograms = mass of an oak tree in kilograms + mass of an opossum in kilograms. This equation has three terms; all with the dimension of mass and units of kilograms; thus, the terms can be added, although the equation itself is nonsense.

Consequently, the requirement that each term must have the same dimensions and units is a necessary, but not a sufficient, condition for a satisfactory equation.

Multiplication and Division

IMPORTANT CONCEPT:
PER LAW

When parameters are multiplied or divided, the dimensions and units are treated with the same operation rules as numerical values.

There are many ways to express the rate at which things are done. Much of our daily life is conducted on a "*per*" or rate basis. We eat 3 meals *per* day, have 5 fingers *per* hand, there are 11 players *per* team in football, 3 feet *per* yard, 4 tires *per* car, 12 fluid ounces *per* canned drink, and 4 people *per* quartet.

Although it is incorrect to add or subtract parameters with different dimensions, it is perfectly permissible to divide or multiply two or more parameters with different dimensions. This is another law of dimensions, the **Per law**.

When we say 65 miles *per* hour, we mean that we travel 65 miles in 1 hour. We could say we travel at 130 miles per 2 hours, and it would mean the same thing. Either way, this rate is expressed by the "*per*" ratio, distance per time.

One of the most useful applications of your knowledge of dimensions is in helping to determine if an equation is dimensionally correct. This is easy to do and only involves the substitution of the dimensions of every parameter into the equation and simplifying the resulting expressions. A simple application will demonstrate this process.

● **EXAMPLE 7-14**

Is the following equation dimensionally correct?

$$t = \sqrt{\frac{d_{final} - d_{initial}}{0.5a}}$$

where t is time
d is distance
a is acceleration
0.5 is unitless

Determine the dimensions of each parameter:

Acceleration	(a)	$\{=\}\ L^1\ T^{-2}$
Distance	(d)	$\{=\}\ L$
Time	(t)	$\{=\}\ T$

Substitute into the equation: $T = \sqrt{(L - L) \left|\dfrac{T^2}{L}\right.}$

Simplifying $T = \sqrt{L \left|\dfrac{T^2}{L}\right.} = \sqrt{T^2} = T$

Yes, the equation is dimensionally correct. Both sides of the equation have the same dimensions.

● **EXAMPLE 7-15**

We can use dimensional arguments to help remember formulas. We are interested in the acceleration of a body swung in a circle of radius (r), at a constant velocity (v). We remember that acceleration depends on r and v, and one is divided by the other, but cannot quite remember how. Is the acceleration (a) given by one of the following?

$$a = \frac{v}{r} \quad \text{or} \quad a = \frac{v}{r^2} \quad \text{or} \quad a = \frac{v^2}{r} \quad \text{or} \quad a = \frac{r}{v} \quad \text{or} \quad a = \frac{r}{v^2} \quad \text{or} \quad a = \frac{r^2}{v}$$

Determine the dimensions of each parameter:

Acceleration	(a)	$\{=\}\ L^1\ T^{-2}$
Radius	(r)	$\{=\}\ L$
Velocity	(v)	$\{=\}\ L^1\ T^{-1}$

Original Equation	Substituting into the Equation	Simplify	Correct?
$a = v/r$	$LT^{-2} = (LT^{-1})\ L^{-1}$	$LT^{-2} = T^{-1}$	No
$a = v/r^2$	$LT^{-2} = (LT^{-1})\ L^{-2}$	$LT^{-2} = L^{-1}\ T^{-1}$	No
$a = v^2/r$	$LT^{-2} = (LT^{-1})^2\ L^{-1}$	$LT^{-2} = LT^{-2}$	Yes
$a = r/v$	$LT^{-2} = L\ (LT^{-1})^{-1}$	$LT^{-2} = T$	No
$a = r/v^2$	$LT^{-2} = L\ (LT^{-1})^{-2}$	$LT^{-2} = L^{-1}\ T^2$	No
$a = r^2/v$	$LT^{-2} = L^2\ (LT^{-1})^{-1}$	$LT^{-2} = LT$	No

COMPREHENSION CHECK 7-14

The power absorbed by a resistor can be given by $P = I^2 R$, where P is power in units of watts [W], I is electric current in amperes [A], and R is resistance in ohms [Ω]. Express the unit of ohms in terms of fundamental dimensions.

COMPREHENSION CHECK 7-15

Indicate whether the following equation is dimensionally consistent (yes or no):

$$v = \sqrt{\frac{PE}{H\rho}}$$

where:

$$v = \text{velocity [ft/s]}$$
$$PE = \text{potential energy [J]}$$
$$H = \text{height [ft]}$$
$$\rho = \text{density [g/cm}^3\text{]}$$

7.8 CONVERSION INVOLVING EQUATIONS

LEARN TO: Solve an equation for a desired quantity using the 3-step procedure
Recognize the importance of converting to base SI units in equation solutions

Engineering problems are rarely as simple as converting from one set of units to another. Normally, an equation is involved in the problem solution. To minimize the likelihood of mistakes, we adopt the following procedure for all problems. While this procedure may seem to overanalyze simple problems, it is relatively foolproof and will become more and more useful as the material progresses in difficulty.

Equation Procedure

1. Given a problem, first convert all parameters into base SI units, combinations of these units, or accepted non-SI units. Use the five-step conversion procedure previously described.
2. Perform all necessary calculations, as follows:
   (a) Determine the appropriate equation.
   (b) Insert the known quantities and units. Be sure to carry the units through until the end!
   (c) Calculate the desired quantity.
   This gives the answer in SI units.
3. Convert the final answer to the required units and express the answer in "reasonable" terms.

● **EXAMPLE 7-16**

On a trip from Alphaville to Betaville, you can take two main routes. Route 1, which goes through Gammatown, is 50 kilometers [km] long; however, you can only drive an average speed of 36 miles per hour [mph]. Route 2 travels along the freeway, at an average speed of 50 mph, but it is 65 km long. How long does it take to complete each route? State the time for each route in minutes [min].

Step One: Convert to Base SI Units		
Method	**Route 1**	**Route 2**
(1) Term to be converted	36 mph	50 mph
(2) Conversion formula (3) Make a fraction (equal to one) (4) Multiply	$\dfrac{36 \text{ mi}}{\text{h}} \Bigg\vert \dfrac{1 \text{ km}}{0.621 \text{ mi}}$	$\dfrac{50 \text{ mi}}{\text{h}} \Bigg\vert \dfrac{1 \text{ km}}{0.621 \text{ mi}}$
(5) Cancel, calculate	58 km/h	81 km/h
Step Two: Calculate		
Method	**Route 1**	**Route 2**
(1) Determine appropriate equation	Distance = (velocity) (time) which can be rewritten as . . . Time = distance/velocity	
(2) Insert known quantities	$\text{Time} = \dfrac{50 \text{ km}}{58 \frac{\text{km}}{\text{h}}}$	$\text{Time} = \dfrac{65 \text{ km}}{81 \frac{\text{km}}{\text{h}}}$
(3) Calculate	Time = 0.86 h	Time = 0.8 h
Step Three: Convert from Base SI Units to Desired Units		
Method	**Route 1**	**Route 2**
(1) Term to be converted	0.86 h	0.8 h
(2) Conversion formula (3) Make a fraction (equal to one) (4) Multiply	$\dfrac{0.86 \text{ h}}{} \Bigg\vert \dfrac{60 \text{ min}}{1 \text{ h}}$	$\dfrac{0.8 \text{ h}}{} \Bigg\vert \dfrac{60 \text{ min}}{1 \text{ h}}$
(5) Cancel, calculate, be reasonable	52 min	48 min

NOTE

$$\frac{\frac{\text{km}}{\text{km}}}{\text{h}} = \frac{\text{km h}}{\text{km}} = \text{h}$$

● **EXAMPLE 7-17**

You are designing a bottle to store juice for a large food manufacturing plant. The bottle is cylindrical in shape, with a 3 inch diameter and a height of 0.45 meters. What is the volume of the bottle in units of cubic centimeters?

The equation for the volume of a cylinder is: $V_{cylinder} = \pi r^2 H$.
Note that several common geometric formulas are provided for you in the end pages of this text.
To solve this problem so the end result is in cubic centimeters, we must convert both the radius and height into units of centimeters before plugging the values into the equation.

Step One: Convert to Base SI Units		
Method	**Diameter**	**Height**
(1) Term to be converted	3 inches	0.45 meters
(2) Conversion formula (3) Make a fraction (equal to one) (4) Multiply	$\dfrac{3\text{ in}}{}\left|\dfrac{2.54\text{ cm}}{1\text{ in}}\right.$	$\dfrac{0.45\text{ m}}{}\left|\dfrac{100\text{ cm}}{1\text{ m}}\right.$
(5) Cancel, calculate	7.62 cm	45 cm
Step Two: Calculate		
(1) Determine appropriate equation	$V_{cylinder} = \pi r^2 H$ $D = 2r \qquad$ so... $r = 1/2\,D$	
(2) Insert known quantities	$r = 1/2\,(7.62\text{ cm}) = 3.81\text{ cm}$ $V = \pi\,(3.81\text{ cm})^2\,(45\text{ cm})$	
(3) Calculate, be reasonable	$V = 2{,}052\text{ cm}^3$	

COMPREHENSION CHECK 7-16

Eclipses, both solar and lunar, follow a cycle of just over 18 years, specifically 6585.32 days. This is called the Saros Cycle. One Saros Cycle after any given eclipse an almost identical eclipse will occur due to fact that the Earth, the Moon, and the Sun are in essentially the same positions relative to each other. The Sun, and the entire solar system, is moving relative to the Cosmic Microwave Background Radiation (the largest detectable frame of reference) at roughly 370 kilometers per second. How far does our solar system travel through the universe in one Saros Cycle? Express your answer in the following units:

(a) meters, with an appropriately chosen prefix;
(b) light-years: one light year = 9.46×10^{15} meters.

COMPREHENSION CHECK 7-17

A basketball has a diameter of approximately 27 centimeters. Find the volume of the basketball in units of gallons.

In-Class Activities

ICA 7-1

Express the following values using scientific notation, engineering notation, and using the correct SI prefix.

Standard	Scientific	Engineering	With Prefix
(a) 389,589,000 J			
(b) 0.0000000008 Pa			

ICA 7-2

Complete the following table:

	Meters	Centimeters	Millimeters	Micrometers	Nanometers
Abbreviation	[m]				
Example	9E-08	9E-06	9E-05	0.09	90
(a)		50			
(b)				5	

ICA 7-3

Complete the following table:

	Inches	Feet	Yards	Meters	Miles
Abbreviation	[in]				
(a)		90			
(b)					2

ICA 7-4

Complete the following table:

	Cubic Inch	Fluid Ounces	Gallon	Liter	Cubic Foot
Abbreviation	[in^3]				
Example	716	400	3.12	11.8	0.414
(a)					3
(b)				5	

ICA 7-5

Complete the following table:

	Miles per Hour	Kilometers per Hour	Yards per Minute	Feet per Second
Abbreviation	[mph] or [mi/h]			
(a)		100		
(b)	55			

ICA 7-6

Complete the following table:

	Gallons per Minute	Cubic Feet per Hour	Liters per Second	Fluid Ounces per Day
Abbreviation	[gpm] or [gal/min]			
(a)		15		
(b)	20			

ICA 7-7

A category F5 tornado can have wind speeds of 300 miles per hour [mph]. What is this velocity in units of meters per second?

ICA 7-8

A new hybrid automobile with regenerative braking has a fuel economy of 55 miles per gallon [mpg] in city driving. What is this fuel economy expressed in units of feet per milliliter?

ICA 7-9

The AbioCor™ artificial heart pumps at a rate of 10 liters per minute. Express this rate in units of gallons per second.

ICA 7-10

If a pump moves water at 2 cubic feet per hour, what is this rate in units of cubic centimeters per second?

ICA 7-11

In China, one "bu" is 1.66 meters. The average height of a human is 5 feet, 7 inches. Convert this height to units of bu.

ICA 7-12

In China, one "cun" is 3.5 centimeters. A "cubit" is defined as 18 inches. Convert 50 cubits to units of cun.

ICA 7-13

In China, one "fen" is defined as 3.3 millimeters. Ten nanometers is the thickness of a cell membrane. Convert 10 nanometers to units of fen.

ICA 7-14

A blink of a human eye takes approximately 300–400 milliseconds. Convert 350 milliseconds to units of shake. One "shake" is equal to 10 nanoseconds.

ICA 7-15

If the SI prefix system was expanded to other units, there would be such definitions as a "milli-hour," meaning 1/1,000 of an hour. Convert 1 millihour to units of shake. One "shake" is equal to 10 nanoseconds.

ICA 7-16

A "jiffy" is defined as 1/60 of a second. Convert 20 jiffys to units of shake. One "shake" is equal to 10 nanoseconds.

ICA 7-17

A "knot" is a unit of speed in marine travel. One knot is 1.852 kilometers per hour. Rather than using the traditional MKS (meter–kilogram–second) unit system, an unusual unit system is the FFF system: furlong–firkin–fortnight. One furlong is equal to 201 meters and one fortnight is 14 days. Convert the speed of 20 knots to units of furlong per fortnight.

ICA 7-18

The Earth's escape velocity is 7 miles per second. Rather than using the traditional MKS (meter–kilogram–second) unit system, an unusual unit system is the FFF system: furlong–firkin–fortnight. One furlong is equal to 201 meters and one fortnight is 14 days. Convert this velocity to units of furlong per fortnight.

ICA 7-19

A manufacturing process uses 10 pound-mass of plastic resin per hour. Rather than using the traditional MKS (meter–kilogram–second) unit system, an unusual unit system is the FFF system: furlong–firkin–fortnight. One firkin is equal to 40 kilograms and one fortnight is 14 days. Convert this rate to units of firkin per fortnight.

ICA 7-20

Determine the fundamental dimensions of the following quantities.

	Quantity	Common Units	Dimensions						
			M	L	T	Θ	N	J	I
(a)	British thermal units per pounds-mass degree Fahrenheit	$\dfrac{BTU}{lb_m \, °F}$							
(b)	joule per gram	$\dfrac{J}{g}$							
(c)	watts per square meter degrees Celsius	$\dfrac{W}{m^2 \, °C}$							

ICA 7-21

Determine the fundamental dimensions of the following quantities.

	Quantity	Common Units	Dimensions						
			M	L	T	Θ	N	J	I
(a)	calories per kilogram kelvin	$\dfrac{cal}{kg\ K}$							
(b)	pounds-mass per square foot hour	$\dfrac{lb_m}{ft^2\ h}$							
(c)	pounds-force per square inch	$\dfrac{lb_f}{in^2}$							

ICA 7-22

Identify the following quantities through the use of fundamental dimensions. Choose from the list (A) - (F) shown

(A) Acceleration   (D) Power
(B) Energy   (E) Pressure
(C) Force   (F) Velocity

(a) mgH where: m = mass [kg] g = gravity [m/s^2] H = height [ft]
(b) $P/(mg)$ where: m = mass [kg] g = gravity [m/s^2] P = power [W]

ICA 7-23

Identify the following quantities through the use of fundamental dimensions. Choose from the list (A) - (F) shown

(A) Acceleration   (D) Power
(B) Energy   (E) Pressure
(C) Force   (F) Velocity

(a) mgv where: m = mass [kg] g = gravity [m/s^2] v = velocity [in/h]
(b) PV where: P = pressure [Pa] V = volume [m^3]

ICA 7-24

For each equation listed, indicate if the equation is a correct mathematical expression based on dimensional considerations.

(a) Accleration = (velocity)^2/(area)$^{1/2}$
(b) Energy = (mass) (speed) (area)$^{1/2}$

ICA 7-25

For each equation listed, indicate if the equation is a correct mathematical expression based on dimensional considerations.

(a) Power = (mass) (velocity)/(time)
(b) Time = (area)$^{1/2}$/(velocity)

ICA 7-26

A circular window has a 10-inch radius. What is the surface area of one side of the window in units of square centimeters?

ICA 7-27

When shipping freight around the world, most companies use a standardized set of containers to make transportation and handling easier. The 40-foot container is the most popular container worldwide. If the container is 2.4 meters wide and has an enclosed volume of 2,385 cubic feet, what is the height of the container in units of inches?

ICA 7-28

A body traveling in a circle experiences an acceleration (a) of $a = v^2/r$, where v is the speed of the body and r is the radius of the circle. We are tasked with designing a large centrifuge to allow astronauts to experience a high "g" forces similar to those encountered on takeoff. One "g" is defined as 9.8 meters per second squared. Design specifications indicate that our design must create at least 5 "g"s. If we use a radius of 30 feet, what is the required speed of the rotating capsule at the end of the arm, in units of meters per second?

ICA 7-29

In NCAA basketball, the center circle diameter which encompasses the free throw line is 3.66 meters. What is the area of the center circle, in units of square feet?

ICA 7-30

Continental drift has an average velocity of 2 inches per year. At this rate, how far would a continental plate move in one hour? Give your answer in units of meters, using an appropriate metric prefix so the answer appears in engineering notation. Assume 1 year = 365 days.

CHAPTER 7 REVIEW QUESTIONS

1. Express the following values using scientific notation, engineering notation, and using the correct SI prefix.

Standard	Scientific	Engineering	With Prefix
(a) 0.0698 m			
(b) 501,000,000,000 g			

2. Express the following values using scientific notation and engineering notation.

Standard	Scientific	Engineering
(a) 35.84 Tm		
(b) 602 fW		

3. Which of the following is the longest distance?

   (a) 26.4 miles
   (b) 40 kilometers
   (c) 2,500 yards
   (d) 100,000 feet

4. Which of the following is the largest volume?

   (a) 50 gallons
   (b) 100 liters
   (c) 1.5 cubic meters
   (d) 2.5 cubic feet

5. In 2001, the first iPod™ by Apple had a rated battery life of 10 hours to run audio files. The 6th model, introduced in 2009, had rated battery life of 36 hours to run audio files. If the average song is 3.5 minutes, how many more songs can you listen to using the 6th model iPod rather than the original iPod on a single battery charge?

6. New plastic fuel tanks for cars can be molded to many shapes, an advantage over the current metal tanks, allowing manufacturers to increase the tank capacity from 77 liters to 82 liters. What is this increase in gallons?

7. The longest sea bridge, the Jiaozhou Bay Bridge in China, spans 26.4 miles. The longest sea bridge in the United States is the Lake Pontchartrian Causeway in Louisiana, which spans 41,940 yards. How much longer is the Jiaozhou Bridge, in units of feet, than the Lake Pontchartrain Causeway?

8. The term "deep sea" refers to everything below a depth of 200 meters. It is estimated more than 90% of the living space on the planet exists at this depth. The deep sea is an area of great interest for explorers. If a submarine dives to a depth of 400 meters, how deep is this in units of miles?

9. Which of the following is the fastest speed?

   (a) 50 centimeters per second
   (b) 2.5 kilometers per hour
   (c) 1 mile per hour
   (d) 125 feet per minute

10. Which of the following is the largest mass flowrate?

   (a) 500 centigrams per hour
   (b) 5 grams per minute
   (c) 80 milligrams per second
   (d) 10 pounds-mass per day

11. Which of the following is the largest volumetric flowrate?

    (a) 10 centiliters per minute
    (b) 1 cubic inch per second
    (c) 10 gallons per hour
    (d) 0.01 cubic foot per minute

12. If a liquid evaporates at a rate of 50 kilograms per minute, what is this evaporation rate in units of pounds-mass per second?

13. If a pump moves water at 70 gallons per minute, what is the volumetric flow rate in units of cubic inches per second?

14. One of the National Academy of Engineering Grand Challenges for Engineering is **Provide Access to Clean Water**. Only 5% of water is used for households—the majority is used for agriculture and industry. It takes 240 gallons of water to produce one pound of rice. How many liters of water are needed to produce one kilogram of rice?

15. One of the National Academy of Engineering Grand Challenges for Engineering is **Provide Access to Clean Water**. Only 5% of water is used for households—the majority is used for agriculture and industry. It takes 1,680 gallons of water to produce one pound of grain-fed beef. How many cubic feet of water are needed to produce one kilogram of beef?

16. One of the National Academy of Engineering Grand Challenges for Engineering is **Provide Access to Clean Water**. Only 5% of water is used for households—the majority is used for agriculture and industry. It is estimated that 528 gallons of water are required to produce food for one person for one day. How many liters per year are required to feed one person?

17. The oxgang is unit of area equal to 20 acres. Express an area of 12 oxgangs in units of square meters.

18. In an effort to modernize the United States interstate system, the Department of Transportation proposes to change speed limits from miles per hour to "flashes." A flash is equal to 10 feet per second. On a car speedometer, what will the new range be in units of "flashes" if the old scale was set to a maximum of 120 miles per hour?

19. Old Mississippi River paddle wheelers routinely measured the river depths to avoid running aground. They used the unit "fathoms," where 1 fathom = 6 feet. The pilot would sing out "mark three" when the river was 3 fathoms deep and "mark twain" at 2 fathoms. The American writer Samuel Clemens took this as his pen name, Mark Twain. If we take 2 fathoms as a new unit, "twain," express 60 miles per hour in units of twains per second.

20. The Units Society Empire (USE) had defined the following set of "new" units: 1 foot = 10 toes. Convert 45 toes to units of meters.

21. The Units Society Empire (USE) had defined the following set of "new" units: 1 mile = 50 yonders. Convert 500 yards to units of yonders.

22. The Units Society Empire (USE) had defined the following set of "new" units: 1 leap = 4 years. Convert 64 leaps to units of months.

23. The Units Society Empire (USE) had defined the following set of "new" units:

Length   1 car = 20 feet
Time   1 class = 50 minutes

Determine X in the following expression: speed limit, 60 miles per hour = X cars per class.

24. The Units Society Empire (USE) had defined the following set of "new" units:

Length   1 stride = 1.5 meters
Time   1 blink = 0.3 seconds

Determine X in the following expression: Boeing 747 cruising speed, 550 miles per hour = X strides per blink.

25. The Units Society Empire (USE) had defined the following set of "new" units:

Length   1 stride = 1.5 meters
Time   1 blink = 0.3 seconds
Mass   1 heavy = 5 kilograms

Determine X in the following expression: force, 1 newton = X heavy stride per blink squared.

26. The Units Society Empire (USE) had defined the following set of "new" units:

Length   1 car = 20 feet
Time   1 class = 50 minutes
Mass   1 light = 2 pound-mass

Determine X in the following expression: force, 1 pound-force = X light car per class squared.

27. Determine the fundamental dimensions of the following quantities.

	Quantity	Common Units	Dimensions						
			M	L	T	Θ	N	J	I
(a)	fuel consumption	kg/(kW h)							
(b)	latent heat	BTU/lb$_m$							
(c)	specific weight	N/m^3							

28. Determine the fundamental dimensions of the following quantities.

	Quantity	Common Units	Dimensions						
			M	L	T	Θ	N	J	I
(a)	molar heat capacity	cal/(mol °C)							
(b)	rate of drying	lb$_m$/(ft^2 h)							
(c)	thermal resistance	(K m^2)/W							

29. Identify the following quantities through the use of fundamental dimensions. Choose from the list (A) - (F) shown

(A) Acceleration   (D) Power
(B) Energy   (E) Pressure
(C) Force   (F) Velocity

(a) $\sqrt{\dfrac{E}{V\rho}}$ where: ρ = density [g/cm^3] E = energy [J] V = volume [m^3]

(b) $\rho\,Q\,g\,H$ where: ρ = density [kg/m^3] Q = volumetric flowrate [gal/s]
                               g = gravity [m/s^2] H = height [in]

30. Identify the following quantities through the use of fundamental dimensions. Choose from the list (A) - (F) shown

(A) Acceleration   (D) Power
(B) Energy   (E) Pressure
(C) Force   (F) Velocity

(a) $\sqrt{\dfrac{F}{A\rho}}$ where: ρ = density [g/cm^3] F = force [N] A = area [m^2]

(b) $E/(m\,H)$ where: E = energy [J] m = mass [g] H = height [ft]

31. Using the following definitions and your knowledge of fundamental dimensions and base units, which of the following are dimensionally equal to length?

Property	Symbol	Typical units	Equivalent units
Acceleration	a	m/s²	
Charge	Q	coulomb [C]	A s
Dynamic viscosity	μ	poise [P]	g/(cm s)
Electric power	P	W	
Mass	m	kg	
Mass Flow Rate	ṁ	kg/s	
Thrust	T	N	
Voltage	V	V	

(a) $\dot{m}/\mu$

(b) VQ/P

(c) $PT/(m\,a)$

32. Using the following definitions and your knowledge of fundamental dimensions and base units, which of the following are dimensionally equal to time?

Property	Symbol	Typical units	Equivalent units
Charge	Q	coulomb [C]	A s
Dynamic viscosity	μ	poise [P]	g / (cm s)
Electric power	P	W	
Kinematic viscosity	ν	stokes [St]	cm²/s
Mass Flow Rate	ṁ	kg /s	
Thrust	T	N	
Voltage	V	V	

(a) $\dot{m}/\mu$

(b) $P/(\nu\,T)$

(c) VQ/P

33. We wish to analyze the velocity (v) of a fluid exiting an orifice in the side of a pressurized tank. The tank contains a fluid to a depth (H) above the orifice. The air above the fluid in the tank is pressurized to a value of (P). We realize the greater the pressure inside, the greater the velocity. We also believe the greater the depth of fluid, the greater the velocity. Examine the equations below and indicate for each if the equation is a valid or invalid equation; justify your answer for each case. In these expressions, g is the acceleration due to gravity and ρ is the fluid density.

(A) $v = \dfrac{P}{\rho} + \sqrt{2gH}$

(B) $v = \sqrt{\dfrac{P}{\rho} + 2H}$

(C) $v = \sqrt{\dfrac{2P}{\rho} + 2gH}$

(D) $v = \sqrt{2P + 2gH}$

34. Wind energy uses large fans to extract energy from the wind and turn it into electric power. Examine the equations below and indicate for each if the equation is a valid or invalid equation; justify your answer for each case. In these expressions, P is the power, η is the efficiency, ρ is the density of the air, A is the area swept out by the fan blades, and v is the velocity of the wind.

(A) $P = \eta\rho A^2 v^2$

(B) $P = \eta\rho A v^2$

(C) $P = \eta\rho A v^3$

(D) $P = \eta\rho^2 A v$

(E) $P = \eta\sqrt{\rho A v^3}$

35. We have encountered some equations in an old set of laboratory notes, each having two terms on the right-hand side of the equation. We realize we cannot read the final variable or variables listed in each equation. Using dimensions and the equation laws, determine the missing variable from the list below, and if that variable is multiplied or divided. In some questions, more than one variable may be required to form the necessary dimensions.

Variable choices:

Area	Acceleration	Density	Height
Mass	Speed	Time	Volume

(a) Distance = (speed) * (time) + (acceleration) ___ (___)
(b) Volume = (dimensionless constant) * (length) * (area) + (speed) ___ (___)
(c) Pressure = (density) * (area)/(time)^2 + (mass) * (acceleration) ___ (___)

36. We have encountered some equations in an old set of laboratory notes, each having two terms on the right-hand side of the equation. We realize we cannot read the final variable or variables listed in each equation. Using dimensions and the equation laws, determine the missing variable from the list below, and if that variable is multiplied or divided. In some questions, more than one variable may be required to form the necessary dimensions.

Variable choices:

Area	Acceleration	Density	Height
Mass	Speed	Time	Volume

(a) Speed = (distance)/(time) + (acceleration) ___ (___)
(b) Energy = (mass) * (speed)^2 + (mass) * (height) ___ (___)
(c) Power = (mass) * (area)/(time)^3 + (mass) * (acceleration) ___ (___)

37. What are the dimensions of the constant coefficient (k) in the following equations?
(a) Energy = k * (mass) * (temperature)
(b) Force = k * (pressure)
(c) Pressure = k * (temperature)/(volume)

38. What are the dimensions of the constant coefficient (k) in the following equations?
(a) Energy = k * (height)
(b) Mass flowrate = k * (velocity) * (area)
(c) Power = k * (mass) * (acceleration) * (temperature)

39. The largest hailstone is the United States was 44.5 centimeters in circumference in Coffeyville, Kansas. What is the diameter of the hailstone in units of inches?

40. The largest hailstone is the United States was 44.5 centimeters in circumference in Coffeyville, Kansas. What is the volume of the hailstone in units of liters?

41. How large a surface area in units of square feet will 1 gallon of paint cover if we apply a coat of paint that is 0.1 centimeter thick?

42. How large a surface area in units of square feet will 1 gallon of paint cover if we apply a coat of paint that is 0.1 inches thick?

43. We know a speed boat can travel at 30 knots. How long (in minutes) will it take to cross the Chesapeake Bay at a place where the bay is 24 miles across? 1 knot = 1 nautical mile per hour; 1 nautical mile = 6,076 feet.

44. In many engineering uses, the value of "g," the acceleration due to gravity, is taken as a constant. However, g is actually dependent upon the distance from the center of the Earth. A more accurate expression for g is:

$$g = g_0 \left(\frac{R_e}{R_e + A} \right)^2$$

Here, g_0 is the acceleration of gravity at the surface of the Earth, A is the altitude, and R_e is the radius of the Earth, approximately 6,380 kilometers. Assume g_0 = 9.8 meters per second squared. What is the value of g at an altitude of 20 miles in units of meters per second squared?

45. In many engineering uses, the value of "g," the acceleration due to gravity, is taken as a constant. However, g is actually dependent upon the distance from the center of the Earth. A more accurate expression for g is:

$$g = g_0 \left(\frac{R_e}{R_e + A} \right)^2$$

Here, g_0 is the acceleration of gravity at the surface of the Earth, A is the altitude, and R_e is the radius of the Earth, approximately 6,380 kilometers. Assume g_0 = 9.8 meters per second squared. If the value of g is 9 meters per second squared, what is the altitude in units of miles?

46. A box has a volume of 10 gallons. If two sides of the box measure 2.4 meters × 2.4 feet, what is the length of the third side of the box in units of inches?

47. We turn on our garden hose and point it straight up. It seems reasonable to assume that the height (H) to which the jet of water rises depends on the initial velocity of the water (v_0) and the acceleration due to gravity (g) as expressed by the relationship

$$H = K \frac{v_0^2}{g}$$

The constant (K) is unitless. If the value of K is 25, what initial velocity, in units of meters per second, will give a water height of 0.5 meters?

CHAPTER 8
UNIVERSAL UNITS

In the chapter on fundamental dimensions, the concepts of derived dimensions and units were introduced. Five of the most common named units were introduced in that chapter, and are so critical they are repeated here as Table 8-1. Recall that numerous common derived dimensions do not have a corresponding derived SI unit. For example, there is no named SI unit for the derived dimension velocity as there is for force (newton) or electrical resistance (ohm).

Table 8-1 **Common derived units in the SI system**

Dimension	SI Unit	Base SI Units	Derived from
Force (F)	newton [N]	$1\ \mathrm{N} = 1\dfrac{\mathrm{kg\ m}}{\mathrm{s}^2}$	$F = ma$ Force = mass times acceleration
Energy (E)	joule [J]	$1\ \mathrm{J} = 1\ \mathrm{N\ m} = 1\dfrac{\mathrm{kg\ m}^2}{\mathrm{s}^2}$	$E = Fd$ Energy = force times distance
Power (P)	watt [W]	$1\ \mathrm{W} = 1\dfrac{\mathrm{J}}{\mathrm{s}} = 1\dfrac{\mathrm{kg\ m}^2}{\mathrm{s}^3}$	$P = E/t$ Power = energy per time
Pressure (P)	pascal [Pa]	$1\ \mathrm{Pa} = 1\dfrac{\mathrm{N}}{\mathrm{m}^2} = 1\dfrac{\mathrm{kg}}{\mathrm{m\ s}^2}$	$P = F/A$ Pressure = force per area
Voltage (V)	volt [V]	$1\ \mathrm{V} = 1\dfrac{\mathrm{W}}{\mathrm{A}} = 1\dfrac{\mathrm{kg\ m}^2}{\mathrm{s}^3\ \mathrm{A}}$	$V = P/I$ Voltage = power per current

8.1 FORCE

LEARN TO: Identify a force quantity when it is expressed in base SI units
Convert from one unit of force to another
Determine the final quantity if given two quantities: force, acceleration, weight

When you push a grocery cart, it moves. If you keep pushing, it keeps moving. The longer you push, the faster it goes; the velocity increases over time, meaning that it accelerates. If you push a full grocery cart that has a high mass, it does not speed up as much, meaning it accelerates less than a cart with low mass. Simply put, the acceleration (a) of a body depends on the force (F) exerted on it and its mass (m). This is a simple form of "Newton's second law of motion" and is usually written as $F = ma$.

The SI unit of force, the **newton** [N], is defined as the force required to accelerate a mass of one kilogram at a rate of one meter per second squared (see Table 8-2). It is named for Sir Isaac Newton (1643–1727). Newton's *Principia* is considered one of the world's greatest scientific writings, explaining the law of universal gravitation and the three laws of motion. Newton also developed the law of conservation of momentum, the law of cooling, and the reflecting telescope. He shares credit for the development of calculus with Gottfried Leibniz.

IMPORTANT CONCEPT

Force =
    mass * acceleration

$F = ma$

SI unit of force =
    newton

Table 8-2 Dimensions of force

Quantity	Common Units	Exponents						
		M	L	T	Θ	N	J	I
Force	N	1	1	−2	0	0	0	0

In the SI system, mass, length, and time are base units and force is a derived unit; force is found from combining mass, length, and time using Newton's second law. The SI system is called "coherent," because the derived unit is set at one by combing base units. The AES system is considered non-coherent as it uses units that do not work together in the same fashion as the SI units do. There are two uses of the term "pound" in the AES system, which occurred in common usage long before Newton discovered gravity. To distinguish mass in pounds and force in pounds, the unit of mass is given as pound-mass (lb_m) and the unit of force is given as pound-force (lb_f). One pound-force is the amount of force needed to accelerate one pound-mass at a rate of 32.2 feet per second squared. Since this relationship is not easy to remember or use in conversions, we will stick with SI units for problem solving, following the procedure discussed in the chapter on fundamental dimensions.

NOTE

In general, a "pound" can be used as a unit of mass or force.

For distinction, the following convention is used:

– pound-mass [lb_m]

– pound-force [lb_f]

Table 8-3

Unit System	Mass	Acceleration	Force	
SI	1 kg	1 m/s^2	1 N = 1 kg m/s^2	** coherent **
AES	1 lb$_m$	32.2 ft/s^2	1 lb$_f$ = 32.2 lb$_m$ ft/s^2	** non-coherent **

● **EXAMPLE 8-1**

A professional archer is designing a new longbow with a full draw weight of 63 pounds-force [lb_f]. The draw weight is the amount of force needed to hold the bowstring at a given amount of draw, or the distance the string has been pulled back from the rest position. What is the full draw weight of this bow in units of newtons [N]?

Method	Steps
(1) Convert term	63 lb$_f$
(2) Apply conversion formula	1 N = 0.225 lb$_f$
(3) Make a fraction	$\dfrac{63\ lb_f}{}\left\vert\dfrac{1\ N}{0.225\ lb_f}\right.$
(4) Multiply	
(5) Cancel, calculate, be reasonable	280 N

● **EXAMPLE 8-2**

A ship is being designed to use an engine that run continuously, providing a small but constant acceleration of 0.06 meters per second squared. If the ship has a mass of 30,000 kilograms, what is the thrust (force) provided by the engines in units of pounds-force?

Step One: Convert to Base SI Units	
No conversion necessary	
Step Two: Calculate	
Method	**Steps**
(1) Determine appropriate equation	$F = ma$
(2) Insert known quantities	$F = \dfrac{30{,}000\ \text{kg}}{}\bigg\vert\dfrac{0.06\ \text{m}}{\text{s}^2}$
(3) Calculate	$F = 1800\ \dfrac{\text{kg m}}{\text{s}^2}$

This is apparently our final answer, but the units are puzzling. If the unit of force is the newton, and if this is a valid equation, then our final result for force should be newtons. If we consider the dimensions of force

Quantity	Common Units	Exponents						
		M	**L**	**T**	**Θ**	**N**	**J**	**I**
Force	N	1	1	−2	0	0	0	0

A unit of force has dimensions $F \{=\} ML/T^2$, which in terms of base SI units would be $F [=] kg\ m/s^2$. As this term occurs so frequently it is given the special name "newton" (see Table 8-1). Anytime we see the term $[kg\ m/s^2]$, we know we are dealing with a force equal to a newton.

(3) Calculate	$\dfrac{1800\ \text{kg m}}{\text{s}^2}\bigg\vert\dfrac{1\ \text{N}}{1\ \frac{\text{kg m}}{\text{s}^2}} = 1800\ \text{N}$

Step Three: Convert from Base SI Units to Desired Units	
Method	**Steps**
(1) Convert term	1800 N
(2) Apply conversion formula	$1\ \text{N} = 0.225\ \text{lb}_f$
(3) Make a fraction	$\dfrac{1800\ \text{N}}{}\bigg\vert\dfrac{0.0225\ \text{lb}_f}{1\ \text{N}}$
(4) Multiply	
(5) Cancel, calculate, be reasonable	$405\ \text{lb}_f$

COMPREHENSION CHECK 8-1

The engine on a spacecraft nearing Mars can provide a thrust of 15,000 newtons. If the spacecraft has a mass of 750 kilograms, what is the acceleration of the spacecraft in miles per hour squared?

8.2 WEIGHT

LEARN TO: Describe the difference between mass and weight
Determine the final quantity if given two quantities: mass, gravity, weight

IMPORTANT CONCEPT

Weight is a FORCE

weight = mass * gravity

$w = mg$

SI unit of weight = newton

NOTE

Objects in space are weightless, not massless.

The **mass** of an object is a fundamental dimension. Mass is a quantitative measure of how much of an object there is, or in other words, how much matter it contains. The **weight** (w) of an object is a force equal to the mass of the object (m) times the acceleration of **gravity** (g).

While mass is independent of location in the universe, weight is dependent upon both mass and gravity (Table 8-4).

On the Earth, the pull of gravity is approximately 9.8 meters per second squared [m/s²]. On the moon, gravity is approximately one-sixth this value, or 1.6 m/s². A one kilogram [kg] object acted on by Earth's gravity would have a weight of 9.8 N, but on the moon it would have a weight of 1.6 N. Unless otherwise stated, assume all examples take place on the Earth.

Table 8-4 Dimensions of weight

Quantity	Common Units	M	L	T	Θ	N	J	I
Weight	N	1	1	−2	0	0	0	0

DEVILISH DERIVATION

- **Mass of an object:** A quantitative measure of how much of an object there is.
- **Weight of an object:** A quantitative measure of the force exerted on the object due to gravity.
  Newton's law of universal gravitation states

$$F = G\frac{m_1 m_2}{r^2}$$

where:
   G is universal gravitational constant

$$G = 6.673 \times 10^{-11}\,(\text{N m}^2)/\text{kg}^2$$

m is the mass
r is the distance between the centers of mass of two bodies

On the Earth, the distance between the center of a body and the center of the earth is approximately the radius of the Earth, r_e.

The mass of one of the bodies can be defined as is the mass of the Earth (with an "e" subscript). Rewrite the equation:

$$F = m\left[G\,\frac{m_e}{r_e^2}\right]$$

The quantity in square brackets is a constant (call it "g"). We call the force "the weight (w) of the body." So,

$$w = mg$$

This is the common equation that relates weight and mass. The value for g is calculated to be 9.8 meters per second squared [m/s²], or 32.2 feet per second squared [ft/s²]. Note that g has the units of acceleration.

● **EXAMPLE 8-3**   What is the weight of a 225-kilogram [kg] bag of birdseed in units of newtons [N]?

Step One: Convert to Base SI Units	
No conversion necessary	

Step Two: Calculate	
Method	**Steps**
(1) Determine appropriate equation	$w = mg$
(2) Insert known quantities	$w = \dfrac{225\ \text{kg}}{}\left|\dfrac{9.8\ \text{m}}{\text{s}^2}\right.$
(3) Calculate, be reasonable	$w = 2{,}205\ \dfrac{\text{kg m}}{\text{s}^2}\left|\dfrac{1\ \text{N}}{\frac{1\ \text{kg m}}{\text{s}^2}}\right. = 2{,}205\ \text{N}$

Step Three: Convert from Base SI Units to Desired Units	
No conversion necessary	

COMPREHENSION CHECK 8-2

The mass of the human brain is 1,360 grams. State the weight of the human brain in units of newtons on the Earth.

COMPREHENSION CHECK 8-3

The mass of the human brain is 1,360 grams. State the weight of the human brain in units of newtons on the moon. The gravity on the moon is 1.6 meters per second squared.

8.3 DENSITY

LEARN TO:	Determine the density in any required units if given specific gravity
	Recall the common values for density of water and the limits of density for solids, liquids, and gasses
	Determine the final quantity if given two quantities: density, mass, volume

IMPORTANT CONCEPT

Density is shown as ρ

$\rho = m/V$

SI unit $= kg/m^3$

Specific weight is shown as γ

$\gamma = w/V$

SI unit $= N/m^3$

Density (ρ, Greek letter rho) is the mass of an object (m) divided by the volume the object occupies (V). Density should not be confused with weight—think of the old riddle: which weighs more, a pound of feathers or a pound of bricks? The answer is they both weigh the same amount, one pound, but the density of each is different. The bricks have a higher density than the feathers, since the same mass takes up less space.

Specific weight (γ, Greek letter gamma) is the weight of an object (w) divided by the volume the object occupies (V) (Table 8-5).

Table 8-5 Dimensions of density and specific weight

Quantity	Common Units	Exponents						
		M	L	T	Θ	N	J	I
Density	kg/m^3	1	−3	0	0	0	0	0
Specific weight	N/m^3	1	−2	−2	0	0	0	0

● **EXAMPLE 8-4**

The density of sugar is 1.61 grams per cubic centimeter [g/cm^3]. What is the density of sugar in units of pound-mass per cubic foot [lb_m/ft^3]?

NOTE

Upon conversion from units of grams per cubic centimeter to pound-mass per cubic foot, the answer should be $\approx$ 60 times larger.

Method	Steps
(1) Term to be converted	$1.61 \ g/cm^3$
(2) Conversion formula	
(3) Make fractions	$1.61\dfrac{g}{cm^3}\left\|\dfrac{2.205 \ lb_m}{1,000 \ g}\right\|\dfrac{1,000 \ cm^3}{0.0353 \ ft^3}$
(4) Multiply	
(5) Cancel, calculate, be reasonable	$101 \ lb_m/ft^3$

● **EXAMPLE 8-5**

The density of a biofuel blend is 0.72 grams per cubic centimeter [g/cm^3]. What is the density of the biofuel in units of kilograms per cubic meter [kg/m^3]?

NOTE

Upon conversion from units of grams per cubic centimeter to kilograms per cubic meter, the answer should be 1,000 times larger.

Method	Steps
(1) Term to be converted	$0.72 \ g/cm^3$
(2) Conversion formula	
(3) Make fractions	$0.72\dfrac{g}{cm^3}\left\|\dfrac{1 \ kg}{1,000 \ g}\right\|\dfrac{100^3 \ cm^3}{1 \ m^3}$
(4) Multiply	
(5) Cancel, calculate, be reasonable	$720 \ kg/m^3$

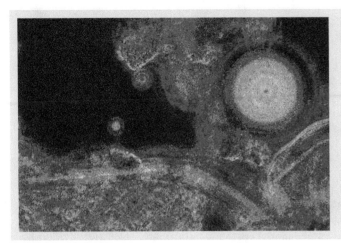

A vast array of valuable compounds can be formed by microbial cultures. Oil produced by the fungi *Pythium irregulare* can be extracted and used for biofuels or pharmaceutical compounds. Biosystems engineers culture the microorganism, design the bioreactor, and extract the valuable compounds using sustainable, ecoprocessing techniques.

Photo courtesy of C. Drapcho

● EXAMPLE 8-6

What is the weight of water, in units of pounds-force [lb_f], in a 55-gallon drum completely full? Assume the density of water to be 1 gram per cubic centimeter. Ignore the weight of the drum.

Step One: Convert to Base SI Units		
Method	**Steps**	
(1) Term to be converted	55 gal	1 g/cm³
(2) Conversion formula (3) Make fractions (4) Multiply	$\dfrac{55 \text{ gal}}{} \left\| \dfrac{1 \text{ L}}{0.264 \text{ gal}} \right\| \dfrac{1 \text{ m}^3}{1,000 \text{ L}}$	$\dfrac{1 \text{ g}}{\text{cm}^3} \left\| \dfrac{1 \text{ kg}}{1,000 \text{ g}} \right\| \dfrac{100^3 \text{ cm}^3}{1 \text{ m}^3}$
(5) Cancel, calculate	0.208 m³	1,000 kg/m³

Step Two: Calculate	
Method	**Steps**
(1) Determine appropriate equation	$w = mg$
(2) Insert known quantities	$w = \dfrac{m}{} \left\| \dfrac{9.8 \text{ m}}{\text{s}^2} \right.$

For Unknown Quantities, Repeat the Process	
Method	**Steps**
(1) Determine appropriate equation	$m = \rho V$
(2) Insert known quantities	$m = \dfrac{1,000 \text{ kg}}{\text{m}^3} \left\| 0.208 \text{ m}^3 \right.$
(3) Calculate, be reasonable	$m = 208 \text{ kg}$
(2) Insert known quantities	$w = \dfrac{208 \text{ kg}}{} \left\| \dfrac{9.8 \text{ m}}{\text{s}^2} \right.$
(3) Calculate	$w = 2,038 \dfrac{\text{kg m}}{\text{s}^2} \left\| \dfrac{1 \text{ N}}{\frac{1 \text{ kg m}}{\text{s}^2}} = 2,038 \text{ N} \right.$

Step Three: Convert from Base SI Units to Desired Units	
Method	**Steps**
(1) Term to be converted	2,038 N
(2) Conversion formula (3) Make a fraction (4) Multiply	$\dfrac{2{,}038\ \text{N}}{}\left\|\dfrac{0.225\ \text{lb}_f}{1\ \text{N}}\right.$
(5) Cancel, calculate, be reasonable	460 lb$_f$

Specific Gravity

IMPORTANT CONCEPT

$$SG = \frac{\rho_{object}}{\rho_{water}}$$

In technical literature, density is rarely given; instead, the **specific gravity** is reported. The specific gravity (SG) of an object is a dimensionless ratio of the density of the object to the density of water (see Table 8-6). It is convenient to list density in this fashion so *any* unit system may be applied by our choice of the units of the density of water. The specific gravities of several common substances are listed in Table 8-7.

Table 8-6 Dimensions of specific gravity

Quantity	Common Units	Exponents						
		M	**L**	**T**	**Θ**	**N**	**J**	**I**
Specific gravity	–	0	0	0	0	0	0	0

IMPORTANT CONCEPT

Density of water

$= 1$ g/cm^3

$= 1$ kg/L

$= 1{,}000$ kg/m^3

$= 62.4$ lb$_m$/ft^3

$= 1.94$ slug/ft^3

Table 8-7 Specific gravity values for common substances

Liquids	SG	Solids	SG
Acetone	0.785	Aluminum	2.70
Benzene	0.876	Baking soda	0.689
Citric acid	1.67	Brass	8.40–8.75
Gasoline	0.739	Concrete	2.30
Glycerin	1.26	Copper	8.96
Iodine	4.93	Gallium	5.91
Mercury	13.6	Gold	19.3
Mineral oil	0.900	Graphite	2.20
Olive oil	0.703	Iron	7.87
Propane	0.806	Lead	11.4
Sea water	1.03	Polyvinyl chloride (PVC)	1.38
Toluene	0.865	Silicon	2.33
Water	1.00	Zinc oxide	5.60

SPECIFIC GRAVITY
LIMITS

Solids > 0.5, < 23

Liquids ~ 1

*exceptions:

  iodine, 4.93

  mercury, 13.6

Gasses ~ 0.001 –
  0.0001

When calculating or considering specific gravities, it is helpful to keep in mind the range of values that you are likely to have.

The densest naturally occurring elements at normal temperature and pressure are osmium and iridium, both with a specific gravity close to 22.6. The *densest substances that a normal person is likely to encounter are platinum (SG = 21.5) and gold (SG = 19.3).* Thus, if you calculate a specific gravity to be higher than about 23, you have almost certainly made an error.

Most liquids are similar to water, with a specific gravity around 1. One notable exception is mercury, with a specific gravity of 13.

On the lower end of the scale, the *specific gravity of air is about 0.001,* whereas hydrogen has a specific gravity of slightly less than 0.0001.

Therefore, if you get a specific gravity value less than about 10^{-4}, you need to check your work very carefully.

● **EXAMPLE 8-7**

The specific gravity of butane is 0.599. What is the density of butane in units of kilograms per cubic meter?

Step One: Convert to Base SI Units	
No conversion needed	

Step Two: Calculate	
Method	**Steps**
(1) Determine appropriate equation	$\rho_{object} = (SG)(\rho_{water})$
(2) Insert known quantities	$\rho_{object} = (0.599)\left(1{,}000\ \dfrac{kg}{m^3}\right)$
(3) Calculate, be reasonable	$\rho_{object} = 599\ \dfrac{kg}{m^3}$

Step Three: Convert from Base SI Units to Desired Units	
No conversion needed	

● **EXAMPLE 8-8**

Mercury has a specific gravity of 13.6. What is the density of mercury in units of slugs per liter?

Step One: Convert to Base SI Units	
No conversion needed	

Step Two: Calculate	
Method	**Steps**
(1) Determine appropriate equation	$\rho_{object} = (SG)(\rho_{water})$
(2) Insert known quantities	$\rho_{object} = (13.6)\left(1.94\ \dfrac{slug}{ft^3}\right)$
(3) Calculate	$\rho_{object} = 26.384\ \dfrac{slug}{ft^3}$

Step Three: Convert from Base SI Units to Desired Units	
Method	**Steps**
(1) Term to be converted	26.384 slug/ft^3
(2) Conversion formula	
(3) Make a fraction	$\dfrac{26.384 \text{ slug}}{\text{ft}^3} \left\vert \dfrac{0.0353 \text{ ft}^3}{1 \text{ L}} \right.$
(4) Multiply	
(5) Cancel, calculate, be reasonable	0.931 slug/L

COMPREHENSION CHECK 8-4

Convert 50 grams per cubic centimeter into units of pounds-mass per cubic foot.

COMPREHENSION CHECK 8-5

A 75-gram cylindrical rod is measured to be 10 centimeters long and 2.5 centimeters in diameter. What is the specific gravity of the material?

8.4 AMOUNT

LEARN TO: Determine the final quantity if given two quantities: amount in grams, amount in moles, molecular weight
Understand the difference between amount of substance and molecular weight
Recall the value and significance of Avogadro's Number

Some things are really very large and some are very small. Stellar distances are so large that it becomes inconvenient to report values such as 235 trillion miles, or 6.4×10^{21} feet when we are interested in the distance between two stars or two galaxies. To make things better, we use a new unit of length that itself is large—the distance that light goes in a year; this is a very long way, 3.1×10^{16} feet. As a result, we do not have to say that the distance between two stars is 620,000,000,000,000,000 feet, we can just say that they are 2 light-years apart.

This same logic holds when we want to discuss very small things such as molecules or atoms. Most often we use a constant that has been named after Amedeo Avogadro, an Italian scientist (1777–1856) who first proposed the idea of a fixed ratio between the amount of substance and the number of elementary particles. The Avogadro constant has a value of 6.022×10^{23} particles per mole. If we have 12 of something, we call it a dozen. If we have 20, it is a score. If we have 6.022×10^{23} of anything, we have a mole. If we have 6.022×10^{23} baseballs, we have a mole of baseballs. If we have 6.022×10^{23} elephants, we have a mole of elephants, and if we have 6.022×10^{23} molecules, we have a mole of molecules. Of course, the mole is never used to define amounts of macroscopic things like elephants or baseballs, being relegated to the realm of the extremely tiny. In the paragraphs below we will see how this rather odd value originated and how this concept simplifies our calculations.

The mass of a nucleon (neutron or proton) is about 1.66×10^{-24} grams. To avoid having to use such tiny numeric values when dealing with nucleons, physicists defined the **atomic mass unit** [amu] to be approximately the mass of one nucleon.

Technically, it is defined as one-twelfth of the mass of a carbon twelve atom. In other words, 1 amu = 1.66×10^{-24} g. The symbol "u" is often used for amu, which is also known as a **Dalton** [Da].

If there is $(1.66 \times 10^{-24}$ g)/(1 amu), then there is (1 amu)/$(1.66 \times 10^{-24}$ g). Dividing this out gives 6.022×10^{23} amu/g. This numeric value is used to define the **mole** [mol]. One mole of a substance (usually an element or compound) contains exactly 6.022×10^{23} fundamental units (atoms or molecules) of that substance. In other words, there are 6.022×10^{23} fundamental units per mole. This is often written as

$$N_A = 6.022 \times 10^{23} \text{ mol}^{-1}$$

As mentioned above, this is called Avogadro's constant or **Avogadro's number**, symbolized by N_A. So why is this important? Consider combining hydrogen and oxygen to get water (H_2O). We need twice as many atoms of hydrogen as atoms of oxygen for this reaction; thus, for every mole of oxygen, we need two moles of hydrogen, since one mole of anything contains the same number of fundamental units, atoms in this case.

The problem is that it is difficult to measure a substance directly in moles, but it is easy to measure its mass. *Avogadro's number affords a conversion path between moles and mass.* Consider hydrogen and oxygen in the above. The atomic mass of an atom in **atomic mass units** [amu] is approximately equal to the number of nucleons it contains. Hydrogen contains one proton, and thus has an atomic mass of 1 amu. We can also say that there is 1 amu per hydrogen atom. Oxygen has an atomic mass of 16; thus, there are 16 amu per oxygen atom. Since atomic mass refers to an individual specific atom, the term **atomic weight** is used, representing the average value of all isotopes of the element. This is the value commonly listed on periodic tables.

Let us use this information, along with Avogadro's number, to determine the mass of one mole of each of these two elements.

$$\text{Hydrogen: } \frac{1 \text{ amu}}{\text{H atom}} \left| \frac{1 \text{ g}}{6.022 \times 10^{23} \text{ amu}} \right| \frac{6.022 \times 10^{23} \text{ atom}}{1 \text{ mol}} = \frac{1 \text{ g}}{1 \text{ mol H}}$$

$$\text{Oxygen: } \frac{16 \text{ amu}}{\text{O atom}} \left| \frac{1 \text{ g}}{6.022 \times 10^{23} \text{ amu}} \right| \frac{6.022 \times 10^{23} \text{ atom}}{1 \text{ mol}} = \frac{16 \text{ g}}{1 \text{ mol O}}$$

The numerical value for the atomic mass of a substance is the same as the number of grams in one mole of that substance, often called the **molar mass**.

Atomic weight = molar mass

Avogadro's number is the link between the two. Hydrogen has a molar mass of 1 gram per mole; oxygen has a molar mass of 16 grams per mole.

When groups of atoms react together, they form molecules. Consider combining hydrogen and oxygen to get water (H_2O). Two atoms of hydrogen combine with one atom of oxygen, so 2 * 1 amu H + 16 amu O = 18 amu H_2O. The **molecular mass** of water is 18 amu. By an extension of the example above, we can also state that one mole of water has a mass of 18 grams, called the **formula weight**.

molecular weight = formula weight

The difference between these ideas is summarized in Table 8-8.

This text assumes that you have been exposed to these ideas in an introductory chemistry class and so does not cover them in any detail. In all problems presented, you will be given the atomic weight of the elements or the formula weight of the molecule, depending on the question asked. This topic is briefly introduced because Avogadro's

NOTE

If Element Z has an atomic mass of X amu, there are X grams per mole of Element Z.

NOTE

If Molecule AB has a molecular weight of X amu, there are X grams per mole of Molecule AB.

number (N_A) is important in the relationship between several constants, including the following:

- The gas constant (R [=] J/(mol K)) and the Boltzmann constant (k [=] J/K), which relates energy to temperature: $R = kN_A$.
- The elementary charge (e [=] C) and the Faraday constant (F [=] C/mol), which is the electric charge contained in one mole of electrons: $F = eN_A$.
- An electron volt [eV] is a unit of energy describing the amount of energy gained by one electron accelerating through an electrostatic potential difference of one volt: $1 \text{ eV} = 1.602 \times 10^{-19}$ J.

Table 8-8 Definitions of "amount" of substance

The quantity . . .	measures the . . .	in units of . . .	and is found by . . .
Atomic mass	Mass of one atom of an individual isotope of an element	[amu]	Direct laboratory measurement
Atomic weight	Average mass of all isotopes of an element	[amu]	Listed on Periodic Table
Molar mass	Mass of one mole of the atom	[g/mol]	Listed on Periodic Table
Molecular mass or molecular weight	Sum of average weight of isotopes in molecule	[amu]	Combining atomic weights of individual atoms represented in the molecule
Formula weight	Mass of one mole of the molecule	[g/mol]	Combining molar mass of individual atoms represented in the molecule

---

● EXAMPLE 8-9

Let us return to the problem of combining hydrogen and oxygen to get water. Assume you have 50 grams of oxygen with which you want to combine the proper mass of hydrogen to convert it completely to water. The atomic weight of hydrogen is 1 and the atomic weight of oxygen is 16.

First determine how many moles of oxygen are present.

$$\frac{50 \text{ g O}}{} \left| \frac{1 \text{ mol O}}{16 \text{ g O}} \right. = 3.125 \text{ mol O}$$

We need twice as many moles of hydrogen as oxygen (H_2O), so we need 6.25 moles of hydrogen. Converting to mass gives

$$\frac{6.25 \text{ mol H}}{} \left| \frac{1 \text{ g H}}{1 \text{ mol H}} \right. = 6.25 \text{ g H}$$

● EXAMPLE 8-10

Acetylsalicylic acid (aspirin) has the chemical formula $C_9H_8O_4$. How many moles of aspirin are in a 1-gram dose? Use the following facts:

- Atomic weight of carbon = 12
- Atomic weight of hydrogen = 1
- Atomic weight of oxygen = 16

First, determine how many grams are in 1 mole of aspirin (determine formula weight).

$$\text{FW of aspirin} = \left[\frac{12\frac{g}{mole}}{1 \text{ molecule C}} \middle| \frac{9 \text{ C molecules}}{} \right] + \left[\frac{1\frac{g}{mole}}{1 \text{ molecule H}} \middle| \frac{8 \text{ H molecules}}{} \right]$$

$$+ \left[\frac{16\frac{g}{mole}}{1 \text{ molecule O}} \middle| \frac{4 \text{ O molecules}}{} \right] = 180 \frac{g}{mole}$$

Finally, convert to moles per dose.

$$\frac{1 \text{ g aspirin}}{\text{dose}} \middle| \frac{1 \text{ mol aspirin}}{180 \text{ g aspirin}} = 5.56 \times 10^{-3} \frac{\text{mol aspirin}}{\text{dose}}$$

● **EXAMPLE 8-11**

Many gases exist as diatomic compounds in nature, meaning two of the atoms are attached to form a molecule. Hydrogen, oxygen, and nitrogen all exist in a gaseous diatomic state under standard conditions.

   Assume there are 100 grams of nitrogen gas in a container. How many moles of nitrogen (N_2) are in the container? Atomic weight of nitrogen = 14.

First, determine how many grams are in 1 mole of diatomic nitrogen (determine the formula weight).

$$\text{FW of } N_2 = \frac{14\frac{g}{mol}}{1 \text{ mol N}} \middle| \frac{2 \text{ mol N}}{} = 28 \frac{g}{mol}$$

Next, convert mass to moles.

$$\frac{100 \text{ grams of } N_2}{} \middle| \frac{\text{mole}}{28 \text{ gram}} = 3.57 \text{ moles } N_2$$

COMPREHENSION CHECK 8-6

Determine the mass in units of grams of 0.025 moles of caffeine (formula: $C_8H_{10}N_4O_2$). The components are hydrogen (formula: H, amu = 1); carbon (formula: C, amu = 12); nitrogen (formula: N, amu = 14); and oxygen (formula: O, amu = 16).

COMPREHENSION CHECK 8-7

Determine the amount in units of moles of 5 grams of a common analgesic acetaminophen (formula: $C_8H_9NO_2$). The components are hydrogen (formula: H, amu = 1); carbon (formula: C, amu = 12); nitrogen (formula: N, amu = 14); and oxygen (formula: O, amu = 16).

8.5 TEMPERATURE

Convert a specific temperature value from one unit of temperature to another
Convert a material property value from one unit of temperature to another
Recall the temperature properties of water and the limits of the four common temperature
scales (°C, °F, K, °R)

NOTE

Human body
~37°C = 98°F

Room temperature
~21°C = 70°F

Melting point of
mercury –39°C =
–38°F

Melting temperature
of lead ~330°C =
620°F

Is 180 really an odd
value? No, not in
Fahrenheit's day.
The number 180 was
familiar to mathematicians and scientists
as the number of
degrees in half a circle
(360/2 = 180).

Temperature was originally conceived as a description of energy: heat (thermal energy) flows spontaneously from "hot" to "cold." But how hot is "hot"? The thermometer was devised as a way to measure the "hotness" of an object. As an object gets warmer, it usually expands. In a thermometer, a temperature is a level of hotness that corresponds to the length of the liquid in the tube. As the liquid gets warmer, it expands and moves up the tube. To give temperature a quantitative meaning, numerous temperature scales have been developed.

Many scientists, including Isaac Newton, have proposed temperature scales. Two scales were originally developed about the same time—**Fahrenheit** [°F] and **Celsius** [°C]—and have become widely accepted in laymen use. These are the most frequently used temperature scales by the general public. Gabriel Fahrenheit (1686–1736), a German physicist and engineer, developed the Fahrenheit scale in 1708. Anders Celsius (1701–1744), a Swedish astronomer, developed the Celsius scale in 1742. The properties of each scale are in Table 8-9.

You may wonder why the Celsius scale seems so reasonable, and the Fahrenheit scale so random. Actually, Mr. Fahrenheit was just as reasonable as Mr. Celsius. Mr. Celsius set the freezing point of water to be 0 and the boiling point to be 100. Mr. Fahrenheit took as 0 a freezing mixture of salt and ice, and as 100 body temperature. With this scale, it just so happens that the freezing and boiling points of water work out to be odd numbers.

Table 8-9 Properties of water

Scale	Freezing Point	Boiling Point	Divisions Between Freezing and Boiling
Fahrenheit [°F]	32	212	180
Celsius [°C]	0	100	100
Kelvin [K]	273	373	100
Rankine [°R]	492	672	180

Some units can cause confusion in calculation. One of those is temperature. One reason for this is that we use temperature in two different ways: (1) reporting an actual temperature value and (2) discussing the way a change in temperature affects a material property. To clarify, we resort to examples.

Calculating Temperature Values

When an actual temperature reading is reported, such as "the temperature in this room is 70°F," how do we determine this reading in another temperature scale? The scales have different zero points, so they cannot be determined using a single conversion factor as done previously but require a formula. Most of you are familiar with the formula to calculate between Fahrenheit and Celsius, but this equation is cumbersome to remember.

$$T[°F] = \frac{9}{5} T[°C] + 32$$

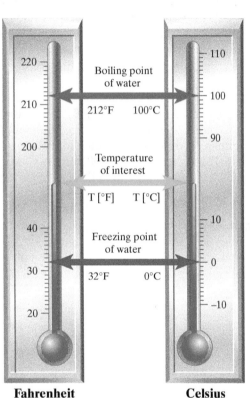

Fahrenheit **Celsius**

Let us imagine we have two thermometers, one with the Fahrenheit scale and the other with the Celsius scale. We set two thermometers side by side so that the freezing point and the boiling point of water are at the same location on both thermometers. We are interested in the relationship between these two scales. From this figure we see that the fraction of the distance from the freezing point to the boiling point in both scales is the same. This means that we can write

$$\frac{T[°F] - 32}{212 - 32} = \frac{T[°C] - 0}{100 - 0}$$

This relationship is really all we need to know to relate a temperature in degrees Fahrenheit to one in degrees Celsius. You can easily do the algebra to calcuate from Fahrenheit to Celsius, or vice versa. By remembering this form, you do not have to remember if the value is 9/5 or 5/9, or to add or subtract 32. This formula is determined by the method of interpolation.

There are numerous other temperature scales, but two are worth mentioning: **kelvin** [K] and **degrees Rankine** [°R]. The kelvin scale is named for First Baron William Thomson Kelvin (1824–1907), an English mathematician and physicist. Kelvin first proposed the idea of "infinite cold," or absolute zero, in 1848, using the Celsius scale for comparison. The Rankine scale is named for William J. M. Rankine (1820–1872), a Scottish engineer and physicist, who proposed an analogy to the kelvin scale, using the Fahrenheit scale. Both men made significant contributions to the field of thermodynamics.

The kelvin and Rankine scales are "absolute," which means that at absolute zero, the temperature at which molecules have minimum possible motion, the temperature is zero. Absolute temperature scales therefore have no negative values. In the kelvin scale, the degree sign is not used; it is simply referred to as "kelvin," not "degrees kelvin." It is the base SI unit for temperature and the most frequently used temperature unit in the scientific community.

EXAMPLE 8-12

The hottest temperature in the United States ever recorded by the National Weather Service, 56.7 degrees Celsius [°C], occurred in Death Valley, California, on July 10, 1913. State this value in units of degrees Fahrenheit [°F].

Method	Steps
(1) Determine appropriate equation	$\dfrac{T[°F] - 32}{212 - 32} = \dfrac{T[°C] - 0}{100 - 0}$
(2) Insert known quantities	$\dfrac{T[°F] - 32}{180} = \dfrac{56.7}{100}$
(3) Calculate, be reasonable	$T = 134°F$

IMPORTANT CONCEPT

When properties that contain temperature are converted:

$$\frac{1°C}{1.8°F} \quad \frac{1K}{1°C} \quad \frac{1°R}{1°F}$$

For this type of conversion, we read the units under consideration as "*per* degree Fahrenheit," with the clue being the word "*per.*"

Conversions Involving Temperature Within a Material Property

When considering how a change in temperature affects a material property, we use a scalar conversion factor. In general, we encounter this in sets of units relating to the property of the material; for example, the units of the thermal conductivity are given by W/(m K), which is read as "watts per meter kelvin." When this is the case, we are referring to the size of the degree, not the actual temperature.

To find this relationship, remember that between the freezing point and the boiling point of pure water, the Celsius scale contains 100 divisions, whereas the Fahrenheit scale contains 180 divisions. The conversion factor between Celsius and Fahrenheit is $100°C \equiv 180°F$, or $1°C \equiv 1.8°F$.

EXAMPLE 8-13

The specific heat (C_p) is the ability of an object to store heat. Specific heat is a material property, and values are available in technical literature. The specific heat of copper is 0.385 J/(g °C), which is read as "joules per gram degree Celsius." Convert this to units of J/(lb$_m$°F), which reads "joules per pound-mass degree Fahrenheit."

NOTE

Specific heat [J/(g K)]
Air = 1.012
Aluminum = 0.897
Copper = 0.385
Helium = 5.1932
Lead = 0.127
Water = 4.184

Method	Steps
(1) Term to be converted	$0.385 \dfrac{J}{g\,°C}$
(2) Conversion formula (3) Make a fraction (4) Multiply	$\dfrac{0.385\,J}{g\,°C}\left\|\dfrac{1,000\,g}{2.205\,lb_m}\right\|\dfrac{1°C}{1.8°F}$
(5) Cancel, calculate, be reasonable	$97 \dfrac{J}{lb_m\,°F}$

A note of clarification about the term "PER"—when reading the sentence: "Gravity on earth is commonly assumed to be 9.8 meters per second squared," there is often little confusion in translating the words to symbols: $g = 9.8$ m/s^2. For a more complex unit, however, this can present a challenge. For example, the sentence "The thermal conductivity of aluminum is 237 calories per hour meter degree Celsius," can be confusing because it can be interpreted as:

$$k = 237 \frac{\text{cal}}{\text{h m °C}} \quad \text{or} \quad k = 237 \frac{\text{cal}}{\text{h}}(\text{m °C}) \quad \text{or} \quad k = 237 \frac{\text{cal}}{\text{h m}}°\text{C}$$

Officially, according to SI rules, when writing out unit names anything following the word "per" appears in the denominator of the expression. This implies the first example listed is correct.

COMPREHENSION CHECK 8-8	The temperature of dry ice is –109.3 degrees Fahrenheit [°F]. Convert this temperature into units of kelvins [K].

COMPREHENSION CHECK 8-9	The specific heat capacity of copper is 0.09 British thermal units per pound-mass degree Fahrenheit [BTU/(lb$_m$ °F)]. Convert into units of British thermal units per gram kelvin [BTU/(g K)].

8.6 PRESSURE

LEARN TO: Determine final quantity if given four of the following: total pressure, hydrostatic pressure, density, gravity, height
Describe Pascal's Law
Recall the common values for atmospheric pressure

IMPORTANT CONCEPT

Pressure = force / area

$$\text{Pa} = \frac{\text{N}}{\text{m}^2}$$

SI unit of pressure = Pascal

Pressure is defined as force acting over an area, where the force is perpendicular to the area. In SI units, a **pascal** [Pa] is the unit of pressure, defined as one newton of force acting on an area of one square meter (Table 8-10). The unit pascal is named after Blaise Pascal (1623–1662), a French mathematician and physicist who made great contributions to the study of fluids, pressure, and vacuums. His contributions with Pierre de Fermat on the theory of probability were the groundwork for calculus.

Table 8-10 Dimensions of pressure

Quantity	Common Units	Exponents						
		M	L	T	Θ	N	J	I
Pressure	Pa	1	−1	−2	0	0	0	0

● **EXAMPLE 8-14**

PRESSURE

1 atm = 1.01325 bar
      = 33.9 ft H_2O
      = 29.92 in Hg
      = 760 mm Hg
      = 101,325 Pa
      = 14.7 psi

An automobile tire is pressurized to a 40 pound-force per square inch [psi or lb_f/in^2]. State this pressure in units of atmospheres [atm].

By examining the "Pressure" box in the conversion table on the inside front cover, we see that the following facts are available for use: 1 atm = 14.7 psi.

Method	Steps
(1) Term to be converted	40 psi
(2) Conversion formula	1 atm = 14.7 psi
(3) Make a fraction	$\dfrac{40\ psi}{}$ $\dfrac{1\ atm}{14.7\ psi}$
(4) Multiply	
(5) Cancel, calculate, be reasonable	2.7 atm

COMPREHENSION CHECK 8-10

If the pressure is 250 feet of water [ft H_2O], what is the pressure in units of inches of mercury [in Hg]?

In this chapter, we consider four forms of pressure, all involving fluids. The general term **fluid** applies to a gas, such as helium or air, or a liquid, such as water or honey.

- **Atmospheric pressure** — the pressure created by the weight of air above us.
- **Hydrostatic pressure** — the pressure exerted on a submerged object by the fluid in which it is immersed.
- **Total pressure** — the combination of atmospheric and hydrostatic pressure.
- **Gas pressure** — the pressure created by a gas inside a closed container.

Atmospheric Pressure

PRESSURE

1 atm ~ 14.7 psi ~ 101 kPa

Atmospheric pressure results from the weight of the air above us, which varies with both altitude and weather patterns. Standard atmospheric pressure is an average air pressure at sea level, defined as one atmosphere [atm], and is approximately equal to 14.7 pound-force per square inch [psi].

Pressure Measurement

When referring to the measurement of pressure, two types of reference points are commonly used.

NOTE

Car tires are inflated with between 30 and 40 psi (gauge pressure).

――――――

"Normal" blood pressure is 120 mm Hg/80 mm Hg (gauge pressure).

Absolute pressure uses a perfect vacuum as a reference point. Most meteorological readings are given as absolute pressure, using units of atmospheres or bars.

Gauge pressure uses the local atmospheric pressure as a reference point. Note that local atmospheric pressure is generally *not* standard atmospheric pressure at sea level. Measurements such as tire pressure and blood pressure are given as gauge pressure.

Absolute pressures are distinguished by an "a" after the pressure unit, such as "psia" to signify "pound-force per square inch absolute." Gauge pressure readings are distinguished by a "g" after the pressure unit, such as "psig" to signify "pound-force per square inch gauge." When using instrumentation to determine the pressure, be sure to note whether the device reads absolute or gauge pressure.

Gauge pressure, absolute pressure, and atmospheric pressure are related by

$$P_{absolute} = P_{gauge} + P_{atmospheric}$$

For example, if we have a reading of 35 psig, this would be 49.7 psia assuming an atmospheric pressure of 14.7 psi.

$$13.5 \text{ psig} + 14.7 \text{ psi} = 49.7 \text{ psia}$$

If a gauge pressure being measured is less than the local atmospheric pressure, this is usually referred to as **vacuum pressure**, and the negative sign is dropped. A perfect vacuum is defined as 0 psia. Thus, a perfect vacuum created at sea level on the Earth would read −14.7 psig, or 14.7 psig vacuum pressure.

As another example, if we have a reading of 10 psig vacuum pressure, this would be 4.7 psia assuming an atmospheric pressure of 14.7 psi.

$$-10 \text{ psig} + 14.7 \text{ psi} = 4.7 \text{ psia}$$

To illustrate the effect of local atmospheric pressure, consider the following scenario. You fill your automobile's tires to 35 psig on the shore of the Pacific Ocean in Peru, and then drive to Lake Titicaca on the Bolivian border at about 12,500 feet above sea level. The absolute pressure in the tires must remain the same in both locations, so your tire pressure now reads about 40 psig due to the decreased atmospheric pressure.

At the shore: 35 psig + 14.7 psi = 49.7 psia
At the lake: 49.7 psia − 9.5 psi = 40.2 psig

Occasionally in industry, it may be helpful to use a point of reference other than atmospheric pressure. For these specific applications, pressure may be discussed in terms of **differential pressure**, distinguished by a "d" after the pressure unit, such as "psid."

Hydrostatic Pressure

Hydrostatic pressure (P_{hydro}) results from the weight of a liquid or gas pushing on an object. *Remember, weight is a force!* A simple way to determine this is to consider a cylinder with a cross-sectional area (A) filled with a liquid of density ρ.

The pressure (P) at the bottom of the container can be found by **Pascal's law**, named after (once again) Blaise Pascal. Pascal's law states the hydrostatic pressure of a fluid is equal to the force of the fluid acting over an area.

IMPORTANT CONCEPT

Pascal's Law
$P_{hydro} = \rho g H$

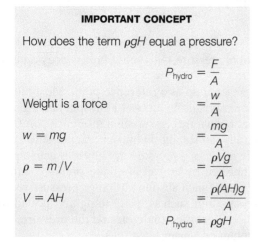

IMPORTANT CONCEPT

How does the term $\rho g H$ equal a pressure?

$$P_{hydro} = \frac{F}{A}$$

Weight is a force

$$= \frac{w}{A}$$

$w = mg$

$$= \frac{mg}{A}$$

$\rho = m/V$

$$= \frac{\rho V g}{A}$$

$V = AH$

$$= \frac{\rho (AH) g}{A}$$

$$P_{hydro} = \rho g H$$

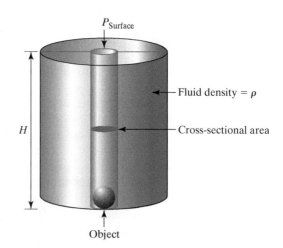

$P_{Surface}$

Fluid density = ρ

H

Cross-sectional area

Object

Recreational scuba diving takes place at depths between 0 and 20 meters. At deeper depths, additional training is usually required because of the increased risk of narcosis, a state similar to alcohol intoxication. The relationship between the depth and the level of narcosis is called the "Martini Effect," as it is said divers feel like they have drunk one martini for every 20 meters they descend.

Photo courtesy of E. Stephan

● EXAMPLE 8-15

We want to know the hydrostatic pressure in a lake at a depth of 20 feet in units of pascals.

For hydrostatic pressure, we need to know the density of the fluid in the lake. Since a density is not specified, we assume the density to be the standard density of water. We want all quantities in units of kilograms, meters, and seconds, so we use a density of 1,000 kilograms per cubic meter for water.

Step One: Convert to Base SI Units	
Method	**Steps**
(1) Term to be converted	20 ft
(2) Conversion formula	
(3) Make a fraction	$\dfrac{20\text{ ft}}{}\left|\dfrac{1\text{ m}}{3.28\text{ ft}}\right.$
(4) Multiply	
(5) Cancel, calculate	6.1 m

Step Two: Calculate	
Method	**Steps**
(1) Determine appropriate equation	$P_{hydro} = \rho g H$
(2) Insert known quantities	$P_{hydro} = \dfrac{1{,}000\text{ kg}}{m^3}\left|\dfrac{9.8\text{ m}}{s^2}\right|\dfrac{6.1\text{ m}}{}$
(3) Calculate, be reasonable	$P_{hydro} = 59{,}760\,\dfrac{kg}{m\,s^2}$

This is apparently our final answer, but the units are puzzling. If the units of pressure are pascals and if this is a valid equation, then our final result for pressure should be pascals. If we consider the dimensions of pressure:

Quantity	Common Units	Exponents			
		M	**L**	**T**	**Θ**
Pressure	Pa	1	−1	−2	0

A unit of pressure has dimensions, $P\{=\}M/(LT^2)$, which in terms of base SI units would be $P[=]kg/(m\ s^2)$. As this term occurs so frequently it is given the special name "pascal." When we see this term, we know we are dealing with a pressure equal to a pascal.

(3) Calculate, be reasonable	$P_{hydro} = 59{,}760\ \dfrac{kg}{m\ s^2}\left\|\dfrac{1\ Pa}{1\ \dfrac{kg}{m\ s^2}}\right. = 59{,}760\ Pa$	

Step Three: Convert from Base SI Units to Desired Units

No conversion needed

Total Pressure

We need to realize that Pascal's law is only a part of the story. Suppose we dive to a depth of 5 feet in a swimming pool and measure the pressure. Now we construct an enclosure over the pool and pressurize the air above the water surface to 3 atmospheres. When we dive back to the 5-foot depth, the pressure will have increased by 2 atmospheres.

Consequently, we conclude that total pressure at any depth in a fluid is the sum of hydrostatic pressure and surface pressure.

IMPORTANT CONCEPT

$P_{total} = P_{surface} + P_{hydro}$

$P_{total} = P_{surface} + \rho g H$

● **EXAMPLE 8-16**

When you dive to the bottom of a pool, at 12 feet under water, how much total pressure do you feel in units of atmospheres?

Step One: Convert to Base SI Units	
Method	**Steps**
(1) Term to be converted	12 ft
(2) Conversion formula	$\dfrac{12\ ft}{}\left\|\dfrac{1\ m}{3.28\ ft}\right.$
(3) Make a fraction	
(4) Multiply	
(5) Cancel, calculate	3.66 m

For hydrostatic pressure, we need to know the density of the fluid in the pool. Since a density is not specified, we assume the density to be the standard density of water. We want all quantities in units of kilograms, meters, and seconds, so we use a density of 1,000 kilograms per cubic meter for water.

For total pressure, we need to know the surface pressure on top of the pool. Since a surface pressure is not specified, we assume the pressure to be 1 atmosphere. We want all quantities in units of kilograms, meters, and seconds, so we use a pressure of 101,325 pascals, or 101,325 kilograms per meter second squared.

Step Two: Calculate	
Method	**Steps**
(1) Determine appropriate equation	$P_{total} = P_{surface} + \rho g H$
(2) Insert known quantities	$P_{total} = \dfrac{101{,}325 \text{ kg}}{\text{m s}^2} + \dfrac{1{,}000 \text{ kg}}{\text{m}^3}\bigg|\dfrac{9.8 \text{ m}}{\text{s}^2}\bigg|3.66 \text{ m}$
(3) Calculate	$P_{total} = 137{,}193\dfrac{\text{kg}}{\text{m s}^2}\bigg|\dfrac{1 \text{ Pa}}{\dfrac{1 \text{ kg}}{\text{m s}^2}} = 137{,}193 \text{ Pa}$

Step Three: Convert from Base SI Units to Desired Units	
Method	**Steps**
(1) Term to be converted	137,193 Pa
(2) Conversion formula	
(3) Make a fraction	$\dfrac{137{,}193 \text{ Pa}}{}\bigg|\dfrac{1 \text{ atm}}{101{,}325 \text{ Pa}}$
(4) Multiply	
(5) Cancel, calculate, be reasonable	1.35 atm

COMPREHENSION CHECK 8-11 An object is completely submerged in a liquid of density 0.75 grams per cubic centimeter at a depth of 3 meters. What is the total pressure on the object? State your answer in atmospheres.

8.7 GAS PRESSURE

LEARN TO: Describe the Ideal Gas Law
Determine final quantity if given three of the following: amount, pressure, temperature, volume
Recall the common values for ideal gas constant

IMPORTANT CONCEPT

Ideal Gas Law

$$PV = nRT$$

Only absolute temperature units (K or °R) can be used in the ideal gas equation.

NOTE

$$R = 8{,}314\ \frac{\text{Pa L}}{\text{mol K}}$$

$$= 0.08206\ \frac{\text{atm L}}{\text{mol K}}$$

Gas pressure results when gas molecules impact the inner walls of a sealed container. The **ideal gas law** relates the quantities of pressure (P), volume (V), temperature (T), and amount (n) of gas in a closed container:

$$PV = nRT$$

In this equation, R is a fundamental constant called the **gas constant**. It can have many different numerical values, depending on the units chosen for pressure, volume, temperature, and amount, just as a length has different numerical values, depending on whether feet or meters or miles is the unit being used. Scientists have defined an "ideal" gas as one where one mole [mol] of gas at a temperature of 273 kelvins [K] and a pressure of one atmosphere [atm] will occupy a volume of 22.4 liters [L]. Using these values to solve for the constant R yields

$$R = \frac{PV}{nT} = \frac{1\ [\text{atm}]}{1\ [\text{mol}]}\frac{22.4\ [\text{L}]}{273\ [\text{K}]} = 0.08206\ \frac{\text{atm L}}{\text{mol K}}$$

Note that we must *use* absolute *temperature units in the ideal gas equation.* We cannot begin with relative temperature units and then convert the final answer. Also, all pressure readings must be in absolute, not gauge, units.

In previous chapters, we have suggested a procedure for solving problems involving equations and unit conversions. For ideal gas law problems, we suggest a slightly different procedure.

Ideal Gas Law Procedure

1. Examine the units given in the problem statement. Choose a gas constant (R) that contains as many of the units given in the problem as possible.
2. If necessary, convert all parameters into units found in the gas constant (R) that you choose.
3. Solve the ideal gas law for the variable of interest.
4. Substitute values and perform all necessary calculations.
5. If necessary, convert your final answer to the required units and apply reasonableness.

● EXAMPLE 8-17

A container holds 1.43 moles of nitrogen (formula: N_2) at a pressure of 3.4 atmospheres and a temperature of 500 degrees Fahrenheit. What is the volume of the container in liters?

Method	Steps
(1) Choose ideal gas constant	Given units: mol, atm, °F, L Select R: 0.08206 $\dfrac{\text{atm L}}{\text{mol K}}$
(2) Convert to units of chosen R	500°F = 533 K
(3) Solve for variable of interest	$V = \dfrac{nRT}{P}$
(4) Calculate	$V = \dfrac{1.43 \text{ mol}}{}\left\|\dfrac{0.08206 \text{ atm L}}{\text{mol K}}\right\|\dfrac{533 \text{ K}}{}\left\|\dfrac{}{3.4 \text{ atm}}\right.$
(5) Convert, be reasonable	$V = 18.4 \text{ L}$

● EXAMPLE 8-18

A container holds 1.25 moles of nitrogen (formula: N_2) at a pressure of 350 kilopascals and a temperature of 160 degrees Celsius. What is the volume of the container in liters?

Method	Steps
(1) Choose ideal gas constant	Given units: mol, Pa, °C, L Select R: 8,314 $\dfrac{\text{Pa L}}{\text{mol K}}$
(2) Convert to units of chosen R	160°C = 433 K
(3) Solve for variable of interest	$V = \dfrac{nRT}{P}$
(4) Calculate	$V = \dfrac{1.25 \text{ mol}}{}\left\|\dfrac{8,314 \text{ Pa L}}{\text{mol K}}\right\|\dfrac{433 \text{ K}}{}\left\|\dfrac{}{350,000 \text{ Pa}}\right.$
(5) Convert, be reasonable	$V = 13 \text{ L}$

● **EXAMPLE 8-19**   A gas originally at a temperature of 300 kelvins and 3 atmospheres pressure in a 3.9-liter flask is cooled until the temperature reaches 284 kelvins. What is the new pressure of gas in atmospheres?

Since the volume and the mass of the gas remain constant, we can examine the ratio between the initial condition (1) and the final condition (2) for pressure and temperature. The volume of the container (V) and the amount of gas (n) are constant, so $V_1 = V_2$ and $n_1 = n_2$.

Method	Steps
(1) Choose ideal gas constant	Given units: mol, K, L Select R: 0.08206 $\dfrac{\text{atm L}}{\text{mol K}}$
(2) Convert to units of chosen R	None needed
(3) Solve for variable of interest, eliminating any variables that remain constant between the initial and final state	$\dfrac{P_1 V_1}{P_2 V_2} = \dfrac{n_1 R T_1}{n_2 R T_2}$ $\dfrac{P_1}{P_2} = \dfrac{T_1}{T_2}$
(4) Calculate	$\dfrac{3 \text{ atm}}{P_2} = \dfrac{300 \text{ K}}{284 \text{ K}}$
(5) Convert, be reasonable	$P = 2.8$ atm

COMPREHENSION CHECK 8-12   A 5-gallon container holds 35 grams of nitrogen (formula: N_2, molecular weight = 28 grams per mole) at a temperature of 400 kelvins. What is the container pressure in units of kilopascals?

COMPREHENSION CHECK 8-13   An 8-liter container holds nitrogen (formula: N_2, molecular weight = 28 grams per mole) at a pressure of 1.5 atmospheres and a temperature of 310 kelvins. If the gas is compressed by reduction of the volume of the container until the gas pressure increases to 5 atmospheres while the temperature is held constant, what is the new volume of the container in units of liters?

8.8   ENERGY

LEARN TO: Determine final quantity if given the other terms in an energy expression
Convert from one unit of energy to another
Select the energy units appropriate to a context

Energy is an abstract quantity with several definitions, depending on the form of energy being discussed. You may be familiar with some of the following types of energy.

IMPORTANT CONCEPT

Work
$$W = F\Delta x$$

Potential Energy
$$PE = mg\Delta H$$

Kinetic Energy, translational
$$KE_T = \tfrac{1}{2}m(v_f^2 - v_i^2)$$

Kinetic Energy, rotational
$$KE_R = \tfrac{1}{2}I(\omega_f^2 - \omega_i^2)$$

Kinetic Energy, total
$$KE = KE_T + KE_R$$

Thermal Energy
$$Q = mC_p\Delta T$$

MOMENT OF INERTIA (I)

m = mass, r = radius

Object	I for KE_R
Cylinder: thin shell	mr^2
Cylinder: solid	$\tfrac{1}{2}mr^2$
Sphere: thin shell	$\tfrac{2}{3}mr^2$
Sphere: solid	$\tfrac{2}{5}mr^2$

Types of Energy

- **Work** (W) is energy expended by exertion of a force (F) over a distance (d). As an example, if you exert a force on (push) a heavy desk so that it slides across the floor, which will make you more tired: pushing it 5 feet or pushing it 50 feet? The farther you push it, the more work you do.
- **Potential energy** (PE) is a form of work done by moving a weight (w)—which is a force—a vertical distance (H). Recall that weight is mass (m) times gravity (g). Note that this is a special case of the work equation, where force is weight and distance is height.
- **Kinetic energy** (KE) is a form of energy possessed by an object in motion. If a constant force is exerted on a body, then by $F = ma$, we see that the body experiences a constant acceleration, meaning the velocity increases linearly with time. Since the velocity increases as long as the force is maintained, work is being done on the object. Another way of saying this is that the object upon which the force is applied acquires kinetic energy, also called **energy of translational motion**. For a nonrotating body moving with some velocity (v) the kinetic energy can be calculated by $KE_T = (\tfrac{1}{2})mv^2$.

  This, however, is not the entire story. A rotating object has energy whether it is translating (moving along a path) or not. If you have ever turned a bicycle upside down, spun one of the wheels fairly fast, then tried to stop it with your hand, you understand that it has energy. This is **rotational kinetic energy**, and for an object spinning in place (but not going anywhere), it is calculated by $KE_R = (\tfrac{1}{2})I\omega^2$. The Greek letter omega (ω) symbolizes angular velocity or the object's rotational speed, typically given in units of radians per second. The moment of inertia (I) depends on the mass and the geometry of the spinning object. The table shown lists the moments of inertia for a few common objects.

  For an object that is rotating and translating, such as a bowling ball rolling down the lane toward the pins, the total kinetic energy is simply the sum of the two:

$$KE = KE_T + KE_R = (\tfrac{1}{2})mv^2 + (\tfrac{1}{2})I\omega^2 = (\tfrac{1}{2})(mv^2 + I\omega^2)$$

- **Thermal Energy** or heat (Q) is energy associated with a change in temperature (ΔT). It is a function of the mass of the object (m) and the specific heat (C_p), which is a property of the material being heated:

$$Q = mC_p\Delta T$$

Where Does $KE = \tfrac{1}{2}mv^2$ Come From?

If a constant force is applied to a body,

- That body will have a constant acceleration (remember $F = ma$).
- Its velocity will increase linearly with time.
- Its average velocity is the average of its initial and final values.

This is	$v = (v_f + v_i)/2$
Distance traveled is	$d = vt$
The work done is	$W = Fd$
	$= (ma)d$
	$= mavt$

Acceleration is the change in velocity over time, or $a = (v_f - v_i)/t$
Substituting for a and v in the work equation

$$W = mavt = m[(v_f - v_i)/t][(v_f + v_i)/2][t]$$
$$W = (\tfrac{1}{2})m(v_f^2 - v_i^2)$$

This is given the name *kinetic energy*, or the energy of motion. Remember, work and energy are equivalent. This expression is for the *translation* of a body only.

ENERGY

J = N m
SI unit of energy = joule

NOTE

1 BTU is ≈ 1,000 times as big as 1 joule.
1 calorie is ≈ 4 times as big as 1 joule.

Calories and BTUs and Joules—Oh My!

The SI unit of work is **joule**, defined as one newton of force acting over a distance of one meter (Table 8-11). The unit is named after James Joule (1818–1889), an English physicist responsible for several theories involving energy, including the definition of the mechanical equivalent of heat and Joule's law, which describes the amount of electrical energy converted to heat by a resistor (an electrical component) when an electric current flows through it. In some mechanical systems, work is described in units of foot pound-force [ft lb_f].

For energy in the form of heat, units are typically reported as British thermal units and calories instead of joules. A **British thermal unit** [BTU] is the amount of heat required to raise the temperature of one pound-mass of water by one degree Fahrenheit. A **calorie** [cal] is amount of heat required to raise the temperature of one gram of water by one degree Celsius.

Table 8-11 **Dimensions of energy**

Quantity	Common Units	Exponents						
		M	L	T	Θ	N	J	I
Work	J	1	2	−2	0	0	0	0
Thermal energy	BTU	1	2	−2	0	0	0	0
	cal	1	2	−2	0	0	0	0

● **EXAMPLE 8-20**

A 50-kilogram load is raised vertically a distance of 5 meters by an electric motor. How much work in units of joules was done on the load?

First, we must determine the type of energy. The parameters we are discussing include mass (kilograms) and height (meters). Examining the energy formulas given above, the equation for potential energy fits. Also, the words "load is raised vertically a distance" fits with our understanding of potential energy.

Step One: Convert to Base SI Units	
No conversion needed	
Step Two: Calculate	
Method	**Steps**
(1) Determine appropriate equation	$PE = mg\Delta H$
(2) Insert known quantities	$PE = \dfrac{50 \text{ kg}}{} \left\vert \dfrac{9.8 \text{ m}}{s^2} \right\vert \dfrac{5 \text{ m}}{}$
(3) Calculate, be reasonable	$PE = 2{,}450 \dfrac{\text{kg m}^2}{s^2}$

This is apparently our final answer, but the units are puzzling. If the units of energy are joules and if this is a valid equation, then our final result for energy should be joules. If we consider the dimensions of energy:

Quantity	Common Units	Exponents			
		M	L	T	Θ
Energy	J	1	2	−2	0

A unit of energy has dimensions $E\{=\} M L^2/T^2$, which in terms of base SI units would be $E[=] kg\ m^2/s^2$. As this term occurs so frequently it is given the special name "joule." Anytime we see this term $(kg\ m^2/s^2)$, we know we are dealing with an energy, equal to a joule.

(3) Calculate, be reasonable	$PE = 2{,}450\ \dfrac{kg\ m^2}{s^2} \left\| \dfrac{1\ J}{1\ \frac{kg\ m^2}{s^2}} \right. = 2{,}450\ J$

Step Three: Convert from Base SI Units to Desired Units
No conversion needed

In the morning, you like to drink your coffee at a temperature of exactly 70 degrees Celsius [°C]. The mass of the coffee in your mug is 470 grams. To make your coffee, you had to raise the temperature of the water by 30 degrees Celsius. How much energy in units of British thermal units [BTU] did it take to heat your coffee? The specific heat of water is 4.18 joules per gram degree Celsius [J/(g °C)].

First, you must determine the type of energy we are using. The parameters discussed include mass, temperature, and specific heat. Examining the energy formulas given above, the equation for thermal energy fits. Also, the words "How much energy . . . did it take to heat your coffee" fits with an understanding of thermal energy.

Step One: Convert to Base SI Units	
No conversion needed	
Step Two: Calculate	
Method	**Steps**
(1) Determine appropriate equation	$Q = mC_p\Delta T$
(2) Insert known quantities	$Q = \dfrac{470\ g}{}\left\| \dfrac{4.18\ J}{g\,°C} \right\| \dfrac{30°C}{}$
(3) Calculate	$Q = 59{,}370\ J$
Step Three: Convert from Base SI Units to Desired Units	
Method	**Steps**
(1) Term to be converted	$59{,}370\ J$
(2) Conversion formula	
(3) Make a fraction	$\dfrac{59{,}370\ J}{}\left\| \dfrac{9.48 \times 10^{-4}\ BTU}{1\ J} \right.$
(4) Multiply	
(5) Cancel, calculate, be reasonable	56 BTU

COMPREHENSION CHECK 8-14

You push an automobile with a constant force of 20 pounds-force until 1,500 joules of energy has been added to the car. How far did the car travel in units of meters during this time? You may assume that frictional losses are negligible.

COMPREHENSION CHECK 8-15

One gram of material A is heated until the temperature rises by 10 kelvins. If the same amount of heat is applied to one gram of material B, what is the temperature rise of material B in units of kelvins?

The specific heat (C_p) of material A = 4 joules per gram kelvin [J/(g K)]
The specific heat (C_p) of material B = 2 joules per gram kelvin [J/(g K)]

8.9 POWER

LEARN TO: Convert from one unit of power to another
Determine the final quantity if given two of the following: energy, power, time

IMPORTANT CONCEPT

Power = energy / time

W = J / s

SI unit of power = watt

Power is defined as energy per time (Table 8-12). The SI unit of power is **watt**, named after James Watt (1736–1819), a Scottish mathematician and engineer whose improvements to the steam engine were important to the Industrial Revolution. He is responsible for the definition of **horsepower** [hp], a unit of power originally used to quantify how the steam engine could replace the work done by a horse.

NOTE

Power is the RATE at which energy is delivered over time.

Table 8-12 **Dimensions of power**

Quantity	Common Units	\multicolumn{7}{c}{Exponents}
		M	L	T	Θ	N	J	I
Power	W	1	2	–3	0	0	0	0

To help understand the relationship between energy and power, imagine the following. Your 1,000-kilogram car has run out of gas on a level road. There is a gas station not far ahead, so you decide to push the car to the gas station. Assume that you intend to accelerate the car up to a speed of one meter per second (about 2.2 miles per hour), and then continue pushing at that speed until you reach the station. Ask yourself the following questions:

- Can I accelerate the car to one meter per second in one minute?
- On the other hand, can I accelerate it to one meter per second in one second?

Most of you would probably answer "yes" to the first and "no" to the second, but why? Well, personal experience! But that is not really an explanation. Since the change in kinetic energy is the same in each case, to accelerate the car in one second, your body would have to generate energy at a rate 60 times greater than the rate required if you accelerated it in one minute. The key word is rate, or how much energy your body can produce per second. If you do the calculations, you will find that for the one-minute scenario, your body would have to produce about $^1/_{90}$ horsepower, which seems quite reasonable. On the other hand, if you try to accomplish the same acceleration in one second, you would need to generate $^2/_3$ horsepower. Are you two-thirds as powerful as a horse?

As another example, assume that you attend a class on the third floor of the engineering building. When you are on time, you take 2 minutes to climb to the third floor. On the other hand, when you are late for class, you run up the three flights in 30 seconds.

- In which case do you do the most work (expend the most energy)?
- In which case do you generate the most power?

● **EXAMPLE 8-22**

A 50-kilogram load is raised vertically a distance of 5 meters by an electric motor in 60 seconds. How much power in units of watts does the motor use, assuming no energy is lost in the process?

This problem was started in Example 8-20. The energy used by the system was found to be 2,450 joules, the analysis of which is not repeated here.

Step One: Convert to Base SI Units	
No conversion needed	
Step Two: Calculate	
Method	**Steps**
(1) Determine appropriate equation	$\text{Power} = \dfrac{\text{energy}}{\text{time}}$
(2) Insert known quantities	$\text{Power} = \dfrac{2{,}450 \text{ J}}{\left\vert 60 \text{ s}\right.}$
(3) Calculate, be reasonable	$\text{Power} = 41\dfrac{\text{J}}{\text{s}} \left\vert \dfrac{1 \text{ W}}{1\,\frac{\text{J}}{\text{s}}}\right. = 41 \text{ W}$
Step Three: Convert from Base SI Units to Desired Units	
No conversion needed	

Note that since power = energy/time, energy = power * time. We pay the electric company for energy calculated this way as kilowatt-hours. If power is constant, we can obtain the total energy involved simply by multiplying the power by the length of time that power is applied. If power is *not* constant, we would usually use calculus to determine the total energy, but that solution is beyond the scope of this book.

COMPREHENSION CHECK 8-16

A motor with a power of 100 watts is connected to a flywheel. How long, in units of hours, must the motor operate to transfer 300,000 joules to the flywheel?

8.10 EFFICIENCY

Recall the limits of efficiency
Determine the final quantity if given three of the following: efficiency, energy, power, time

IMPORTANT CONCEPT

Efficiency is always less than 100%.

Efficiency (η, Greek letter eta) is a measure of how much of a quantity, typically energy or power, is lost in a process. In a perfect world, efficiency would always be 100%. All energy put into a process would be recovered and used to accomplish the desired task. We know that this can never happen, so *efficiency is always less than 100%*. If a machine operates at 75% efficiency, 25% of the energy is lost. This means you have to put in "extra" energy to complete the work.

The use of the terms "input" and "output" require some explanation. The **input** is the quantity of energy or power or whatever required by the mechanism from some source to operate and accomplish its task. The **output** is the amount of energy or power or whatever is actually applied to the task itself by the mechanism. Note that the rated power of a device, whether a light bulb, a motor, or an electric heater, refers to the input power—the power needed to operate the device—not the output power. In an ideal, 100% efficient system, the input and output would be equivalent. In an inefficient system (the real world), the input is equivalent to the sum of the output and the power or energy lost.

IMPORTANT CONCEPT

Efficiency (η) = output/input
Efficiency (η) = output/(output + loss)
Input = quantity required by mechanism to operate
Output = quantity actually applied to task
Loss = quantity wasted during the application

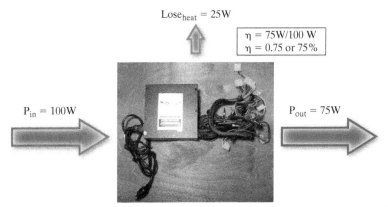

$$\text{Lose}_{heat} = 25W$$

$$\eta = 75W/100\ W$$
$$\eta = 0.75 \text{ or } 75\%$$

$$P_{in} = 100W$$

$$P_{out} = 75W$$

Photo credit: E Stephan

Orders of Magnitude

Table 8-13 gives you an idea of orders of magnitude of power and energy as related to real-world objects and phenomena. All values are approximate and, in most cases, have been rounded to only one significant figure. Thus, if you actually do the calculations from power to energy, you will find discrepancies.

A few things of possible interest:

- U.S. power consumption (all types) is one-fifth of the total world power consumption.
- The Tsar Bomba generated 1.5% of the power of the sun, but only lasted 40 nanoseconds.
- Total human power consumption on the planet is about 0.01% (1/10,000) of the total power received from the sun.

Table 8-13 Order of magnitude for power and energy comparison

Power	"Device"	Energy per Hour	Energy per Year
10 fW	Minimum reception power for cell phone	40 pJ	300 nJ
	Single human cell	4 nJ	30 mJ
10 mW	DVD laser	40 J	300 kJ
500 mW	Cell phone microprocessor	2 kJ	15 MJ
50 W	Modern 2GHz microprocessor	200 kJ	1.5 GJ
100 W	Human at rest	400 kJ	3 GJ
500 W	Human doing strenuous work	2 MJ	15 GJ
750 W	Power per square meter bright sunshine	3 MJ	25 GJ
2 kW	Maximum human power for short period	(NA)	
20 kW	Average U.S. home	80 MJ	600 GJ
100 kW	Typical automobile	400 MJ	3 TJ
150 MW	Boeing 747 jet	500 GJ	5 PJ
1 GW	Large commercial nuclear reactor	4 TJ	30 PJ
20 GW	Three Gorges Hydroelectric Dam (China)	80 TJ	600 PJ
4 TW	U.S. total power consumption	15 PJ	100 EJ
20 TW	Total human power consumption	80 PJ	600 EJ
100 TW	Average hurricane	400 PJ	(NA)
200 PW	Total power received on the Earth from the sun	1 ZJ	6 YJ
5 YW	Largest fusion bomb ever built (Russian Tsar Bomba)	(NA) Total yield 200 PJ	
400 YW	Total power of the sun	10^6 YJ	10^9 YJ

● **EXAMPLE 8-23**

A standard incandescent light bulb has an efficiency of about 5%; thus, $\eta = 0.05$. An incandescent bulb works by heating a wire (the filament) inside the bulb to such a high temperature that it glows white. About 95% of the power delivered to an incandescent bulb is discarded as heat. Only 5% results in "light" energy.

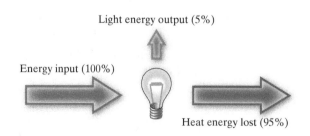

Light energy output (5%)

Energy input (100%)

Heat energy lost (95%)

If a 100-watt bulb is turned on for 15 minutes, how much energy is "lost" as heat during the 15-minute period?

Step One: Convert to Base SI Units	
No conversion needed	
Step Two: Calculate	
Method	**Steps**
(1) Determine appropriate equation	Energy = (Power)(Time)
(2) Insert known quantities	Energy = (Power)(15 min)
For Unknown Quantities, Repeat the Process	
Method	**Steps**
(1) Determine appropriate equation	Input power = output power/efficiency
	"Lost" power = input power − output power
(2) Insert known quantities	100 W = output power/(0.05)
(3) Calculate	Output power = 5 W
	"Lost" power = 100 W − 5 W = 95 W
(2) Insert known quantities	Energy = (95 W)(15 min)
(3) Calculate, be reasonable	$E = 95 \dfrac{J}{s} \left\| \dfrac{15 \text{ min}}{} \right\| \dfrac{60 \text{ s}}{1 \text{ min}}$
	Energy lost = 85,500 J
Step Three: Convert from Base SI Units to Desired Units	
No conversion needed	

● **EXAMPLE 8-24**

Over the past few decades, the efficiency of solar cells has risen from about 10% to the most recent technologies achieving about 40% conversion of solar energy to electricity. The losses are due to several factors, including reflectance and resistive losses, among others.

Assume you have an array of solar cells mounted on your roof with an efficiency of 28%. If the array is delivering 750 watts of electricity to your home, how much solar power is falling on the photoelectric cells?

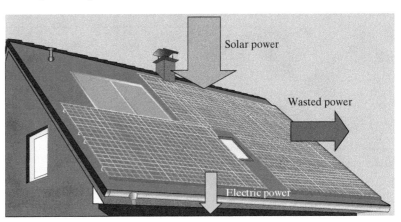

NOTE

How much power is wasted by the array of solar cells? If the array received 2,680 watts and delivered 750 watts, then the difference is 2,680 − 750 = 1,930 watts; thus, 1,930 watts are wasted.

Step One: Convert to Base SI Units	
No conversion needed	
Step Two: Calculate	
Method	**Steps**
(1) Determine appropriate equation	Input power = output power/efficiency
(2) Insert known quantities	Input power = 750 W/0.28
(3) Calculate, be reasonable	Input power = 2,680 W
Step Three: Convert from Base SI Units to Desired Units	
No conversion needed	

● **EXAMPLE 8-25**

If your microwave takes 2 minutes to heat your coffee in Example 8-21, how many watts of power does your microwave require, assuming that it is 80% efficient? Remember that our answer was 59,370 joules, before we converted the final answer to units of BTU.

Step One: Convert to Base SI Units	
No conversion needed	
Step Two: Calculate	
Method	**Steps**
(1) Determine appropriate equation	Input power = output power/efficiency
(2) Insert known quantities	Input power = output power/0.8
For Unknown Quantities, Repeat the Process	
Method	**Steps**
(1) Determine appropriate equation	Output power = energy/time
(2) Insert known quantities	Output power = $\dfrac{59{,}370 \text{ J}}{}\left\vert\dfrac{}{2 \text{ min}}\right\vert\dfrac{1 \text{ min}}{60 \text{ s}}\left\vert\dfrac{1 \text{ W s}}{1 \text{ J}}\right.$
(3) Calculate	Output power = 493 W
(2) Insert known quantities	Input power = 493 W/0.8
(3) Calculate, be reasonable	Input power = 615 W
Step Three: Convert from Base SI Units to Desired Units	
No conversion needed	

COMPREHENSION CHECK 8-17

A motor with an input power of 100 watts is connected to a flywheel. How long, in units of hours, must the motor operate to transfer 300,000 joules to the flywheel, assuming the process is 80% efficient?

COMPREHENSION CHECK 8-18

If a 50-kilogram load was raised 5 meters in 50 seconds, determine the minimum rated wattage of the motor needed to accomplish this, assuming the motor is 80% efficient.

● EXAMPLE 8-26

A simple two-stage machine is shown in the diagram below. Initially, an electric motor receives power from the power grid, accessed by being plugged into a standard electrical wall socket. The power received by the motor from the wall socket is the "input" power or the power the motor uses or requires (Point A).

The spinning drive shaft on the motor can then be used to power other devices, such as a hoist or a vacuum cleaner or a DVD drive; the power available from the spinning shaft is the "output" power of the motor (Point B). In the process of making the drive shaft spin, however, some of the input power is lost (Point C) because of both frictional and ohmic heating as well as other wasted forms such as sound.

Since some energy is being lost as heat or other unusable forms every second of operation (remember, power is energy per time!) the output power *must* be less than the input power—the efficiency of the motor is less than 100%. The power available from the spinning shaft of the motor (Point B) is then used to operate some device: the hoist or vacuum cleaner or DVD drive (Point E). In other words, the output power of the motor is the input power to the device it drives. This device will have its own efficiency, thus wasting some of the power supplied to it by the motor (Point D).

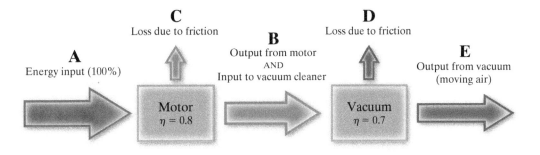

C
Loss due to friction

D
Loss due to friction

B
Output from motor
AND
Input to vacuum cleaner

A
Energy input (100%)

E
Output from vacuum
(moving air)

Motor
$\eta = 0.8$

Vacuum
$\eta = 0.7$

NOTE

The overall efficiency of two linked devices is the product of the two efficiencies.

Assume that a motor with an efficiency of 80% is used to power a vacuum cleaner that has an efficiency of 70%. If the input power to the motor (Point A) is one-half horsepower, what is the output power of the vacuum (Point E)?

The output from the motor (Point B) is $P_B = \eta P_A = 0.8$ (0.5 horsepower) = 0.4 horsepower. This is the input to the vacuum, so the output from the vacuum (Point E) is

$$P_E = \eta P_B = 0.7\,(0.4\,\text{hp}) = 0.28\,\text{hp}$$

What is the overall efficiency of this machine? The input power (Point A) is 0.5 horsepower, and the output power (Point E) is 0.28 horsepower; thus, the efficiency of this linked system is:

$$\eta = P_A/P_E = 0.28\,\text{hp}/0.5\,\text{hp} = 0.56,\ \text{or an efficiency of 56\%}.$$

8.11 ELECTRICAL CONCEPTS

The basic concepts of electricity and electrical devices are perhaps less familiar to most students than are many of the other physical phenomena covered previously in this text. This is due partly to lack of practical experience, and partly to the fact that in general these phenomena are themselves invisible, only their effects being perceptible by people. These effects range from receiving an electric shock to the almost magical performance of touch-screen devices. Table 8-14 summarizes the concepts discussed in this section.

WARNING:

Electrical parameters can get confusing at times since V is used as both a variable name for voltage and for the unit volt, and C is used as a variable name for capacitance as well as the unit coulomb.

Table 8-14 Summary of electrical properties

Property	Symbol	Related Equations	Typical Units	Equivalent Units
Charge	Q	Coulomb's Law: $\lvert F \rvert = k_e \dfrac{\lvert Q_1 Q_2 \rvert}{r^2}$	coulomb [C]	C = A s
Current	I	$Q = I t$	ampere [A]	A = C/s
Voltage	V		volt [V]	V = J/C
Resistance	R	Ohm's Law: $V = I R$	ohm [Ω]	Ω = V/A
Conductance	G	$G = 1/R$	siemens [S]	S = A/V
Electric power	P	$P = V I = I^2 R = V^2/R$	watt [W]	W = V A
Capacitance	C	$Q = C V \quad E_C = \frac{1}{2} C V^2$	farad [F]	F = C/V
Inductance	L	$E_L = \frac{1}{2} L I^2$	henry [H]	H = V s/A

Electric Charge

Electrons and protons, as well as some subatomic particles, have a property known as **electric charge**. On a small scale, charge can be measured in terms of the elementary charge (e). The magnitude of the elementary charge on either an electron or a proton is 1, and by convention, the charge of a proton is called positive ($e = +1$) and that of an electron negative ($e = -1$).

A force acts on a charged particle when in the vicinity of another charged particle. If the charges are alike, both positive or both negative, the force is a repulsive force, and the charges tend to accelerate away from each other. If the charges are unlike, one positive and one negative, the force is attractive with the particles tending to accelerate toward each other.

How big is 6.24×10^{18}? This is estimated to be the number of stars found in 10 million galaxies the size of the Milky Way.

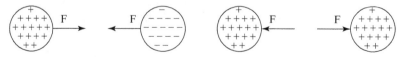

The value of the elementary charge (e) is inconveniently small, so **charge** (Q) is generally quantified using the derived unit **coulomb** [C]. A charge of one coulomb represents the total charge on approximately 6.24×10^{18} protons. Another way to say this: the elementary charge of a single electron is $1/6.24 \times 10^{18} = 1.6 \times 10^{-19}$ C.

NOTE

This is actually a specific case for two charges only. In general, there are more than two charges in three-dimensional space and a three-dimensional vector representation is required. Such mathematics, however, is beyond the scope of this introductory course. You will study vectors in both your calculus courses and in your physics courses. These concepts will then be used in applications specific to your discipline.

The actual force exerted on a charged object varies with both the amount of charge on each object (Q_1 and Q_2) and the distance (r) between the charges. This relationship is defined by **Coulomb's Law**, named after the French physicist Charles-Augustin de Coulomb (1736 – 1806) who first described and quantified the attractive and repulsive electrostatic force.

$$|F| = k_e \frac{|Q_1 \, Q_2|}{r^2}$$

In this equation, k_e is Coulomb's constant, and is approximately equal to $9 \times 10^9 \, \text{N m}^2/\text{C}^2$.

Electric Current

Electric current is superficially analogous to a current of water or other fluid. Just as a current of water is a movement of water molecules in a pipe or channel, electric current is a movement of electric charge in a wire or other solid material.

Electric current (I) is measured in **amperes** [A], one of the base units in the metric system, and is named for Andre-Marie Ampere, (1775 – 1836), the French physicist who is credited with discovering electromagnetism.

The derived unit coulomb is defined in terms of the ampere as one ampere second: $1 \, \text{C} = 1 \, \text{A s}$. This may be easier to understand on an intuitive level by rephrasing this as one ampere equals one coulomb per second: $1 \, \text{A} = 1 \, \text{C/s}$. In other words, a current of one ampere represents a movement of one coulomb of charge past any given point in the wire every second.

To put the magnitude of the ampere in context: for those who have received an electric shock by sticking your finger in a light socket, for instance, you realize the sensation is rather unpleasant. In general, in countries that use 120 volts in domestic appliances, such a shock is typically about 5 milliamperes [mA] or one two-hundredth of an ampere. This level of current is small enough that although unpleasant, your muscles will still respond to the commands from your brain, and you can release the live wire or pull your hand away. However, in circuits powering large appliances such as stoves or air conditioners that use 240 volts, the current from a typical shock is roughly twice the above value, or 10 mA. This is very close to the current level that will overload your nervous system so your muscles will no longer obey and you become unable to let go. This is FAR more dangerous.

When denoting a current on a circuit diagram, an arrow is used to indicate the assumed direction. If the current actually flows the other way, the numeric value will be negative.

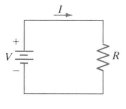

A couple of centuries ago when people were just beginning to seriously experiment with electricity, they hypothesized that there was a flow of some substance from one terminal of their primitive devices to the other. Perhaps needless to say, they knew nothing about electrons, since the structure of the atom was completely unknown at that time. They had a 50-50 chance of correctly guessing the direction this "substance" flowed, but luck was against them and they got it wrong. For many decades, scientists assumed that this substance, called charge, flowed from the terminal they called positive (an excess of charge) to the other terminal they called negative (a deficiency of charge). Eventually, the structure of the atom was deciphered and scientists realized that for many years they had been working with the opposite assumption to the correct one, since in most situations it is electrons flowing from the negative terminal to the positive terminal. As a consequence, even to this day, most engineers solve problems using "conventional current," that assumes charge flows from positive to negative. If you want the actual direction of the flow of electrons, you just multiply the current by minus one.

Voltage

To really understand voltage requires knowledge of the concept of the electric field. This is unfortunately a bit too complicated for the limited time and space we have here, so we will merely attempt to help you develop a feel for how voltage affects other electrical parameters. You will study electric fields in some depth in physics, typically the second physics course, and may learn even more in other courses, particularly if you choose to study electrical or computer engineering.

A somewhat inaccurate explanation of voltage, although one that can be useful in understanding it, is that voltage is what pushes the charges around to create current. In a sense, it quantifies the amount of force that can be exerted on an electric charge by other accumulated charge. In fact, some decades ago, voltage was commonly called electromotive force (EMF), but this has fallen out of favor in most contexts for a variety of reasons, not least of which is that voltage is not a force, being dimensionally quite different.

Voltage (V) is quantified using units of volts [V], and is a measure of how much work is required to move an electric charge in the vicinity of other electric charges. The unit of volt is named for Italian physicist Alessandro Volta, (1745 – 1827), who possibly invented the first chemical battery, called a voltaic pile.

One volt is defined as one joule per coulomb. In other words, if one joule of energy is required to move one coulomb of charge from one place to another, the voltage between those two points is one volt.

Since work is required to move an electric charge in the vicinity of other charges, we might recall the definition of work in another context. Work equals force times the distance through which that force moves an object: $W = F d$. Similarly, work equals charge times the difference in voltage through which that charge moves: $W = Q V$.

One specific case of work is potential energy. If a force is used to raise a mass above the surface of the planet, the work done is stored as energy in the mass of the object being raised. When the object is dropped, the energy will convert form from potential energy to kinetic energy. Similarly, if a bunch of charge is moved closer to an accumulation of like charges, the work done to move the packet of charge is stored as energy in the packet of charge. If a path is provided for the packet of charge to move, the stored energy will be converted into another form, often heat, but it might also include light, sound, chemical energy, etc.

Similar to the need to know whether an object is being lifted (storing potential energy) or is falling (converting the stored energy into kinetic energy), we need to know whether charges are moving toward like charges or away from them. Just like we use an arrow to denote the assumed direction of a current, we need some sort of notation to indicate the assumed polarity of a voltage – which end is assumed to be more positive than the other. This allows us to keep track of whether energy is being stored or released. We do this by placing a plus sign on one side of the device through which the current is flowing and a negative sign on the other end.

Electrical Resistance

Resistance is a measure of how difficult it is to move charges through a material. In some substances, such as many metals, electrons can move quite easily. In other materials such as glass or air, considerable force, thus considerable voltage, is required to make electrons move therein.

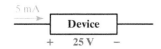

Resistance (R) is quantified using units of ohms [Ω], where one ohm is defined as one volt per ampere. For example, if a 1 volt battery were connected to a device having a resistance of one ohm, one ampere of current would flow through it, assuming the chemical reaction could replenish the charge rapidly enough to maintain such a current. The ohm is named for Georg Simon Ohm, the German physicist who first described the relationship linking voltage, current, and resistance.

Resistance relates the voltage across a device to the current through the device. **Take particular note of the choice of prepositions – across and through**. Understanding this choice will help you understand voltage and current.

Electric current is the movement of charge, typically electrons moving **THROUGH** a substance. Voltage is to some extent a measure of the force being exerted on the moving charges by forces at either end of the device. *This is where it can be a little confusing, particularly without using electric fields in the discussion.* However, imagine that on each side of a device is an accumulation of charge, each exerting a force on the electrons inside the device. Each of those forces might be a "push" or a "pull," and the total force on the electrons in the device is the difference in these forces. The difference in the forces from one side of the device to the other is referred to as the voltage **ACROSS** the device.

As an analogy, if you are trying to push a sofa across the room, but someone else is trying to push the sofa in the opposite direction with the same force, the net force is zero and the sofa does not move. If one person pulls and the other pushes, however, the sofa will move quicker than with either person alone.

Resistance is related to current and voltage by **Ohm's Law: $V = IR$**. Note the following implications of Ohm's Law:

- To maintain a specific current through a resistance requires a voltage proportional to the resistance. A larger resistance makes it harder to "push" the electrons through the device, thus a larger voltage is required.
- Similarly, current is inversely proportional to resistance. For a given voltage, if the resistance increases, the voltage cannot "push" as many electrons through the device per second, so the current must decrease.

In some contexts, it is computationally simpler to use conductance instead of resistance. Conductance (G) is measured in siemens [S] and is simply the reciprocal of resistance: $G = 1/R$. An older unit for conductance that you might find, particularly in older references, is the mho (ohm spelled backwards) and is represented by an upside-down omega [℧]. The unit siemens is named for the German inventor Ernst Werner von Siemens who, among other things, built the first electric elevator and founded the company known today as Siemens AG.

We can talk about a voltage at a point, such as, "the voltage at point A is 15 volts," but such statements are really based on some reference point, often the planet itself, so the statement is really equivalent to something like "the voltage across (or between) point A and ground is 15 volts."

● **EXAMPLE 8-27**

The voltage across a resistor is 15 volts, and the current through it is 6 milliamps [mA]. What is the value of the resistance?

$$V = IR \text{ so } R = \frac{V}{I} = \frac{15\,V}{6\,mA}\left|\frac{1000\,mA}{A}\right| = 2500\,\frac{V}{A}\left|\frac{\Omega A}{V}\right| = 2500\,\Omega = 2.5\,k\Omega$$

COMPREHENSION CHECK 8-19

The current through a 12 kilo-ohms [kΩ] resistor is 25 microamps [μA]. What is the voltage across the resistor?

Electric Power

Conceptually, electric power is perhaps easiest to understand by examining the formula for gravitational potential energy. A mass has its potential energy increased by expending energy to lift it higher above the surface of the planet, since the mass of the object and the mass of the planet are mutually attracting each other.

Similarly, forcing electrons closer to other electrons stores potential energy since they are mutually trying to repel each other. Recall our discussion of batteries. For each electron that is transferred to the negative terminal of the battery by the chemical reaction, a little bit of energy is "stored" in the battery. This is effectively electrical potential energy. The more electrons per second that are jammed together, the more energy per second is stored. Current is measured in charge (electrons) per second, power is proportional to current: $P \propto I$ or $P = XI$, where X is the proportionality constant.

A volt times an ampere is a watt.

$$V = J/C$$
$$A = C/s$$
$$VA = J/s = W$$

Now think back to voltage. Voltage is a measure of how much energy is used to move a given amount of charge: one volt is one joule per coulomb. Therefore, voltage is the proportionality constant and $P = VI$.

● **EXAMPLE 8-28**

A semiconductor diode has 500 millivolts [mV] across it and 700 microamps [μA] of current through it. How much power is the diode absorbing?

$$P = VI = \left(\frac{500\,mV}{}\left|\frac{1\,V}{1000\,mV}\right.\right)\left(\frac{700\,\mu A}{}\left|\frac{1\,A}{1\times10^6\,\mu A}\right.\right)$$

$$= 3.5 \times 10^{-4}\,W = 350\,\mu W$$

For resistors, the electrical power absorbed is usually converted to heat, and we can use Ohm's Law to replace either the voltage or the current in this power relationship:

$$P = VI = (IR)I = I^2R \quad \text{or} \quad P = VI = V(V/R) = V^2/R$$

Note that these two relationships expressed in terms of resistance are only valid for resistors, not for other electrical components. However, it gives us a means to quickly calculate the power absorbed by a resistor when we know only the voltage or current, but not both.

COMPREHENSION CHECK 8-20   A 1000-ohm [Ω] resistor has 120 volts [V] across it. What is the minimum wattage rating of the resistor?

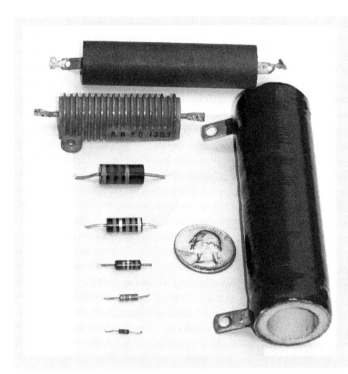

When specifying resistors, both the resistance and the wattage must be given. If you connect a resistor rated at 1 watt in a circuit in which it will have to dissipate 100 watts, it will literally burst into flames, or at least perform an imitation of popcorn by exploding!

From bottom to top, the power rating of these resistors is ⅛ W, ¼ W, ½ W, 1 W, 2 W, 15 W, 25 W, and on the right, 50 W.

Photo credit: W. Park

Capacitance

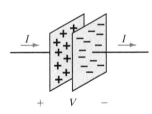

Another simple electrical device is the capacitor. The capacitor is formed by arranging two conducting, low resistance plates very close together, but separated by an insulator with extremely high resistance. Each plate has a wire connected to it. If a current is run into one of the plates of the capacitor, the charges accumulate on that plate since they cannot cross the insulating barrier to the other plate.

When a current enters one plate of the capacitor, the electrons making up the current begin to accumulate on that plate. Since the two plates are separated by an insulator, the electrons cannot cross over to the other plate. While accumulating negative charge on one plate, the negative electrons in the other plate are repelled, leaving behind an overall positive charge. This superficially gives the appearance that the current is going through the capacitor. However, the electrons entering one plate and leaving the other are different electrons, and a charge separation is accumulated on the plates of the capacitor.

The voltage across the capacitor depends not only on the total charge stored, but also on the physical construction of the device, particularly the surface area of the plates. The charge (Q) stored in a capacitor is proportional to the voltage (V) across it: $Q = CV$, where C is the proportionality constant. Note that C must have units of coulombs per volt, and is called capacitance.

NOTE

One farad is a LARGE amount of capacitance. Most capacitors are much smaller than this, and are usually measured in microfarads [μF], nanofarads [nF], or even picofarads [pF].

Capacitance is measured in units of farads [F], where one farad equals one coulomb per volt, or 1 F = 1 C/V. In other words, if a capacitor was storing a charge of one coulomb, and the resulting voltage across its plates was one volt, the capacitance of the device would be one farad.

Since capacitors can contain a separation of charge, they can store energy. The energy stored in a capacitor can be calculated by $E_C = \frac{1}{2} CV^2$. Note that the energy is proportional to the square of the voltage.

● **EXAMPLE 8-29**

A 0.01-microfarad [μF] capacitor is initially completely discharged (no stored charge, thus an initial voltage across it of zero). If a constant current of 4 milliamps [mA] charges the capacitor, how long will be required to change the voltage across it to 5 volts [V]?

Since Q = CV, then C = Q/V.

The total charge delivered by a constant current is Q = It. Inserting this into C = Q/V gives C = It/V.

Solving for t gives t = CV/I.

Therefore,

$$t = \left(\frac{0.01\ \mu F}{}\middle|\frac{1F}{1 \times 10^6\ \mu F}\right)\frac{5\ v}{}\left(\frac{}{4\ mA}\middle|\frac{1000\ mA}{1A}\right) = 1.25 \times 10^{-5}\ \frac{FV}{A}\middle|\frac{C}{FV}\middle|\frac{As}{C} = 12.5\ \mu s$$

COMPREHENSION CHECK 8-21
———

A constant current transfers 12×10^{14} electrons onto one plate of a capacitor in 3 minutes. What is the current, expressed using an appropriate metric prefix?

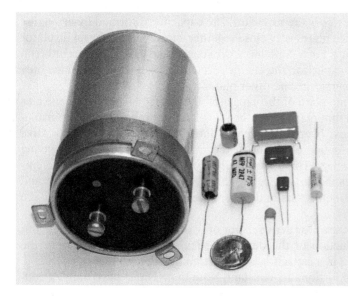

When specifying capacitors, both the capacitance and the maximum voltage must be given. If you connect a capacitor rated at 25 V in a circuit in which it will have 200 V across it, the insulator between the plates will probably fail and the capacitor will be destroyed; it might even explode! The voltage ratings of the capacitors shown range from 25 volts to 500 volts. The big 10,000 μF one on the left is rated at 50 V.

Photo credit: W. Park

Inductance

If a current is moving through a wire, a magnetic field is generated surrounding that wire. If a wire is placed in a CHANGING magnetic field, a current is induced in the wire. This is the physical basis for the final electrical device we will introduce, the inductor.

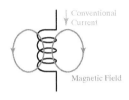

Conventional Current

Magnetic Field

In its simplest form, an **inductor** is just a coil of wire. If a current flows through the coil, the magnetic field generated in each loop adds to the magnetic field generated in every other loop, generating a stronger magnetic field. This is the basis of the electromagnet. Industrial electromagnets can concentrate the magnetic field to a large enough value to pick up huge objects, like cars and trucks. However, in electrical engineering, inductors are more often used for their ability to store energy in the form of a magnetic field.

Note that once a magnetic field has been created in an inductor, if the source of the current that created the magnetic field is removed, the magnetic field will begin to collapse. However, a wire in a **changing** magnetic field such as a collapsing will have a current induced in it, thus allowing the stored energy to be transferred to another place and form.

Inductance (L) is measured in units of **henrys** [H], although the millihenry [mH] or microhenry [μH] is often more convenient. The voltage across an inductor is equal to the inductance of the device times the rate of change of current through the inductor; $V = L\dfrac{dI}{dt}$ for those of you who have begun your study of differential calculus by now. If the current in an inductor changes by one ampere per second, and a voltage is developed across the inductor of one volt, then the inductance is one henry.

Dimensionally, the henry is one volt second per ampere [V s/A]. This can be shown to be dimensionally equal to resistance times time [Ω s] or energy per current squared [J/A^2]. The total energy stored in an inductor can be calculated by $E_L = \dfrac{1}{2}LI^2$. Note that the energy is proportional to the square of the current. You might note the similarity of this to both the formulae for energy stored in a capacitor $E_C = \dfrac{1}{2}CV^2$ and kinetic energy $E = \dfrac{1}{2}mv^2$.

Just as a pendulum transfers energy back and forth between kinetic and potential forms thus creating a physical oscillation, an inductor and a capacitor connected together can swap energy back and forth from a magnetic field to an electric field forming an electrical oscillation. For example, the Theremin, an electronic musical instrument that is played without touching it, relies on such oscillations.

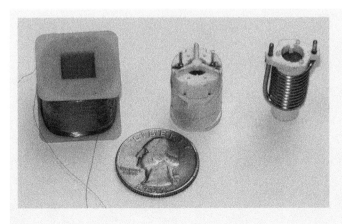

When specifying inductors, both the inductance and the maximum current must be given. If you connect an inductor rated at 5 mA in a circuit which will have 2 amperes through it, the wire will probably melt – a BAD idea!

The inductor shown on the left is wound with many thousands of turns of extremely small wire and its current capacity is rated in microamperes. The one on the right has only ten turns of rather thick wire and can handle about an ampere.

Photo credit: W. Park

● **EXAMPLE 8-30**	The energy stored in a 50 millihenrys [mH] inductor is 75 millijoules [mJ]. If all of this energy is transferred to a 15-microfarad [μF] capacitor, what is the voltage across the capacitor?

$$E_L = E_C \implies E_L = \frac{1}{2}CV^2 \implies V = \sqrt{\frac{2E_L}{C}}$$

$$V = \sqrt{\frac{2(75 \text{ mJ})}{15 \text{ μF}} \left| \frac{1 \times 10^6 \text{ μF}}{1 \text{ F}} \right| \frac{1 \text{ J}}{1000 \text{ mJ}}} = \sqrt{10000 \frac{\text{J}}{\text{F}} \left| \frac{\text{VC}}{\text{J}} \right| \frac{\text{FV}}{\text{C}}} = 100 \text{ V}$$

COMPREHENSION CHECK 8-22	Express $\dfrac{1}{\sqrt{LC}}$ in terms of base SI units, where L is in henrys, and C is in farads.

Table 8-15 Schematic Symbols

Device	Schematic Symbol	Notes
Battery (Single Cell)	V + —|⊢—	The battery terminal with the longer line next to it is always the positive.
Battery (Multi-cell)	+ V —|ı|⊢—	
Resistor	R —⌇⌇⌇—	
Capacitor	C —|⊢ + ↗ *If polarized type*	For polarized capacitors, the positive terminal is the one with the straight line, not the curved line.
Inductor	L ⌇⌇⌇⌇	The inductor symbol can also be drawn with curved bumps rather than loops.

SO WHAT WAS THE ANSWER TO THE BOAT AND THE STONE QUESTION FROM THE INTRODUCTION?

This is a problem that can be analyzed without the need for any equations or formal mathematics. We will start with Archimedes' principle that states simply: "When a body is submerged in a fluid, the buoyancy force (which pushes the body upward) is equal to the weight of the fluid which the body displaces."

If an object is floating at equilibrium in a fluid, the buoyancy force is equal to the weight of the object. The upward buoyancy force and downward weight of the object (remember, weight is a force!) are the same, so the net force on the object is zero. For example, when a 500 pound-mass boat is placed in a pool, its weight acts downward (with a value of 500 pounds-force if at sea level on the Earth), and it sinks deeper and deeper, displacing more and more fluid, until it has displaced 500 pounds-mass of fluid. At that point, the buoyancy force is 500 pounds-force and this opposes the weight of the boat so that it rests at equilibrium.

If the body we place in a fluid weighs more than the fluid it displaces when completely submerged, then the body sinks, but it still experiences a buoyancy force equal to the weight of the fluid displaced. This is one reason astronauts train under water—the net downward force of themselves and of objects they are manipulating is greatly reduced although their mass is the same.

If we place the same 500 pound-mass boat in a pool, and put a 200 pound-mass person in it, the boat will sink in the fluid more deeply than before, until it displaces 700 pound-mass of fluid. At this new level of submergence, the upward and downward forces are equal and the new "system" of boat and person will rest at equilibrium. If we add a stone in the boat, the new system of the boat, the person, and the stone will sink even deeper until it displaces a mass of fluid equal to the combined masses of the boat, the person, and the stone. In each of these situations the displaced fluid has to go some-where, so the level of the liquid in the pool rises.

If we assume that the stone will sink when tossed overboard, it will displace a volume of liquid equal to the volume of the stone. Since the stone is denser than the liquid (has more mass per volume), it now displaces less liquid than it did when it was in the boat. Thus, when the stone is placed in the pool, the water level will drop.

In-Class Activities

ICA 8-1

Complete the following table, using the equation weight = (mass) (gravity) as needed:

	Pound-mass	Kilogram	Newton	Pound-force
Abbreviation		[kg]		
Example	0.33	0.15	1.47	0.33
(a)	10			
(b)			700	

ICA 8-2

Complete the following table, using the equation weight = (mass) (gravity) as needed:

	Slug	Grams	Newton	Pound-force
Abbreviation		[g]		
(a)	50			
(b)			50	

ICA 8-3

If a person weighs 700 newtons, what is the mass of the person in units of pounds-mass?

ICA 8-4

A football lineman weighs 300 pounds-force. What is his mass in units of kilograms?

ICA 8-5

Complete the following table:

	Compound	SG	Density $[lb_m/ft^3]$	Density $[g/cm^3]$	Density $[kg/m^3]$
Example	Ethyl alcohol	1.025	64.0	1.025	1,025
(a)	Tetrachloroethane		100		
(b)	Chloroform	1.489			

ICA 8-6

Complete the following table:

	Compound	SG	Density [lb$_m$/ft^3]	Density [g/cm^3]	Density [kg/m^3]
(a)	Gallium	5.91			
(b)	Aluminum		168.5		

ICA 8-7

If the density of silicon is 10.5 grams per cubic centimeter, what is this in units of pounds-mass per cubic foot?

ICA 8-8

If the density of sodium is 98 kilograms per cubic meter, what is this in units of slugs per gallon?

ICA 8-9

The specific gravity of acetic acid (vinegar) is 1.049. State the density in units of pounds-mass per cubic foot.

ICA 8-10

The specific gravity of iodine is 4.927. State the density in units of slugs per liter.

ICA 8-11

Complete the following table. Assume you have a cube composed of each material, with "length" indicating the length of one side of the cube.

	Material	Mass [g]	Length [cm]	Volume [cm^3]	Density [g/cm^3]
Example	Tungsten	302	2.5	15.6	19.3
(a)	Zinc			25	7.14
(b)	Copper	107			8.92

ICA 8-12

Complete the following table. Assume you have a cylinder, composed of each material, with "radius" and "height" indicating the dimensions of the cylinder.

	Material	Mass [kg]	Radius [m]	Height [m]	Density [kg/m^3]
(a)	Aluminum		1.25	0.75	2,700
(b)	Titanium	8,000		1.0	4,540

ICA 8-13

You have been working to develop a new fictitious compound in the lab. Determine the amount in units of moles of 20 grams of this compound.

The compound has the formula: $X_2Y_2Z_7$, where the components are X, amu = 47; Y, amu = 42; Z, amu = 16.

ICA 8-14

Determine the mass in units of grams of 0.35 moles of a new fictitious compound you have developed in the lab. The formula is $A_5B_8C_2D_3$. The components are A, amu = 3; B, amu = 22; C, amu = 36; and D, amu = 54.

ICA 8-15

Complete the following table:

	Compound	Boiling Temperature			
		[°F]	[°C]	[K]	[°R]
(a)	Acetic acid	180			
(b)	Octane		126		

ICA 8-16

A **eutectic alloy** of two metals contains the specific percentage of each metal that gives the lowest possible melting temperature for any combination of those two metals. Eutectic alloys are often used for soldering electronic components to minimize the possibility of thermal damage. In the past, the most common eutectic alloy used in this application has been 63% Sn, 37% Pb, with a melting temperature of about 361 degrees Fahrenheit. To reduce lead pollution in the environment, many other alloys have been tried, including those in the table below. Complete the following table:

	Compound	Eutectic Temperature			
		[°F]	[°C]	[K]	[°R]
(a)	91% Sn, 9% Zn			472	
(b)	96.5% Sn, 3.5% Ag				890

ICA 8-17

In the Spring of 2004, NASA discovered a new planet beyond Pluto named Sedna. In the news report about the discovery, the temperature of Sedna was reported as "never rising above −400 degrees." What are the units of the reported temperature?

ICA 8-18

Is there a physical condition at which a Fahrenheit thermometer and Celsius thermometer will read the same numerical value? If so, what is this value?

ICA 8-19

Is there a physical condition at which a Fahrenheit thermometer and a Kelvin thermometer will read the same numerical value? If so, what is this value?

ICA 8-20

Complete the table:

	Atmosphere	Pascal	Inches of Mercury	Pound-force per Square Inch
Abbreviation	[atm]			
Example	0.030	3,000	0.886	0.435
(a)			30	
(b)				50

ICA 8-21

If the pressure is 250 feet of water, what is the pressure in units of inches of mercury?

ICA 8-22

If the pressure is 100 millimeters of mercury, what is the pressure in units of atmospheres?

ICA 8-23

Complete the table, using the equation for total pressure:

	Fluid Density [kg/m³]	Height of Fluid [ft]	Surface Pressure [atm]	Total Pressure [atm]
(a)		50	1	2
(b)	1,263		3	5.4

ICA 8-24

Complete the table, using the ideal gas law:

	Compound	Mass [lb$_m$]	MW [g/mol]	Amount [mol]	Pressure [Pa]	Volume [gal]	Temperature [°C]
(a)	Acetylene (C_2H_2)	0.1	26		303,975		−23
(b)	Naphthalene	0.07		0.25	131,723	1.32	

ICA 8-25

Complete the table for specific heat conversions:

	Compound	[cal/(g °C)]	[BTU/(lb$_m$ °F)]	[J/(kg K)]
(a)	Benzene		0.0406	
(b)	Mercury	0.03325		

ICA 8-26

The specific heat of copper is 0.09 British thermal units per pound-mass degree Fahrenheit. Convert this value into units of joules per gram kelvin.

ICA 8-27

The specific heat of helium is 5.24 joules per gram kelvin. Convert this value into units of British thermal units per pound-mass degree Fahrenheit.

ICA 8-28

If a ball is dropped from a height (H) its velocity will increase until it hits the ground (assuming that aerodynamic drag due to the air is negligible). During its fall, its initial potential energy is converted into kinetic energy. If the mass of the ball is doubled, how will the impact velocity change?

ICA 8-29

Which object—A, B, or C—has the most potential energy when held a distance H above the surface of the ground? You must show your work to receive credit.

Object A: mass = 1 kilogram   height = 3 meters
Object B: mass = 1 slug   height = 3 feet
Object C: mass = 1 gram   height = 1 centimeter

ICA 8-30

The specific heats of aluminum and iron are 0.214 and 0.107 calories per gram degree Celsius, respectively. If we add the same amount of energy to a cube of each material of the same mass and find that the temperature of the aluminum increases by 30 degrees Fahrenheit, how much will the iron temperature increase in degrees Fahrenheit?

ICA 8-31

Complete the table for thermal conductivity conversions:

	Compound	[W/(m °C)]	[BTU/(ft h °F)]	[cal/(cm min K)]
(a)	Zinc		122	
(b)	Silver	420		

ICA 8-32

The thermal conductivity of a plastic is 0.325 British thermal units per foot hour degree Fahrenheit. Convert this value in units of watts per meter kelvin.

ICA 8-33

The heat transfer coefficient of steel is 25 watts per square meter degree Celsius. Convert this value into units of calories per square centimeter second kelvin.

ICA 8-34

Complete the table. This problem involves the power required to raise a mass a given distance in a given amount of time assuming 100% efficiency.

	Mass [lb$_m$]	Distance [ft]	Energy [J]	Time [min]	Power [hp]
(a)	220	15		0.5	
(b)		35		2	0.134

ICA 8-35

Complete the table. This problem involves the power required to raise a mass a given distance in a given amount of time.

	Mass [lb$_m$]	Distance [ft]	Energy [J]	Time [min]	Power [hp]	Efficiency [%]
(a)	1,875	145			0.268	85
(b)	200		4,000	1		62

ICA 8-36

You are part of an engineering firm on contract by the U.S. Department of Energy's Energy Efficiency and Renewable Energy task force to develop a program to help consumers measure the efficiency of their home appliances. Your job is to measure the efficiency of stove-top burners. The consumer will place a pan of room temperature water on their stove with 1 gallon of water, record the initial room temperature in units of degrees Fahrenheit, turn on the burner, and wait for it to boil. When the water begins to boil, they will record the time in units of minutes it takes for the water to boil. Finally, they will look up the power for the burner provided by the manufacturer.

Using all of this information provided by the user, determine the efficiency of their burner. Assume the specific heat of water is 4.18 joules per gram degree Celsius.

	Stove Model	Room Temp [°F]	Time to Boil [min]	Rated Burner Power [W]	Efficiency [%]
(a)	Krispy 32-Z	68	21	1,200	
(b)	MegaCook 3000	71	25	1,300	

ICA 8-37

One problem with solar energy is that any given point on the planet is illuminated by the sun for only half of the time at best. It would be helpful, therefore, if there were a simple, affordable, and efficient means for storing any excess energy generated on sunny days for use during the night or on cloudy days.

You are investigating the electrodes used in electrolysis cells as part of a three-stage process for solar energy collection and storage.

1. Convert sunlight to electricity with photovoltaic cells.
2. Use the electricity generated in an electrolysis cell to split water into its component elements, hydrogen and oxygen. The hydrogen can be stored indefinitely. The oxygen can simply be released into the atmosphere.
3. Use a fuel cell to recombine the stored hydrogen with oxygen from the atmosphere to generate electricity.

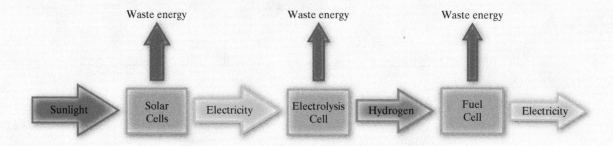

You have obtained an array of new high-efficiency, thin-film photovoltaic cells with an efficiency of 41%. The efficiency of fuel cells varies with the current demands placed on them, but the cells you have obtained yield an overall efficiency of 37% at the anticipated load.

Assume the total solar power on the solar cells is 2,000 watts. You conduct four experiments, each with a different alloy of palladium, platinum, gold, copper, and/or silver for the electrodes in the electrolysis cell. The final output power from the fuel cell is measured for each case, and the results are tabulated below. Determine the efficiency of each electrolysis cell and complete the table.

Alloy	Output Power (P_0) [W]	Electrolysis Cell Efficiency (η)
Alloy A	137	
Alloy B	201	
Alloy C	67	
Alloy D	177	

ICA 8-38

A resistor is dissipating 125 milliwatts [mW] of power. The voltage across the resistor is 12 volts [V].

(a) What is the value of the resistance? Express your answer in units of ohms, using an appropriate prefix.
(b) What is the current through the resistor? Express your answer in units of amperes, using an appropriate prefix.

ICA 8-39

A 3-volt [V] battery delivers a constant current of 100 milliamperes [mA] to the bulb in a flashlight for 20 minutes.

(a) What is the total charge in units of coulombs that passes through the flashlight bulb? Assume conventional current, thus the charge will be positive.
(b) What is the total energy delivered to the flashlight bulb in units of joules?

ICA 8-40

A constant current charges a 20-nanofarad [nF] capacitor to 5 volts [V] in 10 microseconds [μs].

(a) Determine the current. Express your answer in units of amperes, using an appropriate metric prefix.
(b) What is the total energy stored in the capacitor? Express your answer in units of joules, using an appropriate metric prefix.

ICA 8-41

Materials

Bag of cylinders   Scale   Calipers   Ruler

Procedure

For each cylinder, record the mass, length, and diameter in the table provided.

Analysis

- Calculate the volume and density for each cylinder, recording the results in the table provided.
- Rank the rods in order of increasing density, with the least dense rod first on the list.
- Using the density, determine the material of each rod. Your professor will provide you more information on the possible materials in your cylinder bag.

Data Worksheet

Description	Measured Values			Calculated Values	
	Mass	Length	Diameter	Volume	Density
Units					
Rod 1					
Rod 2					
Rod 3					
Rod 4					
Rod 5					

Rank Rods Increasing Density	Density	Material

ICA 8-42

Materials

25 mL graduated cylinder   Scale   Paper towels

Unknown liquids   Basket labeled "Wash"   Water bottle

Wastewater bucket

Procedure

Record the following data in the table provided:

1. Weigh the empty graduated cylinder and record the value.
2. Pour 15 milliliters [mL] of water into the cylinder.
3. Weigh the cylinder with water and record the value.
4. Pour the water into the wastewater bucket.
5. Pour 15 milliliters [mL] of unknown liquid (UL) 1 into a cylinder.
6. Weigh the cylinder with UL 1 and record the value.
7. Pour the UL back into the original container.
8. Place the graduated cylinder in the "Wash" basket if more than one cylinder is available. If only one cylinder is being used, wash the cylinder with water so no trace of the UL is left in the cylinder.
9. Repeat Steps 5–9 with each unknown liquid provided.

Analysis

- Calculate the density and specific gravity for each fluid, recording the results in the table provided.
- Rank the fluids in order of increasing density, with the least dense fluid first on the list.
- Using the specific gravity, determine the type of liquid in each container. Your professor will provide you more information on the possible fluids.

Data Worksheet

Description	Measured			Calculated	
	Total Mass	Volume	Liquid Mass	Density	Specific Gravity
Units					
Empty cylinder					
Water					
UL 1					
UL 2					
UL 3					
UL 4					
UL 5					

Rank Liquids Increasing Density	Density	Liquid

Chapter 8 REVIEW QUESTIONS

1. The space shuttle fleet was designed with two booster stages. If the first stage provides a thrust of 5.25 Mega-newtons and the space shuttle has a mass of 4,470,000 pound-mass, what is the acceleration of the spacecraft in miles per hour squared?

2. The space shuttle fleet was designed with two booster stages. If the first stage provides a thrust of 75 kilo-newtons and the space shuttle has an acceleration of 15,000 miles per hour squared, what is the mass of the spacecraft in units of pounds-mass?

3. The weight of a can of soda on the moon (where the acceleration of gravity is 1.6 meters per second squared) is 0.6 newtons. What is the mass of the can of soda on the Earth in units of kilograms?

4. The weight of a can of soda on the moon (where the acceleration of gravity is 1.6 meters per second squared) is 0.6 newtons. What is the mass of the can of soda on the Earth in units of pounds-mass?

5. A basketball has a mass of approximately 624 grams and a volume of 0.25 cubic feet. Determine the density of the basketball in units of pounds-mass per cubic foot.

6. Consider the following strange, but true, units:

   1 arroba = 11.5 kilograms   1 peck = 9 liters

   A basketball has a mass of approximately 624 grams and a volume of 0.25 cubic feet. Determine the density of the basketball in units of arroba per peck.

7. Consider the following strange, but true, units:

   1 batman = 3 kilograms   1 hogshead = 63 gallons

   A basketball has a mass of approximately 624 grams and a volume of 0.25 cubic feet. Determine the density of the basketball in units of batman per hogshead.

8. A cube of material X, 1 inch on all sides, has a mass of 0.05 kilograms. Determine the specific gravity of material X.

9. The specific gravity of gold is 19.3. What is the length of one side of a 0.4 kilogram cube of solid gold, in units of inches?

10. The density of gasoline is 0.72 grams per cubic centimeter. What is the mass in units of kilograms of a 5-gallon container filled completely with gasoline? Ignore the mass of the container.

11. A lab reports the density of a new element is X kilograms per cubic foot and Y grams per cubic meter. Which of the following statements is true?
    (A) $X > Y$ **(C)** $X = Y$
    (B) $X < Y$ **(D)** Cannot be determined

12. The Eco-Marathon is an annual competition sponsored by Shell Oil, in which participants build special vehicles to achieve the highest possible fuel efficiency. The Eco-Marathon is held around the world with events in the United Kingdom, Finland, France, Holland, Japan, and the United States.

    A world record was set in Eco-Marathon by a French team in 2003 called Microjoule with a performance of 10,705 miles per gallon. The Microjoule runs on ethanol. If the cars are given 100 grams of ethanol (specific gravity = 0.789) and drive until the fuel runs out, how far did the Microjoule drive in kilometers?

13. A golden bar of metal (5 centimeters by 18 centimeters by 4 centimeters) being transported by armored car is suspected of being fake, made from a less valuable metal with a thin coating of pure gold. The bar is found to have a mass of 2.7 kilograms. If the specific gravity of gold is 19.3, is the bar fake? Justify your answer.

14. A rod on the surface of Jupiter's moon Callisto has a volume of 0.3 cubic meters. Determine the weight of the rod in units of pounds-force. The density is 4,700 kilograms per cubic meter. Gravitational acceleration on Callisto is 1.25 meters per second squared.

Courtesy of W. Park

15. A substance used to remove the few remaining molecules from a near vacuum by reacting with them or adsorbing them is called a getter. There are numerous materials used and several ways of deploying them within a system enclosing a vacuum, but here we will look at a common method used in vacuum tubes, once the workhorse of electronics but now relegated to high-end audio systems and other niche markets. In vacuum tubes, after the air is evacuated with a vacuum pump, getters are usually deposited inside the hemispherical top by flash deposition. Assume that it is desired to flash deposit 1.5×10^{-3} moles of a getter onto the hemispherical top of a vacuum tube with an inside diameter of three-quarters of an inch. For each of the following getter materials, how thick will the coating be? Report your answers using meters with an appropriately chosen prefix.

The 12AX7 is a very common dual triode vacuum tube first developed for audio applications in the mid-1940s and still in common use in guitar amplifiers.

Getter Material	Specific Gravity	Atomic Weight [g/mol]
Aluminum	2.7	26.981
Barium	3.51	137.33
Calcium	1.55	40.078

16. The largest temperature decline during a 24-hour period was 56 degrees Celsius in Browning, Montana. Express this as degrees Fahrenheit per minute.

17. The largest temperature decline during a 24-hour period was 56 degrees Celsius in Browning, Montana. Express this as degrees Rankine per second.

18. If we increase the temperature in a reactor by 90 degrees Fahrenheit, how many degrees Celsius will the temperature increase?

19. We are making a cup of coffee and want the temperature to be just right, so we measure the temperature with both Fahrenheit and Celsius thermometers. The Fahrenheit meter registers 110 degrees Fahrenheit, but you prefer to it to be slightly hotter at 119 degrees Fahrenheit, so we heat it up a little. How much will the Celsius thermometer increase when we make this change?

20. Which of the following plastics has the highest melting temperature? You must prove your answer for credit!
(A) Acrylic at 150 degrees Fahrenheit.
(B) Polyethylene terephthalate (PET) at 423 kelvins.
(C) High-density polyethylene (HDPE) at 710 degrees Rankine.

21. The tiles on the space shuttle are constructed to withstand a temperature of 1,950 kelvins. What is the temperature in units of degrees Fahrenheit?

22. The boiling point of propane is −43 degrees Celsius. What is the temperature in units of degrees Fahrenheit?

23. We want to construct a thermometer using mercury (Hg). As the mercury in the bulb is heated, it expands and moves up the thin capillary tube connected to the bulb. The symbol used for the coefficient of volume expansion of a substance due to a temperature increase is β. It is used in the following equation:

$$\Delta V = \beta V (\Delta T)$$

Here, ΔV is the increase in volume, V is the original volume, and ΔT is the temperature increase. The value of β for mercury is 1.8×10^{-4} [1/degree Celsius]. If the bulb contains 0.2 milliliters and the tube has a diameter of 0.2 millimeters, how much will the mercury rise in the tube in units of centimeters if we increase the temperature from 30 degrees Fahrenheit to 70 degrees Fahrenheit?

24. You are designing a new thermometer using Galinstan®, an alloy of gallium, indium, and tin that is liquid at normal living temperatures. The specific alloy used has a coefficient of thermal expansion $\beta = 190 \times 10^{-6}$ [1/kelvin].

The change in volume (ΔV) for a given change in temperature (ΔT) can be determined by
$$\Delta V = \beta V (\Delta T)$$

Here, ΔV is the increase in volume, V is the original volume, and ΔT is the temperature increase. The thermometer will contain two cubic centimeters of Galinstan®, most of which is in the "bulb" or reservoir that is connected to a capillary tube up which the liquid moves as it expands. If your design specifications are to have a 2-millimeter change in the position of the liquid in the capillary tube for each degree Fahrenheit change in temperature, what is the diameter of the capillary tube, assuming it has a circular cross section?

25. A "normal" blood pressure is 120 millimeters of mercury (systolic reading) over 80 millimeters of mercury (diastolic reading). Convert 120 millimeters of mercury into units of pounds-force per square inch.

26. A "normal" blood pressure is 120 millimeters of mercury (systolic reading) over 80 millimeters of mercury (diastolic reading). Convert 80 millimeters of mercury into units of pascals.

27. A car tire is inflated to 30 pounds-force per square inch. If the tire has an area of 0.25 square feet in contact with the road, how much force is exerted by all four tires? Express your answer in units of pounds-force.

28. The force on the inside of a cork in a champagne bottle is 10 pound-force. If the cork has a diameter of 0.5 inches, what is the pressure inside the bottle in units of feet of water?

29. If a force of 15 newtons is applied to a surface and the pressure is measured as 4,000 pascals, what is the area of the surface in units of square meters?

30. A sensor is submerged in a silo to detect any bacterial growth in the stored fluid. The stored fluid has a density of 2.2 grams per cubic centimeters. What is the hydrostatic pressure felt by the sensor at a depth of 30 meters in units of atmospheres?

31. One of the National Academy of Engineering Grand Challenges for Engineering is **Develop Carbon Sequestration Methods**. The NAE defines carbon sequestration as "capturing the carbon dioxide produced by burning fossil fuels and storing it safely away from the atmosphere." The most promising storage location is underground, possibly in sedimentary brine formations. You are assigned to develop instrumentation to measure the properties of a brine formation, located 800 meters deep. Assume the instruments will feel an equivalent amount of pressure to the amount of hydrostatic pressure felt at the bottom of an 800-meter high column of brine, with a specific gravity of 1.35. To what hydrostatic pressure, in units of atmospheres, must the instrumentation be built to withstand?

32. A cylindrical tank filled to a height of 25 feet with tribromoethylene has been pressurized to 3 atmospheres ($P_{surface} = 3$ atmospheres). The total pressure at the bottom of the tank is 5 atmospheres. Determine the density of tribromoethylene in units of kilograms per cubic meter.

33. A submersible vehicle is being designed to operate in the Atlantic Ocean. Density of ocean water is 1.025 grams per cubic centimeter. For a maximum depth of 300 feet, what is the total pressure the hull of the submersible must be designed to withstand? Give your answer in units of pounds-force per square inch.

34. NASA is designing a mission to explore Titan, the largest moon of Saturn. Titan has numerous hydrocarbon lakes containing a mix of methane and ethane in unknown proportions. As part of the mission, a small submersible vehicle will explore Kraken Mare, the largest of these lakes, to determine, among other things, how deep it is. Assuming that the maximum depth of Kraken Mare is less than 400 meters, how much pressure in atmospheres must the submersible be designed to withstand? Assume the surface pressure on Titan is 147 kilopascals, the surface temperature is 94 kelvins, and the gravity is 1.35 meters per second squared. The specific gravity of liquid methane is 0.415 and the specific gravity of liquid ethane is 0.546.

35. Airspeed (v), is determined from dynamic pressure using the following formula: $P_{dynamic} = \frac{1}{2}\rho v^2$. Determine the dynamic pressure, in units of pascals, for an aircraft moving at an airspeed of 600 miles per hour. Air density is 1.20 kilograms per cubic meter.

36. When a flowing fluid is stopped, its pressure increases. This is called stagnation pressure. The stagnation pressure is determined by: $P_{stagnation} = \frac{1}{2}\rho v^2 + P_{surface}$, where ρ is the fluid density, v the fluid speed, and $P_{surface}$ the atmospheric pressure. Calculate the stagnation pressure in units of atmospheres for acetone flowing at 15 feet per second. Assume the density of acetone to be 785 kilograms per cubic meter.

37. When a flowing fluid is stopped, its pressure increases. This is called stagnation pressure. The stagnation pressure is determined by $P_{stagnation} = \frac{1}{2} \rho v^2 + P_{surface}$, where ρ is the fluid density, v is the fluid speed, and $P_{surface}$ is the atmospheric pressure. If the stagnation pressure is 18 pounds-force per square inch, what is the fluid speed in units of feet per minute? Assume the fluid is methyl ethyl ketone (MEK), with a density of 805 kilograms per cubic meter.

38. A 10-liter flask contains 1.3 moles of an ideal gas at a temperature of 20 degrees Celsius. What is the pressure in the flask in units of atmospheres?

39. A 10-liter flask contains 5 moles of gas at a pressure of 15 atmospheres. What is the temperature in the flask in units of kelvins?

40. An ideal gas in a 1.25-gallon container is at a temperature of 125 degrees Celsius and pressure of 2.5 atmospheres. If the gas is oxygen (formula: O_2, molecular weight = 32 grams per mole), what is the mass of gas in the container in units of grams?

41. A 5-liter container holds nitrogen (formula: N_2, molecular weight = 28 grams per mole) at a pressure of 1.1 atmospheres and a temperature of 400 kelvins. What is the mass of nitrogen in the container, in units of grams?

42. An ideal gas, kept in a 5-liter container at 300 kelvins, exhibits a pressure of 2 atmospheres. If the volume of the container is decreased to 2.9 liters, but the temperature remains the same, what is pressure in the new container in units of atmospheres?

43. An ideal gas is kept in a 10-liter container at a pressure of 1.5 atmospheres and a temperature of 310 kelvins. If the gas is compressed until its pressure is raised to 3 atmospheres while holding the temperature constant, what is the new volume in units of liters?

44. A container holding 1.5 moles of oxygen (formula: O_2, molecular weight = 32 grams per mole) at a pressure of 1.5 atmospheres and a temperature of 310 kelvins is heated to 420 kelvins, while maintaining constant volume. What is the new pressure inside the container in units of pascals?

45. Which of the following requires the expenditure of more work? You must show your work to receive credit.
   (A) Lifting a 100-newton weight a height of 4 meters.
   (B) Exerting a force of 50 pounds-force on a sofa to slide it 30 feet across a room.

46. A 10-gram rubber ball is released from a height of 6 meters above a flat surface on the moon. Gravitational acceleration on the moon is 1.62 meters per second squared. Assume that no energy is lost from frictional drag. What is the velocity, in units of meters per second, of the rubber ball the instant before it strikes the flat surface?

47. If a ball is dropped from a height (H) its velocity will increase until it hits the ground (assuming that aerodynamic drag due to the air is negligible). During its fall, its initial potential energy is converted into kinetic energy. If the ball is dropped from a height of 800 centimeters, and the impact velocity is 41 feet per second, determine the value of gravity in units of meters per second.

48. A ball is thrown vertically into the air with an initial kinetic energy of 2,500 joules. As the ball rises, it gradually loses kinetic energy as its potential energy increases. At the top of its flight, when its vertical speed goes to zero, all of the kinetic energy has been converted into potential energy. Assume that no energy is lost to frictional drag, etc. How high does the ball rise in units of meters if it has a mass of 5 kilograms?

49. A robotic rover on Mars finds a spherical rock with a diameter of 10 centimeters. The rover picks up the rock and lifts it 20 centimeters straight up. The resulting potential energy of the rock relative to the surface is 2 joules. Gravitational acceleration on Mars is 3.7 meters per second squared. What is the specific gravity of the rock?

50. If a person weighs 200 pounds-mass, how fast must they run in units of meters per second to have a kinetic energy of 1,000 calories?

51. Measurements indicate that boat A has twice the kinetic energy of boat B of the same mass. How fast is boat A traveling if boat B is moving at 30 knots? 1 knot = 1 nautical mile per hour; 1 nautical mile = 6,076 feet.

52. If a 10-kilogram rotating solid cylinder moves at a velocity (v), it has a kinetic energy of 36 joules. Determine the velocity the object is moving in units of meters per second if the kinetic energy is given by $KE = \frac{1}{2} mv^2 + \frac{1}{4} mv^2$.

53. We go out to sunbathe on a warm summer day. If we soak up 100 British thermal units per hour of energy, how much will the temperature of 132 pound-mass person increase in 2 hours in units of degrees Celsius? We assume that since our bodies are mostly water they have the same specific heat as water. The specific heat of water is 4.18 joules per gram degree Celsius.

54. A 3-kilogram projectile traveling at 100 meters per second is stopped by being shot into an insulated tank containing 100 kilograms of water. If the kinetic energy of the projectile is completely converted into thermal energy with no energy lost, how much will the water increase in temperature in units of degrees Celsius? The specific heat of water is 1 calorie per gram degree Celsius.

55. The maximum radius a falling liquid drop can have without breaking apart is given by the equation $R = \sqrt{\sigma/(g\rho)}$, where σ is the liquid surface tension, g is the acceleration due to gravity, and ρ is the density of the liquid. For bromine at 20 degrees Celsius, determine the surface tension (σ) in units of joules per meter squared if the maximum radius of a drop is 0.8 centimeter and the specific gravity of the liquid is 2.9.

56. The maximum radius a falling liquid drop can have without breaking apart is given by the equation $R = \sqrt{\sigma/(g\rho)}$, where σ is the liquid surface tension, g is the acceleration due to gravity, and ρ is the density of the liquid. For acetone at 20 degrees Celsius, determine the surface tension (σ) in units of joules per meter squared if the maximum radius of a drop is 1 centimeter and the specific gravity of the liquid is 0.785.

57. When we drive our car at 100 feet per second, we measure an aerodynamic force (called drag) of 66 pounds-force that opposes the motion of the car. How much horsepower is required to overcome this drag?

58. The power required by an airplane is given by $P = Fv$, where P is the engine power, F is the thrust, and v is the plane speed. At what speed will a 500-horsepower engine with 1,000 pounds-force of thrust propel the plane?

59. The power required by an airplane is given by $P = Fv$, where P is the engine power, F is the thrust, and v is the plane speed. What horsepower is required for 1,000 pounds-force of thrust to propel a plane 400 miles per hour?

60. The power required by an airplane is given by $P = Fv$, where P is the engine power, F is the thrust, and v is the plane speed. Which of the following planes has the most power? You must show your work to receive credit.

Plane A: Thrust = 2,000 pounds-force   Speed = 200 meters per second

Plane B: Thrust = 13,000 newtons   Speed = 500 feet per second

61. When gasoline is burned in the cylinder of an engine, it creates a high pressure that pushes on the piston. If the pressure is 100 pound-force per square inch, and it moves the 3-inch diameter piston a distance of 5 centimeters in 0.1 seconds, how much horsepower does this action produce?

62. A 100-watt motor (60% efficient) is used to raise a 100-kilogram load 5 meters into the air. How long, in units of seconds, will it take the motor to accomplish this task?

63. A 100-watt motor (60% efficient) is available to raise a load 5 meters into the air. If the task takes 65 seconds to complete, how heavy was the load in units of kilograms?

64. You need to purchase a motor to supply 400 joules in 10 seconds. All of the motors you can choose from are 80% efficient. What is the minimum wattage on the motor you need to choose?

65. A robotic rover on Mars finds a spherical rock with a diameter of 10 centimeters. The rover picks up the rock and lifts it 20 centimeters straight up. The rock has a specific gravity of 4.75. The gravitational acceleration on Mars is 3.7 meters per second squared. If the robot's lifting arm has an efficiency of 40% and required 10 seconds to raise the rock 20 centimeters, how much power (in watts) did the arm use?

66. Consider the following strange, but true, unit:

    1 donkeypower = 0.33 horsepower

    A certain motor is rated to supply an input power of 2,500 calories per minute at an efficiency of 90%. Determine the amount of output power available in units of donkeypower.

67. When boiling water, a hot plate takes an average of 8 minutes and 55 seconds to boil 100 milliliters of water. Assume the temperature in the lab is 75 degrees Fahrenheit. The hot plate is rated to provide 283 watts. The specific heat capacity of water is 4.18 joules per gram degree Celsius. How efficient is the hot plate?

68. When boiling water, a hot plate takes an average of 8 minutes and 55 seconds to boil 100 milliliters of water. Assume the temperature in the lab is 75 degrees Fahrenheit. The hot plate is rated to provide 283 watts. If we wish to boil 100 milliliters of acetone using this same hot plate, how long do we expect the process to take? Acetone has a boiling point of 56 degrees Celsius. The specific heat capacity of water is 4.18 joules per gram degree Celsius. Acetone has a specific gravity of 0.785 and a specific heat capacity of 2.15 joules per gram degree Celsius. [*Hint:* You must determine the efficiency of the hotplate.]

69. You are part of an engineering firm on contract by the U.S. Department of Energy's Energy Efficiency and Renewable Energy task force to measure the power efficiency of home appliances. Your job is to measure the efficiency of stove-top burners. In order to report the efficiency, you will place a pan containing one gallon of room temperature water on their stove, record the initial room temperature, turn on the burner, and wait for it to boil. When the water begins to boil, you will record the time it takes the water to boil and look up the power for the burner provided by the manufacturer. The specific heat capacity of water is 4.18 joules per gram degree Celsius. After measuring the following stove-top burners, what is the efficiency of each burner?

Room Temp [°F]	Time to Boil [min]	Rated Burner Power [W]
(a) 72	21	1500
(b) 69	18	1350

70. The power available from a wind turbine is calculated by the following equation:

$$P = \frac{1}{2} A \rho v^3$$

where P = power [watts], A = sweep area (circular) of the blades [square meters], ρ = air density [kilograms per cubic meter], and v = velocity [meters per second]. The world's largest sweep area wind turbine generator in Spain has a blade diameter of 420 feet. The specific gravity of air is 0.00123. Assuming a velocity of 30 miles per hour and the power produced is 5 megawatts, determine the efficiency of this turbine.

71. A constant voltage of 5 volts [V] is applied across a 250-millihenry [mH] inductor until the current through the inductor is 200 microamperes [μA].

    (a) For how many seconds was the voltage applied to the inductor? Express your answer using an appropriate metric prefix.
    (b) What is the total energy stored in the inductor? Express your answer in units of joules, using an appropriate metric prefix.

72. A 10,000-microfarad [μF] capacitor is charged to 25 volts [V]. If the capacitor is completely discharged through an iron rod 0.2 meters long and 0.25 centimeter in diameter, resulting in 90% of the stored energy being transferred to the rod as heat, how much does the temperature of the rod increase? Give your answer in kelvins.
    Data you may need:
    Specific gravity of iron: $SG = 7.874$
    Specific heat of iron: $C_P = 0.450 \, J/(g\,K)$

Chapter 9
DIMENSIONLESS NUMBERS

NOTE

Within this text, dimensions are shown in braces { } and units in brackets [ ].

Recall that in the previous chapter on Fundamental Dimensions and Base Units, we discussed the concept of dimensions. A **dimension** is a measurable physical idea; it generally consists solely of a word description with no numbers. A **unit** allows us to quantify a dimension, to state a number describing how much of that dimension exists in a specific situation. Units are defined by convention and related to an accepted standard. Table 9-1 shows the seven base units and their corresponding fundamental dimensions.

Table 9-1 **Fundamental dimensions and base units**

Dimension	Symbol	Unit	Symbol
Length	L	meter	m
Mass	M	kilogram	kg
Time	T	second	s
Temperature	Θ	kelvin	K
Amount of substance	N	mole	mol
Light intensity	J	candela	cd
Electric current	I	ampere	A

9.1 CONSTANTS WITH UNITS

LEARN TO: Understand the concept of physical constants
Recognize the difference between fundamental constants and material constants

For some constants, their values are always the same regardless of the situation. Examples include the universal gravitational constant and the ideal gas law constant. Several fundamental constants used in various engineering applications are found in Table 9-2 and the back cover of the textbook.

You will encounter many of these constants in your later studies of engineering. Two that you may already be familiar with are described below.

Table 9-2 Selected Fundamental Constants

Property	Symbol	Value
Avogadro constant	N_A	$6.022 \times 10^{23}\,\text{mol}^{-1}$
Boltzmann constant	k	$1.38065 \times 10^{-23}\,\text{J/K}$
Faraday constant	F	$9.65 \times 10^4\,\text{C/mol}$
Ideal gas law constant	R	8314 (Pa L)/(mol K) 0.08206 (atm L)/(mol K)
Planck constant	h	$6.62 \times 10^{-34}\,\text{Js}$
Speed of light in a vacuum	c	$3 \times 10^8\,\text{m/s}$
Stefan-Boltzmann constant	σ	$5.67 \times 10^{-8}\,\text{W/(m}^2\,\text{K}^4)$
Universal gravitational constant	G	$6.67 \times 10^{-11}\,\dfrac{\text{Nm}^2}{\text{kg}^2}$

Universal Gravitation Constant

When the centers of two bodies of mass (m_1 and m_2) are separated by some radius (r), then the force (F) tending to pull them toward each other is given by **Law of Universal Gravitation**, named after Isaac Newton, the famous English scientist who is responsible for the concepts of gravitation, laws of motion, and, along with Gottfried Leibniz, differential calculus. The **universal gravitational constant** (G) is a proportionality constant.

$$F = G\frac{m_1 m_2}{r^2}$$

Ideal Gas Law Constant

The **ideal gas law** relates the quantities of pressure (P), volume (V), temperature (T) and amount (n) of gas in a container. This law was first proposed by Benoît Clapeyron, a French engineer who made great contributions to the field of thermodynamics. The **ideal gas law constant** (R) is the relationship found by "ideal" gas behavior, where 1 mole [mol] of gas occupies a volume of 22.4 liters [L] at a temperature of zero degrees Celsius [°C] and a pressure of 1 atmosphere [atm].

$$PV = nRT$$

Another type of "constant" maintains the same value as long as the physical situation remains the same. These "constants" are found in equations that describe how matter and/or energy behave and are a property of the material involved. Several simple examples of how varying conditions cause changes in such "constants" are given below and summarized in Table 9-3. The values of many constants are well documented and are readily available in the literature.

Several of these have been discussed previously in the chapter on Universal Units; a short reminder is provided here.

Acceleration of Gravity

If the Law of Universal Gravitation is written for a small body (subscript b) and the earth (subscript e) as we hold the body close to the earth we obtain the equation shown at the right. Since the term in parentheses is a constant specific to the earth,

Table 9-3 Selected material constants

Property	Symbol	Typical Units	Material	Value
Gravitational acceleration	g	$\dfrac{m}{s^2}$	Earth	9.8
			moon	1.6
Density	ρ	$\dfrac{g}{cm^3}$	air	0.00129
			mercury	13.6
			silicon carbide	3.1
			water	1.0
Specific heat	C_p	$\dfrac{J}{gK}$	air	1.005
			mercury	0.14
			silicon carbide	0.75
			water	4.18
Thermal conductivity	k	$\dfrac{W}{mK}$	air	0.0243
			mercury	8.34
			silicon carbide	120
			water	0.607

we can replace the three parameters in parentheses by a single constant, called **gravity** (g).

$$F = m_b\left(G\frac{m_e}{r_e^2}\right) = m_b g$$

If the values for universal gravitational constant, the mass and the radius of the Earth are substituted into the expression in parenthesis, the resulting value for g will be 9.8 meters per second squared. If you go to Earth's moon, the terms represented by m_e and r_e are much smaller, and gravity in this case is about one-sixth of the value on Earth, or about 1.6 meters per second squared.

Density

The relationship between the mass (m) of an object and the volume (V) the object occupies is called **density** (ρ, Greek letter rho) and has a dimension of mass per volume. For example, the density of potassium is 0.86 grams per cubic centimeter, whereas the density of gold is 19.3 grams per cubic centimeter.

$$\rho = \frac{m}{V}$$

Usually, values listed for density will vary somewhat from the "standard" values, depending on conditions of temperature and pressure. For example under typical conditions of 20°C, a cubic centimeter of air has a mass of about 0.0013 grams. However, at −50°C, a cubic centimeter of air has a mass of 0.0015 grams.

Specific Heat

The **specific heat** of a material indicates how much energy must be added to a given mass of material in order to cause the temperature to increase by a specified amount. To be a bit more precise, the thermal energy (Q) associated with a change in temperature (ΔT) is a function of the mass of the object (m) and the specific heat (C_p).

$$Q = mC_p\Delta T$$

For example, to raise the temperature of one gram of liquid mercury by 1 degree Celsius requires 0.14 joules of energy ($C_p = 0.14 \text{ J}/(\text{g}^\circ\text{C})$). For comparison, liquid water has a specific heat of $C_p = 4.18 \text{ J}/(\text{g}^\circ\text{C})$. This means that water requires 30 times as much energy to increase its temperature by one degrees Celsius compared with the same mass of mercury. This high value of specific heat is one of the reasons that liquid water is critically important to life as we know it.

Thermal Conductivity

When one side of an object is hotter than the other side, heat will flow spontaneously through the object from the high temperature to the low temperature in a phenomenon called **conduction**. The rate of heat transfer (Q/t) is a function of the cross-sectional area (A), the distance across which the heat travels (d), and the difference between the high temperature and the low temperature (ΔT). This model is called **Fourier's Law**, named for Joseph Fourier, a French physicist who made many contributions to heat flow and mathematics. Thermal conductivity (κ) is a material property that denotes the ability of a material to conduct heat. A material with a high thermal conductivity readily transports heat whereas a material with a low thermal conductivity retards heat flow.

$$\frac{Q}{t} = -\kappa A \frac{\Delta T}{d}$$

9.2 COMMON DIMENSIONLESS NUMBERS

LEARN TO: Understand when a quantity is dimensionless

NOTE

A dimensionless number is not able to be described by any dimension, but rather by the lack of dimensions.

Sometimes, we form the ratio of two parameters, where each parameter has the same dimensions. Sometimes, we form a ratio with two groups of parameters, where each group has the same dimensions. The final result in both cases is dimensionless.

Pi (π): One example is the parameter π, used in the calculation of a circumference or area of a circle. The reason π is dimensionless is that it is actually defined as the ratio of the circumference (C) of a circle to its diameter (D):

$$\pi = \frac{C}{D} = \frac{\text{circumference}}{\text{diameter}} \{=\} \frac{\text{length}}{\text{length}} = \frac{L^1}{L^1} = L^0$$

The ratio of one length to another length yields a dimensionless ratio. We can see this in another way through reversing the process. For the circumference of a circle:

$$C = \pi D$$

and if dimensions are inserted,

$$\{L^1\} = \pi \{L^1\}$$

This equation is dimensionally correct only if π has no dimensions. The same result is obtained for the equation of the area of a circle.

$$A = \pi r^2$$

Inserting dimensions:

$$\{L^2\} = \pi\{L^1\}\ \{L^1\} = \pi\{L^2\}$$

Again, this equation is dimensionally correct only if π is dimensionless.

Specific Gravity (SG): The specific gravity is the ratio of the density of an object to the density of water.

$$\text{Specific gravity} = \frac{\text{density of the object}}{\text{density of water}} = \frac{\text{mass/volume}}{\text{mass/volume}} \ \{=\} \frac{\{M/L^3\}}{\{M/L^3\}} = \{M^0L^0\}$$

Mach Number (Ma): We often describe the speed at which an airplane or rocket travels in terms of the Mach number, named after Ernst Mach, an Austrian physicist. This number is the ratio of the speed of the plane compared with the speed of sound in air.

$$\text{Mach number} = \frac{\text{speed of the object}}{\text{speed of sound in air}} \ \{=\} \frac{\{L/T\}}{\{L/T\}} = \{L^0T^0\}$$

Table 9-4 Some common dimensionless parameters

Name	Phenomena Ratio	Symbol	Expression
Coefficient of friction	Sideways force (F)/weight of object (w) [object static or kinetic (object sliding)]	μ_{st} and μ_k	F/w
Drag coefficient	Drag force (F_d)/inertia force (ρ, density; ν, speed; A, body area)	C_d	$F_d/(\tfrac{1}{2}\rho\nu^2 A)$
Mach number	Object speed (ν)/speed of sound (ν_{sound})	Ma	ν/ν_{sound}
Pi	Circle circumference (C)/circle diameter (D)	π	C/D
Poisson's ratio	Transverse contraction (ε_{trans})/ longitudinal extension (ε_{long})	ν	$\varepsilon_{trans}/\varepsilon_{long}$
Specific gravity	Object density/density of water	SG	ρ/ρ_{H_2O}

COMPREHENSION CHECK 9-1

The heat loss (Q/t, in units of joules per second) from the surface of a hot liquid is given by:

$$\frac{Q}{t} = hA(T-T_0)$$

Express the parameter (h) in fundamental dimensions if the area (A) is given in units of square meters. Both the temperature of the liquid (T) and the ambient temperature (T_0) are measured in degrees Celsius.

(A) MT^{-3} **(C)** $ML^2T^{-1}\Theta$

(B) $MT^{-3}\Theta$ **(D)** Dimensionless

COMPREHENSION CHECK 9-2

A simple expression for the velocity of molecules in a gas is:

$$v = K\sqrt{\frac{P}{\rho}}$$

In terms of fundamental dimensions, what are the dimensions of the constant K if the velocity (v) is given in meters per second, pressure (P) in pascals, and density (ρ) in grams per cubic centimeter?

(A) $L^{-1}T$ (C) $L^{-2}T$
(B) LT^{-1} (D) Dimensionless

We must remind ourselves that it is essential to use the appropriate dimensions **and** units for every parameter. Suppose that we are interested in computing the sine of an angle. This can be expressed as a dimensionless number by forming the ratio of the length of the opposite side divided by the length of the hypotenuse of a right triangle.

$$\sin(x) = \frac{\text{length opposite side}}{\text{length hypotenuse}} \{=\} \frac{L}{L} = L^0$$

In addition to the ratio of two lengths, you will know from one of your math classes that the sine can be also be expressed as an infinite series given by:

$$\sin(x) = x - \frac{x^3}{3!} + \frac{x^5}{5!} - \frac{x^7}{7!} + \cdots$$

LAW OF ARGUMENTS

Any function that can be computed using a series must employ a *dimensionless* argument.

This includes all the trigonometric functions, logarithms, and e^x, where e is the base of natural logarithms.

Let us suppose that the argument x had the units of length, say, feet. The units in this series would then read as:

$$\text{ft} - \frac{\text{ft}^3}{3!} + \frac{\text{ft}^5}{5!} - \frac{\text{ft}^7}{7!} + \cdots$$

We already know that we cannot add two terms unless they have the same units; recall the Plus law from the chapter on Fundamental Dimensions. The only way we can add these terms, all with different exponents, is if each term is dimensionless. Consequently, when we calculate $\sin(x)$, we see that the x must be dimensionless, which is why we use the unit of radians. This conclusion is true for any function that can be computed using a series form, leading to the **Law of Arguments**.

● **EXAMPLE 9-1**

What are the dimensions of k in the following equation, where d is distance and t is time?

$$d = Be^{kt}$$

Since exponents must be dimensionless, the product of k and t must not contain any dimensions. The dimensions of time are {T}

$$kT^1 \{=\} M^0 L^0 T^0 \Theta^0$$

Solving for k yields:

$$k \{=\} T^{-1}$$

k is expressed in dimensions of inverse time or "per time."

COMPREHENSION CHECK 9-3

What are the dimensions of the value "6" in the following equation, assuming T is temperature [kelvin] and P is algae population [gram per milliliter of lake water]?

$$T = 102\, e^{-6P}$$

9.3 DIMENSIONAL ANALYSIS

LEARN TO: Understand the reasoning behind using dimensional analysis to simplify problem solutions

Dimensionless quantities are generated as a result of a process called **dimensional analysis**. As an example, suppose we want to study rectangles, assuming that we know nothing about rectangles. We are interested in the relationship between the area of a rectangle (A), the width of the rectangle (W), and the perimeter of the rectangle (P). We cut out a lot of paper rectangles and ask students in the class to measure the area, the perimeter, and the width (Table 9-5).

If we graph the area against the perimeter, we obtain Figure 9-1

From this, we see that the data are scattered. We would not have a great deal of confidence in drawing conclusions about how the area depended on the perimeter of

Table 9-5 Rectangle measurements

Perimeter (P) [cm]	Area (A) [cm²]	Width (W) [cm]
4.02	1.0	1.1
8.75	4.7	1.9
6	2.3	1.55
13.1	6.0	1.1
17.75	19	5.25
10.25	1.2	0.25
12.1	3.0	5.5
6	0.3	2.9
16.25	15.4	5.1
17	7.8	1.05

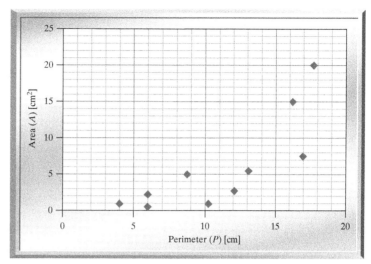

Figure 9-1 Graph of rectangle data

the rectangle. The best we could do is to make a statement such as, "It seems that the larger the perimeter, the larger the area." However, close examination of the data table shows that as the perimeter increases from 8.75 to 10.25 centimeters and from 16.25 to 17 centimeters, the area actually decreases in each case. One reason for this problem is that our plot has omitted one important parameter: the width.

Analysis shows that one way in which to generalize plots of this type is to create dimensionless parameters from the problem variables. In this case, we have perimeter with dimension of length, width with the dimension of length, and area with the dimension of length squared. A little thought shows that we could use the ratio of P/W (or W/P) instead of just P on the abscissa. The ratio W/P has the dimensions of length/length, so it is dimensionless. It does not matter whether this is miles/miles, or centimeters/centimeters, the ratio is dimensionless. Similarly, we could write $A/(W^2)$, and this would also be dimensionless.

These ratios are plotted and shown in Figure 9-2. The scatter of Figure 9-1 disappears and all the data appear along a single line.

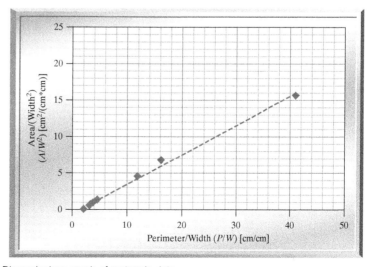

Figure 9-2 Dimensionless graph of rectangle data

To understand how to read data from Figure 9-2, let us examine the following question. If a rectangle has a perimeter of 20 feet and a width of 2 feet, what is the area?

Step A: $P/W = (20 \text{ ft})/(2 \text{ ft}) = 10$ (with no units).

Step B: From the chart, at a P/W value of 10, we read a value from the line of $A/(W^2) = 3.5$.

Step C: Calculate A from this as $A = 3.5 * (2 \text{ ft} * 2 \text{ ft}) = 14 \text{ ft}^2$.

Some of you may be thinking that we made this problem unnecessarily difficult. After all, anyone who manages to get to college knows that the "sensible" measurements to make are length, width, and area. However, many phenomena are far more complicated than simple rectangles, and it is often not at all obvious what parameters should be measured to characterize the behavior of the system we are studying. In situations of this type, dimensionless analysis can become a powerful tool to help us understand *which* parameters affect the behavior of the system and *how* they affect it. With this in mind, let us look at a slightly more complicated example.

● **EXAMPLE 9-2**

A not-so-famous scientist, Dr. Triticale, decided to apply his scientific skills to cooking. He had always been fascinated with the process of cooking pancakes, so it seemed reasonable that he start there. He wanted to learn how to flip the flapjacks in a graceful arc in the air and then catch them.

He spent long summer days pondering this process until he finally was able to produce a list of the parameters that he felt were important. He kept asking himself, "If I change this parameter, will the trajectory of the pancake change?" If he could answer "Yes!" or even "Probably," he then considered the parameter as important enough to include on his list. As he saw it, these parameters were:

Speed of the frying pan, *U*	Mass of the flapjack, *m*
Height of the flip, *H*	Gravity (it pulls the flapjack back down), *g*

He then wrote this dependency in equation form as $H = f:(U, m, g)$.

Dr. Triticale realized that while he felt that gravity was important, it would not be easy to change the value of gravity in his tests (he could have gone to a high mountain or the moon, but this was too hard). His plan was to do many tests (and consequently eat many pancakes). He would make many measurements for many different flipping speeds and pancake masses, and try to fit a curve to the data.

Based on his work with conversion factors and his knowledge of the Per law, he reasoned that it is acceptable to multiply parameters with different dimensions. It is also fine to raise a parameter (and its associated units) to a power. Based on his understanding of the Plus law, he knew it is not acceptable to add parameters with different dimensions.

Using this information, he decided that it would be permissible to try to "fit" the dependence of pancake flipping to the important parameters raised to different powers and multiplied together. This would create a single term like $k_1 U^{a_1} m^{b_1} g^{c_1}$.

He also knew that if this term were made to have the same dimensions as H, it just might be a legitimate expression. In fact, if this were the case, he could use many terms, each of which had the dimensions of H and add them all together. While this might not be a valid equation, at least it would satisfy the Per and Plus laws, and with many terms he would have a good chance of his equation fitting the data. So, he boldly decided to try the following series:

$$H = k_1 U^{a_1} m^{b_1} g^{c_1} + k_2 U^{a_2} m^{b_2} g^{c_2} + k_3 U^{a_3} m^{b_3} g^{c_3} + \cdots$$

He needed to determine the values of the dimensionless k constants as well as all of the exponents. He knew that all the terms on the right-hand side must have the same dimensions, or they could not be added together. He also knew that the dimensions on the left and right sides must match.

With this, he then realized that he could examine the dimensions of any term on the right-hand side since each had to be the same dimensionally. He did this by comparing a typical right-hand term with the left-hand side of the equation, or

$$H = kU^a m^b g^c$$

The next step was to select the proper values of a, b, and c, so that the dimensions of the right-hand side would match those on the left-hand side. To do this, he substituted the dimensions of each parameter:

$$L^1 M^0 T^0 = \{LT^{-1}\}^a \{M\}^b \{LT^{-2}\}^c = \{L\}^{a+c} \{M\}^b \{T\}^{-a-2c}$$

For this to be dimensionally correct, the exponents for L, M, and T on the right and left would have to match, or

$$L: 1 = a + c \quad M: 0 = b \quad T: 0 = -a - 2c$$

This yields

$$a = 2 \quad b = 0 \quad c = -1$$

From this, Dr. Triticale settled on a typical term as

$$k\, U^2 m^0 g^{-1}$$

Finally, he wrote the "curve fitting" equation (with a whole series of terms) as

$$H = \sum_{i=1}^{\infty} k_1 U^2 g^{-1} + k_2 U^2 g^{-1} + k_3 U^2 g^{-1} + \cdots = \frac{U^2}{g} \sum_{i=1}^{\infty} k_i = (K)\left(\frac{U^2}{g}\right)$$

Now, armed with this expression, he was sure that he could flip flapjacks with the best, although he knew that he would have to conduct many experiments to make sure the equation was valid (and to determine the value of K). What he did not realize was that he had just performed a procedure called "dimensional analysis."

9.4 RAYLEIGH'S METHOD

LEARN TO: Determine appropriate dimensionless numbers using Rayleigh's Method
Understand the physical significance of the Reynolds Number as it applies to pipe flow
Determine final quantity if given four of following: density, diameter, Reynolds Number, velocity, viscosity

In this section we formalize the discussion presented in Example 9-2 by introducing a method of dimensional analysis devised by Lord Rayleigh, John William Strutt, the third Baron Rayleigh. Three detailed examples illustrate his approach to dimensionless analysis:

■ Example 9-3, in which we analyze factors affecting the distance traveled by an accelerating object

- Example 9-4, in which we determine the most famous named dimensionless number, Reynolds number
- Example 9-5, in which we simplify one use of Rayleigh's method

No matter the problem, the way we solve it stays the same:

Rayleigh's Method

Step 1: Write each variable and raise each to an unknown exponent (use *all* the variables, even the dependent variable). Order and choice of exponent do not matter.

Step 2: Substitute dimensions of the variables into Step 1. Be sure to raise each dimension to the proper exponent groups from Step 1.

Step 3: Group by dimension.

Step 4: Exponents on each dimension must equal zero for dimensionless numbers, so form a set of equations by setting the exponent groups from Step 3 for each dimension equal to zero.

Step 5: Solve the simultaneous equations (as best as you can).

  Hint: Number of unknowns – number of equations = number of groups

Step 6: Substitute results of Step 5 back into Step 1 exponents.

Step 7: Group variables by exponent. These resulting groups are your dimensionless numbers.

Step 8: Be sure to *check* it out!! Are *all* of the ratios really dimensionless?

  Hint: If the resulting groups are *not* dimensionless, you most likely goofed in either Step 2 or Step 5!

Rayleigh's analysis is quite similar to the Buckingham Pi method, another method to determine dimensionless groups. Rayleigh's method is, however, a bit more direct and often seems less "mysterious" to those who are new to dimensional analysis. Both methods use a general form with multiplied and exponentiated variables. Any inspection of physics, engineering, and mathematical texts reveal many examples of this form of equation governing a myriad of behaviors.

● **EXAMPLE 9-3**

To develop an understanding of how initial velocity, acceleration, and time all affect the distance traveled by an accelerating object, we conduct some experiments and then analyze the resulting data. We asked a student to conduct a series of tests for us. She observed 25 different moving bodies with a wide range of initial speeds and different accelerations. For each, she measured the distance the bodies traveled for some prescribed time interval. Results are given in Table 9-6.

Table 9-6 Position of a body as a function of initial velocity, acceleration, and time

Test	Initial Velocity (v_0) [m/s]	Acceleration (a) [m/s²]	Time (t) [s]	Distance (d) [m]
1	3	1	6	36
2	3	2	6	54
3	1.5	5	6	99
4	5	4	6	44
5	5	3	8	136

Test	Initial Velocity (v_0) [m/s]	Acceleration (a) [m/s^2]	Time (t) [s]	Distance (d) [m]
6	5	5	2	20
7	10	1	9	131
8	14	2	11	275
9	20	3	4	104
10	10	2	4	56
11	10	4	3	48
12	10	6	2	32
13	5	2	2	14
14	8	2	10	180
15	12	2	4	64
16	6	1	4	32
17	2	2	9	99
18	3	3	12	252
19	6	4	6	108
20	15	5	2.4	50
21	4	7	7.2	210
22	2	2	8	80
23	9	8	6.2	210
24	6.7	2	1.7	14
25	3.1	2	10	131

In addition, we would like to use this data set to help make predictions of the distance traveled by other bodies under different conditions. For example, we might want to answer the following question:

■ What is the acceleration needed to travel 4,800 meters in 200 seconds, if the initial velocity is 8 meters per second?

There are several independent variables (initial velocity, acceleration, and time), so it is not obvious what to plot. We can write the dependency as

$$d = f: (v_0, a, t)$$

We anticipate that it is difficult to draw conclusions regarding the interdependence of all of these variables. Realizing this, we plot distance against time without worrying about the initial velocity and the acceleration.

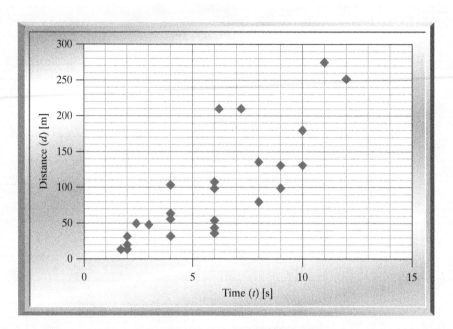

It seems that, in general, the longer one travels, the farther one goes. Upon closer inspection, however, it is obvious that this is not always the case. For example, for a travel time of 6 seconds, the distance traveled varies from about 25 to 210 meters. Since enough tests were not conducted with systematic variation of the initial velocity or acceleration, it is not possible to do much better than this. We certainly have no hope of answering the questions above with any confidence. In addition, since the values are so scattered, we realize that we have no good way to determine if any of our measurements were "bad."

With this disheartening conclusion, we perform a dimensional analysis in an attempt to place the parameters into fewer groups. The immediate problem we face is how to combine the parameters to give dimensionless groups. For rectangles, this was relatively easy to do by inspection. The parameters in this new problem are slightly more complicated, and although we might find suitable groups by inspection, as the problems become a lot harder (and they will), we need some sort of standard method, or algorithm, to define suitable dimensionless groups.

This technique is relatively simple and comprises the following eight steps:

Step 1: Raise each variable to a different unknown power, using symbols for the power variables that do not already appear in the problem, and then multiply all of these individual terms together. For example, since the current problem has both an a and d used as variables, we should not use a and d for the powers; hence we choose the letters p through s for the exponents. The order in which we list the variables and assign exponents is completely random.

This gives us the term: $d^p v_0^q a^r t^s$.

Step 2: Substitute the correct dimensions for each variable.

$$\{L\}^p \left\{\frac{L}{T}\right\}^q \left\{\frac{L}{T^2}\right\}^r \{T\}^s$$

Step 3: Expand the expression to have each dimension as a base raised to some power.

$$\{L\}^{p+q+r} \{T\}^{-q-2r+s}$$

Step 4: *For the expression in Step 3 to be dimensionless, each exponent must equal zero, or*

$$p + q + r = 0 \text{ and } -q - 2r + s = 0$$

Step 5: *Solve for the exponents. In this case, we have two equations and four unknowns, so it is not possible to solve for all the unknowns in terms of an actual number. We must be satisfied with finding two of the exponents in terms of the other two. This might seem problematic, but we will find that this not only is not a difficulty, but also is quite common in this type of analysis.* **Note that there are many ways to do this and all will lead to two dimensionless ratios. If you do not like the plot you get from doing it one way, try solving for different exponents and see if that provides a better plot. All will be correct, but some are easier to use than others.** *Although several procedures will lead to solutions, in general, we will solve for one of the variables, and then substitute into the other equations to reduce the number of variables. If a variable appears in all or most of the equations, that may be a good one to begin with.*

In our example, we solve the second equation for q.

$$q = -2r + s$$

Substituting for q *into the other equation gives*

$$p - 2r + s + r = 0$$

thus,

$$p = r - s$$

At this point, we have defined p *and* q *in terms of the other two variables,* r *and* s.

Step 6: *Substitute into the original expression.*

$$d^{r-s}v_0^{-2r+s}a^r t^s$$

Note that all of the exponents are now expressed in terms of only two variables, r *and* s.

Step 7: *Simplify by collecting all terms associated with the remaining exponential variables (*r *and* s *in this case).*

$$\left(\frac{da}{v_0^2}\right)^r \left(\frac{tv_0}{d}\right)^s$$

Step 8: *The simplification in Step 7 gives the dimensionless ratios we are looking for. Dropping the exponents assumed in Step 1 gives the following groups:*

$$\left(\frac{da}{v_0^2}\right) \text{ and } \left(\frac{tv_0}{d}\right)$$

We need to double-check to make sure that both the groups are dimensionless. Before plotting them, we make two additional observations. (1) The variables of distance and initial velocity appear in both quantities. This may not always be desirable. (2) The initial velocity appears in the denominator of the first ratio. This may cause problems if we are examining data in which the initial velocity is very small, making the ratio very large. While dimensional analysis is much more involved than the examples given here, there are several important facts for you to remember.

First, since the results of the dimensional analysis produces dimensionless ratios, these ratios may be used as they appear above or they may be inverted. In other words, for this example, we can use $\frac{da}{v_0^2}$ or $\frac{v_0^2}{da}$ equally well.

To eliminate the problem of very small initial velocity values, the second form is preferable for our work here. As a side note, if we are interested in the behaviors at very small times, then we would prefer for time to appear in the numerator of the second ratio.

Second, it is permissible to alter the form of one of the ratios by multiplying it by the other one or by the inverse of the other one or by the other one squared, etc. This will change the form of the first ratio and may produce results that are easier to interpret. A simple example can be used to show this. For the two ratios here, multiply the first ratio by the second ratio squared. This yields a "new" first ratio as $[(at^2)/d]$ and this could be used along with the second ratio $[(tv_0)/d]$. This result may have the advantage of initial velocity appearing in only one of the ratios.

To continue this example, we create a worksheet with the four columns of data and then add two extra columns, one for each of the two dimensionless ratios $[v_0^2/(da)]$ and $[(v_0t)/d]$. Once this is done, it is a straightforward matter to plot one against the other. This result is shown below:

NOTE
There seems to be one "bad" data point. Would you have been able to pick out this point from the original data or from the dimensional plot?

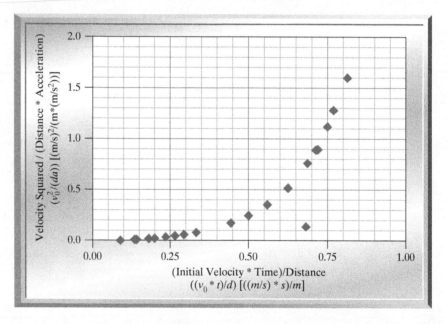

Now the scatter from the original dimensional plot is gone, and all but one data point seems to lie on a smooth curve. We can use this plot to determine the relationship between distance traveled, acceleration, time, and initial velocity. Let us see how to do this for the question we posed earlier.

What acceleration is required to go 4,800 meters in 200 seconds if the initial car velocity is 8 meters per second?

On the abscissa: [(8 m/s) (200 s)]/(4,800 m) = 0.33
Reading from the graph: $v_0^2/(da) = 0.075$
Solving for acceleration: a = $(8 \text{ m/s})^2/(0.075)$ (4,800 m) = 0.18 m/s^2

Several important conclusions can be drawn from this exercise.

- Dimensionless parameters often allow us to present data in an easily interpretable fashion when the "raw" data have no recognizable pattern.
- When we use the exponent approach to find dimensionless parameters, we need to remember that the exponents could be either positive or negative. Thus, in the case of the rectangle, P/W is just as good as W/P. You can always try both to see which gives the best-looking results. The choice is yours, and sometimes depends on whether one of the variables goes to zero; since you cannot divide by zero, that variable should not be in the denominator, if possible.
- If we "collapse" the data by using dimensionless parameters so that a single curve can fit through the resulting points, *bad data points will usually become obvious*.
- Finally, this approach can reduce literally thousands of different measurements into one simple curve. In the case of the car, the single line we obtained will work for all possible combination of times, initial velocities, accelerations, and distance. If we used dimensional plots, we would need more plots, with many lines on each plot. This would require an entire book of plots rather than the single plot with a single line that we obtained above by dimensionless ratios.

● **EXAMPLE 9-4**

To classify the smoothness of a flowing fluid, Osborne Reynolds developed the now famous dimensionless quantity of **Reynolds number**. His theory stated that the smoothness or roughness (a lot of eddies or swirling) of a fluid depended upon:

How fast the fluid was moving (velocity)	$v \, [=] \, \mathrm{m/s}$
The density of the fluid	$\rho \, [=] \, \mathrm{kg/m^3}$
The diameter of the pipe	$D \, [=] \, \mathrm{m}$
How hard it was to move the fluid (viscosity)	$\mu \, [=] \, \mathrm{g/(cm \, s)}$

Reynolds knew the smoothness depended upon these quantities:

$$\text{Smoothness of the flow} = f: (v, \rho, D, \mu)$$

But how did they depend on one another? We could write the four variables above as

$$v^a \rho^b D^c \mu^d$$

and if this was dimensionless, it would appear as $M^0 \, L^0 \, T^0$.

To make this grouping dimensionless, first we substitute in the dimensions of the four variables to obtain:

$$\left\{\frac{L}{T}\right\}^a \left\{\frac{M}{L^3}\right\}^b \{L^c\} \left\{\frac{M}{LT}\right\}^d = M^{b+d} L^{a-3b+c-d} T^{-a-d}$$

If this is to be dimensionless, then the exponents on all of the dimensions must equal zero, therefore:

$M:$ $b + d = 0$
$L:$ $a - 3b + c - d = 0$
$T:$ $-a - d = 0$

This gives three equations in four unknowns, so we will have to solve for three of the variables in terms of the fourth. In this example, we solve for the three unknowns a, b, c in terms of d:

$M:$ $b = -d$
$T:$ $a = -d$
$L:$ $c = -a + 3b + d = d - 3d + d = -d$

Substituting these back into the original parameters gives:

$$v^{-d}\rho^{-d}D^{-d}\mu^{d}$$

We see that there is one dimensionless group, since all the parameters have an exponent of d. We can write

$$\frac{\mu}{v\rho D}\{=\}\frac{\frac{M}{LT}}{\frac{L}{T}\frac{M}{L^3}L}$$

Since the variables of diameter and velocity can approach zero, the Reynolds number is commonly written as follows:

$$Re = \frac{\rho D v}{\mu}$$

If the Reynolds number has a value less than 2,000, the flow is described as **laminar**, *meaning it moves slowly and gently with no mixing or churning. If the Reynolds number has a value greater than 10,000, the flow is described as* **turbulent**, *meaning it moves quickly with much mixing and churning (lots of eddies) occurring. The region in between 2,000 and 10,000 is called the* **transition region**.

NOTE

The Reynolds number is used to describe fluid flow.

$Re < 2,000$ = laminar

$2,000 < Re < 10,000$ = transitional

$Re > 10,000$ = turbulent

● EXAMPLE 9-5

Suppose we conduct an experiment with a ball that we throw from the top of a tall tower of height H. We throw it directly downward with some initial velocity v, and then measure the elapsed time t until it hits the ground. We vary the initial height and the initial velocity. The variables of interest in this problem are H, v, and t. A little thought leads us to include g, since it is the force of gravity that causes the ball to fall in the first place.

Using Rayleigh's method, find a set of dimensionless ratios that can be used to correlate our data.

Step 1: *Write each variable and raise each to an unknown exponent (use all the variables, even the dependent variable).*

$$t^a H^b v^c g^d$$

Step 2: *Substitute dimensions of the variables into Step 1. Be sure to raise each dimension to the proper exponent from Step 1.*

$$t^a\{=\}T^a \quad H^b\{=\}L^b \quad v^c\{=\}L^cT^{-c} \quad g^d\{=\}L^dT^{-2d}$$

Step 3: *Group by dimension.*

$$L^{b+c+d}T^{a-c-2d}$$

Step 4: *Exponents on each dimension must equal zero for dimensionless numbers! Form a set of equations by setting the exponents for each dimension equal to zero.*

$$b + c + d = 0 \quad a - c - 2d = 0$$

Step 5: *Solve the simultaneous equations (as best as you can).*

$$b = -c - d \quad a = c + 2d$$

Step 6: *Substitute results of Step 5 back into Step 1 exponents.*

$$t^{c+2d}\, H^{-c-d}\, v^c\, g^d$$

Step 7: *Group variables by exponent. These resulting groups are your dimensionless numbers.*

$$\left[\frac{v\,t}{H}\right]^c \qquad \left[\frac{g\,t^2}{H}\right]^d$$

Step 8: *Be sure to* check *it out!! Are all of the ratios really dimensionless?*

COMPREHENSION CHECK 9-4

The Euler number is a function of the pressure drop, velocity, and density. Determine the form of the Euler number with Rayleigh's method.

Pressure drop	ΔP	pascal
Density	ρ	grams per cubic centimeter
Velocity	v	meters per second

NOTE

We are not sure that the results of this technique are *physically correct*, only that they are *dimensionally correct*.

At the beginning of the analysis, when in doubt about the importance of a parameter, put it in the list of important parameters.

Always remember that we initiate this procedure simply by providing a list of parameters we think are important to the situation at hand. If we omit an important parameter, our final result will not be physically correct, even if it is dimensionally correct. Consequently, if we select an improper parameter, then when tests are conducted, we will discover that it was not important to the problem and we can drop it from further consideration. *We cannot decide whether any variable is important until we conduct some experiments.*

Consequently, if we are *sure* that a parameter is important, then we know it should *not* drop from the analysis. The only way it can be retained is if at least one other parameter contains the missing dimension. In this case, we need to ask ourselves what other parameters might be important, add them to our list, and rework the analysis.

Dimensional analysis helps us organize data by allowing us to plot one-dimensionless parameter against another, resulting in one line on a single plot. This is a powerful result, and reduces a problem of multiple initial parameters to one containing only two. This discussion leads to the **Problem Simplification Rule**:

By performing dimensional analysis of the parameters, we can generally find dimensionless groupings to effectively reduce the number of parameters, facilitating the presentation of interdependencies and often simplifying the problem.

In-Class Activities

ICA 9-1

Complete the following table.

	Quantity	SI Units	Dimensions						
			M	L	T	Θ	N	J	I
Example	Acoustic impedance	(Pa s)/m	1	−2	−1	0	0	0	0
(a)	Circuit resistance	V/A							
(b)	Luminous efficacy	cd/W							
(c)	Molar concentration	mol/L							
(d)	Thermal conductivity	cal/(cm s °C)							

ICA 9-2

Complete the following table.

	Quantity	SI Units	Dimensions						
			M	L	T	Θ	N	J	I
Example	Acoustic impedance	(Pa s)/m	1	−2	−1	0	0	0	0
(a)	Inductance	J/A^2							
(b)	Luminous energy	cd s							
(c)	Molarity	mol/kg							
(d)	Wire resistivity	Vm/A							

ICA 9-3

Calculate the numerical value of each of the dimensionless parameters listed in the table. Be sure to check that the ratio is actually dimensionless after you insert the values.

	Situation	Name	Expression	Value
(a)	Hot water	Prandtl number, Pr	$\dfrac{\mu C_p}{k}$	
(b)	Sphere in air	Drag coefficient, C_D	$\dfrac{F}{\frac{1}{2}\rho v_a^2 A}$	
(c)	Water in a river	Froude number, Fr	$\dfrac{v_W}{\sqrt{gH}}$	

Properties and definitions for this problem:

Property	Symbol	Units	Air	Water
Density	ρ	slugs/ft^3	0.002378	1.94
Dynamic viscosity	μ	kg/(m s)	2×10^{-5}	4×10^{-4}
Thermal conductivity	k	W/(m K)	0.025	0.7
Specific heat	C_p	cal/(g °C)	0.24	1

Property	Symbol	Units	Value
Silhouette Area of object	A	in^2	120
Water depth	H	m	3
Water speed	v_w	cm/s	210
Air speed	v_a	mph	60
Drag Force on sphere	F	N	30

ICA 9-4

Calculate the numerical value of each of the dimensionless parameters listed in the table. Be sure to check that the ratio is actually dimensionless after you insert the values.

	Situation	Name	Expression	Value
(a)	Air over a flat plate	Nusselt number, Nu	$\dfrac{hL}{k}$	
(b)	Water: Effect of surface tension	Weber number, We	$\dfrac{\rho v_W^2 d}{\sigma}$	
(c)	Wind making a wire "sing"	Strouhal number, St	$\dfrac{\omega D_{wire}}{v_a}$	

Properties and definitions for this problem:

Property	Symbol	Units	Air	Water
Density	ρ	slugs/ft^3	0.002378	1.94
Heat transfer coefficient	h	W/(m^2 °C)	20	---
Thermal conductivity	k	W/(m K)	0.025	0.7
Surface tension	σ	dynes/cm	----	70

Property	Symbol	Units	Value
Plate length	L	ft	2
Depth of water film	d	cm	3
Water speed	v_w	cm/s	210
Air speed	v_a	mph	60
Oscillation frequency	ω	Hz (or cycles/s)	140
Wire diameter	D_{wire}	mm	20

ICA 9-5

A fluid with a specific gravity of 0.91 and a viscosity of 0.38 pascal seconds is pumped through a 25-millimeter diameter smooth pipe at an average velocity of 2.6 meters per second. Determine the Reynolds number in the pipe for the system and indicate if the flow is laminar, transitional, or turbulent.

ICA 9-6

Brine, with a density of 1.25 grams per cubic centimeter and a viscosity of 0.015 grams per centimeter second is pumped through a 5-centimeter radius steel pipe at an average velocity of 15 centimeters per second. Determine the Reynolds number in the pipe for the system and indicate if the flow is laminar, transitional, or turbulent.

ICA 9-7

When a simple turbine is used for mixing, the following variables are involved:

Power requirement	P	watt
Shaft speed	N	hertz
Blade diameter	D	meters
Blade width	W	meters
Liquid density	ρ	kilograms per meter cubed

Determine a set of dimensionless groups for the turbine, using Rayleigh's method.

ICA 9-8

We assume that the total storm water runoff (R, given in volume units) from a plot of land depends on the length of time that it rains (t), the area of the land (A), and the rainfall rate (r, given in inches per hour).

Rainfall Rate (r) [in/h]	Land Area (A) [acres]	Rainfall Duration (t) [h]	Measured Runoff (R) [ft³]
0.50	2	3.0	49
0.30	14	2.5	172
0.78	87	4.1	4,563
0.15	100	2.2	541
0.90	265	0.4	1,408
0.83	32	7.6	3,310
1.40	18	1.8	744
0.22	6	4.7	102
0.67	26	3.1	886
0.48	62	4.9	2,392

(a) Using the data, construct a plot of the runoff versus the time that it rains. You should see that this plot is of little help in understanding the relationships between the various parameters.

(b) Using this plot, estimate the total runoff from 200 acres if rain falls for 3 hours at a rate of 1.2 inches per hour. Is this even possible using this plot?

(c) Using the variables in the table, complete a dimensional analysis to help you plot the data. You should obtain two dimensionless ratios. Plot these, with the ratio containing the total runoff on the ordinate. This plot should collapse the values to a single line. Draw a smooth curve through the values.

(d) Use this line to answer question (b) again.

ICA 9-9

We are interested in analyzing the velocity of a wave in water. By drawing a sketch of the wave, and labeling it, we decide that the velocity depends on the wavelength (λ), the depth of the water (H), the density of the water (ρ), and the effect of gravity (g). We have measured wave speeds in many situations; the data are given below.

Water Depth (H) [m]	Wave Length (λ) [m]	Velocity (v) [m/s]
1.0	10.0	7.4
1.0	20.0	7.7
2.0	30.0	10.8
9.0	40.0	18.7
0.2	13.0	3.5
4.0	24.0	13.6
18.0	20.0	14.0
0.3	2.6	4.0
33.0	30.0	17.1
5.0	15.0	11.9

(a) Construct a plot of wave velocity versus either wave length or water depth. You will see substantial scatter.

(b) Using your plot, estimate the wave velocity for a wave length of 25 meters in water that is 25 meters deep. Is this even possible using this plot?

(c) Perform a dimensional analysis on the parameters (v, ρ, H, g, and λ). After calculating the new dimensionless ratio values, make a dimensionless plot.

(d) Recalculate the answer to question (b).

Chapter 9 REVIEW QUESTIONS

1. While researching fluid dynamics, you come across a reference to the dimensionless number called the *Grashof number,* given by the equation below.

$$Gr = \frac{g\,\beta\,(T_S - T_b)\,D^3}{\nu^2}$$

where:

D = pipe diameter [=] ft
g = acceleration due to gravity [=] m/s^2
T = temperature of the surface (T_s) and bulk fluid (T_b) [=] K
ν = kinematic viscosity [=] cm^2/s

What are the **dimensions** of beta, β?

2. While researching fluid dynamics, you come across a reference to the dimensionless number called the *capillary number,* given by the equation below.

$$Ca = \frac{\mu\,v}{\gamma}$$

where:

μ = fluid viscosity [=] g/(m s)
v = velocity [=] ft/s

What are the **dimensions** of gamma, γ?

3. While researching fluid dynamics, you come across a reference to the dimensionless number called the *Laplace number,* given by the equation below.

$$La = \frac{\delta\,\rho\,L}{\mu^2}$$

where:

ρ = fluid density [=] kg/m^3
μ = fluid viscosity [=] g/(m s)
L = length [=] ft

What are the **dimensions** of delta, δ?

4. The Arrhenius number (Ar) is the dimensionless parameter describing the ratio of activation energy to thermal energy, often used in chemistry. It depends on the following quantities:

E_a = activation energy [=] J/mol
R = ideal gas constant [=] (atm L)/(mol K)
T = temperature [=] K

Use your knowledge of dimensions to determine the proper form of the Arrhenius number.

(A) $Ar = \dfrac{E_a}{RT}$

(B) $Ar = E_a RT$

(C) $Ar = \dfrac{RT^2}{E_a}$

(D) $Ar = \dfrac{E_a T}{R}$

5. The Biot number (Bi) is the dimensionless parameter describing if the temperature of an object will vary significantly in space. It depends on the following quantities:

h = heat transfer coefficient $[=]$ W/(m^2 °C)

L_C = characteristic length = Volume of object/Surface Area of object $[=]$ m^3/m^2 = m

k = thermal conductivity $[=]$ W/(m K)

Use your knowledge of dimensions to determine the proper form of the Biot number.

(A) $Bi = \dfrac{h\,L_c}{k}$

(B) $Bi = h\,L_c\,k$

(C) $Bi = \dfrac{k\,L_c}{h}$

(D) $Bi = \dfrac{h\,k}{L_c^2}$

6. A biodegradable fuel having a specific gravity of 0.95 and a viscosity of 0.04 grams per centimeter second is draining by gravity from the bottom of a tank. The drain line is a plastic 3-inch diameter pipe. The velocity is 5.02 meters per second. Determine the Reynolds number in the pipe for the system and indicate if the flow is laminar, in transition, or turbulent.

7. A sludge mixture having a specific gravity of 2.93 and a viscosity of 0.09 grams per centimeter second is pumped from a reactor to a holding tank. The pipe is a 2½-inch diameter pipe. The velocity is 1.8 meters per second. Determine the Reynolds number in the pipe for the system and indicate if the flow is laminar, in transition, or turbulent.

8. Water (specific gravity = 1.02; viscosity = 0.0102 grams per centimeter second) is pumped through a 0.5-meter diameter pipe. If the Reynolds number is 1,800 for the system, determine the velocity of the water in units of meters per second.

9. Water (specific gravity = 1.02; viscosity = 0.0102 grams per centimeter second) is pumped through 0.5-meter diameter pipe. If the Reynolds number is 5,800 for the system, determine the velocity of the water in units of meters per second.

10. The Peclet number is used in heat transfer in general and forced convection calculations in particular. It is a function of the two other dimensionless groups, the Reynolds number and the Prandlt number. Determine the functional form of these dimensionless groups, using Rayleigh's method. The problem depends on the following variables:
   - Liquid density, ρ $[=]$ kg/m^3
   - Specific heat of liquid, C_p $[=]$ J/(g °C)
   - Liquid viscosity, μ $[=]$ kg/(m s)
   - Thermal diffusivity, α $[=]$ m^2/s
   - Thermal conductivity of the plate, k $[=]$ W/(m °C)
   - Distance from edge of the plate, x $[=]$ m
   - Liquid velocity, v $[=]$ m/s

11. When a fluid flows slowly across a flat plate and transfers heat to the plate, the following variables are important. Analyze this system using Rayleigh's method.
   - Liquid density, ρ $[=]$ kg/m^3
   - Specific heat of liquid, C_p $[=]$ J/(g °C)
   - Liquid viscosity, μ $[=]$ kg/(m s)
   - Thermal conductivity of the plate, k $[=]$ W/(m °C)
   - Heat transfer coefficient, h $[=]$ W/(m^2 °C)
   - Distance from edge of the plate, x $[=]$ m
   - Liquid velocity, v $[=]$ m/s

12. In modeling the flow of liquid in a piping system, you decide to try to develop some dimensionless groups to determine the interaction between variables. You decide the following variables are important:

- volumetric flowrate, Q [=] gallons per minute
- kinematic viscosity, ν [=] centimeters squared per second
- dynamic viscosity, μ [=] pascal seconds
- density, ρ [=] kilograms per cubic meter
- velocity, v [=] feet per second
- diameter, D [=] millimeters
- mass of fluid, m [=] kilograms

Use Rayleigh's Method to determine a set of dimensionless groups.

13. A projectile is fired with an initial velocity (v_0) at an angle (θ) with the horizontal plane. Find an expression for the range (R). The data are given in the table below. Use the data in the table to create one or more *dimensional* plots (e.g., launch speed on the abscissa and range on the ordinate). From these plots, answer the following questions.

Launch Angle (θ) [°]	Launch Speed (v_0) [m/s]	Measured Range (R) [m]
4	70	73
50	50	230
3	50	30
45	18	32
37	27	75
35	60	325
22	8	4.4
10	30	34
88	100	77
45	45	210

(a) If the launch speed is 83 meters per second and the launch angle is 64 degrees, what is the range? You will likely find it difficult to provide a good estimate of the range, but do the best you can.

(b) Complete a dimensional analysis of this situation. In this case, you would assume that the important parameters are θ, v_0, and R. Upon closer examination, however, it would seem that the range on Earth and on the moon would be different. This suggests that gravity is important, and that you should include g in the list of parameters. Finally, since it is not clear how to include θ, you could omit it and replace the velocity by v_x and v_z, where x is the distance downrange and z the height. You should use this information to determine dimensionless parameters. Also, you must decide how the lengths in R and g should appear. When you complete the analysis, you should find that these four parameters will be grouped into a single dimensionless ratio.

(c) Use the data from the table to calculate the numerical value of the ratio for each test. Note that $v_x = v \cos(\theta)$ and that you can find a similar expression for v_z. Insert these expressions into your dimensionless ratio.

(d) Assuming that you performed the dimensional analysis correctly, you should find that the ratio you obtained will always give the same value (at least nearly, within test-to-test error). Calculate the average value of the tests, and if it is nearly an integer, use the integer value.

(e) Finally, set this ratio equal to this integer, and then solve for the range R. Write your final equation for the range (i.e., R = xxxxx). Now using this equation, answer question (a) again.

14. The drag on a body moving in a fluid depends on the properties of the fluid, the size and the shape of the body, and probably most importantly, the velocity of the body. We find that for high velocities, the fluid density is important but the "stickiness" (or viscosity) of the fluid is not. The frontal area of the object is important. You might expect that there will be more drag on a double-decker bus moving at 60 miles per hour than on a sports car moving at 60 miles per hour.

The table below gives some data for tests of several spheres placed in air and in water. The terminal velocity, the point at which the velocity becomes constant when the weight is balanced by the drag, is shown.

Object	Drag (F) [lb$_f$]	Velocity (v) [ft/s]	Diameter (D) [in]	Fluid
Table tennis ball	0.005	12	1.6	Air
Bowling ball	6	60	11	Air
Baseball	0.18	41	3	Air
Cannon ball	33	174	9	Air
Table tennis ball	0.0028	0.33	1.6	Water
Bowling ball	12.4	3.1	11	Water
Baseball	0.31	1.7	3	Water
Cannon ball	31	6.2	9	Water

(a) Plot the drag on the ordinate and the velocity of the object on the abscissa for each fluid on a separate plot. Use the graphs to answer the following question: What is the drag on a baseball in gasoline (specific gravity = 0.72) at a speed of 30 feet per second? You may struggle with this, but do the best you can.

(b) Now complete a dimensional analysis of this situation and replot the data. First, recognize that the important parameters are the ball diameter (use the silhouette area of a circle), the density of the fluid, the drag, and the velocity. You will find a single dimensionless ratio that combines these parameters.

(c) Compute the value of this ratio for the eight tests. Be sure in your analysis that you use consistent units so that the final ratio is truly unitless.

(d) Use this result to help you answer question (a) again.

Part 3

SCRUPULOUS WORKSHEETS

Scrupulous: **scroop·yə·ləs** ~ adjective;
definition _____

LEARNING OBJECTIVES

The overall learning objectives for this part include:

Chapter 10:
- Use Microsoft Excel to enhance problem solution techniques, including entering, sorting, and formatting data in a worksheet;
- Applying functions, including mathematical, statistical, and trigonometric;
- Read, write, and predict conditional statements, lookup functions, and data validation statements;
- Use conditional formatting, sorting, and filtering to aid in problem solutions.

Chapter 11:
- Use graphical techniques to create "proper" plots, sketch functions, and determine graphical solutions to problems.
- Create and format data into graphs using Microsoft Excel.

Chapter 12:
- Describe and interpret mathematical models in terms of physical phenomena.
- Given a graph, determine the type of trendline shown and interpret the physical parameters of the experimental system.

Chapter 13:
- Determine an appropriate mathematical model to describe experimental data using physical knowledge and logarithmic plots, then apply the model to form graphical solutions to engineering problems.
- Given a logarithmic plot, determine the equation of the trendline.
- Use Microsoft Excel to model experimental data by creating logarithmic plots.

Chapter 14:
- Apply basic concepts of statistics to experimental data.
- Use statistical and graphical functions and in Microsoft Excel and MATLAB to enhance solution techniques.

Microsoft Excel is a worksheet computer program used internationally for an incalculable number of different applications. A **worksheet** is a document that contains data separated by rows and columns. The idea of using a worksheet to solve different types of problems originated before the advent of computers in the form of bookkeeping ledgers. The first graphical worksheet computer program for personal computers, VisiCalc, was released in 1979 for the Apple II® computer.

Figure P3-1 Comparison of VisiCalc and Excel interfaces.

Modern worksheet computer programs like Excel are significantly more powerful than earlier versions like VisiCalc; a comparison of the interface is shown in Figure P3-1. Excel contains text-formatting controls, built-in functions to perform common calculations, and a number of different plotting capabilities that make it an extremely powerful data analysis tool for engineers. Part 3 introduces the Microsoft Excel interface, the formatting controls used to create organized worksheets, and many built-in functions to assist in analyzing data or performing calculations on data contained in the worksheet.

A successful engineer must rely on knowledge of the way things work in order to develop solutions to problems, whether ameliorating climate change or trapping cockroaches. In many cases, the behavior of systems or phenomena can be described mathematically. These mathematical descriptions are often called mathematical models. The variables in the model vary with respect to one another in the same way that the corresponding parameters of the real physical system change.

As a very simple example, imagine you are driving your car on a country road at a constant speed of 30 miles per hour. You know that at this speed, you travel one-half mile every minute. If you drive at this speed for 44 minutes, you cover a distance of 22 miles.

A mathematical model for this is $d = 0.5t$, where d is distance in miles, t is time in minutes, and the value 0.5 has units of miles per minute. If you substitute *any* number of minutes in this equation for time (including 44), the distance (in miles) will be exactly half of the time numerical value. This allows you to predict what would happen in the "real world" of cars and roads without having to actually go out and drive down the road to determine what would happen if you drove 30 miles per hour for 44 minutes.

Needless to say, the mathematical descriptions for some physical systems can be extremely complicated, such as models for the weather, global economic fluctuations, or the behavior of plasma in an experimental fusion reactor.

As it turns out, a significant number of phenomena important in engineering applications can be described mathematically with only three simple types of models. Also in Part 3, we introduce these three models and their characteristics, as well as discuss the use of Excel to determine a mathematical model from a set of data determined by experimentation.

A few notes about this section of the book:

■ Within the examples given in this portion of the text, note that any information you are asked to type directly into Excel will be found in quotations. Do not type the quotation marks, type only the information found within the quotation marks.

■ In hardcopy, the data needed to create a chart will be shown in columns or rows, depending on the size of the data, to efficiently use space and save a few trees by using less textbook paper. In the worksheets containing the starting data online, the data will be shown in columns.

■ Files available online are indicated by the symbol.

■ ✎ This symbol indicates directions for an important process to follow. Step-by-step instructions are given once for each procedure.

■ ⌘ This symbol indicates special instructions for Mac OS users.

TIME MANAGEMENT

If you are using this text sequentially, by this point you are probably starting to feel a bit overwhelmed with all you need to do. While many introductory textbooks cover time management during the first few weeks of the semester, the authors have found it more useful to cover it a little later. In week 2 of your first semester of college, you are probably feeling like you still have things under control and do not need help. By week 10, however, you may be struggling to keep everything together and are more open to try some time management suggestions. Please note these are just suggestions and each person must develop a time management system that works best for him or her. It may take you a few attempts to find a process you can actually use, so keep making adjustments until you find your own personal solution.

There are 24 hours in each day, and 7 days in a week. Each week, you have 168 hours, or an estimated 170 hours, to spend doing something—sleeping, going to class, doing homework, or attending a football game. How do you spend all this time?

■ To get enough rest, you should sleep at least 7 hours every night, or about 50 hours every week.

■ If you spend 1 hour for each meal during the day, about 20 hours of your week will be spent eating.

■ If you allow 1 hour per day for personal hygiene and a few hours for laundry (your classmates will thank you for showering and having clean clothes), this takes about 10 hours per week.

■ Attending class is critical, and with lectures and labs you are probably in the classroom for 20 hours.

■ If you spend the maximum recommended study time on each course, this will take another 30–45 hours each week.

So what is left? Actually, quite a bit of time remains: 30 hours. While that may not seem like much, remember we assumed the maximum limits in our analysis.

■ It may only take you 30 minutes each day to get showered and dressed, saving you 3.5 hours per week.

■ Your lab may be canceled, freeing up an additional 3 hours.

■ While there are weeks when it will be necessary to study the maximum amount, this will also be balanced by weeks when you can study the minimum amount.

How, exactly, can you balance this "free" time with the "required" time? To be successful at time management, you must plan. If you carve out 1 hour each week to determine your plan for the upcoming days, you will be able to find time to work in any activities you want to do and still find time to study, eat, and sleep. Here, we present a PLAN with four steps: Prioritize, Leave time for fun, Anticipate delays, and No—learn to say it.

Prioritize

Ask:

- What must be completed this week (required assignments)?
- What can I begin to work on for next week (upcoming project, exams)?
- What would be nice to do if I have the time (recommended problems, reading)?

Rules:

- Schedule all courses in your plan. Attend every class. Be sure to include travel time, especially if you are commuting.
- Select a study time for each class and stick to it. As a general rule, plan for 2–3 hours of studying for each hour in class. For a 15-credit-hour course load, this is 30–45 hours.
- Determine when you can study best. Are you an early riser or a night owl?
- Be specific in your plan. Listing "Read Chapter 2, pages 84–97" is much better than "Read chemistry." Break down large projects into smaller tasks, each with a deadline.
- Do not study more than 2 hours at a time without a break. Pay attention to how long it takes you to become distracted easily.
- Schedule time daily to read course e-mail and check any online course management system.
- If you are working during college, do not forget to schedule in this time. As a general rule, you should not plan to work more than 10 hours per week while taking a 15-credit-hour course load. If you are working more, you may want to consult your financial aid office for advice.

Leave Time for Fun (and Chores)

Ask:

- What has to get done this week (chores)?
- What activities do I want to take part in (fun stuff you really want to do)?
- What would be nice to do if I have time (fun stuff if you have time)?

Rules:

- Schedule time for planning each week. Adopt your weekly schedule to meet the upcoming week deadlines and assignments.
- Schedule time for meals. Relax and talk with friends, read an engrossing book. Do not study during meals!
- Schedule time for sleep. Stick to this schedule—you will feel better if you go to sleep and awake each day at the same time . . . yes, even on weekends!
- Schedule time for physical activity. This can be hitting the gym, playing intramurals, or taking a walk. Staying healthy will help you stay on track.
- Schedule time for chores, such as laundry and paying bills.

- Allow time for technology on a limited basis. If you have a favorite TV show, schedule time to watch. If you want to surf on a social network, do so for a limited time each day.
- Plan outings. Colleges are wonderful resources for arts, music, theater, and athletics. Explore and find activities to enjoy, but do not compromise study time.
- Leave some open time. It is not necessary to schedule every minute of every day. Free time is a wonderful stress reliever!

Anticipate Delays

Ask:

- What can go wrong this week?
- What activities will alter my plans?

Rules:

- Plan time for "Murphy's Law": broken computers, running out of paper, getting sick, or helping a friend. If none occur, you will have extra hours in your plan.
- Leave time to proofread your work, or better yet, have someone else help you. Utilize your course teaching assistants, professor, or college academic facilities to assist you in polishing your final product.
- Plan to finish large projects 1 week before they are due to allow for any unexpected delays.

NO—Learn to Say it!

Ask:

- Will this activity help me reach my goal?
- If I do this activity, what will alter in my plan?

Rules:

- Schedule social activities around academics. Say "no" if you are not finished with your coursework.
- Remember, you are here to get an education. Employers will not care that you attended every basketball game or that you have 10,000 online friends if you have poor grades.

CHAPTER 10
EXCEL WORKBOOKS

The following is an example of the level of knowledge of Excel needed to proceed with this chapter. *If you are not able to quickly recreate an Excel Worksheet similar to the one shown, including equations and formatting, please review worksheet basics in the appendix materials online before proceeding.*

Begin with a new worksheet. Add correct header information (date, name, course, purpose / problem statement).

In Row 5, add the following headers:

- Mass (m) [g]
- Height (H) [ft]
- Potential Energy (PE) [J]
- Time (t) [min]
- Power (P) [W]

Color the cells of Row 5 the cell shade and font color of your choice.

Add the following data:

Mass [g]	Height [ft]	Time [min]
10	5	1
50	8	0.5
75	10	2.5

Calculate the corresponding potential energy and power terms in Row 6. Be sure to watch your units!

Choose an appropriate (reasonable) way to display the data in terms of number format.

Copy the equations from Row 6 down to Row 8 using the fill handle.

Add a border to all cells in Columns A – E, Rows 5 – 8.

Center all the information within each column.

A sample worksheet is shown below.

	A	B	C	D	E
1	Date		Course - Section		Name
2	Purpose: This worksheet demonstrates the skills necessary to proceed with the Excel Workbooks chapter.				
3					
4					
5	Mass (m) [g]	Height (H) [ft]	Potential Energy (PE) [J]	Time (t) [min]	Power (P) [W]
6	10	5	0.15	1	0.002
7	50	8	1.20	0.5	0.040
8	75	10	2.24	2.5	0.015

10.1 CELL REFERENCES

LEARN TO: Create an Excel worksheet that implements relative, absolute, and mixed cell addressing

Understand how formulas execute when written and copied using cell addressing

● **EXAMPLE 10-1**

Suppose we are given a list of XY coordinates in a worksheet. We want to calculate the distance between each point. We can find the distance between two XY coordinates by using Pythagoras' theorem:

$$d = \sqrt{(x_2 - x_1)^2 + (y_2 - y_1)^2}$$

	A	B	C	D	E	F	G	H	I
2	This example demonstrates how to handle Excel's order of operations and cell references.								
3									
4									
5		Point 1			Point 2				
6	X	Y		X	Y				
7	27	20		25	10				
8	25	4		7	8				
9	4	6		24	3				
10	25	26		13	24				
11	19	24		26	1				
12	29	10		0	5				
13	7	29		13	13				
14	3	20		19	16				
15	20	7		5	17				
16	20	26		19	3				
17	13	15		13	14				
18	23	22		17	25				
19	3	27		10	22				
20	30	16		30	17				
21									

To solve this problem, we must adhere to the default behavior of Excel to properly calculate the distance between the coordinates. First, we must observe the order of operations that Excel follows to determine how we need to write our equations. Second, we must determine how to use **cell references** to translate the x_2, x_1, y_2, and y_1 values in the equation shown above into locations in our worksheet.

Let us rewrite Pythagoras' theorem in the notation shown above using what we know about order of operations in Excel:

$$d = ((x_2 - x_1)\wedge 2 + (y_2 - y_1)\wedge 2)\wedge (1/2)$$

Let us calculate the distance between Point 1 and Point 2 in column G. In cell G7, we need to translate the equation into an equation that replaces the x_1, y_1 and x_2, y_2 variables with addresses to cells in the worksheet. Since each row represents a single calculation, we know that for the first data pair, x_1 is located in cell A7, y_1 is in B7, x_2 is in D7, and y_2 is in E7.

The equation we need to type into cell G7 becomes

$$= ((D7 - A7)^2 + (E7 - B7)^2)^{(1/2)}$$

If we copy that equation down for the other pairs of XY coordinates, our sheet should now contain a column of all the distance calculations.

	A	B	C	D	E	F	G	H	I
1	Distance Between XY Coordinates								
2	This example demonstrates how to handle Excel's order of operations and cell references.								
3									
4									
5		Point 1			Point 2				
6	X	Y		X	Y		Distance		
7	27	20		25	10		10.20		
8	25	4		7	8		18.44		
9	4	6		24	3		20.22		
10	25	26		13	24		12.17		
11	19	24		26	1		24.04		
12	29	10		0	5		29.43		
13	7	29		13	13		17.09		
14	3	20		19	16		16.49		
15	20	7		5	17		18.03		
16	20	26		19	3		23.02		
17	13	15		13	14		1.00		
18	23	22		17	25		6.71		
19	3	27		10	22		8.60		
20	30	16		30	17		1.00		
21									

Suppose we start off with a slightly modified worksheet that requires us to calculate the distance between all the points in the first column of XY values to a single point in the second column.

We can calculate the distance between all the points in the first column to the single point through the use of absolute addressing. An **absolute address** *allows an equation to reference a single cell that will remain constant regardless of where the equation is copied in the worksheet. An absolute reference is indicated by a dollar sign ($) in front of the row and column designators. In this example, we want to use an absolute reference on cells D7 and E7 in all distance calculations. The equation we need to type in cell G7 becomes:*

$$= (($D$7 - A7)^2 + ($E$7 - B7)^2)^{(1/2)}$$

	A	B	C	D	E	F	G	H	I
1	Distance Between XY Coordinates								
2	This example demonstrates how to handle Excel's order of operations and cell references.								
3									
4									
5		Point 1			Point 2				
6	X	Y		X	Y		Distance		
7	27	20		25	10		10.20		
8	25	4					6.00		
9	4	6					21.38		
10	25	26					16.00		
11	19	24					15.23		
12	29	10					4.00		
13	7	29					26.17		
14	3	20					24.17		
15	20	7					5.83		
16	20	26					16.76		
17	13	15					13.00		
18	23	22					12.17		
19	3	27					27.80		
20	30	16					7.81		
21									

Relative Addressing

- A **relative cell address** used in a formula will always *refer to the cell in the same relative position* to the cell containing the formula, no matter where the formula is copied in the worksheet. For example, if "=B2" is typed into cell C4 and then copied to cell C7, the formula in cell C7 would read "=B5". In this case, the cell reference is to call the cell two rows up and one cell to the left.
- When we insert or change cells, the formulas automatically update. This is one of a worksheet's major advantages: easily applying the same calculation to many different sets of data.

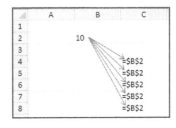

SHORTCUT

To change the method of addressing, highlight the cell address within the formula and hit F4 to cycle through the addressing choices.

= B2
= $B$2
= B$2
= $B2

Absolute Addressing

- Absolute addressing is indicated by the presence of a dollar sign ($) immediately before both the column and row designators in the formula (e.g., $C$5; $AB$10).
- An **absolute cell address** will *always refer to the same cell* if the formula is copied to another location. For example, if "=$B$2" is typed into cell C4 and then copied to cell C7, the formula in cell C7 would read "=$B$2".

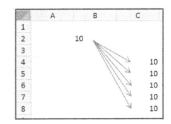

Mixed Addressing

- In **mixed addressing**, *either the row or the column designator is fixed* (by the $), but the other is relative (e.g., $C5; AB$10; $AB10).
- It may not be immediately obvious why this capability is desirable, but many problems are dramatically simplified with this approach. We will study this in more detail later.

COMPREHENSION CHECK 10-1

Type "5" in cell E22 and "9" in cell E23; type "=E22 + 4" in cell F22. Copy cell F22 to cell F23.

- Is this an example of absolute, mixed, or relative addressing?
- What is displayed in cell F23?

COMPREHENSION CHECK 10-2

Type "20" into cell G22 and "=$G$22 + 10" in cell H22. Copy cell H22 down to row 26 using the fill handle.

- Is this an example of absolute, mixed, or relative addressing?
- What is displayed in cell H26?

COMPREHENSION CHECK 10-3

Type "25" into cell A28 and "=A$28 + 5" in cell D28. Copy cell D28 down to row 30 using the fill handle. Copy cell D28 across to column F using the fill handle.

- Is this an example of absolute, mixed, or relative addressing?
- What is displayed in cell D30? What is displayed in cell F28?

COMPREHENSION CHECK 10-4

Type "=$A28 + 5" in cell G28. Copy cell G28 down to row 30 using the fill handle. Copy cell G28 across to column J using the fill handle.

- Is this an example of absolute, mixed, or relative addressing?
- What is displayed in cell G30? What is displayed in cell J28?

10.2 FUNCTIONS IN EXCEL

LEARN TO: Properly use Excel functions, especially those listed in tables in this section
Understand limitations of certain functions, especially trig function arguments
Given an Excel equation with built-in functions, predict the output

Hundreds of functions are built into Excel. Tables 10-1 through 10-4 list a few functions commonly used in engineering applications. Table 10-5 contains common error messages you may encounter. There are several things you should note when using these functions.

- You must make certain to *use the correct name of the function.* For example, the average function is written as AVERAGE and cannot be abbreviated AVE or AVG.

- *All functions must be followed by parentheses.* For example, the value of π is given as PI(), with nothing inside the parentheses.

- The *argument* of the function (the stuff in the parentheses) can include numbers, text, expressions, or cell references, as long as they are appropriate for the function.

- Many functions can *accept a list or range of cells as the argument.* These can be expressed as a list separated by commas [e.g., A6, D7, R2, F9], as a rectangular block designated by the top-left cell and bottom-right cell separated by a colon [e.g., D3:F9], or as a mixed group [e.g., A6, R2, D3:F9]. To insert cells into a formula, type the formula up to the open parenthesis and select the desired cells. You can also type in the references directly into the formula.

- Most functions will also *accept another function as the argument.* These can be fairly simple [e.g., SIN (RADIANS (90))] or more complicated [e.g., AVERAGE (SQRT(R2), COS(S4 + C4), MIN (D3:F9) + 2)].

- Some functions, such as trigonometric functions, require specific arguments. *Trigonometric functions must have an argument in units of radians, not units of degrees.* Be sure you are aware of any limitations of the functions you are using. Look up an unfamiliar function in the **HELP** menu.

- Note that *some functions can be expressed in several different ways.* For example, raising the number 2 to the fifth power can be written as $= 2\wedge5$ or as POWER(2,5).

Table 10-1 Trigonometric functions in Excel

Function as Written in Excel	Definition
ACOS (cell)	Calculates the inverse cosine of a number (also ASIN)
COS (angle in radians)	Calculates the cosine of an angle (also SIN)
DEGREES (angle in radians)	Converts radians to degrees
PI()	Calculates pi (π) to about 15 significant figures
RADIANS (angle in degrees)	Converts degrees to radians

Table 10-2 Mathematical functions in Excel

Function as Written in Excel	Definition
EXP (cell)	Raises e (base of the natural log) to the power "cell"
POWER (cell, power)	Raises the cell to "power"
PRODUCT (cells)	Finds the product of a list of cells
SQRT (cell)	Finds the square root of cell
SUM (cells)	Finds the sum of a list of cells

Table 10-3 Statistical functions in Excel

Function as Written in Excel	Definition
AVERAGE (cells)	Finds the mean or average value of a list of cells
MAX (cells)	Finds the maximum value in a list of cells
MEDIAN (cells)	Finds the median value of a list of cells
MIN (cells)	Finds the minimum value in a list of cells
STDEV.P (cells)	Finds the standard deviation value of a list of cells
VAR.P (cells)	Finds the variance value of a list of cells

Table 10-4 **Miscellaneous functions in Excel**

Function as Written in Excel	Definition
COUNT (cells)	Counts number of cells that are not blank and that do not contain an error
COUNTIF (cells, criteria)	Counts number of cells that meet the stated criteria, such as a numerical value, text, or a cell reference
COUNTIFS (cells1, criteria1, cells2, criteria2, . . .)	Counts number of cells that meet multiple stated criteria, such as a numerical value, text, or a cell reference
INTERCEPT (*y* values, *x* values)	Calculates linear line for range of (x, y) pairs and returns the intercept value of y (where $x = 0$)
ROUND (cell, number of decimal places)	Rounds a number to a specific number of decimal places
SLOPE (*y* values, *x* values)	Calculates linear line for range of (x, y) pairs and returns the slope value
TRUNC (cell, number of digits)	Truncates a number to a specific number of digits

Table 10-5 **Common error messages in Excel and possible solutions**

Error	Explanation	Possible Fix	Example
#####	Column is not wide enough to display a number	Make column wider	−125,000,500 will not fit in a cell with a standard width
#DIV/0!	Formula has resulted in division by zero	Check values in denominator of formula contained in the cell	If cell A1 contains 12 and cell A2 is empty, the formula =A1/A2 will return #DIV/0!
#NAME?	Excel does not recognize something you have typed	Check spelling! Check operators for missing : Check for missing " " around text	Formula names: MXA should be MAX PI should be PI() Range of cells: A2B3 should be A2:B3
#NULL!	You specify a set of cells that do not intersect	Check formulas for spaces, missing commas	= SUM(A2:A5 B4:B6) will return this error; fix as = SUM(A2:A5,B4:B6)
#VALUE!	Formula contains invalid data types	Arguments of functions must be numbers, not text Sometimes, part of a required function is missing; check for all required elements	If cell A2 contains "2 grams" and cell A3 contains 3, the formula = A2 + A3 will result in this error since A2 is text (the word grams makes the cell text, not a number) = VLOOKUP(A2:B5,2,FALSE) will result in this error since a lookup function must contain four parts in the argument, not three
#N/A	Formula has called a value that is not available	Check for lookup value in data table (see Section 10.4)	If A2 contains 11, and the data table contains values 1 to 10 in the first column, this error will appear since the value 11 is not in the first column of the data table
#REF!	Invalid cell reference	Check operators for missing * or / Check formula for data table size and number of column to return (see Section 10.4)	Operators: (A7)(B6) should be (A7)*(B6) = VLOOKUP(A2,A2:B5,3,FALSE) will return this error because there are not three columns available in the lookup table
#NUM!	Formula results invalid numeric values	Check numerical result expected is between -1×10^{307} and 1×10^{307}	If the calculation results in a value outside the range given, such as 2×10^{400}, this error will appear

Handling Calculation Errors: IFERROR

Especially when dealing with worksheets that rely on user interaction to create meaningful information or analysis, there are often scenarios that will result in calculations that are not possible or might result in an error in a cell calculation. If you see cells in your worksheet that contain values like #DIV/0!, #N/A, or other messages that begin with the # symbol, that means that Excel was not able to calculate or look up the expression typed into the cell. The IFERROR function will allow the programmer of an Excel worksheet to specify what value should appear in a cell if there is a calculation error in the worksheet. The IFERROR function is often used when dealing with lookup statements or iterative expressions where error messages in cells might throw off the intended result of the calculation. For example, if you type = A1/A2 into cell B1 and it results in #DIV/0! you could type the following instead:

$$= \text{IFERROR(A1/A2,0)}$$

This function will check to see if A1/A2 results in an error message. If it does not generate an error, the resulting value of A1/A2 will appear in the cell, otherwise the value 0 will appear in the cell. It is worth noting that "0" in the formula above can be replaced with any valid Excel commands, including function calls, conditional statements, lookup statements, or simple hardcoding a value like 0 as shown above. For example, all of the following are valid IFERROR expressions:

$$= \text{IFERROR(A1/A2,MAX(A1,A2))}$$

$$= \text{IFERROR(IF(B2<3,A1/A2,B2),0)}$$

$$= \text{IFERROR(VLOOKUP(B2,A15:F20,3,FALSE),0)}$$

In the final example, if the lookup value of B2 is not found in the table located in A15:F20, the formula will return the value 0 rather than the error message #N/A.

● EXAMPLE 10-2

Assume we are studying the number of accidents that occur during different times of the day. Using the data given in the Excel workbook collected each week for two years, we want to use Excel to analyze our data to determine the average, minimum, or maximum number of accidents, as well as a few other items that might be of significance.

	A	B	C	D	E	F	G
1	Vehicular Accidents						
2	This worksheet demonstrates the proper use of Excel functions						
3							
4	Week	Number Accidents	Total Accidents		Samples Greater than Mean		
5	Y1 - 1	161	Total Samples				
6	Y1 - 2	209	Mean				
7	Y1 - 3	212	Median		Samples Between	180	200
8	Y1 - 4	62	Variance				
9	Y1 - 5	154	Standard Deviation				
10	Y1 - 6	68					
11	Y1 - 7	249					
12	Y1 - 8	33					
13	Y1 - 9	86					

Total accidents: = SUM (B5:B108)
Total samples: = COUNT (B5:B108)
Mean: = AVERAGE (B5:B108)
Median: = MEDIAN (B5:B108)
Variance: = VAR.P (B5:B108)
Standard deviation: = STDEV.P (B5:B108)

Note that decimal values appear when we calculate the mean, median, variance, and standard deviation of the accident data. Since it makes sense to round these values up to the nearest whole number, we need to type those functions as the argument to a rounding function. Start by modifying the equation for the mean by typing the **ROUND** *function. Notice that as you start typing the ROUND function in the cell, a drop-down menu with a list of all of the functions that start with the letters ROUND appears below the cell. Note that Excel contains a function called* **ROUNDUP** *that will round a number up to the nearest whole value away from zero.*

Total Accidents	15124	Samples Greater than Mean
Total Samples	104	
Mean	=round	
Median	ROUND	Rounds a number to a specified number of digits	2
Variance	ROUNDDOWN	
Standard Deviation	ROUNDUP	

After we select the ROUNDUP function, a new box below the cell documents the arguments the function requires. Note that we need to provide the value we want to round as the first argument and the number of decimal places to which we want to round the number (in this case, 0).

Total Accidents	15124	Samples Greater than Mean
Total Samples	104	
Mean	=roundup(	
Median	ROUNDUP(**number**, num_digits)	Between
Variance	4229.95562	
Standard Deviation	65.038109	

The new function we need to type ultimately becomes

= ROUNDUP (AVERAGE (B5:B108), 0)

Repeat this with the equations for calculating the median, variance, and the standard deviation.

Suppose we want to determine how many of the samples reported accidents greater than the calculated average number of accidents. Note that the **COUNTIF** *function requires a "criteria" argument, which can take on a number of different values. For example, if we want to count the number of values greater than 200 in the range B5:B108, we need to type the criteria ">200" (in double quotes) as the 2nd argument to the COUNTIF function.*

= COUNTIF (B5:B108,">200")

In this example, we want to compare our COUNTIF result to a value calculated in a different cell. Since we cannot type cell references inside of double quotes (">E21"), we need to use the **ampersand** *operator (&) to* **concatenate** *the logical operator to the cell reference (">"&E21).*

Samples Greater than Mean: = COUNTIF (B5:B108,">"&D6)

Similarly, we could use the **COUNTIFS** *function to calculate the number of samples that have a number of accidents between (and including) 180 and 200. COUNTIFS is a* *special function that contains a variable number of arguments, with a minimum of two arguments required (range1, criteria1) to use the function. Since we have two criteria that must be met (>180 and <200), we must pass in four arguments to the COUNTIFS function (range1, critera1, range2, criteria2). In this example, range1 and range2 must be the same range of cells since we are enforcing the criteria on the same set of data. We will place the bounds in the worksheet as follows:*

Lower Bound in F7: 180   Upper Bound in G7: 200

Samples Between: = COUNTIFS (B5:B108,">="&F7, B5:B108, "<="&G7)

Your final worksheet should appear as shown.

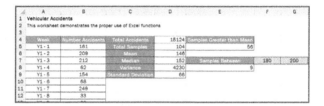

COMPREHENSION CHECK 10-5

Launch a new worksheet. Type the following Excel expressions into the specified cells. Be certain you understand *why* each of the following yields the specific result. Note that not all functions shown in this table are valid Excel functions. If the formula returns an error, how can the formula be changed to correctly display the desired result?

In Cell . . .	Enter the Formula . . .	The Cell Will Display . . .
A1	= SQRT (144)	
A2	= MAX (5, 8, 20/2, 5 + 6)	
A3	= AVERAGE (5, SQRT(100), 15)	
A4	= POWER (2, 5)	
A5	= PI()	
A6	= PI	
A7	= PRODUCT (2, 5, A2)	
A8	= SUM (2 + 7, 3 * 2, A1:A3)	
A9	= RADIANS (90)	
A10	= SIN (RADIANS (90))	
A11	= SIN (90)	
A12	= ACOS (0.7071)	
A13	= DEGREES(ACOS(0.7071))	
A14	= CUBRT(27)	

● **EXAMPLE 10-3**

The maximum height (*H*) an object can achieve when thrown can be determined from the velocity (*v*) and the launch angle with respect to the horizontal (*θ*):

$$H = \frac{v^2 \sin (\theta)}{2g}$$

Note the use of a cell (E7) to hold the value of the acceleration due to gravity. This cell will be referenced in the formulae instead of our inserting the actual value into the formulae. This will allow us to easily work the problem in a different gravitational environment (e.g., Mars) simply by changing the one cell containing the gravitational constant.

	A	B	C	D	E	F	G
1	Basic Examples of Trig Functions and Cell Addressing						
2	The following data is used to illustrate built-in trig functions and mixed references						
3							
4							
5							
6							
7	Planet	Earth		Gravity (g)	9.8	[m/s²]	
8							
9	Velocity	Angle (θ) [degrees]					
10	(v)[m/s]	50	60	70	80		
11	10						
12	12						
13	14						
14	16						
15	18						
16	20						
17							

For the following, assume that the angle 50° is in cell B10. After setting up the column of velocities and the row of angles, we type the following into cell B11 (immediately below 50°)

= $A11^2 * SIN (RADIANS (B$10)) / (2*$E$7)

Note the use of absolute addressing (for gravity) and mixed addressing (for angle and velocity). For the angle, we allow the column to change (since the angles are in different columns) but not the row (since all angles are in row 10). For the velocity, we allow the row to change (since the velocities are in different rows) but the column is fixed (since all velocities are in column A). This allows us to write a single formula and replicate it in both directions.

The sine function requires an argument in units of radians, and the angle is given in units of degrees in the problem statement. In this example, we used the RADIANS function to convert from degrees into radians. Another method is to use the relationship 2π radians is equal to 360 degrees, or

= $A11^2 * SIN ((2 * PI() / 360) * B$10) / (2*$E$7)

We replicate the formula in cell B11 across the row to cell E11, selecting all four formulae in row 11 and replicating to row 16. If done correctly, the values should appear as shown.

Velocity (v) [m/s]	Angle (θ) [°]			
	50	60	70	80
20	3.91	4.42	4.79	5.02
12	5.63	6.36	6.90	7.24
14	7.66	8.66	9.40	9.85
16	10.01	11.31	12.27	12.86
18	12.66	14.32	15.53	16.28
20	15.63	17.67	19.18	20.10

Here, we consider the planet to be Mars with a gravity of 3.7 meters per second squared in cell E7. The worksheet should automatically update, and the values should appear as shown.

Velocity (v) [m/s]	Angle (θ) [°]			
	50	60	70	80
10	10.35	11.70	12.70	13.31
12	14.91	16.85	18.29	19.16
14	20.29	22.94	24.89	26.08
16	26.50	29.96	32.51	34.07
18	33.54	37.92	41.14	43.12
20	41.41	46.81	50.79	53.23

Now, we consider the planet to be Moon with a gravity of 1.6 meters per second squared in cell E7. The worksheet should automatically update, and the values should appear as shown.

Velocity (v) [m/s]	Angle (θ) [°]			
	50	60	70	80
10	23.94	27.06	29.37	30.78
12	34.47	38.97	42.29	44.32
14	46.92	53.04	57.56	60.32
16	61.28	69.28	75.18	78.78
18	77.56	87.69	95.14	99.71
20	95.76	108.25	117.46	123.10

COMPREHENSION CHECK 10-6

As part of the design of a high performance engine, you are analyzing properties of spherical ceramic ball bearings. Since many ceramic materials are considerably less dense than the metals typically used in such applications, the centrifugal load added by the bearings can be significantly reduced by the use of ceramics.

	A	B	C	D	E	F	G
1							
2		Mass of Ball Bearings (m) [g]					
3		Specific Gravity					
4	Radius (r) [cm]	3.12	3.18	3.22	3.31	3.37	
5	1.00	13.1	13.3	13.5	13.9	14.1	
6	1.05	15.1	15.4	15.6	16.1	16.3	
7	1.10	17.4	17.7	18.0	18.5	18.8	
8	1.15	19.9	20.3	20.5	21.1	21.5	
9	1.20	22.6	23.0	23.3	24.0	24.4	
10	1.25	25.5	26.0	26.3	27.1	27.6	
11	1.30	28.7	29.3	29.6	30.5	31.0	

Which of the following could be typed in cell B5 and copied across to cell F5, then down to cell F11 to calculate the masses of the various ball bearings shown in the table? If more than one answer is correct, indicate all that apply.

A. = 4/3 * PI * $A5^3 * $B4
B. = 4/3 * PI() * $A5^3 * B$4
C. = 4/3 * PI() * $A$5^3 * $B$4
D. = 4/3 * PI * A$5^3 * B$4
E. = 4/3 * PI() * A5^3 * B4

10.3 LOGIC AND CONDITIONALS

LEARN TO: Create IF statements in Excel to create conditional results
Generate compound logic to develop complex conditions
Predict the output of an IF statement

Outside of the realm of computing, logic exists as a driving force for decision making. Logic transforms a list of arguments into outcomes based on a decision.

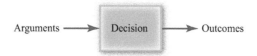

Some examples of everyday decision making:

- If the traffic light is red, stop. If the traffic light is yellow, slow down. If the traffic light is green, go.

  Argument: three traffic bulbs   Decision: is bulb lit?   Outcomes: stop, slow, go

- If the milk has passed the expiration date, throw it out; otherwise, keep the milk

  Argument: expiration date   Decision: before or after?   Outcomes: garbage, keep

To bring decision making into our perspective on problem solving, we need to first understand how computers make decisions. **Boolean logic** exists to assist in the decision-making process, where each argument has a binary result and our overall outcome exhibits binary behavior. **Binary behavior**, depending on the application, is any sort of behavior that results in two possible outcomes.

In computing, we often refer to the outcome of Boolean calculations as "yes" and "no." Alternatively, we may refer to the outcomes as "true" and "false," or "1" and "0."

To determine the relationship between two cells (containing numbers or text), we have a few operators, listed in Table 10-6, that allow us to compare two cells to determine whether or not the comparison is true or false.

Table 10-6 **Relational operators in Excel**

Operator	Meaning
>	Greater than
<	Less than
> =	Greater than or equal to
< =	Less than or equal to
=	Equal to
< >	Not equal to

These relational operators are usually placed between two different cells to determine the relationship between the two values. This expression of **cell–operator–cell** is typically called a **relational expression**. If more than two relational expressions are needed to form a decision, relational expressions can be combined by means of logical operators to create a **logical expression**. To connect the Boolean arguments to make a logical decision, we have a few logical operators that allow us to relate our arguments to determine a final outcome.

NOTE

AND is true if and only if all arguments are true.

OR is true if at least one of the arguments is true.

- **AND:** The AND logical operator enables us to connect two Boolean arguments and return the result as TRUE if and only if *both* Boolean arguments have the value of TRUE. In Excel, the AND function accepts more than two arguments and is TRUE if all the arguments are TRUE.
- **OR:** The OR logical operator enables us to connect two Boolean arguments and return the result as TRUE if *only one* of the Boolean arguments has the value of TRUE. In Excel, the OR function accepts two or more arguments and is TRUE if at least one of the arguments is TRUE.
- **NOT:** The NOT logical operator enables us to invert the result of a Boolean operation. In Excel, the NOT function accepts one argument. If the value of that argument is TRUE, the NOT function returns FALSE. Likewise, if the argument of the function is FALSE, the NOT function returns TRUE.

Conditional statements are commands that give some decision-making authority to the computer. Specifically, the user asks the computer a question using conditional statements, and then the computer selects a path forward based on the answer to the question. Sample statements are given below:

- If the water velocity is fast enough, switch to an equation for turbulent flow!
- If the temperature is high enough, reduce the allowable stress on this steel beam!

- If the RPM level is above red line, issue a warning!
- If your grade is high enough on the test, state: You Passed!

In these examples, the comma indicates the separation of the condition and the action that is to be taken if the condition is true. The exclamation point marks the end of the statement. Just as in language, more complex conditional statements can be crafted with the use of "else" and "otherwise" and similar words. In these statements, the use of a semicolon introduces a new conditional clause, known as a nested conditional statement. For example:

- If the collected data indicate the process is in control, continue taking data; otherwise, alert the operator.
- If the water temperature is at or less than 10 degrees Celsius, turn on the heater; or else if the water temperature is at or greater than 80 degrees Celsius, turn on the chiller; otherwise, take no action.

Single Conditional Statements

In Excel, conditional statements can be used to return a value within a cell based upon specified criteria. The IF conditional statement within Excel takes the form

$$= IF \text{ (logical test, value if true, value if false)}$$

Every statement must contain three and only three parts:

1. **A logical test, or the question to be answered**
   The answer to the logical test must be TRUE or FALSE.
   Is the flow rate in Reactor #1 higher than Reactor #5?

2. **A TRUE response**, if the answer to the question is yes
   Show the number 1 to indicate Reactor #1.

3. **A FALSE response**, if the answer to the question is no
   Show the number 5 to indicate Reactor #5.

The whole statement for the above example would read:

$$= IF \text{ (B3 > B4, 1, 5)}$$

	A	B	C
1			
2			
3	Reactor #1 Flowrate	10	[gpm]
4	Reactor #5 Flowrate	25	[gpm]
5	Maximum Flowrate in Reactor #	5	

Special Things to Note

- **To leave a cell blank, type a set of quotations with nothing in between ("").** For example, the statement $= IF \text{ (C3>10, 5, "")}$ is blank if C3 is less than 10.
- **For display of a text statement, the text must be stated within quotes** (*"text goes in here"*). For example, the statement $= IF \text{ (E5 > 10, 5, "WARNING")}$ would display the word WARNING if E5 is less than 10.

EXAMPLE 10-4 For the following scenarios, write a conditional statement to be placed in cell B5 to satisfy the conditions given. Below each statement are sample outcomes of the worksheet in different scenarios.

(a) Display the pressure difference between upstream station 1 (displayed in cell B3) and downstream station 2 (displayed in cell B4) if the pressure difference is positive; otherwise, display the number 1.

	A	B	C
1			
2			
3	Station #1 Pressure	2.4	[atm]
4	Station #2 Pressure	2.8	[atm]
5	Pressure Difference	1	[atm]

	A	B	C
1			
2			
3	Station #1 Pressure	3.2	[atm]
4	Station #2 Pressure	2.8	[atm]
5	Pressure Difference	0.4	[atm]

Answer: $= IF((B3 - B4) > 0, B3 - B4, 1)$

(b) Display the value of the current tank pressure if the current pressure is less than the maximum tank pressure; otherwise, display the word "MAX".

	A	B	C
1		ˎ	
2			
3	Maximum Tank Pressure	5	[atm]
4	Current Tank Pressure	2	[atm]
5	Pressure Status	2	[atm]

	A	B	C
1			
2			
3	Maximum Tank Pressure	5	[atm]
4	Current Tank Pressure	10	[atm]
5	Pressure Status	MAX	[atm]

Answer: $= IF (B3 > B4, B4, "MAX")$

(c) If the sum of the temperature values shown in cells B2, B3, and B4 is greater than or equal to 100, leave the cell blank; otherwise, display a warning to the operator that the temperature is too low.

	A	B	C
1			
2	Temperature Reading #1	25	[°C]
3	Temperature Reading #2	50	[°C]
4	Temperature Reading #3	45	[°C]
5	Cumulative Temperature		

	A	B	C
1			
2	Temperature Reading #1	25	[°C]
3	Temperature Reading #2	10	[°C]
4	Temperature Reading #3	45	[°C]
5	Cumulative Temperature	Too Low	

Answer: $= IF (SUM(B2:B4) >= 100, "", "Too Low")$

COMPREHENSION CHECK 10-7

Evaluate the following expressions. What is the final results that would occur when the formula is evaluated using the worksheet shown?

Comparison A: = IF (B5 > B6, B7, "")

Comparison B: = IF (B2 + B3 <= 2*B9, B3 + B4, MIN(B2:B9))

Comparison C: = IF (B9 <> B8, "B9", B9 / B8)

	A	B	C	D	E	F
1						
2	Value 1	4				
3	Value 2	13			Comparison A	
4	Value 3	19			Comparison B	
5	Value 4	18			Comparison C	
6	Value 5	21				
7	Value 6	10				
8	Value 7	6				
9	Value 8	17				

Nested Conditional Statements

If more than two outcomes exist, the conditional statements in Excel can be nested. The nested IF conditional statement within Excel can take the form

> = IF(logical test #1, value if #1 true, IF (logical test #2, value if #2 true, value if both false))

Note that the number of parenthesis must match (open and closed) and must be placed in the proper location. Recall that every statement must contain three and only three parts. For the first IF statement, they are:

1. **The first logical test, or the first question to be answered**
   The answer to the logical test must be TRUE or FALSE.
   Is the score for Quiz #1 less than the score for Quiz #2?

2. **A true response**, or what to do if the answer to the first question is yes
   Show the score for Quiz #1.

3. **A false response**, or what to do if the answer to the first question is no
   Proceed to the logical question for the second IF statement.

For the second IF statement, the three parts are:

1. **The second logical test, or the second question to be answered**
   The answer to the logical test must be TRUE or FALSE.
   Is the score for Quiz #2 less than the score for Quiz #1?

2. **A true response**, or what to do if the answer to the second question is yes
   Show the score for Quiz #2.

3. **A false response**, or what to do if the answer to the second question, and by default both questions, is no
   Show the text "Equal".

The whole statement typed in cell B5 for the above example would read

= IF (B3 < B4, B3, IF (B3 > B4, B4, "Equal"))

	A	B	C
1			
2			
3	Quiz Grade #1	70	
4	Quiz Grade #2	70	
5	Lowest Quiz Score	Equal	

	A	B	C
1			
2			
3	Quiz Grade #1	90	
4	Quiz Grade #2	70	
5	Lowest Quiz Score	70	

	A	B	C
1			
2			
3	Quiz Grade #1	50	
4	Quiz Grade #2	70	
5	Lowest Quiz Score	50	

There can be a maximum of 64 nested IF statements within a single cell. The nested IF can appear as either the true or false response to the first IF logical test. In the above example, only the false response option is shown.

● **EXAMPLE 10-5** Write the conditional statement to display the state of water (ice, liquid, or steam) based upon temperature displayed in cell B4, given in degrees Celsius. Below are sample outcomes of the worksheet in different scenarios.

	A	B	C
1			
2			
3			
4	Temperature of Mixture	75	[°C]
5	State of Mixture	Liquid	

	A	B	C
1			
2			
3			
4	Temperature of Mixture	110	[°C]
5	State of Mixture	Steam	

	A	B	C
1			
2			
3			
4	Temperature of Mixture	10	[°C]
5	State of Mixture	Ice	

Here, there must be two conditional statements because there are three responses:

- *If the temperature is less than or equal to zero, display "Ice";*
- *If the temperature is greater than or equal to 100, display "Steam";*
- *Otherwise, display "Liquid".*

Answer: = IF(B4 <= 0, "Ice", IF (B4 >= 100, "Steam", "Liquid"))

COMPREHENSION CHECK 10-8

Continue the example in CC 10-6 above. The following is typed into cell G5, then copied down to cell G11:

$$= IF(MAX(B5:F5)>AVERAGE(\$D\$5:\$D\$11), IF$$
$$MIN(B5:F5)>AVERAGE(\$D\$5:\$D\$11),"X","Z"),"Y")$$

(a) Which of the following will appear in cell G7?
(b) Which of the following will appear in cell G8?
(c) Which of the following will appear in cell G9?

Choose from:

A. X
B. Y
C. Z
D. An error message will appear
E. The cell will be blank

▲	A	B	C	D	E	F	G
1							
2		Mass of Ball Bearings (m) [g]					
3		Specific Gravity					
4	Radius (r) [cm]	3.12	3.18	3.22	3.31	3.37	
5	1.00	13.1	13.3	13.5	13.9	14.1	
6	1.05	15.1	15.4	15.6	16.1	16.3	
7	1.10	17.4	17.7	18.0	18.5	18.8	
8	1.15	19.9	20.3	20.5	21.1	21.5	
9	1.20	22.6	23.0	23.3	24.0	24.4	
10	1.25	25.5	26.0	26.3	27.1	27.6	
11	1.30	28.7	29.3	29.6	30.5	31.0	

Compound Conditional Statements

If more than two logic tests exist for a single condition, conditional statements can be linked together by AND, OR, and NOT functions. Up to 255 logical tests can be compared in a single IF statement (only two are shown in the box below). The compound IF conditional statement takes the form

---

= IF (AND (logical test #1, logical test #2), value if both tests are true, value if either test is false)

= IF (OR (logical test #1, logical test #2), value if either test is true, value if both tests are false)

● EXAMPLE 10-6

Write the conditional statement that meets the following criteria:

(a) If the product has cleared all three quality checks (given in cells B2, B3, and B4) with a score of 80 or more on each check, mark the product as "OK" to ship; otherwise, mark the product as "Recycle."

	A	B	C
1			
2	Quality Check #1 Rating	90	
3	Quality Check #2 Rating	80	
4	Quality Check #3 Rating	85	
5	Mark Product	OK	

	A	B	C
1			
2	Quality Check #1 Rating	60	
3	Quality Check #2 Rating	80	
4	Quality Check #3 Rating	85	
5	Mark Product	Recycle	

Answer: = IF(AND (B2 >= 80, B3 >= 80, B4 >= 80),"OK", "Recycle")

(b) If the product has cleared all three quality checks (given in cells B2, B3, and B4) with a minimum score of 80 on each check, mark the product as "OK" to ship; otherwise, if the product scored a 50 or below on any check, mark the product as "Rejected"; otherwise, mark the product as "Rework."

	A	B	C
1			
2	Quality Check #1 Rating	90	
3	Quality Check #2 Rating	80	
4	Quality Check #3 Rating	85	
5	Mark Product	OK	

	A	B	C
1			
2	Quality Check #1 Rating	40	
3	Quality Check #2 Rating	80	
4	Quality Check #3 Rating	85	
5	Mark Product	Rejected	

	A	B	C
1			
2	Quality Check #1 Rating	60	
3	Quality Check #2 Rating	80	
4	Quality Check #3 Rating	85	
5	Mark Product	Rework	

Answer: = IF(AND (B2 >= 80, B3 >= 80, B4 >= 80), "OK", IF (OR (B2 <= 50, B3 <= 50, B4 <= 50), "Rejected", "Rework"))

COMPREHENSION CHECK 10-9

Continue the example in CC 10-6 above. Which of the following could be typed in cell H7 that will result in OK appearing in H7 if the mass in cell C7 is between 17.5 grams and 20 grams inclusive, but leave H7 blank otherwise? If more than one answer is correct, check all that apply.

A. =IF(C7<17.5 OR C7>20),"","OK")
B. =IF(OR(C7<17.5,C7>20),"","OK")
C. =(IF(C7<17.5) OR IF(C7>20),"","OK")
D. =IF(C7<17.5,"", IF(C7>20,"","OK"))
E. =IF(C7<17.5,"OK", IF(C7>20,"OK",""))

⟋	A	B	C	D	E	F	G
1							
2	Mass of Ball Bearings (m) [g]						
3		Specific Gravity					
4	Radius (r) [cm]	3.12	3.18	3.22	3.31	3.37	
5	1.00	13.1	13.3	13.5	13.9	14.1	
6	1.05	15.1	15.4	15.6	16.1	16.3	
7	1.10	17.4	17.7	18.0	18.5	18.8	
8	1.15	19.9	20.3	20.5	21.1	21.5	
9	1.20	22.6	23.0	23.3	24.0	24.4	
10	1.25	25.5	26.0	26.3	27.1	27.6	
11	1.30	28.7	29.3	29.6	30.5	31.0	

10.4 LOOKUP AND DATA VALIDATION

LEARN TO: Use a lookup function to merge data given two data tables with at least one common field
Predict the output if given a lookup statement
Create a validation protocol for data

The lookup function enables Excel to locate information from a table of data in a worksheet. There are two lookup functions: VLOOKUP, which searches vertically, and HLOOKUP, which searches horizontally. In the following example, we focus on VLOOKUP, but the same principles could easily be applied to HLOOKUP. To use the VLOOKUP function, we need to pass in four different arguments:

VLOOKUP (lookup_value, table_array, col_index_num, [range_lookup])

- The *lookup_value* argument is the value we want to look up in the table. Typically, this value is a string, but it can be a numerical value. Note that whatever we use as the *lookup_value*, Excel will perform a case-insensitive search of the data for the value, which means that any special characters used in the string, like punctuation or spaces, must appear the same in the *lookup_value* and the table, and must be a unique identifier in the first column of the table.
- The *table_array* is the range of cells that encapsulates the entire data table we want to search. Since we are using VLOOKUP, it is important to realize that our *table_array* must have at least two columns of data. Note that the *lookup_value* we are passing in to the VLOOKUP function will only search the first column of the *table_array*, so it might be necessary to move the data around.
- The *col_index_num* argument is the column number that contains the data we want as a result of our search. By default, Excel will refer to the first column where the *lookup_value* is located as the number 1, so the *col_index_num* will typicallly be a number greater than 1.

- The last argument, [***range_lookup***], is an optional argument as indicated by the square brackets. This argument tells the function what type of search to perform and can only take on two values: TRUE or FALSE. In most cases, you will want to list this as FALSE.

  - Passing in TRUE tells Excel to conduct an approximate search of the data. That is, Excel will search the data table for the largest value that is less than the *lookup_value* and use that result as the selected value. Note that for an approximate search, the first column of the *table_array* must be sorted in ascending order.
  - Passing in FALSE tells Excel to conduct an exact search of the data. The data need not be sorted for this option. If an exact match is not found, the function returns an error.
  - If we do not specify TRUE or FALSE, Excel attempts to match the data exactly, and if a match is not found, Excel returns an approximate value. This may give undesired results. It is good practice to tell Excel which searching algorithm to use to search the *table_array*.

Assume we are given the following table of data on students. To determine what Sally's eye color is from (column C) in cell A5, we could type

$$= \text{VLOOKUP (\"Sally\", A1:D4, 3, FALSE)}$$

since the data are unsorted and we are looking for an exact match on Sally.

	A	B	C	D
1	Joe	18	Blue	EE
2	John	19	Brown	ME
3	Sally	18	Brown	IE
4	Julie	18	Blue	CE

● EXAMPLE 10-7

Digital audio is a relatively new medium for storing and reproducing music. Before albums were sold on CD and other digital media formats, analog recordings were commonly sold as vinyl records, 8-track tapes, and cassette tapes. We want to build a worksheet to help us compare these different media formats to observe how information storage has progressed over the past 50 years. Note the following media equivalencies:

- A 74-minute CD (44.1 kilohertz, 2 channel, 16-bit digital audio) can hold 650 MB of data.
- A single-sided, single-layer DVD can hold 4.7 GB of data (~4,813 MB, 547 minutes of 44.1 kilohertz, 2 channel, 16-bit digital audio).
- A single-sided, single-layer Blu-ray disc can hold 25 GB of data (~25,600 MB, 2,914 minutes of 44.1 kilohertz, 2 channel, 16-bit digital audio).
- A 7-inch vinyl record recorded at 45 rpm can hold 9 minutes of music.
- A 7-inch vinyl record recorded at $33\frac{1}{3}$ rpm can hold 12 minutes of music.
- A 12-inch vinyl record recorded at 45 rpm can hold 24 minutes of music.
- A 12-inch vinyl record recorded at $33\frac{1}{3}$ rpm can hold 36 minutes of music.
- An 8-track tape can hold 46 minutes of music.
- A typical cassette tape can hold 60 minutes of music.

To determine audio equivalencies between these different storage formats, we first create a worksheet. We want to allow the user to input the media type and quantity of the desired format to be converted. To complete the comparison, it would seem like each calculation requires a statement with nine questions to ask (Is it a CD? Is it a DVD? Is it a Blu-ray? . . .).

	A	B	C	D	E
1	Digital Audio Media				
2	This worksheet demonstrates the use of VLOOKUP and data validation				
3					
4					
5	Quantity	Format	is equivalent to	Quantity	Format
6					CD
7					DVD
8					Blu-ray Disc
9	Storage Information				7" @ 45 rpm
10	Format	Length [min]			7" @ 33 1/3 rpm
11	CD	74			12" @ 45 rpm
12	DVD	547			12" @ 33 1/3 rpm
13	Blu-ray Disc	2914			8-track tape
14	7" @ 45 rpm	9			Cassette tape
15	7" @ 33 1/3 rpm	12			
16	12" @ 45 rpm	24			
17	12" @ 33 1/3 rpm	36			
18	8-track tape	46			
19	Cassette tape	60			

Rather than requiring the user to type the name of the media each time (CD, DVD, Blu-ray, etc), Excel can do **data validation**, *so we can give the user of our worksheet a drop-down menu from which to select the media. We need to add a table that contains the name of each media type along with the length of the audio we can fit on each media. We will place this table below our initial data, in cells A10:B19.*

Next, we need to calculate the quantity of each item. Since the name of the media will appear in cell B6, we use that as the lookup value in our VLOOKUP statement. To calculate the quantity for each equivalent media, we look up the length of the format specified in B6, divide that by the length of each media given in column E, and multiply that by the number of the original media provided in A6. Note that we need to round this number up since it does not make sense to have a noninteger value in our count.

For CDs, the calculation in Cell D6 should be

$$= \text{ROUNDUP (VLOOKUP (\$B\$6, \$A\$11:\$B\$19, 2, FALSE)/}$$
$$\text{VLOOKUP (E6, \$A\$11:\$B\$19, 2, FALSE) *\$A\$6, 0)}$$

The next step to finish our worksheet is to include a drop-down menu of the different media formats. To insert data validation on the media format, we click Cell B6 and go to **Data > Data Tools > Data Validation.**

The **Data Validation** *window is displayed. Under the* **Settings** *tab, the* **Allow:** *menu lets us specify the type of data that can be provided in the cell we selected. Since we want to restrict the data to a list of values, we select* **List**.

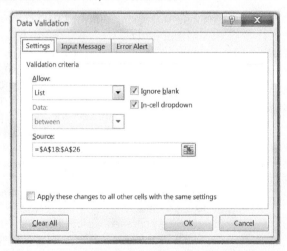

Under the **Source**: option, we select the range of all of the media types, $A$11:$A$19, and click **OK** to close the Data Validation window.

Notice the drop-down handle next to cell B6. When the user of the worksheet clicks B6, a drop-down menu appears that lists all of the possible media types so that the user can quickly select an item from the list. Furthermore, this feature prevents the user from typing items that are not on the list, making a typo, or entering any other information that will cause an error in calculations that rely on the value in B6.

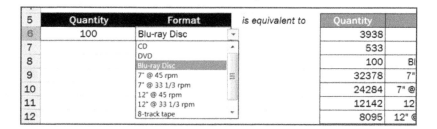

In addition to controlling the input type to a cell, it is also possible to give feedback to the person using the worksheet using pop up messages. In this example, the quantity cannot be a negative number, so we need to bring up the Data Validation window again and restrict the input to only allow whole numbers that are greater than or equal to zero.

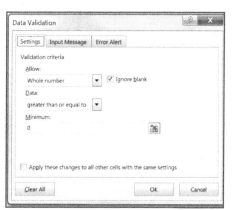

Next, we need to click the Input Message tab to type in a message that will appear below the cell when the person using our worksheet clicks on the cell to type in a quantity.

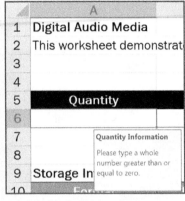

Finally, we need to click the Error Alert tab to provide the message that should pop up when an invalid number is typed into the cell.

COMPREHENSION CHECK 10-10

This is a continuation of the worksheet you created in Example 10-3. Modify it to use VLOOKUP and data validation to allow the user of the worksheet to select the planet and automatically fill in the gravity for each planet.

Planet	Gravity (g) [m/s^2]
Earth	9.8
Jupiter	24.8
Mars	3.7
Mercury	3.7
Moon	1.6
Neptune	11.2
Pluto	0.7
Saturn	10.4
Uranus	8.9
Venus	8.9

10.5 CONDITIONAL FORMATTING

LEARN TO: Use conditional formatting in Excel to facilitate data analysis
Use conditional formatting to apply multiple rules to create compound logic analysis

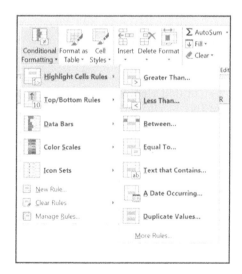

You can use conditional formatting to change the font color or background of a cell based upon the values found in that cell. As an example:

- On a blank worksheet, type the value of 20 in cell A4, a value of 30 in cell B4, and a value of 50 in cell C4.
- Select cells A4 to C4.
- Select **Home** > **Styles** > **Conditional Formatting**.
- On the first drop-down menu, choose **Highlight Cells Rules**.
- On the second drop-down menu, choose **Less Than**.

The choice of "less than" will combine the next two boxes into a single box. You can enter a number or formula, or reference a cell within the worksheet.

For this example, enter the value "25." Note: If you enter a formula, the same rules apply for absolute and relative referencing. In addition, if you select a cell within the worksheet, the program automatically defaults to an absolute reference.

- Select the formatting you want to apply when the cell value meets the condition or the formula returns the value TRUE using the dropdown menu shown after the word "with". The default is set to "Light Red Fill with Dark Red Text". You can change the font, border, or background of the cell using the **Custom Format** option. For this example, choose a green background on the Fill tab. When you are finished, click **OK**.

■ To add another condition, simply repeat the process. As another example, make it greater than 40, with a font of white, bolded on a red background.

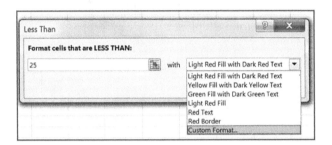

Your worksheet should now look like the one shown. If none of the specified conditions are TRUE, the cells keep their existing formats.

	A	B	C
1			
2			
3			
4	20	30	50
5			
6			

● **EXAMPLE 10-8**

Let us assume we want to build an interactive worksheet that changes the format of a cell to model the behavior of a traffic light. We want the user to input the number of seconds it takes for a light (which is initially green) to turn red. In addition, the user must also be able to provide the "warning" so that the light can switch from green to yellow and then to red.

■ The green light (bottom) will only be lit if the time remaining is greater than the warning time.
■ The yellow light (middle) will only be lit if the time remaining is greater than 0 seconds, but less than the warning time.
■ The red light (top) will only be lit if the time remaining is 0 seconds.

Before we set up the conditional formatting for each cell, we need to write IF statements in the light cells that will be used as a trigger for conditional formatting.

For Cell E5 (the red light): = IF(A5 = 0, "R", "")
For Cell E9 (the yellow light): = IF(AND (A5 <= B5, A5 > 0), "Y", "")
For Cell E13 (the green light): = IF(A5 > B5, "G", "")

Next, we add a set of conditional formatting rules for each cell.
For the red light, we click E5 and create two rules:

■ *Highlight Cells Rules > Text that Contains and enter a letter R in the appropriate field, setting the formatting to red color and red text. Note the text and fill are the SAME color red.*

■ *Highlight Cells Rules* > *New Rule.* Under *Select a Rule Type:* choose *Format only cells that contain.* Under the *Edit the Rule Description:* in the first drop down menu choose *Blanks.* Set the format to black fill with black text.

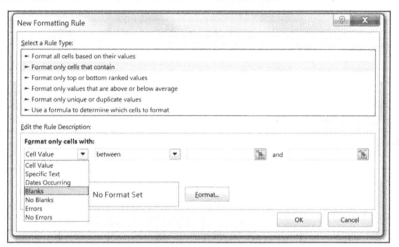

For the yellow light, we click E9 and repeat this process to turn the fill color yellow when cell has the letter "Y" in the text. For the green light, we click E13 and repeat this process to turn the fill color green when cell has the letter "G" in the text.

The final worksheet should appear as shown. Note that cell formats should change when the time remaining changes.

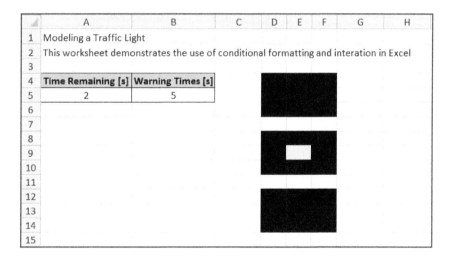

This is a continuation of the worksheet you created in Example 10.3. Modify it to highlight all heights greater than 100 meters with a light blue background and all heights less than 25 meters with a dark blue background with a white font.

10.6 SORTING AND FILTERS

LEARN TO: Use Excel to sort data with multiple levels of sorting
Use Excel to filter data based on specified criteria
Use the SUBTOTAL function to analyze filtered data

Excel provides a number of built-in tools for sorting and filtering data in a worksheet. This section describes how to use these tools effectively without causing unintended side effects.

Each year, the federal government publishes a list of fuel economy values. The complete lists for recent years can be found at www.fueleconomy.gov/feg. A partial list of 2013 vehicles is shown below. In the table, MPG = miles per gallon.

Make	Model	MPG City	MPG Highway	Annual Fuel Cost
Jeep	Grand Cherokee 4WD	16	23	$2,900
BMW	X5 xDrive 35i	16	23	$3,100
Honda	Civic Hybrid	44	44	$1,250
Volkswagen	Jetta 2.5L	24	31	$2,100
Ford	Mustang	15	26	$2,900
Bentley	Continental GTC	14	24	$3,450
Honda	Fit	28	35	$1,800

Given this information, assume you are to present it with some sort of order. What if you want to sort the data on text values (Make or Model) or numerical values (MPG City, MPG Highway, Annual Fuel Cost), or what if you want to view only certain vehicles that meet a certain condition?

Sorting Data in a Worksheet

- Select the cells to be sorted. You can select cells in a single column or row, or in a rectangular group of cells.
- Select **Home** > **Editing** > **Sort & Filter**. By default, two commonly used sorting tools (Sort A to Z and Sort Z to A) appear, in addition to a button for Custom Sort. With a group of cells selected, the common sorting tools will sort according to the values in the leftmost column. If the leftmost column contained numerical values, the options would have read Sort Smallest to Largest/Largest to Smallest. Since it is often desired to involve multiple sorting conditions, click **Custom Sort**.
- The sorting wizard is displayed as shown below. If your selected group of cells had a header row (a row that displays the names of the columns and not actual data) the "My data has headers" checkbox should be selected.

By default, Excel automatically detects whether the top row of your selected data is a header or a data row. Since you selected the data including the header rows, the "Sort by" drop-down menu will contain the header names. If you had not included the header row, the "Sort by" drop-down menu would show the column identifiers as options. It is good practice to select the headers in addition to the data to make sorting easier to understand.

- Assume you want to sort the list alphabetically (A to Z) by the make, then by smallest-to-largest annual fuel cost. Click the **Add Level** button to add two levels of sorting since there are two conditions. In the sorting wizard, the topmost sorting level will be the sort applied first, and then the next level will sort each data group that forms from the first sort. In the example, there is more than one Honda vehicle, so the second level will place the Civic Hybrid above the Fit, since the Civic Hybrid has a smaller annual fuel cost.

The resulting sorted data appear as shown.

	A	B	C	D	E
1	Fuel Economy of Vehicles				
2	This worksheet demonstrates the use of sorting and filtering in Excel				
3					
4	Make	Model	MPG City	MPG Highway	Annual Fuel Cost
5	Bentley	Continental GTC	14	24	$3,450
6	BMW	X5 xDrive 35i	16	23	$3,100
7	Ford	Mustang	15	26	$2,900
8	Honda	Civic Hybrid	44	44	$1,250
9	Honda	Fit	28	35	$1,800
10	Jeep	Grand Cherokee 4WD	16	23	$2,900
11	Volkswagen	Jetta 2.5L	24	31	$2,100

NOTE

To "undo" a sort, either choose the "Undo" arrow button on the top menu or use CTRL+Z.

It is important to be sure to select all of the data when using the sort functions because it is possible to corrupt your data set. To demonstrate, select only the first three columns (Make, Model, MPG City) and sort the data smallest to largest on the MPG City column.

Notice after sorting that the last two columns (MPG Highway, Annual Fuel Cost) are not the correct values for the vehicle. There is no way to recover the original association if you were to save the file and open it at a later time, so it is critical that when using the built-in sorting functions, you verify the correctness of your data before saving your workbook. In this case, you can click Excel's Undo button or CTRL+Z to unapply the last sort.

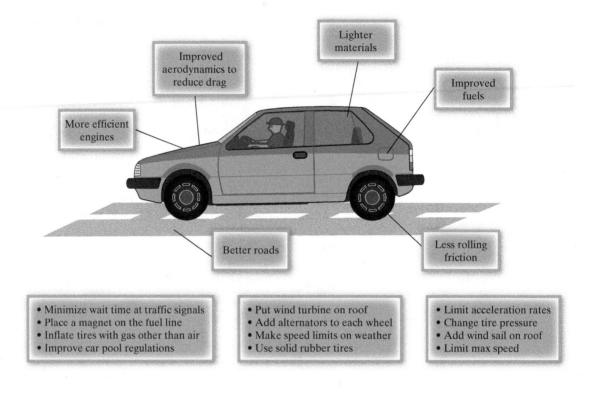

Improving automotive gas mileage, while keeping costs under control, is a complex puzzle, involving many different types of engineers. Above are some ways to possibly improve fuel efficiency. Some really work, some are false claims, and some are fictitious. Can you tell the difference? What other ways can you think of to improve today's automobiles?

COMPREHENSION CHECK 10-12

In 1980, the Environmental Protection Agency (EPA) began the Superfund Program to help cleanup highly polluted areas of the environment. There are over 1,300 Superfund sites across the country. Not all Superfund sites are from deliberate pollution. Some sites are old factories, where chemicals were dumped on the ground; landfills where garbage was dumped along with other poisonous waste; remote places where people secretly dumped hazardous waste because they did not know what to do with it; or old coal, iron ore, or silver mines.

According to the EPA (http://www.epa.gov/superfund/index.htm), the following groundwater contaminants were found in South Carolina Superfund sites in Greenville, Pickens, Oconee, and Anderson counties.

- Sort by city in ascending order. Examine the result: Which city appears first?
- Sort again: first by city in descending order, then by site name in descending order. Examine the results: Which site name now appears first?

■ Sort again by contaminant in ascending order, then by site name in ascending order. Examine the results: Which site name appears last?

Contaminants	Site Name	City
Polycyclic aromatic hydrocarbons	Sangamo Weston	Pickens
Volatile organic compounds	Beaunit Corporation	Fountain Inn
Polycyclic aromatic hydrocarbons	Beaunit Corporation	Fountain Inn
Polycyclic aromatic hydrocarbons	Para-Chem Southern, Inc.	Simpsonville
Volatile organic compounds	Golden Strip Septic Tank Service	Simpsonville
Volatile organic compounds	Para-Chem Southern, Inc.	Simpsonville
Metals	Para-Chem Southern, Inc.	Simpsonville
Polycyclic aromatic hydrocarbons	Rochester Property	Travelers Rest
Volatile organic compounds	Sangamo Weston	Pickens
Polychlorinated biphenyl	Sangamo Weston	Pickens
Metals	Rochester Property	Travelers Rest
Metals	Golden Strip Septic Tank Service	Simpsonville
Metals	Beaunit Corporation	Fountain Inn
Volatile organic compounds	Rochester Property	Travelers Rest

Filtering Data in a Worksheet

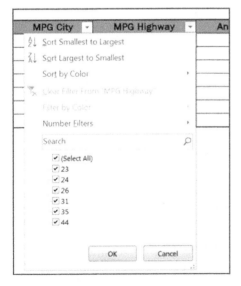

Assume you want to look only at a specific portion of the data set and hide all the other rows of data. For example, you might want to look only at Honda vehicles or all vehicles that have an MPG City rating between 10 and 15 MPG. Excel has a built-in filtering capability by which you can conditionally display rows in a data set.

■ Select the header row for a data set and click the **Sort & Filter** button in the **Home** > **Editing** ribbon. Click the **Filter** option to enable filtering for each column of data. Each column label contains a drop-down menu with various sorting options, as well as a number of different approaches for filtering.

• For data sets that contain a small number of options, use the checkboxes in the drop-down filter to manually check certain options to display.

• For numerical values, use the Number Filters submenu to filter on certain conditional expressions. The Custom Filter option in the Number Filters submenu lets you combine up to two logical expressions to filter a single column of data.

Assume you want to revisit your fuel economy data set and add in a number of statistical functions to assist in analysis.

	A	B	C	D	E
1	Fuel Economy of Vehicles				
2	This worksheet demonstrates the use of sorting and filtering in Excel				
3					
4	Make	Model	MPG City	MPG Highway	Annual Fuel Cost
5	Jeep	Grand Cherokee 4WD	16	23	$2,900
6	BMW	X5 xDrive 35i	16	23	$3,100
7	Honda	Civic Hybrid	44	44	$1,250
8	Volkswagen	Jetta 2.5L	24	31	$2,100
9	Ford	Mustang	15	26	$2,900
10	Bentley	Continental GTC	14	24	$3,450
11	Honda	Fit	28	35	$1,800
12					
13		Average	22	29	$2,500
14		Min	14	23	$1,250
15		Max	44	44	$3,450

Suppose you filter the data set to look only at the Honda vehicles.

	A	B	C	D	E
1	Fuel Economy of Vehicles				
2	This worksheet demonstrates the use of sorting and filtering in Excel				
3					
4	Make	Model	MPG City	MPG Highway	Annual Fuel Cost
7	Honda	Civic Hybrid	44	44	$1,250
11	Honda	Fit	28	35	$1,800
12					
13		Average	22	29	$2,500
14		Min	14	23	$1,250
15		Max	44	44	$3,450

Notice that the statistical calculations at the bottom are still referencing the entire data set, even though, because of the filter, only a subset of the data is displayed. For data comparisons, this will be a valuable side effect; however, if you want the calculations to apply only to the visible data, you will need to use built-in functions other than the traditional functions (AVERAGE, MIN, MAX).

Using the SUBTOTAL Function

The **SUBTOTAL** function allows the worksheet to dynamically recalculate expressions generated with a filtered list. In the example where only Honda vehicles are selected, only the two visible vehicles will be used in the calculations, if you modify your worksheet to use the SUBTOTAL function instead of the traditional statistical functions. To use the SUBTOTAL function, pass in two different arguments:

```
= SUBTOTAL (function_num, range)
```

- The *function_num* argument is a number associated to various built-in Excel functions. Table 10-7 lists the available functions for use with the SUBTOTAL function.
- The *range* argument is the range of cells to which the function should be applied.

Table 10-7 **Available functions in SUBTOTAL**

function_num	Function	Definition
1	AVERAGE	Computes the average value of the range
2	COUNT	Counts the number of cells in the range that contain numbers
3	COUNTA	Counts the number of nonempty cells in the range
4	MAX	Calculates the maximum value of the range
5	MIN	Calculates the minimum value of the range
6	PRODUCT	Calculates the product of each number in the range
7	STDEVP	Calculates the standard deviation of the numbers in the range
8	SUM	Calculates the sum of all of the numbers in the range
9	VARP	Calculates the variance of the numbers in the range

In the example, use the following calculation in cell C13 to calculate the average of MPG City:

$$= \text{AVERAGE}(C5{:}C11)$$

The AVERAGE function corresponds to function_num 1, so the resulting calculation in cell C13 using the SUBTOTAL function would appear as follows:

$$= \text{SUBTOTAL}(1, C5{:}C11)$$

After you modified all of the statistical calculations in the worksheet to use the SUBTOTAL function, the sheet should appear as shown in the examples below. Note that the values recalculate automatically according to the filtered data.

Filter on Make: Honda Only

	A	B	C	D	E
1	Fuel Economy of Vehicles				
2	This worksheet demonstrates the use of sorting and filtering in Excel				
3					
4	Make	Model	MPG City	MPG Highway	Annual Fuel Cost
7	Honda	Civic Hybrid	44	44	$1,250
11	Honda	Fit	28	35	$1,800
12					
13		Average	36	40	$1,525
14		Min	28	35	$1,250
15		Max	44	44	$1,800

Filter on Annual Fuel Cost: Less than $3,000

	A	B	C	D	E
1	**Fuel Economy of Vehicles**				
2	This worksheet demonstrates the use of sorting and filtering in Excel				
3					
4	**Make**	**Model**	**MPG City**	**MPG Highway**	**Annual Fuel Cost**
5	Jeep	Grand Cherokee 4WD	16	23	$2,900
7	Honda	Civic Hybrid	44	44	$1,250
8	Volkswagen	Jetta 2.5L	24	31	$2,100
9	Ford	Mustang	15	26	$2,900
11	Honda	Fit	28	35	$1,800
12					
13		Average	25	32	$2,190
14		Min	15	23	$1,250
15		Max	44	44	$2,900

In-Class Activities

ICA 10-1

The worksheet shown below was designed to calculate the total pressure felt by an object submerged in a fluid as a function of the depth the object is submerged. The user will enter the surface pressure (in units of atmospheres), specific gravity of the fluid, and the gravity of the planet (in units of meters per second squared) – all user input is shown in red. The worksheet will calculate the surface pressure in units of pascals, density of the fluid in kilograms per cubic meter, and depth in units of feet – all conversions are shown in orange. Finally, the worksheet will calculate the total pressure in units of atmospheres.

	A	B	C	D
1				
2				
3				
4	Surface Pressure	(Psurface)	2	[atm]
5	Specific Gravity of Fluid	(SG)	1.26	[–]
6	Gravity	(g)	9.8	[m / s^2]
7				
8	Surface Pressure	(Psurface)		[Pa]
9	Density of Fluid	(ρ)		[kg / m^3]
10				
11	Depth (H) [ft]	Depth (H) [m]	Total Pressure (P) [atm]	
12	1			
13	10			
14	20			
15	30			
16	40			
17	50			
18	60			
19	70			
20	80			
21	90			
22	100			

(a) What formula should be typed in cell C8 to convert the surface pressure in cell C4 from atmospheres to pascals?

(b) What formula should be typed in cell C9 to determine the density in units of kilograms per cubic meter?

(c) What formula should be typed into cell B12 that can then be copied down Column B to convert the depth from units of feet to units of meters?

(d) What formula should be typed into cell C12 that can then be copied down Column C to calculate the total pressure in units of atmospheres?

ICA 10-2

The worksheet provided was designed to calculate the total pressure felt by an object submerged in a fluid as a function of the depth the object is submerged.

The user will enter the surface pressure (in units of atmospheres), specific gravity of the fluid, and the gravity of the planet (in units of meters per second squared) – all user input is shown in red.

The worksheet will calculate the surface pressure in units of pascals, density of the fluid in kilograms per cubic meter, and depth in units of feet – all conversions are shown in orange. Format the pressure and density to a whole number, and the height in meters to three decimal places.

Finally, the worksheet will calculate the total pressure in units of atmospheres; format to two decimal places.

Complete the starting Excel file to meet these criteria. A sample worksheet is shown below for comparison.

	A	B	C	D
1				
2				
3				
4	Surface Pressure	(Psurface)	2	[atm]
5	Specific Gravity of Fluid	(SG)	1.26	[–]
6	Gravity	(g)	9.8	[m / s^2]
7				
8	Surface Pressure	(Psurface)	202650	[Pa]
9	Density of Fluid	(ρ)	1260	[kg / m^3]
10				
11	Depth (H) [ft]	Depth (H) [m]	Total Pressure (P) [atm]	
12	1	0.30	2.04	
13	10	3.05	2.37	
14	20	6.10	2.74	
15	30	9.15	3.11	
16	40	12.20	3.49	
17	50	15.24	3.86	
18	60	18.29	4.23	
19	70	21.34	4.60	
20	80	24.39	4.97	
21	90	27.44	5.34	
22	100	30.49	5.72	

ICA 10-3

Some alternate energy technologies, such as wind and solar, produce more energy than needed during peak production times (windy and sunny days), but produce insufficient energy at other times (calm days and nighttime). Many schemes have been concocted to store the surplus energy generated during peak times for later use when generation decreases. One scheme is to use the energy to spin a massive flywheel at very high speeds, then use the rotational kinetic energy stored to power an electric generator later.

The worksheet shown below was designed to calculate how much energy is stored in flywheels of various sizes. The speed of the flywheel (revolutions per minute) is to be entered in cell B2, and the density of the flywheel in cell B4. A formula in cell B3 converts the speed into units of radians per second. There are 2π radians per revolution of the wheel.

To simplify the computations, the stored energy was calculated in three steps. The first table calculates the volumes of the flywheels, the second table uses these volumes to calculate the masses of the flywheels, and the third table uses these masses to determine the stored rotational kinetic energy.

Note that in all cases, changing the values in cells B2 and/or B4 should cause all appropriate values to be automatically recalculated.

⁄	A	B	C	D	E	F	G	H	I
1									
2	Speed (v) [rpm]	15,000		Volume (V) [m³]			Height (H) [m]		
3	Speed (ω) [rad/s]	1571		Diameter (D) [m]	0.3	0.6	0.9	1.2	1.5
4	Density (ρ) [kg/m³]	8000		0.2	0.009	0.019	0.028	0.038	0.047
5				0.4	0.038	0.075	0.113	0.151	0.188
6				0.6	0.085	0.170	0.254	0.339	0.424
7				0.8	0.151	0.302	0.452	0.603	0.754
8				1.0	0.236	0.471	0.707	0.942	1.178
9									
10				Mass (m) [kg]			Height (H) [m]		
11				Diameter (D) [m]	0.3	0.6	0.9	1.2	1.5
12				0.2	75	151	226	302	377
13				0.4	302	603	905	1206	1508
14				0.6	679	1357	2036	2714	3393
15				0.8	1206	2413	3619	4825	6032
16				1.0	1885	3770	5655	7540	9425
17									
18				Kinetic Energy (KE) [J]			Height (H) [m]		
19				Diameter (D) [m]	0.3	0.6	0.9	1.2	1.5
20				0.2	4.65E+05	9.30E+05	1.40E+06	1.86E+06	2.33E+06
21				0.4	7.44E+06	1.49E+07	2.23E+07	2.98E+07	3.72E+07
22				0.6	3.77E+07	7.53E+07	1.13E+08	1.51E+08	1.88E+08
23				0.8	1.19E+08	2.38E+08	3.57E+08	4.76E+08	5.95E+08
24				1.0	2.91E+08	5.81E+08	8.72E+08	1.16E+09	1.45E+09
25				Average KE [J]	9.11E+07	1.82E+08	2.73E+08	3.64E+08	4.55E+08
26				Max – Min KE [J]	1.08E+09				

(a) What should be typed in cell B3 to convert revolutions per minute in cell B2 into radians per second?

(b) What should be typed into cell E4 that can then be copied through the rest of the first table to calculate the flywheel volumes? Assume the shape of the flywheel to be a cylinder.

(c) What should be typed into cell E12 that can then be copied through the rest of the second table to calculate the flywheel masses?

(d) What should be typed into cell E20 that can then be copied through the rest of the third table to calculate the kinetic energies stored in the flywheels? The rotational kinetic energy is given by the formula: $KE_{Rot} = (I\omega^2)/2 = (mr^2\omega^2)/4$

(e) What should be typed into cell E25 that can then be copied through Row 25 to determine the average kinetic energy at each height (in each column)?

(f) What should be typed into cell E26 to determine the difference between the maximum kinetic energy and 800 times the minimum kinetic energy given in the table?

ICA 10-4

The worksheet shown was designed to calculate the cost of material necessary to purchase to produce a given number of parts. The user will enter the specific gravity of the material, the diameter of the cylindrical part in units of inches, the cost of the raw material in dollars per pound-mass, and the number of parts to be manufactured – all user input is shown in red. The worksheet will calculate the radius of the cylindrical part in units of centimeters and the density of the fluid in grams per cubic centimeter – all conversions are shown in orange.

The worksheet will determine the volume and mass of a single part for a given height. Finally, the worksheet will determine the total mass of material needed to produce the desired number of parts in units of pounds-mass, and the total material cost.

The total material cost appears twice. In cells E13 to E20, a formula is written to determine the cost. In cells B26 to B33, the cells simply reference the corresponding cell in the table above. For example, in cell B26 the formula = E13 appears.

In the bottom table, the total cost for "N" parts is determined by the formula:

Total Cost = Total Material Cost + (Energy Cost + Labor Cost) × Number of Parts

	Height (H) [cm]	Volume (V) [cm^3]	Mass (m) [g]	Mass (M_N) [lb_m] for N parts	Total Material Cost (MC) [$]
Specific Gravity of Material	(SG)	1.50	[–]		
Diameter	(D)	4.0	[in]		
Cost of Raw Material	(C)	$2.25	[$ / lb_m]		
Number of Parts	(N)	150	[–]		
Radius	(R)		[cm]		
Density of Fluid	(ρ)		[g / cm^3]		

Height (H) [cm]	Volume (V) [cm^3]	Mass (m) [g]	Mass (M_N) [lb_m] for N parts	Total Material Cost (MC) [$]
1				
2				
3				
5				
6				
8				
10				
12				

Labor Cost	(LC)	$1.50	[$ / part]

Height (H) [cm]	Total Cost of N Parts	Energy Cost (EC) [$ / part]			
	Total Material Cost (MC) [$]	$0.05	$0.10	$0.20	$0.40
1					
2					
3					
5					
6					
8					
10					
12					

(a) What should be typed in cell C9 to determine the radius in the correct units?

(b) What should be typed into cell B13 that can then be copied down Column B to determine the volume of a cylindrical part in units of cubic centimeters?

(c) What should be typed into cell C13 that can then be copied through down Column C to calculate the mass of each part in unit of grams?

(d) What should be typed into cell D13 that can then be copied down Column D to calculate the total mass needed to produce N parts in units of pounds-mass?

(e) What should be typed into cell E13 that can then be copied down Column E to calculate the total material cost?

(f) What should be typed into cell C26 that can then be copied through C26 to F33 given the energy cost in row 25 and labor cost in cell C22 to calculate the total cost of producing N parts?

ICA 10-5

The worksheet shown was designed to calculate the cost of material necessary to purchase to produce a given number of parts. The user will enter the specific gravity of the material, the diameter of the cylindrical part in units of inches, the cost of the raw material in dollars per pound-mass, and the number of parts to be manufactured – all user input is shown in red. The worksheet will calculate the radius of the cylindrical part in units of centimeters and the density of the fluid in grams per cubic centimeter – all conversions are shown in orange.

The worksheet will determine the volume and mass of a single part for a given height. Finally, the worksheet will determine the total mass of material needed to produce the desired number of parts in units of pounds-mass, and the total material cost.

The total material cost appears twice. In cells E13 to E20, a formula is written to determine the cost. In cells B26 to B33, the cells simply reference the corresponding cell in the table above. For example, in cell B26 the formula = E13 appears.

In the bottom table, the total cost for "N" parts is determined by the formula:

Total Cost = Total Material Cost + (Energy Cost + Labor Cost) × Number of Parts

A sample worksheet is shown below for comparison.

Height (H) [cm]	Volume (V) [cm^3]	Mass (m) [g]	Mass (M_N) [lb_m] for N parts	Total Material Cost (MC) [$]
Specific Gravity of Material (SG)		1.50	[--]	
Diameter (D)		4.0	[in]	
Cost of Raw Material (C)		$2.25	[$/lb_m]	
Number of Parts (N)		150	[--]	
Radius (R)		5.08	[cm]	
Density of Fluid (ρ)		1.5	[g/cm^3]	

Height (H) [cm]	Volume (V) [cm^3]	Mass (m) [g]	Mass (M_N) [lb_m] for N parts	Total Material Cost (MC) [$]
1	81.07	121.61	40	$90.50
2	162.15	243.22	80	$181.00
3	243.22	364.83	121	$271.50
5	405.37	608.05	201	$452.50
6	486.44	729.66	241	$543.00
8	648.59	972.88	322	$724.00
10	810.73	1216.10	402	$905.00
12	972.88	1459.32	463	$1,086.01

Labor Cost (LC) | $1.75 | [$/part]

Height (H) [cm]	Total Cost of N Parts — Total Material Cost (MC) [$]	Energy Cost (EC) [$/part] $0.05	$0.10	$0.20	$0.40
1	$90.50	$360.50	$388.00	$383.00	$413.00
2	$181.00	$451.00	$458.50	$473.50	$503.50
3	$271.50	$541.50	$549.00	$564.00	$594.00
5	$452.50	$722.50	$730.00	$745.00	$775.00
6	$543.00	$813.00	$820.50	$835.50	$865.50
8	$724.00	$994.00	$1,001.50	$1,016.50	$1,046.50
10	$905.00	$1,175.00	$1,182.50	$1,197.50	$1,227.50
12	$1,086.01	$1,356.01	$1,363.51	$1,378.51	$1,408.51

ICA 10-6

Refer to the following worksheet. The following expressions are typed into the Excel cells indicated. Write the answer that appears in the cell listed. If the cell will be blank, write "BLANK" in the answer space. If the cell will return an error message, write "ERROR" in the answer space.

	A	B	C	D	E	F	G	H
1								
2								
3	Fluid Type	Benzene			Fluid Type	Olive Oil		
4	Density (ρ)	0.879	[g / cm^3]		Density (ρ)	0.703	[g / cm^3]	
5	Viscosity (μ)	6.47E-03	[g / (cm s)]		Viscosity (μ)	1.01	[g / (cm s)]	
6								
7	Velocity (v)	15	[cm / s]		Velocity (v)	50	[cm / s]	
8								
9	Pipe Diameter	Reynolds Number			Pipe Diameter	Reynolds Number		
10	(D) [cm]	(Re) [--]			(D) [cm]	(Re) [--]		
11	1.27	2,588			1.27	44		
12	2.54	5,176			2.54	88		
13	3.81	7,764			3.81	133		
14	5.08	10,352			5.08	177		
15	6.35	12,940			6.35	221		
16	7.62	15,529			7.62	265		

	Expression	Typed into Cell
(a)	= IF (B4 > F4, B3, "F3")	D4
(b)	= IF (B7/2 > F7/10, " ", B7*2)	H7
(c)	= IF (B11 < F11, "B11", IF (B11 > F11, SUM(B11, F11), F11))	D11
(d)	= IF (AND(B4 < F4,B5 < F5), B3, MAX(F11:F16))	D9
(e)	= IF(OR(E16/2^2 > E15*2,E11+E12 < E14),F4*62.4,F4*1000)	H16

ICA 10-7

Write the output value that would appear in a cell if the equation was executed in Excel. You should answer these questions WITHOUT actually using Excel, as practice for the exam. If the cell will appear blank, write "BLANK" in the space provided.

= IF (AND (A1/A2 > 2, A2 > 3), A1, A2)		Output
(a)	A1 = 30 A2 = 5	
(b)	A1 = 5 A2 = 1	

= IF (SIN (A1*B1/180) < 0.5, PI(), IF (SIN (A1*B1/180) > 1, 180/A1,""))		Output
(c)	A1 = 30 B1 = PI()	
(d)	A1 = 5 B1 = PI()	

ICA 10-8

Write the output value that would appear in a cell if the equation was executed in Excel. You should answer these questions WITHOUT actually using Excel, as practice for the exam. If the cell will appear blank, write "BLANK" in the space provided.

= IF (OR (C1 > D3, D3 < E1), "YES", "NO")			Output
(a)	C1 = 10	E1 = −5	D3 = 0.1*C1^(−5*E1)
(b)	C1 = 10	E1 = 5	D3 = 0.1*C1^(−5*E1)

= IF (AND (G4/H3 > 2, H3 > 3), G4, MAX (2, G4, H3, 5*J2-10))			Output
(c)	G4 = 30	H3 = 5	J2 = 2
(d)	G4 = 10	H3 = 8	J2 = 10

ICA 10-9

Refer to the following worksheet. In all questions, give the requested answers in Excel notation, indicating EXACTLY what you would type into the cell given to properly execute the required procedures.

	A	B	C	D	E	F	G
1							
2							
3	Height (H) [ft]	5				Width (W) [ft]	
4					1	1.5	2
5							
6	Volume (V)	Radius (r)	Area (A)		Length [ft]		
7	[ft^3]	[ft]	[ft^2]	[cm^2]	(L1)	(L2)	(L3)
8	79		70.5				
9	1		7.9				
10	55		58.8				
11	13		28.6				
12	39		49.5				
13	9		23.8				
14	63		62.9				
15	23		38.0				
16	72		67.3				
17	27		41.2				
18	67		64.9				

(a) In Column B, you wish to determine the radius of a cylinder. The volume (Column A) and height (Cell B3) have been provided. Recall the volume of a cylinder is given by $V = \pi r^2 H$. Assume you will write the formula in Cell B8 and copy it down the column to Cell B100. In the expression, fill in the blanks with any Excel functions and fill in the boxes with any dollar signs necessary for relative, mixed or absolute references.

$$= \underline{\hspace{1cm}}(\square A\square 8 \: / \: (\underline{\hspace{0.5cm}} * \square B\square 3) \underline{\hspace{0.3cm}}) \underline{\hspace{0.6cm}}$$

(b) In Column C, the area of a cylinder corresponding to the radius (in Column B) and the height (Cell B3) has been determined in units of square feet. In Column D, you wish to express these values in units of square centimeters. Fill in any Excel mathematical operators or parenthesis for the expression to correctly complete this conversion.

$$= \: C8\underline{\hspace{0.5cm}}2.54\underline{\hspace{0.5cm}}2\underline{\hspace{0.5cm}}12\underline{\hspace{0.5cm}}2$$

(c) In Columns E-G, we wish to determine the dimensions of a rectangular container with the same volume as the cylinders given in Column A. The rectangle will be the same height as the cylinder (Cell B3) but have three possible widths (contained in Cells E_4–G_4). Fill in the boxes below with any dollar signs necessary for relative, mixed, or absolute references to allow the expression to determine the length in Cell E8, and by copied across to Columns F and G, then down all three columns to Row 100.

$$= \square A\square 8/(\square B\square 3*\square E\square 4)$$

(d) In Column H, we wish to tell the user how the length and radius of the different containers compare. Fill in the IF-statement below for Cell H8 to display the maximum value of the length calculations (Cells E8 through G8) if the maximum value of the length calculations is greater than the corresponding radius calculation, otherwise display the letter R.

$$= \: IF(\_(1)\_, \: \_(2)\_, \: \_(3)\_)$$

(e) Fill in the if-statement below for Cell J8 to display the sum of Length 1 and Length 2 if the sum of these lengths is greater than Length 3; otherwise, leave it blank.

$$IF(\_(1)\_, \: \_(2)\_, \: \_(3)\_)$$

ICA 10-10

Give all answers in EXACT Excel notation, as if you were instructing someone EXACTLY what to type into Excel. Be sure to use the values given in the worksheet as cell references and not actual numerical values in the formula. Use absolute, mixed or relative addressing as required.

	A	B	C	D	E	F	G	H
1								
2		Ideal Gas Constant (R)	8,314	[(Pa L)/(K mol)]				
3		Amount of substance (n)	2	[mol]				
4		Molecular weight (MW)	28	[g / mol]				
5		Mass of substance (m)		[g]				
6								
7		Temperature (T) [°F]	Temperature (T) [K]	Volume (V) [ft³]	Volume (V) [L]	Pressure (P) [Pa]	Pressure Warning	Volume Warning
8		25		1				
9		30		1.2				
10		35		1.4				
11		40		0.84				
12		45		0.75				

(a) What would you type into cell C5 to calculate the mass of gas in the container?

(b) What would you type into cell C8 so that you could copy the cell down to cell C12 to calculate all corresponding values of temperature, converting the temperatures given in Column B from units of degrees Fahrenheit to units of kelvins?

(c) What would you type into cell E8 so that you could copy the cell down to cell E12 to calculate all corresponding values of volume, converting the volumes given in Column D from units of cubic feet to units of liters?

(d) What would you type into cell F8 so that you could copy the cell down to cell F12 to calculate all corresponding values of pressure using the ideal gas law, solving for pressure in units of pascals?

(e) What conditional statement would you type in cell G8 so that you could copy the cell down to cell G12 to display the words "Too High" if the pressure from the ideal gas calculation is equal to or greater than 500,000 pascals? If the pressure is less than this value, the cell should remain blank.

(f) What conditional statement would you type in cell H8 so that you could copy the cell down to cell H12 to display the words "Bigger" if the corresponding value in Column E is greater than 5 gallons, "Smaller" if the value in Column E is less than 1 gallon, or display the actual value of the volume, in units of gallons, if the value is between 1 and 5 gallons?

ICA 10-11

A bioengineer conducts clinical trials on stressed-out college students to see if a sleep aid will help them fall asleep faster. She begins the study by having 20 students take a sleep aid for seven days and records through biofeedback the time when they fall asleep. To analyze the data, she sets up the following worksheet. Evaluate the expressions below; state what will appear in the cell when the command is executed. Column I contains the average time each student took to fall asleep during the seven-day trial. Column J contains any adverse reactions the students experienced (H = headache; N = nausea).

(a) Column K will contain the rating of the time it took the student to fall asleep compared with the control group, who did not take the medication. The statement as it appears in cell K14 is given below. What will appear in cell K14 when this statement is executed?

$$= IF > (I14 > \$I\$2 + \$I\$3, \text{"MORE"}, IF (I14 < \$I\$2 - \$I\$3, \text{"LESS"}, \text{""}))$$

(b) Column L groups the participants into three groups according to their reaction to the drug and the time it took them to fall asleep. Assume the statement for part (a) is executed in Column K. The statement as it appears in cell L7 is given below. What will appear in cell L7 when this statement is executed?

$$= IF (AND (K7 = \text{"MORE"}, J7 = \text{"H"}), \text{"MH"}, IF (AND (K7 = \text{"MORE"}, J7 = \text{"N"}), \text{"MN"}, \text{""}))$$

(c) Suppose the formula in Column L was changed to regroup the participants. The statement as it appears in cell L9 is given below. In Excel, this statement would appear as a continuous line, but here it is shown on two lines for space. What will appear in cell L9 when this statement is executed?

$$= IF (AND (K9 = \text{"MORE"}, OR (J9 = \text{"H"}, J9 = \text{"N"})), \text{"SEVERE"},$$
$$IF (OR (J9 = \text{"H"}, J9 = \text{"N"}), \text{"MILD"}, IF (K9 = \text{"LESS"}, \text{"HELPFUL"}, \text{""})))$$

(d) Suppose the formula in part (c) was copied into cell L16. What would appear in cell L16 when this statement is executed?

(e) Suppose the formula in part (c) was copied into cell L18. What would appear in cell L18 when this statement is executed?

	A	B	C	D	E	F	G	H	I	J	K	L
1						Control Group Data						
2						Overall Average			35	[min]		
3						Standard Deviation			4	[min]		
4												
5						Number of Minutes to Fall Asleep						
6	Patient	Day 1	Day 2	Day 3	Day 4	Day 5	Day 6	Day 7	Average	Reaction	Time	Group
7	A	45	39	83	47	39	25	42	46	H		
8	B	35	75	15	36	42	12	29	35			
9	C	42	32	63	45	37	34	31	41	N		
10	D	14	25	65	38	53	33	32	37	H		
11	E	14	71	48	18	29	14	24	31			
12	F	14	25	29	24	18	24	15	21	H N		
13	G	31	14	42	19	28	17	21	25			
14	H	12	24	32	42	51	12	16	27	H N		
15	I	28	29	44	15	43	15	22	28	N		
16	J	21	19	35	41	34	25	18	28	H		
17	K	44	36	51	39	30	26	25	36			
18	L	38	43	36	59	14	34	18	35	N		
19	M	19	15	63	50	55	27	31	37	H		

ICA 10-12

Refer to the worksheet shown, set up to calculate the displacement of a spring. Hooke's law states the force (F, in newtons) applied to a spring is equal to the stiffness of the spring (k, in newtons per meter) times the displacement (x, in meters): $F = kx$.

	A	B	C	D	E	F	G	H
1								
2	Spring Code	Stiffness [N/m]	Maximum Displacement [mm]			Spring Code	Stiffness [N / m]	Maximum Displacement [mm]
3	3-Blue ▾	50	20			1-Blue	10	40
4						1-Black	25	60
5	Mass [g]	Displacement [cm]	Warning			2-Blue	30	25
6	25	0.49				2-Black	40	60
7	50	0.98				2-Red	20	30
8	75	1.47				3-Blue	50	20
9	100	1.96				3-Red	40	30
10	125	2.45	Too Much Mass			3-Green	60	10
11	150	2.94	Too Much Mass					
12	175	3.43	Too Much Mass					
13	200	3.92	Too Much Mass					
14	225	4.41	Too Much Mass					
15	250	4.90	Too Much Mass					
16	275	5.39	Too Much Mass					
17	300	5.88	Too Much Mass					
18								

Cell A3 contains a data validation list of springs. The stiffness (cell B3) and maximum displacement (cell C3) values are found using a VLOOKUP function linked to the table shown at the right side of the worksheet. These data are then used to determine the displacement of the spring at various mass values. A warning is issued if the displacement determined is greater than the maximum displacement for the spring. Use this information to determine the answers to the following questions.

(a) Write the expression, in Excel notation, that you would type into cell B6 to determine the displacement of the spring. Assume you will copy this expression to cells B7 to B17.

(b) Fill in the following information in the VLOOKUP function used to determine the maximum displacement in cell C3 based on the choice of spring in cell A3.

$$= \text{VLOOKUP}(\underline{\quad(1)\quad}, \underline{\quad(2)\quad}, \underline{\quad(3)\quad}, \underline{\quad(4)\quad})$$

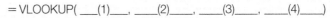

$\dfrac{N}{m} x = F$

$20 x = F$

(c) Fill in the following information in the IF function used to determine the warning given in cell C6, using the maximum displacement in cell C3. Assume you will copy this expression to cells C7 to C17.

$$= IF(\underline{\quad(1)\quad}, \underline{\quad(2)\quad}, \underline{\quad(3)\quad})$$

ICA 10-13

You are interested in analyzing different implant parts being made in a bioengineering production facility. The company has the ability to make 9 different parts for shoulder, knee, or hip replacement.

On the worksheet shown, you have created a place for the user to choose the body location (shoulder, knee, or hip) in cell B5 using a data validation list. Once the body location is set, a list of material choices will appear in cells D5 to F5. The user can choose a material in cell B6 using a data validation list. If the material chosen does not match one of the possible choices in cell D5 to F5, a warning will be issued for the user to choose another material.

In cell B9, the user will choose if the part is size small (S), medium (M), or large (L) using a data validation list. Based upon body location and size, the part number will adjust automatically using a VLOOKUP function. After the part number has been determined, the material weight (cell B11) and part volume (cell B12) will adjust automatically using a VLOOKUP function.

The user will enter the number of desired parts in cell B14. If the user requests more than 250 parts, a warning of "Too Many" will be issued; if the user requests less than 20 parts, a warning of "Too Small" will be issued in cell C14.

The amount of material to be ordered will be determined in cell B16 by multiplying the number of parts and the material weight. The cost of the material to be ordered will be determined in cell B17. If the order cost is greater than $1000, a request to "Check with Purchasing" will appear; otherwise, the cost of the order will appear. Finally, in cell B18 the amount of boxes needed for shipping will appear determined by number of parts requested and number of parts per box, based on the part number chosen in cell B10.

Lookup functions in Excel contain four parts.

$$= VLOOKUP(\underline{\quad(1)\quad}, \underline{\quad(2)\quad}, \underline{\quad(3)\quad}, \underline{\quad(4)\quad})$$

(a) Fill in the following information in the VLOOKUP function used to determine third possible material choice in cell F5 based on the choice of body location in cell B5.

An IF statement in Excel contains three parts. Fill in the following information in the IF function used to determine the following conditions:

$$= IF(\underline{\quad(1)\quad}, \underline{\quad(2)\quad}, \underline{\quad(3)\quad})$$

(b) In cell C6, the a warning is issued to the user if the material chosen in cell B6 does not match the list of materials provided in cell D5 to F5. Fill in the IF statement used to create this error message, containing a complex IF test using AND or OR.

A nested IF statement in Excel contains three parts per IF statement. Fill in the following information in the IF function used to determine the following conditions:

$$= IF(\underline{\quad(1a)\quad}, \underline{\quad(2a)\quad}, IF(\underline{\quad(1b)\quad}, \underline{\quad(2b)\quad}, \underline{\quad(3b)\quad}))$$

(c) In cell B14, the user can enter the number of parts needed in production. If this value is more than 250 parts, a warning will appear in Cell C14 telling the user the quantity is too high; if the value is less than 20, a warning will tell the user the quantity is too small; otherwise, the cell remains blank.

(d) In order for Excel to display the correct number of boxes needed, the following functions are tried. Which one will correctly display the number of boxes needed to ship the parts?

(A) = B14/VLOOKUP(B10,J1:L10,3,FALSE)

(B) = ROUND(B14/VLOOKUP(B10,J1:L10,3,FALSE),0).

(C) = ROUNDDOWN(B14/VLOOKUP(B10,J1:L10,3,FALSE),0)

(D) = ROUNDUP(B14/VLOOKUP(B10,J1:L10,3,FALSE),0)

(E) = TRUNC(B14/VLOOKUP(B10,J1:L10,3,FALSE),0)

Body Location	Part Size	Part Number	Material Weight [lbm]	Number / Box	Part Volume [cin]	Energy Cost / Part
Shoulder	S	JB2	0.45	78	5.5	0.1
Shoulder	M	JB3	0.15	24	3.5	0.04
Shoulder	L	JB5	0.15	55	3.5	0.09
Hip	L	KA9	0.05	64	1.5	0.02
Hip	M	KA11	0.1	82	2.5	0.05
Hip	S	KA2	0.4	36	6	0.02
Knee	M	DS3	0.5	65	1.5	0.07
Knee	S	DS7	0.3	98	1.5	0.05
Knee	L	DS8	0.4	93	5	0.04

Body Location	Shoulder	Material Choices:	AuZn-4	WC-2	CuAg-5
MATERIAL	PdSi3	Wrong Material Match / Choose Again			
Cost / lbm of material	$ 22.00				
Part Size	L				
Part Number	JB5				
Material Weight [lbm]	0.15				
Part Volume [cin]	3.5				
Number of Parts	800	Too Many			
Amount of Mat'l to Order [lbm]	45				
Cost of Mat'l to Order [$]	$990.00				
Amount of Boxes Needed	6				

Material	Material Cost / lbm
AuZn-4	$ 5.00
WC-2	$ 17.00
CuAg-5	$ 7.00
PdSi-3	$ 22.00
PdSi-5	$ 2.00
ZnCd-2	$ 18.00
CoNi-7	$ 24.00
CoAg-12	$ 8.00
CdAl-2	$ 13.00
PtZn-4	$ 19.00
PtC-9	$ 6.00
MnPd-8	$ 25.00
WTi-3	$ 3.00
ScCo-4	$ 6.00
ZrW-8	$ 7.00
MnRh-5	$ 13.00
PdCd-7	$ 11.00

Body Location	Material Choice		
Shoulder	AuZn-4	WC-2	CuAg-5
Knee	ZnCd-2	CoNi-7	PtC-9
Hip	PtZn-4	PtC-9	MnPd-8

ICA 10-14

You have a large stock of several values of inductors and capacitors, and are investigating how many possible combinations of a single capacitor and a single inductor chosen from the ones you have in stock will give a resonant frequency between specified limits.

Create two cells to hold a minimum and maximum frequency the user can enter.

Incorrect Data:

Allowable Range	
f_{min} [Hz]	f_{max} [Hz]
2,500	1,000

Correct Data:

Allowable Range	
f_{min} [Hz]	f_{max} [Hz]
2,500	7,777

Calculate the resonant frequency (f_R) for all possible combinations of one inductor and one capacitor, rounded to the nearest integer. For a resonant inductor/capacitor circuit, the resonant frequency in hertz [Hz] is calculated by

$$f_R = \frac{1}{2\pi\sqrt{LC}}$$

In this equation, L is the inductance in units of henry [H] and C is the capacitance in units of farads [F]. Note that the capacitance values in the table are given in microfarads. Automatically format each result to indicate its relation to the minimum and maximum frequency values as listed below.

■ $f_R > f_{MAX}$: The cell should be shaded white with light grey text and no border.

■ $f_R < f_{MIN}$: The cell should be shaded light grey with dark grey text and no border.

■ $f_{MIN} < f_R < f_{MAX}$: The cell should be shaded white with bold black text and a black border.

If done properly, the table should appear similar to the table below for $f_{MIN} = 2,500$ and $f_{MAX} = 7,777$.

After you have this working properly, modify the frequency input cells to use data validation to warn the user of an invalid value entry.

Resonant Frequency (f_R) [Hz]	Capacitance (C) [μF]							
Inductance (L) [H]	0.0022	0.0082	0.05	0.47	0.82	1.5	3.3	10
0.0005	151748	78601	31831	10382	7860	**5812**	**3918**	2251
0.002	75874	39301	15915	**5191**	**3930**	**2906**	1959	1125
0.01	33932	17576	**7118**	2322	1758	1299	876	503
0.05	15175	7860	**3183**	1038	786	581	392	225
0.068	13012	**6740**	**2729**	890	674	498	336	193
0.22	**7234**	**3747**	1517	495	375	277	187	107
0.75	**3918**	2029	822	268	203	150	101	58

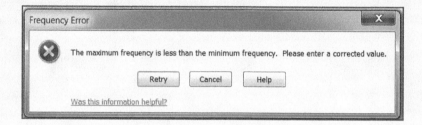

ICA 10-15

We accidentally drop a tomato from the balcony of a high-rise apartment building. As it falls, the tomato has time to ponder some physics and says, "You know, the distance I have fallen equals $\frac{1}{3}$ gravity times the time I have fallen squared." Create a worksheet to solve the question of when the tomato goes splat.

■ The user will input the initial balcony height in units of feet. Use data validation to set a limit for the height of 200 feet.

■ Place the acceleration due to gravity in a cell under the balcony height and not within the formulas themselves. *Be sure to watch the units for this problem!*

■ Column A will be the distance the tomato falls, starting at a distance of zero up to a distance of 200 feet, in 5-foot increments.

■ Column B will show the calculated time elapsed at each distance fallen.

■ Column C will display the status of the tomato as it falls.
  • If the tomato is still falling, the cell should display the distance the tomato still has to fall.
  • If the tomato hits the ground, the cell should display "SPLAT" on a red background.
  • SPLAT should appear once; the cells below are blank.

Test your worksheet using the following conditions:

I. At a balcony height of 200 feet, the tomato should splat at a time of 3.52 seconds.
II. At a balcony height of 50 feet, the tomato should splat at a time of 1.76 seconds.

ICA 10-16

You are interested in calculating the best place to stand to look at a statue. Where should you stand so that the angle subtended by the statue is the largest?

At the top of the worksheet, input the pedestal height (P) and the statue height (S).

In Column A, create a series of distances (d) from the foot of the statue, from 2 feet to 40 feet by 2-foot increments.

In Column B, calculate the subtended angle in radians using the following equation:

$$\theta = \tan^{-1}\left(\frac{P + S}{d}\right) - \tan^{-1}\left(\frac{P}{d}\right)$$

Photo courtesy of E. Stephan

In Column C, write a function to change the angles in Column B from radians to degrees. At the bottom of Column C, insert a function to display the maximum value of all the angles.

In Column D, use a conditional statement whose output is blank except at the single distance where the angle is a maximum; at the maximum, print "Stand Here." This font should be in the color of your choice, not the default black text.

Test your worksheet using the following conditions:

I. At a pedestal height of 20 feet and a statue height of 10 feet, the subtended angle is 11.5 degrees and you should stand 24 feet from the statue.

II. At a pedestal height of 30 feet and a statue height of 20 feet, the subtended angle is 14.5 degrees and you should stand 38 feet from the statue.

ICA 10-17

Many college students have compact refrigerator-freezers in their dorm room. The data set provided is a partial list of energy efficient models less than 3.6 cubic feet [cft], according to the American Council for an Energy Efficient Economy (www.aceee.org). Complete the analysis below.

We would like to compute the cost to run each model for a year. Assume that it costs $0.086 per kilowatt-hour [kWh]. Create a new column, "Annual Energy Cost [$/year]," that calculates the annual energy cost for each refrigerator.

(a) Sort the first table by energy usage, with the model with the highest kilowatt-hour rating listed first. Which model appears first?

(b) Sort by the volume in ascending order and the annual energy cost in ascending order. Which model appears first?

(c) Assume we want to restrict our selection to refrigerators that can contain more than 2.5 cubic feet. Which models appear in the list?

(d) Assume we want to restrict our selection to refrigerators that can contain more than 2.5 cubic feet and only require between 0 and 300 kilowatt-hours per year. Which models appear in the list?

ICA 10-18

The complexity of video gaming consoles has evolved over the years. The data set provided is a list of energy usage data on recent video gaming consoles, according to the Sust-It consumer energy report data (www.sust-it.net).

Compute the cost to run each gaming console for a year, including the purchase price. Assume that it costs $0.086 per kilowatt-hour [kWh]. Create a new column, "Cost + Energy [$/yr]," that calculates the total (base + energy) cost for each gaming console.

On average, a consumer will own and operate a video gaming console for four years. Calculate the total carbon emission [kilograms of carbon dioxide, or kg CO_2] for each gaming console over the average lifespan; put the result in a column labeled "Average Life Carbon Emission [kg CO_2]." If these steps are completed correctly, the first year cost for the Microsoft Xbox 360 should be $410.36 and the Average Life Carbon Emissions should be 207.88 kilograms of carbon dioxide.

(a) Sort the table by total cost, with the console with the highest total cost listed first. Which console appears first?

(b) Sort by the original cost in ascending order and the average life carbon emission in ascending order. Which console appears last?

(c) Restrict your selection to video game consoles that originally cost $300. Which models appear in the list?

(d) Restrict your selection to video game consoles that originally cost less than or equal to $300 and have an average life carbon emission less than or equal to 25 kg CO_2. Which models appear in the list?

Chapter 10 REVIEW QUESTIONS

1. With current rocket technology, the cost to lift one kilogram of mass to geosynchronous orbit (GSO) is about $20,000. Several other methods of lifting mass into space for considerably less cost have been envisioned, including the Lofstrom loop, the orbital airship, and the space elevator.

   In space elevators, a cargo compartment (climber) rides up a slender tether attached to the Earth's surface and extending tens of thousands of miles into space. Many designs provide power to the climber by beaming it to a collector on the climber using a laser of maser.

   The leftmost column of the table should contain efficiencies from 0.5% to 2% in 0.25% increments. The top row of the table should list electricity prices from 4 cents to 14 cents per kilowatt-hour with 2 cent increments. Each row of the table thus represents a specific efficiency and each column represents a specific electricity cost. The intersection of each row and column should contain the corresponding total cost of the electricity used to lift one kilogram to GSO.

   Assume that the total change in the potential energy of an object lifted from sea level to GSO is 50 megajoules per kilogram.

   Any constants and conversion factors used should appear as properly labeled constants in individual cells, and your formulae should reference these. Conversions and constants should NOT be directly coded into the formulae. You are expected to use absolute, relative, and mixed cell addressing as appropriate.

   Test case: If electricity costs 18 cents per kilowatt-hour and the conversion efficiency is 3%, the electricity to lift one kilogram to GSO would cost $83.33.

2. A history major of your acquaintance is studying agricultural commerce in nineteenth century Wales. He has encountered many references to "hobbits" of grain, and thinking that this must be some type of unit similar to a bushel (rather than a diminutive inhabitant of Middle Earth), he has sought your advice because he knows you are studying unit conversions in your engineering class.

   He provides a worksheet containing yearly records for the total number of hobbits of three commodities sold by a Mr. Thomas between 1817 and 1824, and has asked you to convert these to not only cubic meters, but also both U.S. and imperial bushels.

	A	B	C	D	E	F	G	H	I	J	K	L	M
			Barley				Wheat				Oats		
	Year	Hobbits	Imp. Bushels	US Bushels	Cubic Meters	Hobbits	Imp. Bushels	US Bushels	Cubic Meters	Hobbits	Imp. Bushels	US Bushels	Cubic Meters
7	1817	106				154				203			
8	1818	118				145				187			
9	1819	98				167				167			
10	1820	137				124				199			
11	1821	102				105				210			
12	1822	142				168				147			
13	1823	93				132				186			
14	1824	117				136				193			
15													
16		Hobbit	Imp. Bushels	US Bushels	Cubic Meters								
17		1											

After a little research, you find that the hobbit was equal to two and a half imperial bushels, the imperial bushel equals 2,219 cubic inches, and the U.S. bushel equals 2,150 cubic inches.

First, you create a table showing the conversion factors from hobbits to the other units, including comments documenting the conversion. You then use these calculated conversion factors to create the rest of the table.

3. You want to set up a worksheet to investigate the oscillatory response of an electrical circuit. Create a worksheet similar to the one shown, including the proper header information.

4			
5			
6			
7	**Neper Frequency (α_0)**	25	[rad/s]
8	**Resonant Frequency (ω_0)**	400	[rad/s]
9	**Initial Voltage (V_0)**	15	[V]
10			
11	Damped Frequency (ω_d)		[rad/s]
12			
13			
14	**Time (t) [s]**	**Voltage (V) [V]**	
15			

First, calculate another constant, the damped frequency ω_d, which is a function of the neper frequency (α_0) and the resonant frequency (ω_0). This can be calculated with the formula

$$\omega_d = \sqrt{\omega_0^2 - \alpha_0^2}$$

Next, create a column of times (beginning in A15) used to calculate the voltage response, ranging from 0 to 0.002 seconds at an increment of 0.0002 seconds.

In column B, calculate the voltage response with the following equation, formatted to one decimal place:

$$V = V_0 e^{-\alpha_0 t} \cos(\omega_d t)$$

Test Cases: Use the following to test your worksheet.

I. Change neper frequency to 200 radians per second, resonant frequency to 800 radians per second, and initial voltage to 100 volts. At a time of 0.0008 seconds, the voltage should be 69.4 V.

II. Change neper frequency to 100 radians per second, resonant frequency to 600 radians per second, and initial voltage to 100 volts. At a time of 0.0008 seconds, the voltage should be 82.2 V.

4. A phase diagram for carbon and platinum is shown. Assuming the lines shown are linear, we can say the mixture has the following characteristics:

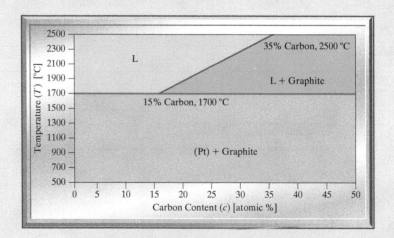

- Below 1,700°C, it is a mixture of solid platinum and graphite.
- Above 1,700°C, there are two possible phases: a liquid (L) phase and a liquid (L) + graphite phase. The endpoints of the division line between these two phases are labeled on the diagram.

Use the workbook provided to determine the phase of a mixture, given the temperature and carbon content.

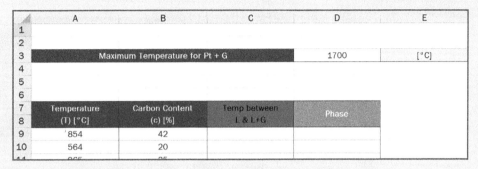

	A	B	C	D	E
1					
2					
3	Maximum Temperature for Pt + G			1700	[°C]
4					
5					
6					
7	Temperature	Carbon Content	Temp between	Phase	
8	(T) [°C]	(c) [%]	L & L+G		
9	854	42			
10	564	20			

(a) Write the equation to describe the temperature of the dividing line between the liquid (L) region and the liquid (L) + graphite region in Column C. Reference the carbon content found in Column B as needed. Add any absolute reference cells you feel are needed to complete this calculation.

(b) Write the conditional statement to determine the phase in Column D. For simplicity, call the phases Pt + G, L, and L + G. For points on the line, YOU can decide which phase they are included in.

(c) Use conditional formatting to indicate each phase. Provide a color key.

5. A simplified phase diagram for cobalt and nickel is shown. Assuming the lines shown are linear, we can say the mixture has the following characteristics:

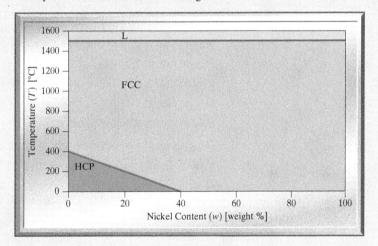

- Above 1,500°C, it is a liquid.
- Below 1,500°C, there are two possible phases: face-centered cubic (FCC) phase and hexagonal close-packed (HCP) phase.

Use the workbook provided to determine the phase of a mixture, given the temperature and nickel content.

	A	B	C	D	E
1					
2					
3	Minimum Temperature for Liquid			1500	[°C]
4					
5					
6					
7	Temperature	Nickel Content	Temp Between	Phase	
8	(T) [°C]	(w) [%]	HCP & FCC		
9	543	74			
10	1028	4			
11	1326	69			

(a) Write the mathematical equation to describe the dividing line between the HCP region and the FCC region in Column C. Reference the nickel content found in Column B as needed. Add any absolute reference cells you feel are needed to complete this calculation.

(b) Write the conditional statement to determine the phase in Column D. For simplicity, call the phases HCP, FCC, and L. For points on the line, YOU can decide which phase they are included in.

(c) Use conditional formatting to indicate each phase. Provide a color key.

6. You enjoy drinking coffee but are particular about the temperature (T) of your coffee. If the temperature is greater than or equal to 70 degrees Celsius [°C], the coffee is too hot to drink; less than or equal to 45°C is too cold by your standards. Your coffee pot produces coffee at the initial temperature (T_0). The cooling of your coffee can be modeled by the equation below, where time (t) and the cooling factor (k) are in units per second:

$$T = T_0 e^{-kt}$$

(a) At the top of the worksheet, create an area where the user can modify four properties of the coffee. For a sample test case, enter the following data.

  ■ Initial temperature (T_0); for the initial problem, set to 80°C.

  ■ Cooling factor (k); set to 0.001 per second [s^{-1}].

  ■ Temperature above which coffee is "Too Hot" to drink (T_{hot}); set to 70°C.

  ■ Temperature below which coffee is "Too Cold" to drink (T_{cold}); set to 45°C.

(b) Create a temperature profile for the coffee:

  ■ In column A, generate a time range of 0–300 seconds, in 15-second intervals.

  ■ In column B, generate the temperature of the coffee, using the equation given and the input parameters set by the user (T_0 and k).

(c) In column B, the temperature values should appear on a red background if the coffee is too hot to drink, and a blue background if it is too cold using conditional formatting.

(d) In column C, create a warning next to each temperature that says "Do not Drink" if the calculated temperature in column B is too hot or too cold in comparison with the temperature values the user enters.

A sample worksheet is shown below for the test case described in Part (a).

Coffee Parameters		
Initial Temperature (T_0)	80	[°C]
Cooling Factor (k)	0.001	[1/s]
Too Hot Temperature (T_{hot})	70	[°C]
Too Cold Temperature (T_{cold})	45	[°C]

Time [s]	Temperature [deg C]	Warning!
0	80	Do not Drink
15	79	Do not Drink
30	78	Do not Drink
45	76	Do not Drink
60	75	Do not Drink
75	74	Do not Drink
90	73	Do not Drink
105	72	Do not Drink
120	71	Do not Drink
135	70	
150	69	
165	68	
180	67	

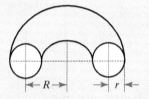

7. In the 1950s, a team at Los Alamos National Laboratories built several devices they called "Perhapsatrons," thinking that PERHAPS they might be able to create controllable nuclear fusion. After several years of experiments, they were never able to maintain a stable plasma and abandoned the project.

   The perhapsatron used a toroidal (doughnut-shaped) plasma confinement chamber, similar to those used in more modern Tokamak fusion devices. You have taken a job at a fusion research lab, and your supervisor asks you to develop a simple spreadsheet to calculate the volume of a torus within which the plasma will be contained in a new experimental reactor.

   (a) Create a simple calculator to allow the user to type in the radius of the tube (r) in meters and the radius of the torus (R) in meters and display the volume in cubic meters.
   (b) Data validation should be used to assure that $R > r$ in part (a).
   (c) Create a table that calculates the volumes of various toruses with specific values for r and R. The tube radii (r) should range from 5 centimeters to 100 centimeters in increments of 5 centimeters. The torus radii (R) should range from 1.5 meters to 3 meters in increments of 0.1 meters.

   The volume of a torus can be determined using $V = 2\pi^2 R r^2$. A sample worksheet for parts (a) and (b) is shown below.

Tube Radius (r) [m]	Torus Radius (R) [m]	Torus Volume (V) [m³]
2	1	79.0

Microsoft Excel   ✕

❌ The value you entered is not valid.

A user has restricted values that can be entered into this cell.

[Retry] [Cancel] [Help]

Was this information helpful?

Use the following phase diagram for Questions 8–9.

The phase diagram below for the processing of a polymer relates the applied pressure to the raw material porosity.

- Region A or B = porosity is too high or too low for the material to be usable.
- Region C = combinations in this region yield material with defects, such as cracking or flaking.
- Region D = below a pressure of 15 pound-force per square inch [psi] the polymer cannot be processed.
- Region E = optimum region to operate.

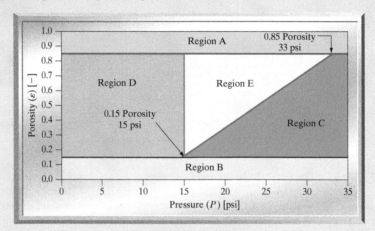

There are often multiple ways to solve the same problem; here we look a few alternative ways to determine the phase of the material and the processibility of the material.

8. (a) In Column C, develop the equation for the line dividing the phases of Region E and Region C. Assume it was written in cell C9 and copied to Column C.

(b) In Column D, write an expression to determine the phase of the material (Phase A–Phase E).

(c) In Column E, write an expression to determine if the material is processible.

(d) When the conditions of Phase E are met, the cell should be highlighted by conditional formatting. Provide a color key.

	A	B	C	D	E
1					
2					
3		Porosity Upper Limit [%]		85	
4		Porosity Lower Limit [%]		15	
5		Pressure Limit [psi]		15	
6					
7	Pressure	Porosity	Porosity between	Phase	Is Material able to
8	(P) [psi]	(ε) [%]	C and E		be Processed?
9	16	91			
10	17	60			
11	18	20			

9. (a) In Column A and Column B, use data validation to restrict the user from entering values outside the valid parameter ranges—pressure: 0–35 psi and porosity: 0–100%.

(b) In Column C, develop the equation for the line dividing the phases of Region E and Region C.

(c) In Column D, write an expression to determine the phase of the material (Phase A–Phase E).

(d) In Column E, write an expression to determine if the material is processible.

(e) When the conditions of Phase E are met, the cell should be highlighted by conditional formatting.

(f) Write an expression in Column F to tell the user why the material was rejected. For example, under the conditions of pressure = 25 psi and porosity = 40%, the statement might say "Porosity too low."

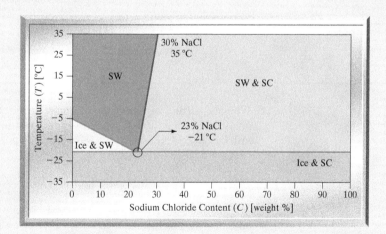

	A	B	C	D	E	F
1						
2						
3	Porosity Upper Limit [%]			85		
4	Porosity Lower Limit [%]			15		
5	Pressure Limit [psi]			15		
6						
7	Pressure	Porosity	Porosity between			
8	(P) [psi]	(c) [%]	C and E			
9	50	68				
10						
11						
12						

Use the following phase diagram for Questions 10–11.

The following phase diagram is for salt water. There are four possible phases, which depend on the temperature and the sodium chloride content (NaCl).

- Ice and SC = Mixed ice and salt crystals.
- Ice and SW = Ice and saltwater.
- SW = Saltwater.
- SW and SC = Saltwater and salt crystals.

There are often multiple ways to solve the same problem; here we look a few alternative ways to determine the phase of the mixture.

10. (a) In Column C, develop the equation for the line dividing the phases of the ice–saltwater mix and the saltwater. Assume it was written in cell C11 and copied down.

(b) In Column D, develop the equation for the line dividing the phases of the saltwater and the saltwater–salt crystals mix. Assume it was written in cell D11 and copied down.

(c) In Column E, write an expression to determine the phase of the mixture.

(d) Use conditional formatting to highlight the various phases. Provide a color key.

	A	B	C	D	E
1					
2					
3					
4					
5					
6					
7	Upper Limit of Mixed Ice and Salt Crystals			-21	[°C]
8					
9	NaCl [%]	Temp [°C]	Dividing Temp [° C]		Phase
10			Ice and SW to SW	SW to SW and SC	
11	84	31			
12	60	-17			
13	81	-17			
14	41	17			

11. (a) In Column A and Column B, use data validation to restrict the user from entering values outside the valid parameter ranges: NaCl (%): 0–100%; Temp [°C]: −35°C to 35°C.
   (b) In Column C, develop the equation for the line dividing the phases of the ice–saltwater mix and the saltwater.
   (c) In Column D, develop the equation for the line dividing the phases of the saltwater and the saltwater–salt crystals mix.
   (d) In Column E, write an expression to determine the phase of the mixture.
   (e) Use conditional formatting to highlight the various phases. Provide a color key.

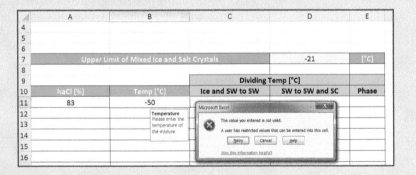

	A	B	C	D	E
4					
5					
6					
7	Upper Limit of Mixed Ice and Salt Crystals			-21	[°C]
8					
9			Dividing Temp [°C]		
10	NaCl [%]	Temp [°C]	Ice and SW to SW	SW to SW and SC	Phase
11	83	-50			
12					
13					
14					
15					
16					

12. When liquid and vapor coexist in a container at equilibrium, the pressure is called vapor pressure. Several models predict vapor pressure. One, called the *Antoine equation*, first introduced by Ch. Antoine in 1888, yields vapor pressure in units of millimeters of mercury [mm Hg].

$$P = 10^{\left(A - \frac{B}{T+C}\right)}$$

The constants A, B, and C are called the *Antoine constants*; they depend on both fluid type and temperature. Note that "B" and "C" must be in the same units as temperature and "A" is a dimensionless number, all determined by experiment.

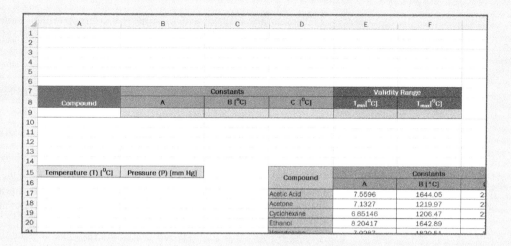

Create a worksheet using the provided template. The Antoine constants, located in cells D17 to I24 of the workbook provided, should automatically fill in after the user selects one from a drop-down menu in Cell A9 of the compounds shown below. (*Hint:* Use data validation and lookup expressions.)

Next, create a column of temperature (*T*) beginning at –100 degrees Celsius and increasing in increments of 5 degrees Celsius until a temperature of 400 degrees Celsius.

In column B, calculate the vapor pressure (*P*, in millimeters of mercury, [mm Hg]) using the Antoine equation, formatted to four decimal places. If the equation is outside the valid temperature range for the compound, the pressure column should be blank.

13. The ideal gas law assumes that molecules bounce around and have negligible volume themselves. This is not always true. To compensate for the simplifying assumptions of the ideal gas law, the Dutch scientist Johannes van der Waals developed a "real" gas law that uses several factors to account for molecular volume and intermolecular attraction. He was awarded the Nobel Prize in 1910 for his work. The *van der Waals equation* is as follows:

$$\left(P + \frac{an^2}{V^2}\right)(V - bn) = nRT$$

P, *V*, *n*, *R*, and *T* are the same quantities as found in the ideal gas law. The constant "*a*" is a correction for intermolecular forces [atm L^2/mol^2], and the constant "*b*" accounts for molecular volume [L/mol]. Each of these factors must be determined by experiment.

Create a worksheet using the provided template. The molecular weight, "*a*," and "*b*" should automatically fill in after the user selects the type of gas in cell B7. (*Hint:* Use data validation and lookup expressions using the data found in the table located in E7 to H26 in the workbook provided.) The user will also set the quantity of gas and the temperature of the system.

Next, create a column of volume beginning in A21 at 0.5 liters and increasing in increments of 0.1 liters to a volume of 5 liters.

In column B, calculate the pressure (P, in atmospheres [atm]) using the ideal gas law.

In column C, calculate the pressure (P, in atmospheres [atm]) using the van der Waals equation.

14. One of the NAE Grand Challenges for Engineering is **Engineering the Tools of Scientific Discovery**. According to the NAE website: "Grand experiments and missions of exploration always need engineering expertise to design the tools, instruments, and systems that make it possible to acquire new knowledge about the physical and biological worlds."

Solar sails are a means of interplanetary propulsion using the radiation pressure of the sun to accelerate a spacecraft. The table contained in the starting Excel file shows the radiation pressure at the orbits of the eight planets.

NOTE

The astronomical unit (AU) is the average distance from the Earth to the Sun.

Create a table showing the area in units of square meters of a solar sail needed to achieve various accelerations for various spacecraft masses at the distances from the sun of the various planets. Your solution should use data validation and VLOOKUP to select a planet and the corresponding radiation pressure. The columns of your table should list masses of the spacecraft (including the mass of the sail) ranging from 100 to 1,000 kilograms in increments of 100 kilograms. The rows should list accelerations from 0.0001 to 0.001 g in increments of 0.001 g, where "g" is the acceleration of Earth's gravity, 9.8 meters per second squared. All constants and conversion factors should be placed in individual cells using appropriate labels, and all formulae should reference these cells and NOT be directly coded into the formulae. You should use absolute, relative, and mixed addressing as appropriate.

15. A hands-on technology museum has hired you to do background research on the feasibility of a new activity to allow visitors to assemble their own ferrite core memory device—a technology in common use until the 1970s, and in specialized applications after that. The computers onboard the early space shuttle flights used core memory due to their durability, non-volatility, and resistance to radiation—core memory recovered from the wreck of the Challenger still functioned.

Ferrite core memory comprises numerous tiny ferrite rings ("cores") in a grid, each of which has either two or three wires threaded through it in a repeating pattern and can store a single bit, or binary digit—a 0 or a 1. Since the cores were typically on the order of one millimeter in diameter, workers had to assemble these under microscopes.

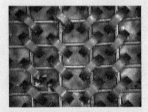

Photo courtesy of W. Park

After investigating ferrite materials, you find several that would be suitable for fabrication of the cores. The museum staff has decided to have the visitors assemble a 4×4 array (16 cores—actual devices were MUCH larger) and anticipate that 2,500 people will assemble one of these over the course of the project. Assuming that the cores are each cylindrical rings with a hole diameter half that of the outside diameter of the ring and a thickness one-fourth the outside diameter, you need to know how many grams of ferrite beads you need to purchase with 10% extra beyond the specified amount for various core diameters and ferrite materials. You also wish to know the total cost for the beads.

Using the provided online worksheet that includes a table of different ferrite material densities and costs, use data validation to select one of the materials from the list, then create a table showing the number of pounds of cores for core diameters of 1.2 to 0.7 millimeter in 0.1 millimeter increments as well as the total cost. For cores with a diameter less than 1 millimeter, there is a 50% manufacturing surcharge, thus the smallest cores cost more per gram. Include table entries for individual core volume and total volume of all cores. Your worksheet should resemble the example below.

	A	B	C	D	
1					
2					
3					
4			Cost of Ferrite Cores for Ha		
5					
6	Ferrite Compound	Specific Gravity	Cost per Gram [$/g]		Fer Comp
7	CMP C	3.73	$ 32.50		CM
8					CM
9	Sets needed	2500			CM
10	Cores per set	16			CM
11	Total Cores	40,000			CM
12	Total + 10%	44,000			CM
13					
14				Core Outs	
15			0.7	0.8	0
16	Volume of one core [mm³]		0.0505	0.0754	0.1
17	Volume of all Cores [mm³]		2,222	3,318	4.7
18	Mass of Cores [g]		8.29	12.37	17
19	Cost of Cores [$]		$ 404.11	$ 603.21	$ 8

16. A substance used to remove the few remaining molecules from a near vacuum by reacting with them or adsorbing them is called a getter. There are numerous materials used and several ways of deploying them within a system enclosing a vacuum, but here we will look at a common method used in vacuum tubes, once the workhorse of electronics but now relegated to high-end audio systems and other niche markets. In vacuum tubes, after the air is evacuated with a vacuum pump, getters are usually deposited on the inside of the tube, often at the top, by flash deposition.

Assume we are investigating getter materials for use in vacuum tubes with various inside diameters and hemispherical tops. The getter will be flash deposited on this hemispherical area.

We wish to set up a worksheet that will allow the user to select a getter material from a menu using data validation, and produce a table showing the number of moles of that material and the thickness of the deposited film for various masses of material from 20 to 300 milligram with 20 milligram increments and various tube inside diameters from 0.6 to 1.2 inches by 0.1 inch. Your final worksheet should appear similar to the example shown below. A starting worksheet including the table of possible materials and their specific gravities and atomic weights is available online.

Photo courtesy of W. Park

	A	B	C	D	E
1					
2					
3					
4	Getter Material	Specific Gravity	Atomic Weight [g/mol]		Getter Material
5	Sodium	0.968	22.99		Barium
6					Aluminum
7					Sodium
8					Strontium
9					Calcium
10					Magnesium
11					
12	Getter Thickness [µm]			Vacuum Tube	
13	Mass [mg]	Moles	0.6	0.7	0.8
14	20	8.70E-04	56.6	41.6	31.9
15	40	1.70E-03	113.3	83.2	63.7
16	60	2.60E-03	169.9	124.8	95.6

EXCEL

one can tell at a glance what value a specific set of colors means. For the novice, however, trying to read color codes can be a bit challenging.

Begin with the worksheet template provided. In the worksheet, the user will enter a resistance value as the first two digits and a multiplier, both selected using a drop-down menu created through data validation. The resistance should be calculated as the first two digits times the multiplier.

The worksheet should automatically determine the First Digit and the Second Digit of the value entered in cell E7, using the built-in functions LEFT and RIGHT. The number of zeros should be determined using the lookup function.

Finally, the worksheet should determine the corresponding resistance band color using the Color Code table. The cells should automatically change to the correct color when the digits or multiplier are changed using conditional formatting.

For example, a resistance of 4,700 ohms [Ω] has first digit 4 (yellow), second digit 7 (violet), and 2 zeros following (red). A resistance of 56 Ω would be 5 (green), 6 (blue), and 0 zeros (black); 1,000,000 Ω is 1 (brown), 0 (black), and 5 zeros (green). Particularly note that if the second digit is zero, it does not count in the multiplier value. There are numerous explanations of the color code on the web if you need further information or examples.

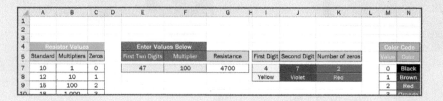

19. Download the starting file, and complete the following commands using the data provided.

(a) Indicate the following using conditional formatting commands of your choice. Each condition below should appear in a unique format.

- Length shown in Column B is greater than 6 inches or less than 4 inches.
- Width shown in Column C is less than 2.5 inches.
- Inner radius shown in Column D is above average for the inner radius values.
- Outer radius shown in Column E is below average for the outer radius values.
- Volume shown in Column F is less than 10 cubic inches or greater than 20 cubic inches.

(b) For the following conditions, in Column H use an IF statement to indicate the Status:

- If length is less than 4 inches or width is less than 2.5 inches, list the status as "Too Small."
- Otherwise, if twice the inner radius is greater than the outer radius, list the status as "Off Center."
- Otherwise, if the volume is greater than 20 cubic inches or the mass is greater than 3,000 grams, list the status as "Too Large."
- Otherwise, if none of these conditions are true, leave the cell blank.

(c) For the following conditions, in Column J use an IF statement to indicate the Action Code:

- If the status is "Too Small" or "Too Large," list as action code as a numerical value of one.
- If the status is "Off Center," list as action code as a numerical value of two.
- If none of these conditions are met, list as action code as a numerical value of three.

(d) Use a conditional formatting icon set in Column I to indicate the following:

- Status as green for action code 3.
- Status as yellow for action code 2.
- Status as red for action code 1.

(e) Count the following items, showing the results somewhere above the data table. Be sure to indicate each counted item with an appropriate label.

- Indicate the number of items classified as each action code, such as how many items are listed as 1.
- Indicate number of parts when the length is greater than 6 inches.
- Indicate number of parts when the volume is less than 10 cubic inches or greater than 20 cubic inches. As a hint, use two "COUNT" functions and add them together.

(f) Sort the worksheet in the following order: Length, increasing and simultaneously then Outer Radius, decreasing. Be careful to select only the data and not the entire worksheet.

(g) Set the worksheet controls to be filtered in the header row. Filter the worksheet so only parts of length 2.80, 5.20, and 7.15 inches are shown.

CHAPTER 11
GRAPHICAL SOLUTIONS

Often, the best way to present technical data is through a "picture." But if not done properly, it is often the worst way to display information. As an engineer, you will have many opportunities to construct such pictures. If technical data are presented properly in a graph, it is often possible to explain a point in a concise and clear manner that is impossible any other way.

11.1 GRAPHING TERMINOLOGY

LEARN TO: Identify the abscissa and the ordinate of a graph
Identify the independent and dependent variables in a problem

MNEMONIC

Within the alphabet:

a comes before o

h comes before v

x comes before y

Therefore:

Abscissa = Horizontal axis

Ordinate = Vertical axis

Abscissa is the horizontal axis; **ordinate** is the vertical axis. Until now, you have probably referred to these as "x" and "y." This text uses the terms *abscissa* and *ordinate*, or *horizontal* and *vertical*, since x and y are only occasionally used as variables in engineering problems.

The **independent** variable is the parameter that is controlled or whose value is selected in the experiment; the **dependent** variable is the parameter that is measured corresponding to each set of selected values of the independent variable. Convention usually shows the independent variable on the abscissa and the dependent variable on the ordinate.

Data sets given in tabular form are commonly interpreted and graphed with the leftmost column or topmost row as the independent variable and the other columns or rows as the dependent variable(s). For the remainder of this text, if not specifically stated, assume that the abscissa variable is listed in the leftmost column or topmost row in a table of data values.

Time	Distance (d) [m]	
(t) [s]	Car 1	Car 2
Abscissa	Ordinate	Ordinate

Time (t) [s]		Abscissa
Distance	Car 1	Ordinate
(d) [m]	Car 2	Ordinate

11.2 PROPER PLOTS

We call graphs constructed according to the following rules **proper plots**:

- **Label both axes clearly.** Three things are required unless the information is unavailable: category (e.g., Time), symbol used (t), and units [s]. Units should accompany all quantities when appropriate, enclosed in square brackets [ ].
- **Select scale increments (both axes) that are easy to read and interpolate between.** With a few exceptions, base your scale on increments of 1, 2, 2.5, and 5. You can scale each value by any power of 10 as necessary to fit the data. Avoid unusual increments (such as 3, 7, 15, or 6.5).

Increment	Sequence				
1	0	10	20	30	40
5	0.05	0.10	0.15	0.20	0.25
2.5	−2,500	0	2,500	5,000	7,500
2	6×10^{-5}	8×10^{-5}	1×10^{-4}	1.2×10^{-4}	1.4×10^{-4}

In this final case, reading is easier if the axis is labeled something like Time (t) [s] $\times 10^{-4}$ so that only the numbers 0.6, 0.8, 1.0, 1.2, and 1.4 show on the axis.

- **Provide horizontal and vertical gridlines** to make interpolation easier to aid the reader in determining actual numerical values from the graph.

When minor gridlines are present, the reader should be able to easily determine the value of each minor increment. For example, examine the graphs shown in Figure 11-1. In which graph is it easier to determine the abscissa value for the blue point? In the graph on the left, the abscissa increment can easily be determined as 0.1 meters. In the graph on the right, it is more difficult to determine the increment as 0.08 meters.

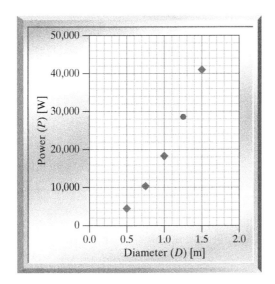 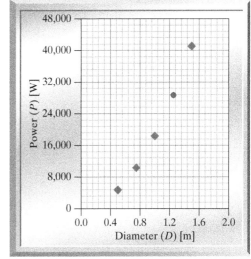

Figure 11-1 Example of importance of minor gridline spacing.

- **Provide a clear legend** describing each data set of multiple data sets shown. Do not use a legend for a single data set. Legends may be shown in a stand-alone box or captioned next to the data set. Both methods are shown in Figure 11-2.
- **Show measurements as symbols. Show calculated or theoretical values as lines.** Do not display symbols for calculated or theoretical values. A symbol shown on a graph indicates that an experimental measurement has been made (see Figure 11-3).

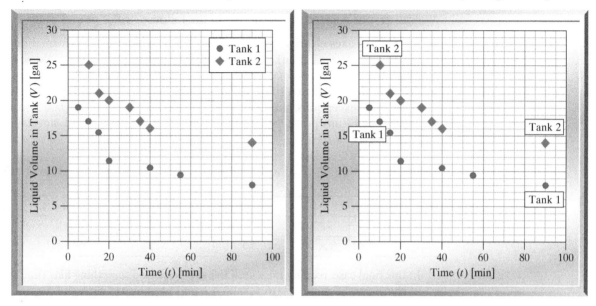

Figure 11-2 Options for displaying legends.

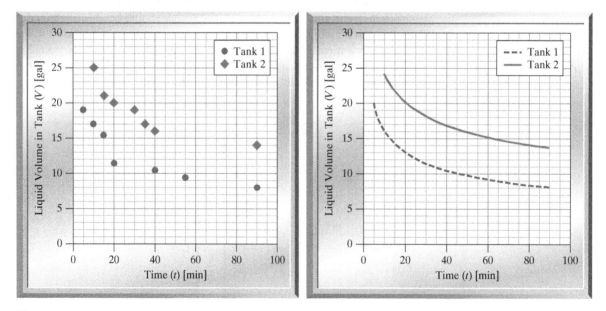

Figure 11-3 Illustration of experimental data (shown as points) versus theoretical data (shown as lines).

- **Use a different symbol shape and color** for each experimental data set and a different line style and color for each theoretical data set. **Never use yellow and other light pastel colors**. Remember that when graphs are photocopied, all colored lines become black lines. Some colors disappear when copied and are hard to see in a projected image. For example, in Figure 11-4, left, it is much easier to distinguish between the different lines than in the figure on the right.

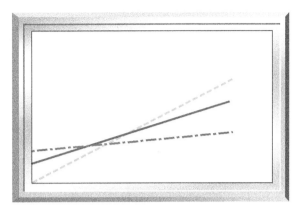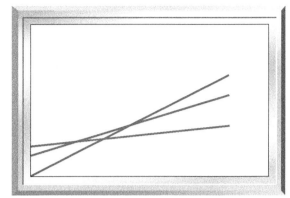

Figure 11-4 Example of importance of different line types.

- ■ When placing a graph within a document:
  - ■ **Produce graphs in portrait orientation** whenever possible within a document. Portrait orientation does not necessarily mean that the graph is distorted to be taller than it is wide; it means that readers can study the graph without turning the page sideways.
  - ■ **Be sure the graph is large enough to be easily read.** The larger the graph, the more accurate the extracted information.
  - ■ **Caption with a brief description.** The restating of "*d* versus *t*" or "distance versus time" or even "the relationship between distance and time" does not constitute a proper caption. The caption should give information about the graph to allow the graph to stand alone, without further explanation. It should include information about the problem that does not appear elsewhere on the graph. For example, instead of stating "distance versus time," better choices would be "Lindbergh's Flight across the Atlantic," "The Flight of Voyager I," or "Walking between Classes across Campus, Fall 2008." When including a graph as part of a written report, place the caption below the graph.

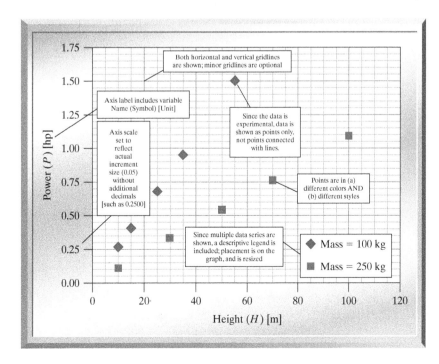

Figure 11-5 Example of a proper plot, showing multiple experimental data sets.

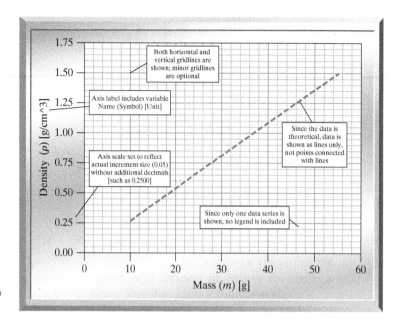

Figure 11-6 Example of a proper plot, showing a single theoretical data set.

Figure 11-7 below is an example of a poorly constructed plot. Some problems with this plot are listed below:

- It is a plot of distance versus time, but is it the distance of a car, a snail, or a rocket? What are the units of distance—inches, meters, or miles? What are the units of time—seconds, days, or years? Is time on the horizontal or vertical axis?
- Two data sets are shown, or are there three? Why is the one data set connected with a line? Is it a trendline? Is the same data set shown in the triangles? What do the shaded and open triangles represent—different objects, different trials of the same object, or modifications to the same object?
- Lack of gridlines and strange axis increments makes it difficult to interpolate between values. What is the location of the blue dot?

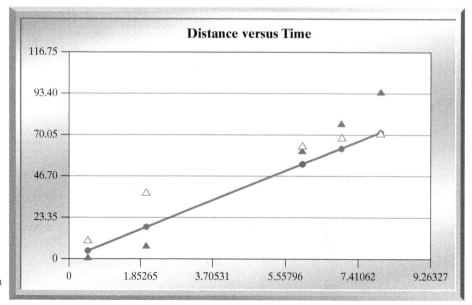

Figure 11-7 Example of a poorly constructed graph.

● **EXAMPLE 11-1**

When attempting to stop a car, a driver must consider both the reaction time and the braking time. The data are taken from www.highwaycode.gov.uk. Create a proper plot of these experimental data, with speed on the abscissa.

Vehicle Speed (v) [mph]	Distance	
	Reaction (d_r) [m]	Braking (d_b) [m]
20	6	6
30	9	14
40	12	24
50	15	38
60	18	55
70	21	75

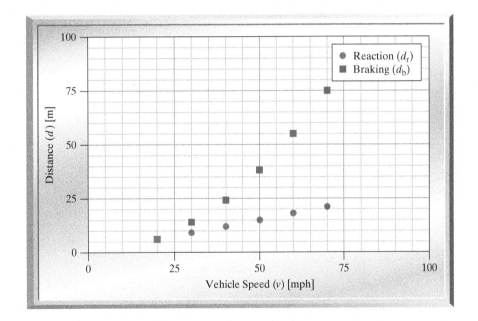

Figure 11-8 At various speeds, the necessary reaction time and braking time needed to stop a car.

● **EXAMPLE 11-2**

Ohm's law describes the relationship between voltage, current, and resistance within an electrical circuit, given by the equation $V = IR$, where V is the voltage [V], I is the current [A], and R is the resistance [Ω]. Construct a proper plot of the theoretical voltage on the ordinate versus current, determined from the equation, for the following resistors: 3,000 Ω, 2,000 Ω, and 1,000 Ω. Allow the current to vary from 0 to 0.05 A.

Note that while the lines were probably generated from several actual points along each line for each resistor, the points are not shown; only the resulting line is shown since the values were developed from theory and not from experiment. If you create a plot like this by hand, you would first put in a few points per data set, then draw the lines and erase the points so that they are not shown on the final graph.

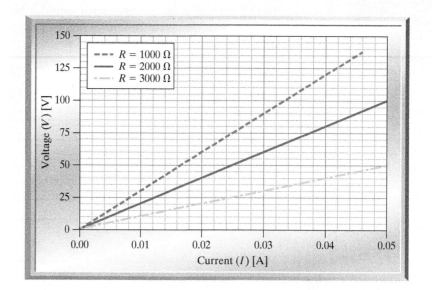

Figure 11-9 Ohm's law determined for a simple circuit to compare three resistor values.

COMPREHENSION CHECK 11-1

In the following experimental data plot, identify violations of the proper plot rules.

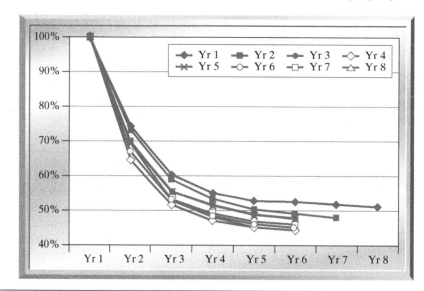

COMPREHENSION CHECK 11-2

In the following experimental data plot, identify violations of the proper plot rules.

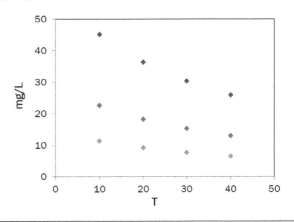

COMPREHENSION CHECK 11-3

In the following theoretical data plot, identify violations of the proper plot rules.

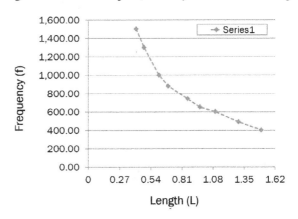

COMPREHENSION CHECK 11-4

In the following theoretical data plot, identify violations of the proper plot rules.

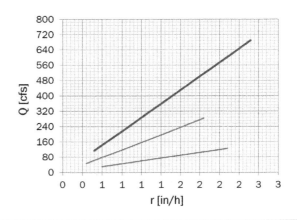

11.3   AVAILABLE GRAPH TYPES IN EXCEL

LEARN TO: Recognize the different types of graph available in Excel, and when to use each type
Understand the difference between a scatter plot and a line plot
Understand the concept of categorical data

The following is an example of the level of knowledge of Excel needed to proceed. *If you are not able to quickly recreate the following exercise in Excel, please review graphing basics in the appendix materials online before proceeding.*

Two graphs are given here; they describe the draining of tanks through an orifice in the bottom. When the tank contains a lot of liquid, the pressure on the bottom is large and the tank empties at a higher rate than when there is less liquid. The first graph shows actual data obtained from two different tanks. These data are given in the table below. The second plot shows curves (developed from theoretical equations) for two tanks. The equations for these curves are also given. Create these graphs exactly as shown, with matching legend, axis limits, gridlines, axis labels, symbol and line types and colors.

Experimental data for first graph:

Time (t) [min]	5	10	15	20	40	55	90
Volume Tank #1 (V1) [gal]	19.0	17.0	15.5	11.5	10.5	9.5	8.0

Time (t) [min]	10	15	20	30	35	40	90
Volume Tank #2 (V2) [gal]	25	21	20	19	17	16	14

Theoretical equations for second graph (with t in minutes):

- Tank 1: Volume remaining in tank 1 [gal] $V = 33\, t^{-0.31}$
- Tank 2: Volume remaining in tank 2 [gal] $V = 44\, t^{-0.26}$

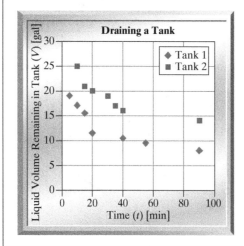
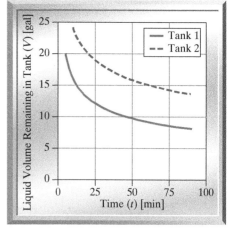

You can create many different types of charts in Excel. Usually, you will only be concerned with a few main types, shown in Table 11-1.

Table 11-1 Common chart types available in Excel

A **scatter plot** is a graph that numerically represents two-dimensional (2-D) theoretical or experimental data along the abscissa and ordinate of the graph. It is most commonly used with scientific data. To create a scatter plot, you specify each pair in the graph by selecting two identically sized columns or rows of data that represent the (x, y) values of each experimental symbol or point on a theoretical expression.

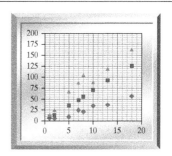

A scatter plot can be shown as discrete data points (used to show experimental data) or lines (used to show theoretical expressions). Excel will also show discrete data points connected by lines; the authors of this text do not find this type of chart particularly useful and do not discuss this type of chart.

The step size of both axes is evenly spaced as determined by the user and can be customized to show all or part of a data set plotted on a graph.

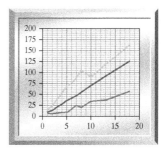

Use a scatter plot to visualize your data when you want to:

- Observe mathematical phenomena and relationships among different data sets
- Interpolate or extrapolate information from data sets
- Determine a mathematical model for a data set, using trendlines

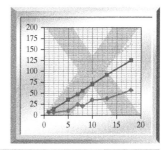

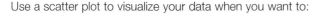

A **line plot** is a graph that visualizes a one-dimensional (1-D) set of theoretical or experimental data.

A line plot can be shown as points connected by lines, lines only, or in three dimensions (3-D).

The y-axis values of a line plot are spaced as determined by the user; however, the x-axis of a line plot is not. As shown in the graphs to the right, a line plot places each discrete element evenly along the x-axis regardless of the actual step-spacing of the data.

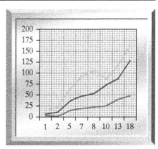

Use a line plot to visualize your data when you want to:

- Display any evenly spaced data
- Visualize time-series data taken at even intervals
- Display categorical data (e.g., years, months, days of the week)

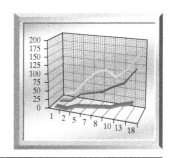

(continued)

Table 11-1 **Common chart types available in Excel (*continued*)**

A **column graph** is used for displaying various types of categorical data.

The y-axis increments are spaced evenly, but the x-axis spacing has no meaning since the items are discrete categories. As a rule of thumb, a column graph can be used to represent the same information shown on a line plot.

A column plot can be shown as bars, cylinders, or cones; as a clustered group or stacked; or in 1-D or 3-D.

Use a column graph to visualize your data when you want to:

- Display any categorical data
- Observe differences between categories

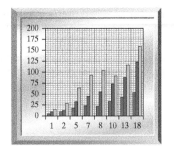

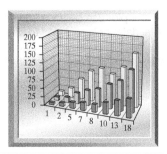

A **bar graph** is identical to a column graph, with the x- and y-categories reversed; the x-category appears on the ordinate and the y-category appears on the abscissa. Because of the similarity, only column graphs are covered in this text.

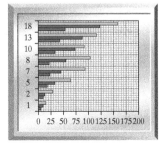

A **pie graph** is used on a single column or row of nonnegative numbers, graphed as a percentage of the whole. It is typically used for categorical data, with a maximum of seven categories possible.

A pie graph can be shown in 1-D or 3-D, with either the percentages or the raw data displayed with the category names.

Use a pie graph to visualize your data when you want to:

- Display categorical data as part of a whole
- Observe differences between categories

Pie charts are similar in form to column and bar charts; they are not covered in this text.

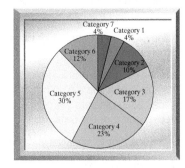

11.4 GRAPH INTERPRETATION

LEARN TO: Calculate the area under a curve and describe its meaning
Calculate the slope of a line and describe its meaning
Understand the technical terms derivative and integral, with respect to graph interpretation

A graph conveys a great deal of information in a small amount of space. By being able to interpret a graph, you can infer the story behind the lines. In addition to the value of the slope of the line, the shape of the line contains useful information.

● **EXAMPLE 11-3**

Hourglass. *Courtesy of Thayer's Gifts, Greenwood, SC. Photo: W. Park*

Assume your company is designing a series of hourglasses for the novelty market, such as tourist attraction sales. You have determined that your prototype hourglass allows 275 cubic millimeters of sand to fall from the top to the bottom chamber each second. What volume of sand would be needed if the "hourglass" really measured a period of 10 minutes?

There are 60 seconds per minute, thus 10 minutes is 600 seconds. The sand flows at a rate of 275 cubic millimeters per second for 600 seconds, thus the total volume of sand is 165,000 cubic millimeters.

$$(275 \text{ mm}^3/\text{s})(600 \text{ s}) = 165,000 \text{ mm}^3 \text{ or } 165 \text{ cm}^3$$

Let us consider the same problem graphically. Since the flow rate of sand is constant, a graph of flow rate with respect to time is simply a horizontal line. Now consider the area under the flow rate line. The area of a rectangle is simply the width times the height. If we make a point of using the units on each axis as well as the numeric values, we get

$$((275-0) \text{ mm}^3/\text{s})((10-0) \text{ min*}60 \text{ s/min}) = (275 \text{ mm}^3/\text{s})(600 \text{ s}) = 165,000 \text{ mm}^3$$

This is exactly the same result we got above. In other words, the volume of sand is the area under the line.

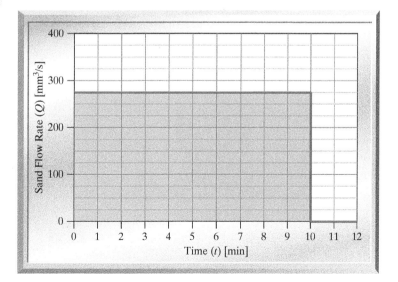

Figure 11-10 Sand in an hourglass.

This seems like much more effort than the straightforward calculation we did originally, so why should we bother with the graph? Let us look at a slightly more complicated situation.

● **EXAMPLE 11-4**

Assume a container is being filled with sand. Initially, the sand enters the container at 100 grams per second, but the rate of filling decreases linearly for 20 seconds, then stops. The final rate of sand into the container just before it stops is 25 grams per second. How much sand enters the container during the 20 seconds involved?

NOTE

When discussing a rate of mass per time, such as grams per second, the quantity is referred to as the **mass flow rate**, symbolized by $\dot{m}$. When discussing a rate of volume per time, such as gallons per minute [gpm], this quantity is referred to as **volumetric flow rate**, symbolized by Q.

Let us compute the area under the line shown in Figure 11-11, being sure to include units, and see what we get. We can break this area into a rectangle and a triangle, which will make the calculation a bit easier.

■ *The area of the rectangle at the base (below $\dot{m} = 25$) is ((25−0) grams/second) ((20−0) seconds) = 500 grams.*
■ *The area of the triangle is 0.5 ((100−25) grams per second) ((20−0) seconds) = 750 grams.*
■ *The total area is 1,250 grams, the total mass of sand in the container after 20 seconds.*

Again, many of you have realized that there is a much easier way to obtain this result. Simply find the average flow rate (in this case: 62.5 grams per second) and multiply by the total time.

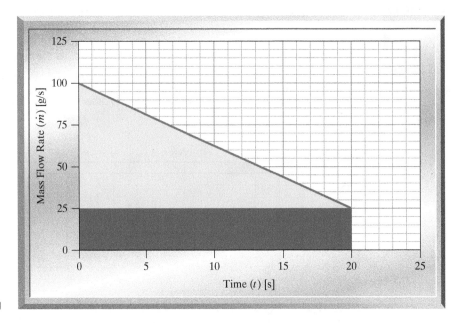

Figure 11-11

However, what if the parameter plotted on the vertical axis was not a simple straight line? Consider the following example.

● **EXAMPLE 11-5**   What if the parameter plotted on the vertical axis was not a simple straight line or straight-line segments? For example, the flow rate of liquid out of a pipe at the bottom of a cylindrical barrel follows an exponential relationship. Assume the flow rate out of a tank is given by $Q = 4\,e^{-t/8}$ gallons per minute. A graph of this is shown in Figure 11-12.

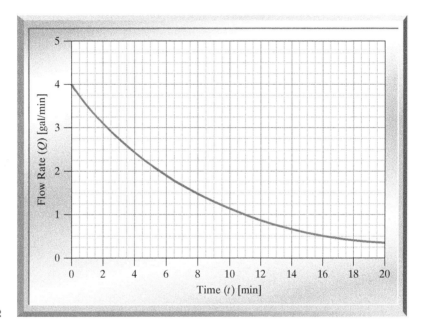

Figure 11-12

Although we might be able to make a reasonable estimate of the area under the curve (the total volume of water that has flowed out of the tank) simple algebra is insufficient to arrive at an accurate value. Those of you who have already studied integral calculus should know how to solve this problem. However, some students using this text may not have progressed this far in math, so we will have to leave it at that. It is enough to point out that there are innumerable problems in many engineering contexts that require calculus to solve. To succeed in engineering, you must have a basic understanding of calculus.

● **EXAMPLE 11-6**

From the past experience of driving an automobile down a highway, you should understand the concepts relating acceleration, velocity, and distance. As you slowly press the gas pedal toward the floor, the car accelerates, causing both the speed and the distance to increase. Once you reach a cruising speed, you turn on the cruise control. Now, the car is no longer accelerating and travels at a constant velocity while increasing in distance. These quantities are related through the following equations:

$$\text{velocity} = (\text{acceleration})(\text{time}) \quad v = (a)(t)$$
$$\text{distance} = (\text{velocity})(\text{time}) \quad\quad d = (v)(t)$$

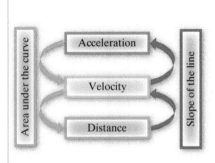

If we create a graph of velocity versus time, the form of the equation tells us that acceleration is the slope of the line. Likewise, a graph of distance versus time has velocity as the slope of the line.

However, if we had a graph of velocity versus time and we wanted to determine distance, how can we do this? The distance is determined by how fast we are traveling times how long we are traveling at that velocity; we can find this by determining the area under the curve of velocity versus time. Likewise, if we had a graph of acceleration versus time, we could determine the velocity from the area under the curve. In technical terms, the quantity determined by the slope is referred to as the **derivative**; the quantity determined by the area under the curve is referred to as the **integral**.

In the graph shown in Figure 11-13, we drive our car along the road at a constant velocity of 60 miles per hour [mph]. After 1.5 hours, how far have we traveled?

The area under the curve, shown by the rectangular box, is:

$$\text{Area of the rectangle} = (\text{height of rectangle})(\text{width of rectangle})$$
$$= (60 - 0\,mph)(1.5 - 0\,h)$$
$$= 90\,miles$$

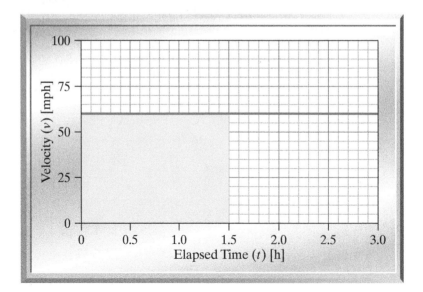

Figure 11-13 Example of distance calculation from area under velocity versus time graph.

**COMPREHENSION
CHECK** 11-5

Use the graph to answer the following questions.

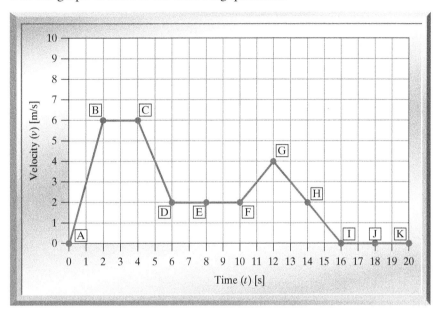

(a) What is the distance traveled by the vehicle when it reaches point C?
(b) What is the distance traveled by the vehicle when it reaches point F?

11.5 MEANING OF LINE SHAPES

LEARN TO: Recognize linear and non-linear curves, and interpret the slope and area of the curve
Understand the special linear cases, vertical lines and horizontal lines
Understand the physical meanings of the four combinations of curves with concavity

In addition to the value of the slope of the line, the shape of the line contains useful information. In Figure 11-13, the speed is shown as a horizontal line. This implies that it has a constant value; it is not changing over time. The slope of this line is zero, indicating that the acceleration is zero. Table 11-2 contains the various types of curve shapes and their physical meanings.

Table 11-2 What do the lines on a graph mean?

If the graph shows a . . .	. . . it means that the dependent variable . . .	Sketch
horizontal line	The variable is not changing. The slope (the derivative) is zero. The area under the curve (the integral) is increasing at a constant rate.	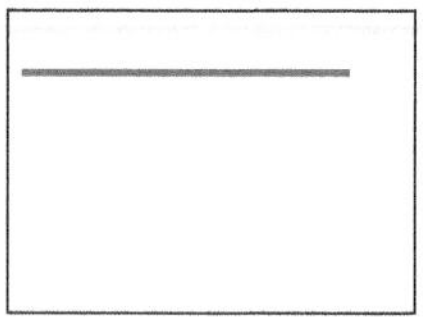
vertical line	The variable has changed "instantaneously." The slope (the derivative) is "undefined" (infinite). The area under the curve is undefined (zero).	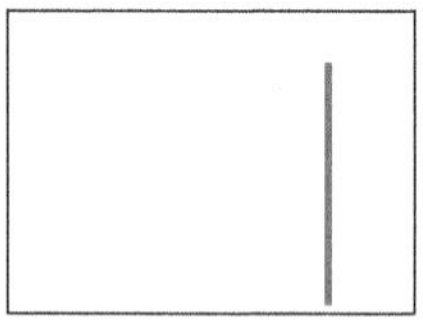
straight line, positive or negative slope neither horizontal nor vertical	The variable is changing at a constant rate. The slope (the derivative) is constant and non-zero. The area under the line (the integral) is increasing. If the slope is positive, the rate of increase is increasing. If the slope is negative, the rate of increase is decreasing. If the negative slope line goes below zero, the area will begin to decrease.	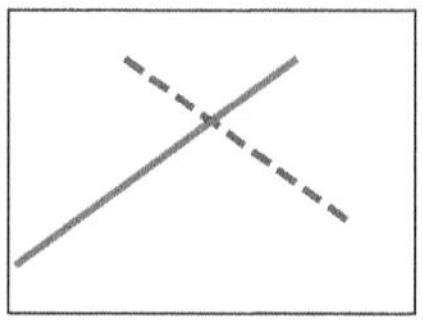
curved line concave up, increasing trend	The variable is increasing at an increasing rate. The slope of the curve (the derivative) is positive and increasing. The area under the curve (the integral) is increasing at an increasing rate.	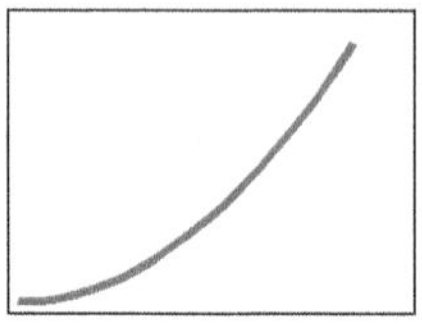
curved line concave down, increasing trend	The variable is increasing at a decreasing rate. The slope of the curve (the derivative) is positive and decreasing. The area under the curve (the integral) is increasing at an increasing rate.	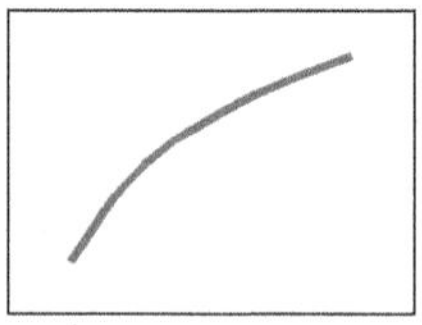
curved line concave up, decreasing trend	The variable is decreasing at a decreasing rate. The slope of the curve (the derivative) is negative with a decreasing magnitude. The area under the curve (the integral) is increasing at a decreasing rate.	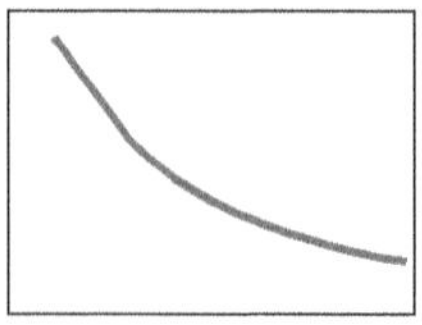
curved line concave down, decreasing trend	The variable is decreasing at an increasing rate. The slope of the curve (the derivative) is negative with an increasing magnitude. The area under the curve (the integral) is increasing at a decreasing rate.	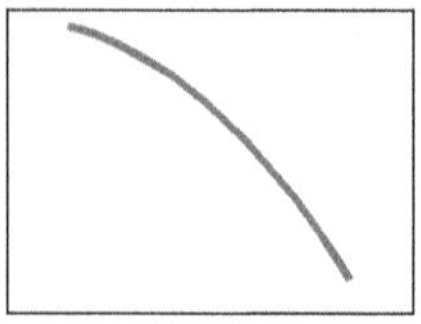

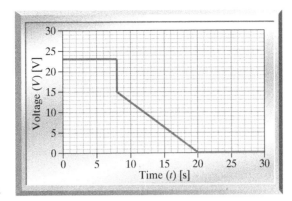

Figure 11-14

In Figure 11-14, the voltage is constant from time = 0 to 8 seconds, as indicated by the horizontal line at 23 volts. At time = 8 seconds, the voltage changes instantly to 15 volts, as indicated by the vertical line. Between time = 8 seconds and 20 seconds, the voltage decreases at a constant rate, as indicated by the straight line, and reaches 0 volts at time = 20 seconds, where it remains constant.

In Figure 11-15, the force on the spring increases at an increasing rate from time = 0 until 2 minutes, then remains constant for 1 minute, after which it increases at a decreasing rate until time = 5 minutes. After 5 minutes, the force remains constant at about 6.8 newtons.

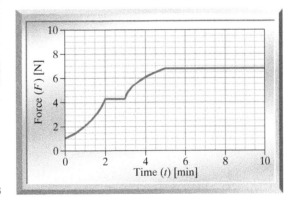

Figure 11-15

The height of a blimp is shown in Figure 11-16. The height decreases at an increasing rate for 5 minutes, then remains constant for 2 minutes. From time = 7 to 10 minutes, its height decreases at a decreasing rate. At time = 10 minutes, the height remains constant at 10 meters.

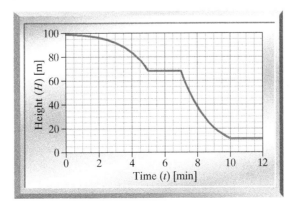

Figure 11-16

● **EXAMPLE 11-7**   The Mars Rover travels slowly across the Martian terrain collecting data, yielding the following velocity profile. Use this graph to answer the following questions.

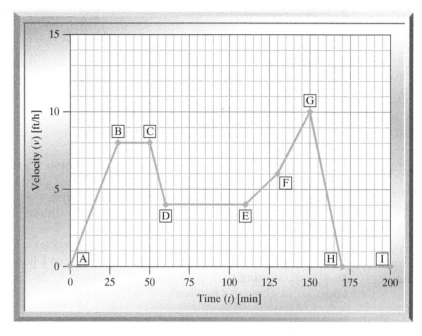

Figure 11-17

Between points (D) and (E), the acceleration of the Rover is _____.

The velocity profile between points (D) and (E) is flat, indicating that the velocity is not changing. Acceleration is the derivative of velocity with respect to time; so acceleration is ZERO.

If the graph shows a . . .	. . . it means that the dependent variable . . .	Sketch
horizontal line	The variable is not changing. The slope (the derivative) is zero. The area under the curve (the integral) is increasing at a constant rate.	

The value of acceleration of the Rover between points (G) and (H) is _____ ft/h².

Acceleration is the slope of the line of the velocity versus time graph. The slope between (G) and (H) is found by:

$$((10-0)\ ft/h)/(((170-150)\ min)*60\ min/h) = 30\ ft/h^2$$

Between points (E) and (F), the distance traveled by the Rover is _____.

The velocity profile between points (E) and (F) is increasing at a constant rate. Distance is the integral of velocity with respect to time; so the distance is INCREASING at an INCREASING rate.

If the graph shows a . . .	. . . it means that the dependent variable . . .	Sketch
straight line, positive or negative slope neither horizontal nor vertical	The variable is changing at a constant rate. The slope (the derivative) is constant and non-zero.	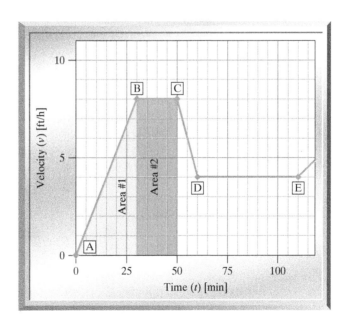
	The area under the line (the integral) is increasing. If the slope is positive, the rate of increase is increasing.	

The distance the Rover has traveled from the start of the trip to point (C) is _____ ft.

Distance is the area under the curve of the velocity versus time graph. The area defined from point (A) to point (C) can be divided into two geometric shapes:

From (A) to (B) = Area is a Triangle = 1/2 base * height
Area #1 = 1/2 (8−0) ft/h* (30−0) min* 1h/60 min = 2 ft

From (B) to (C) = Area is a Rectangle = base * height
Area #2 = (8−0) ft/h* (50−30) min * 1h/60 min = 2.67 ft

Total distance = Area #1 + Area #2 = 2 ft + 2.67 ft = 4.67 ft

Figure 11-18

COMPREHENSION CHECK 11-6

Use the graph to answer the following questions. Choose from the following answers:

1. Zero
2. Positive and constant
3. Positive and increasing
4. Positive and decreasing
5. Negative and constant
6. Negative with increasing magnitude
7. Negative with decreasing magnitude
8. Cannot be determined from information given

NOTE

The rate of change (derivative) of acceleration is called JERK.

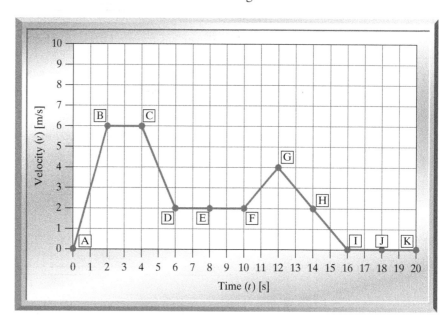

(a) Between points (A) and (B), the acceleration is ____
(b) Between points (B) and (C), the acceleration is ____
(c) Between points (C) and (D), the acceleration is ____
(d) Between points (D) and (E), the distance is ____
(e) Between points (F) and (G), the distance is ____
(f) Between points (G) and (H), the distance is ____

11.6 GRAPHICAL SOLUTIONS

LEARN TO: Use a graph of expressions to identify the overlapping points
Show fixed costs, variable cost, sales price, revenue, and profit graphically
Identify the breakeven point of an economic process (if one exists)

When you have two equations containing the same two variables, it is sometimes desirable to find values of the variables that satisfy both equations. Most of you have studied methods for solving simultaneous linear equations—however, most of these methods apply only to linear equations and do not work if one or both of the equations is nonlinear. It also becomes problematic if you are working with experimental data.

For systems of two equations, or data sets in two variables, you can use a graphical method to determine the value or values that satisfy both. The procedure is simply to graph the two equations and visually determine where the curves intersect. This may be nowhere, at one point, or at several points.

● EXAMPLE 11-8

We assume that the current through two electromagnets is given by the following equations

$$\text{Electromagnet A: } I = 5t + 6$$
$$\text{Electromagnet B: } I = -3t + 12$$

We want to determine when the value of the current through the electromagnets is equal.

Graphing both equations gives Figure 11-19. Recall that data derived from a theoretical equation is shown as lines only, without any points.

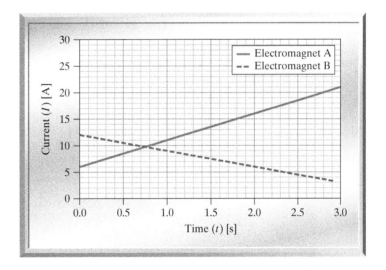

Figure 11-19

The two lines cross at time 0.75 seconds (approximately), and the current at this time is approximately 9.7 amperes. The larger we make this graph and the more gridlines we include, the more accurately we can determine the solution.

Solution: t = 0.75 seconds, I = 9.7 amperes.

Using Graphs in Economic Analysis

Breakeven analysis determines the quantity of product a company must make before they begin to earn a profit. Two types of costs are associated with manufacturing: fixed and variable. **Fixed costs** include equipment purchases, nonhourly employee salaries, insurance, mortgage or rent on the building, etc., or "money we must spend just to open the doors." **Variable costs** depend on the production volume, such as material costs, hourly employee salaries, and utility costs. The more product produced, the higher the variable costs become.

Total cost = Fixed cost + Variable cost * Amount produced

The product is sold at a **selling price**, creating **revenue**.

Revenue = Selling price * Amount sold

Any excess revenue remaining after all production costs have been paid is **profit**. Until the company reaches the breakeven point, they are operating at a **loss** (negative profit), where the money they are bringing in from sales does not cover their expenses.

Profit = Revenue − Total cost

The **breakeven point** occurs when the revenue and total cost lines cross, or the point where profit is zero (not negative or positive). These concepts are perhaps best illustrated through an example.

● EXAMPLE 11-9

Let the amount of product we produce be G [gallons per year]. Consider the following costs:

- Fixed cost: $1 million
- Variable cost: 10 cents/gallon of G
- Selling price: 25 cents/gallon of G

Plot the total cost and the revenue versus the quantity produced. Determine the amount of G that must be produced to breakeven. Assume we sell everything we make.

The plot of these two functions is shown in Figure 11-20. The breakeven point occurs when the two graphs cross, at a production capacity of 6.7 million gallons of G.

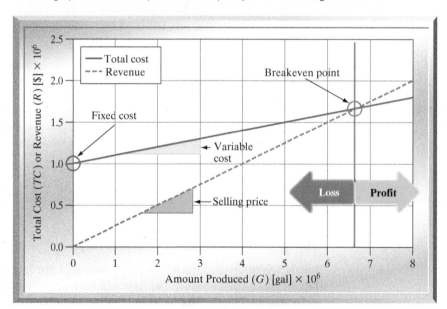

Figure 11-20 Breakeven analysis definitions.

● EXAMPLE 11-10

In creating electrical parts for a Mars excursion module, you anticipate the costs of production shown in the graph. In your analysis, you assume the following costs of production:

- Labor cost = $1.20 / part
- Energy cost = $0.60 / part

Use this graph to answer the following questions.

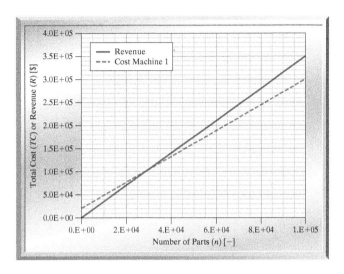

Figure 11-21

What is the material cost per part?

Variable cost is the slope of the total cost line.
*Total cost = Fixed cost + Variable cost * Amount produced*

$$Slope\ total\ cost = \frac{3E5 - 2E4}{1E5 - 0} = \frac{\$2.80}{part}$$

The material cost is one of three costs that make up the variable cost.
Variable cost = Material cost + Labor cost + Energy cost
Solving for Material cost:

$$Material\ cost = \frac{\$2.80}{part} - \frac{\$1.20}{part} - \frac{\$0.60}{part} = \frac{\$1.00}{part}$$

What is the selling price of each part?

Selling price is the slope of the revenue line.
*Revenue = Selling price * Amount sold*

$$Slope\ revenue = \frac{3.5E5 - 0}{1E5 - 0} = \frac{\$3.50}{part}$$

You decide to consider a second option, with a fixed cost of $50,000 and a variable cost of $2.00 / part. Draw the total cost line for Machine #2 on the graph.

To draw the total cost line, two points are needed if the line is linear.
At n = 0 parts, the total cost = fixed cost = $50,000.
At n = 100,000 parts,
the total cost = $50,000 + ($2.00/part) (100,000 parts) = $250,000.

To ensure the line is linear, it is a good idea to test at least one more point to make sure if falls along this line.

At n = 40,000 parts,
the total cost = $50,000 + ($2.00/part)(40,000 parts) = $130,000.

Connecting a line through these points yields the green, dot-dash line shown below.

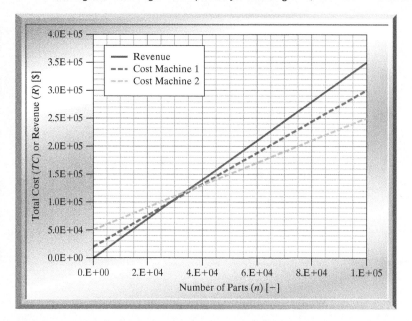

Figure 11-22

What is the profit of each machine at 80,000 parts?

Profit is the difference between the cost and revenue lines. If the cost line is above the revenue line, the process is operating at a loss. If the cost line is below the revenue line, the process is operating at a profit. Examining the graph at 80,000 parts, both cost lines are below the revenue line, so both machines are operating at a profit.

The difference for Machine 1 is 4 minor gridlines. Each ordinate minor gridline on the graph is $1E4. The profit for Machine 1 is $40,000.

The difference for Machine 2 is 7 minor gridlines. The profit for Machine 2 is $70,000.

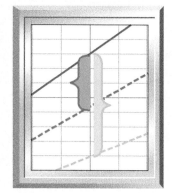

Figure 11-23

If the selling price is decreased by $0.50 per part, what will happen to the breakeven point for Machine #1?

(A) It will move to the left, indicating the breakeven will occur sooner than originally shown

(B) It will move to the right, indicating the breakeven will occur later than originally shown

(C) It will not change the breakeven point

In the revenue line, the larger the slope, the higher the angle of line, the higher the selling price. A decrease in selling price translates graphically to a slope at a lower angle. If the slope of the revenue line decreases, the number of parts required to breakeven will increase, shifting the breakeven point to the right.

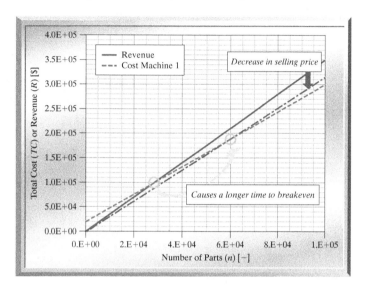

Figure 11-24

COMPREHENSION CHECK 11-7

You are working for a tire manufacturer, producing wire to be used in the tire as a strengthening agent. You are considering implementing a new machining system, and you must present a breakeven analysis to your boss. You develop the graph, showing two possible machines that you can buy.

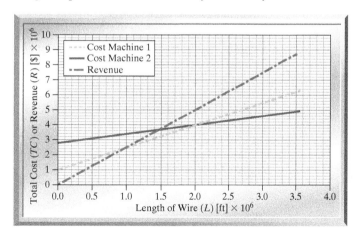

(a) Which machine has a higher fixed cost?
(b) Which machine has a lower variable cost?
(c) How much wire must be produced on Machine 1 to breakeven?
(d) If you make 3 million feet of wire, which machine will yield the highest profit?
(e) Which machine has the lower breakeven point?

You want to install a solar panel system on your home. According to one source, if you install a 40-square foot system, the cost curve is shown in the graph.

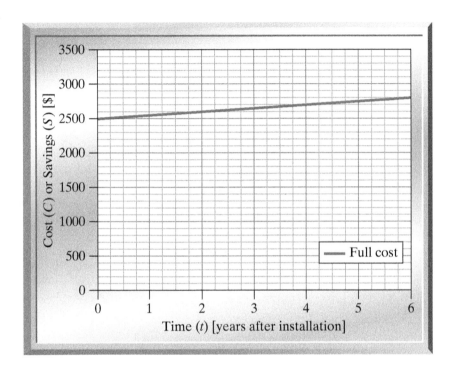

(a) List the fixed cost and the variable cost for this system.

(b) If the source claims that you can breakeven in 3.5 years, how much savings are you generating per year (or, what is the slope of the savings curve or the "revenue" that you generate by installing the system)? Draw the "revenue" curve on the graph and use it to answer this question.

(c) If you receive a Federal Tax Credit for "going green," you can save 30% on the initial fixed cost. With this savings, how long does it take to breakeven? Draw this operating cost curve, labeled "Credit Cost" on the graph and use it to answer this question.

(d) With the new tax credit, at what time do you reach a savings of $1000?

● **EXAMPLE 11-11**

The semiconductor diode is sort of like a one-way valve for electric current: it allows current to flow in one direction, but not the other. In reality, the behavior of a diode is considerably more complicated. In general, the current through a diode can be found with the **Shockley equation**,

$$I = I_0 \left(e^{\frac{V_D}{nV_T}} - 1 \right)$$

where I is the current through the diode in amperes; I_0 is the saturation current in amperes, constant for any specific diode; V_D is the voltage across the diode in volts; and V_T is the thermal voltage in volts, approximately 0.026 volts at room temperature. The emission coefficient, n, is dimensionless and constant for any specific diode; it usually has a value between 1 and 2.

The simple circuit shown has a diode and resistor connected to a battery. For this circuit, the current through the resistor can be given by:

$$I = \frac{V - V_D}{R}$$

where I is the current through the resistor in milliamperes [mA], V is the battery voltage in volts [V], V_D is the voltage across the diode in volts, and R is the resistance in ohms [Ω].

In this circuit, the diode and resistor are in series, which implies that the current through them is the same. We have two equations for the same parameter (current), both of which are a function of the same parameter (diode voltage). We can find a solution to these two equations, and thus the current in the circuit, by graphing both equations and finding the point of intersection. For convenience of scale, the current is expressed in milliamperes rather than amperes.

Plot these two equations for the following values and determine the current.

$$I_0 = 0.01 \text{ mA}$$
$$V = 3 \text{ V}$$
$$R = 24 \text{ }\Omega$$
$$nV_T = 0.04 \text{ V}$$

NOTE

This example demonstrates the graphical solution of simultaneous equations when one of the equations is nonlinear. We do not expect you to know how to perform the involved circuit analyses. Those of you who eventually study electronics will learn these techniques in considerable detail.

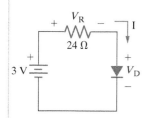

The point of intersection shown in Figure 11-25 is at $V_D = 0.64$ V and $I = 100$ mA; thus, the current in the circuit is 100 mA or 0.1 A.

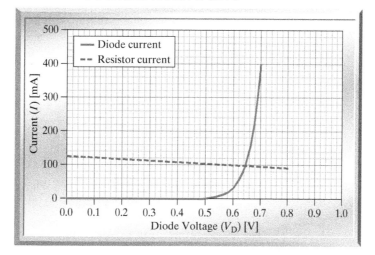

Figure 11-25

In-Class Activities

For questions ICA 11-1 to ICA 11-9, your instructor will determine if you should complete this question by hand or using Excel. If you must complete this problem by hand, a blank graph has been provided online.

ICA 11-1

Joule's first law relates the heat generated to current flowing in a conductor. It is named after James Prescott Joule, the same person for whom the unit of Joule is named. Use the following experimental data to create a scatter graph of the power (P, on the ordinate) and current (I, on the abscissa).

Current (I) [A]	0.50	1.25	1.50	2.25	3.00	3.20	3.50
Power (P) [W]	1.20	7.50	11.25	25.00	45.00	50.00	65.00

ICA 11-2

Data for a wind turbine is shown below. Use the following experimental data to create a scatter plot of the power (P, on the ordinate) and velocity (v, on the abscissa).

Velocity (v) [m/s]	5	8	12	15	19	23
Power (P) [W]	15	60	180	400	840	1500

ICA 11-3

There is a large push in the United States currently to convert from incandescent light bulbs to compact fluorescent bulbs (CFLs). The lumen [lm] is the SI unit of luminous flux (LF), a measure of the perceived power of light. To test the power usage, you run an experiment and measure the following data. Create a proper plot of these experimental data, with electrical consumption (EC) on the ordinate and LF on the abscissa.

	Electrical Consumption [W]	
Luminous Flux [lm]	Incandescent 120 V	Compact Fluorescent
80	16	
200		4
400	38	8
600	55	
750	68	13
1,250		18
1,400	105	19

ICA 11-4

Your team has designed three tennis ball launchers, and you have run tests to determine which launcher best meets the project criteria. Each launcher is set to three different launch angles, and the total distance the ball flies through the air is recorded. These experimental data are summarized in the table. Plot all three sets of data on a scatter plot, showing one data set for each of the three launchers on a single graph. Launch angle should be plotted on the horizontal axis.

Launcher 1		Launcher 2		Launcher 3	
Launch Angle (θ) [°]	Distance (d) [ft]	Launch Angle (θ) [°]	Distance (d) [ft]	Launch Angle (θ) [°]	Distance (d) [ft]
20	5	10	10	20	10
35	10	45	25	40	20
55	12	55	18	50	15

ICA 11-5

Plot the following pairs of functions on a single graph. The independent variable (angle) should vary from 0 to 360 degrees on the horizontal axis.

(a) $\sin \theta, -2 \sin \theta$ **(c)** $\sin \theta, \sin \theta + 2$

(b) $\sin \theta, \sin 2\theta$ **(d)** $\sin \theta, \sin (\theta + 90)$

ICA 11-6

Plot the following pairs of functions on a single graph. The independent variable (angle) should vary from 0 to 360 degrees on the horizontal axis.

(a) $\cos \theta, \cos 3\theta$ **(c)** $\cos \theta, \cos (2\theta) + 1$

(b) $\cos \theta, \cos \theta - 3$ **(d)** $\cos \theta, 3 \cos (2\theta) - 2$

ICA 11-7

You need to create a graph showing the relationship of an ideal gas between pressure (P) and temperature (T). The ideal gas law relationship: $PV = nRT$. The ideal gas constant (R) is 0.08206 atmosphere liter per mole kelvin. Assume the tank has a volume (V) of 12 liters and is filled with nitrogen. The initial temperature (T) is 270 kelvin and the initial pressure (P) is 2.5 atmospheres. First, determine the number of moles of gas (n). Then, create a graph to model the gas as the temperature increases from 270 to 350 kelvin.

ICA 11-8

The decay of a radioactive isotope can be modeled using the following equation, where C_0 is the initial amount of the element at time zero and k is the half-life of the isotope. Create a graph of the decay of Isotope A [$k = 1.48$ hours]. Allow time to vary on the abscissa from 0 to 5 hours with an initial concentration of 10 grams of Isotope A.

$$C = C_0 e^{-t/k}$$

ICA 11-9

In researching alternate energies, you find that wind power is calculated by the following equation:

$$P = \frac{1}{2} A \rho v^3$$

where

- P = power [watts]
- A = sweep area (circular) of the blades [square meters]
- ρ = air density [kilograms per cubic meter]
- v = velocity [meters per second]

The specific gravity of air is 0.00123 and the velocity is typically 35 meters per second. Create a graph of the theoretical power (P, in units of watts) as a function of the blade diameter (D, in units of meters). Allow the diameter to be graphed on the abscissa and vary from 0.5 to 1.5 meters. The following graph applies to ICA 11-10 to 11-13.

ICA 11-10

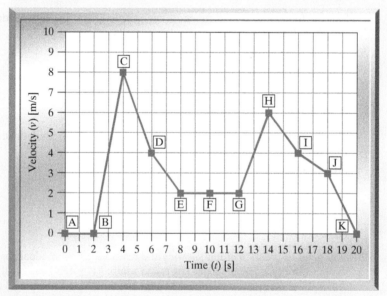

Answer the following questions using the graph. Choose from the following answers.

1. Zero
2. Positive and constant
3. Positive and increasing
4. Positive and decreasing
5. Negative and constant
6. Negative with increasing magnitude
7. Negative with decreasing magnitude
8. Cannot be determined from information given

(a) Between points (A) and (B), the acceleration is
(b) Between points (C) and (D), the acceleration is
(c) Between points (G) and (H), the acceleration is
(d) Between points (B) and (C), the distance is
(e) Between points (F) and (G), the distance is
(f) Between points (I) and (J), the distance is

ICA 11-11

Answer the following questions using the graph. Choose from the following answers.

1. Zero
2. Positive and constant
3. Positive and increasing
4. Positive and decreasing
5. Negative and constant
6. Negative with increasing magnitude
7. Negative with decreasing magnitude
8. Cannot be determined from information given

(a) Between points (B) and (C), the acceleration is
(b) Between points (F) and (G), the acceleration is
(c) Between points (I) and (J), the acceleration is
(d) Between points (A) and (B), the distance is
(e) Between points (C) and (D), the distance is
(f) Between points (G) and (H), the distance is

ICA 11-12

Use the graph to determine the following numerical values and appropriate units:

(a) Between points (A) and (B), the acceleration is
(b) Between points (I) and (J), the acceleration is
(c) At point (G), the total distance traveled is
(d) At point (K), the total distance traveled is

ICA 11-13

Use the graph to determine the following numerical values and appropriate units:

(a) Between points (C) and (D), the acceleration is
(b) Between points (F) and (G), the acceleration is
(c) At point (E), the total distance traveled is
(d) At point (I), the total distance traveled is

ICA 11-14

Use the graph on the next page to determine which statements about the two vehicles are true?

(a) At point B, the distance traveled by Vehicle 1 is equal to the distance traveled by Vehicle 2.
(b) At point B, the velocity of Vehicle 1 is equal to the velocity of Vehicle 2.
(c) The average acceleration of Vehicle 1 between points B and C is equal to the average acceleration of Vehicle 2 between points D and E.
(d) At point E, the distance traveled by Vehicle 1 is greater than the distance traveled by Vehicle 2.
(e) At point E, the velocity of Vehicle 1 is greater than the velocity of Vehicle 2.
(f) The average acceleration of Vehicle 1 between points E and F is greater than to the average acceleration of Vehicle 2 between points E and F.

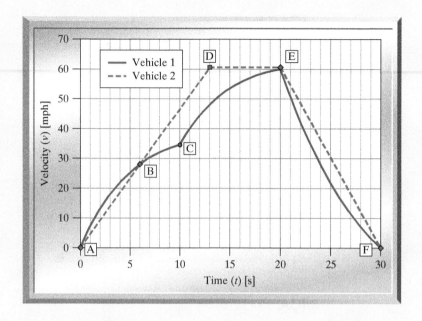

ICA 11-15

The graph shows the power delivered to a motor over a period of 50 seconds. The power gradually increases to 200 watts and then remains constant until the power is turned off at 50 seconds.

(a) What is the total energy absorbed by the motor during the 50 second period shown?

(b) What is the rate of change of power delivery during the first 10 seconds?

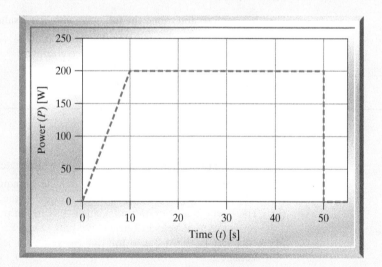

ICA 11-16

The music industry in the United States has had a great deal of fluctuation in profit over the past 20 years due to the advent of new technologies such as peer-to-peer file sharing and mobile devices such as the iPod and iPhone. The following graph displays data from a report published by eMarketer in 2009 about the amount U.S. consumers spend on digital music files and physical music formats (CDs, records, cassette tapes, etc.), where the values for 2009–2013 are reported as projections and for 2008 is reported using actual U.S. spending measurements.

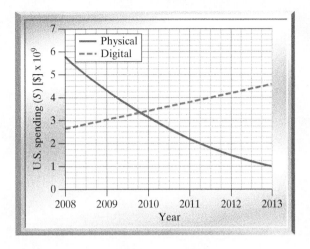

(a) According to the study, when will the sale of physical media be equivalent to the sale of digital audio files?

(b) When will the sales of digital audio files exceed that of physical media by $1 billion?

(c) If the physical media sales were $2 billion higher than the trend displayed on the graph, when would the sale of digital audio files exceed physical media?

(d) If the digital audio file sales were $1 billion lower than the trend displayed on the graph, when would the sale of digital audio files exceed physical media?

ICA 11-17

You are working for a chemical manufacturer, producing solvents used to clean lenses for microscopes. You are working on determining the properties of three different solvent blends. You develop the following chart, showing the evaporation of the three blends.

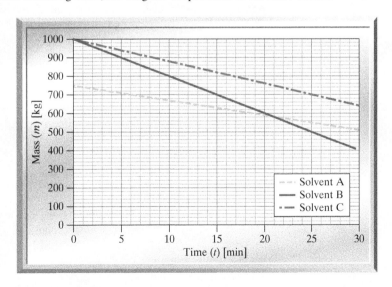

(a) Which solvent evaporates at the slowest rate?

(b) Which solvent evaporates at the fastest rate?

(c) What is the initial mass of Solvent A? Be sure to include units.

(d) What is the rate of solvent evaporation of Solvent A? Be sure to include units.

ICA 11-18

Use the accompanying graph to answer the following questions. Assume the company makes 30,000 parts per month of Product A and 17,500 parts per month of Product B.

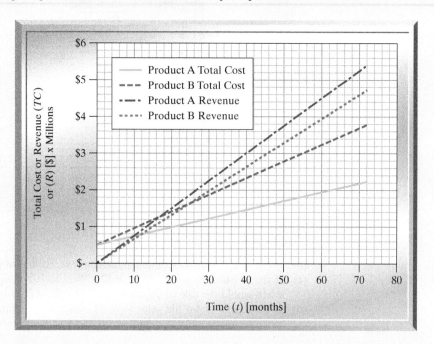

(a) Which product has the higher variable cost, and what is this value in units of dollars per part?

(b) Which product has the higher selling price, and what is this value in units of dollars per part?

(c) Which product has the faster breakeven time, and what is this value in units of months?

(d) At six years, which product makes more profit and what is this value in units of dollars?

(e) If the fixed cost of product B is increased to $1,000,000 and the selling price is increased by $0.75 / part, what is the new breakeven point in units of months?

ICA 11-19

A company designs submersible robots with a new design for the robots that increases the rate of production. A new facility for manufacturing the submersible robots is constructed at a cost of $100,000,000. A contract is negotiated with a materials supplier (Supplier A) to provide all of the raw material and construction labor necessary for $250 per robot. The robots will be sold for $500 each.

(a) How many robots must be manufactured and sold to breakeven?

(b) How many robots must be manufactured and sold to make a profit of $100,000,000?

(c) An alternative materials supplier (Supplier B) comes along with a quote for the labor and material cost at $400 per robot, but only requires $50,000,000 to build a submersible robot construction facility. How many robots must be manufactured and sold to breakeven for this alternative supplier?

(d) Which supplier will generate a profit of $20,000,000 with fewer robots produced?

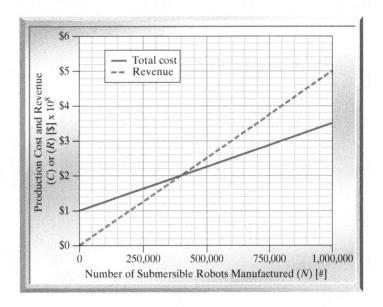

ICA 11-20

Your company is manufacturing a complex part from an advanced material. Assume the initial setup cost to manufacture these parts is $750,000, and each part costs $500 to make.

(a) Create a proper plot of this total cost curve, labeled "Cost Proposal A".

(b) If the company wishes to break even after selling 1,000 parts, sketch the revenue curve on the graph.

(c) What is the sales price per unit in this case?

(d) How many units must the company sell in order to make a profit of $500,000? Indicate this location on graph.

(e) The company is considering a change in the process to reduce the manufacturing cost by $100 per part, with the same fixed cost as Proposal A. Sketch the total cost curve for this situation, labeled "Cost Proposal B".

(f) What is the breakeven point for Cost Proposal B if the revenue curve remains the same for the new processing change? Indicate this location on the graph.

ICA 11-21

Using the list provided, you may be assigned a topic for which to create a graph. You must determine the parameters to graph and imagine a set of data to show on the chart. A blank grid has been provided below and online; you may use one of these grids, or use graph paper as directed by your instructor.

1. Air temperature
2. Airplane from airport to airport
3. Baking bread
4. Bird migration
5. Boiling water in a whistling teapot
6. Bouncing a basketball
7. Brushing your teeth
8. Burning a pile of leaves

9. Burning candle
10. Climbing a mountain
11. Cooking a Thanksgiving turkey
12. Daily electric power consumption
13. Detecting a submarine by using sonar
14. Diving into a swimming pool
15. Drag racing
16. Driving home from work

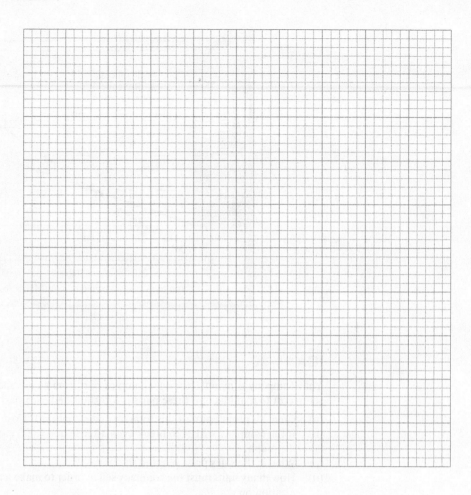

17. Dropping ice in a tub of warm water
18. Engineer's salary
19. Exercising
20. Feedback from an audio system
21. Fishing
22. Flight of a hot air balloon
23. Football game crowd
24. Formation of an icicle
25. A glass of water in a moving vehicle
26. Hammering nails
27. Leaves on a tree
28. Letting go of a helium balloon
29. Marching band
30. Moving a desk down a staircase
31. Oak tree over the years
32. Oil supply
33. Person growing up
34. Playing with a yo-yo
35. Plume from a smokestack
36. Pony Express
37. Popping corn
38. Pouring water out of a bottle

39. Power usage on campus
40. Pumping air into a bicycle tire
41. Rain filling a pond
42. Recycling
43. River in a rainstorm
44. Skipping a stone on water
45. Sleeping
46. Snoring
47. Snow blowing over a roof
48. Solar eclipse
49. Sound echoing in a canyon
50. Space station
51. Spinning a hula-hoop
52. Student attention span during class
53. Studying for an exam
54. The moon
55. Throwing a ball
56. Thunderstorm
57. Traffic at intersections
58. Train passing through town
59. Using a toaster
60. Washing clothes

ICA 11-22

Materials

Balloons (2)	Stopwatch (2)	String (40 inches)	Tape measure

Part I: Blowing Up a Balloon

One team member is to inflate one balloon, a second team member is to time the inhalation stage (how long it takes to inhale a single breath), and a third team member is to time the exhalation stage (how long it takes to exhale a single breath into the balloon). A fourth team member is to measure the balloon size at the end of each inhale/exhale cycle, using the string to measure the balloon circumference.

Record the observations on a worksheet similar to the following one for three complete inhale/exhale cycles or until the balloon appears to be close to maximum volume, whichever occurs first. Repeat the entire balloon inflation process for a second balloon; average the times from the balloons to obtain the time spent at each stage and the average circumference at each stage. Calculate the balloon volume at each stage, assuming the balloon is a perfect sphere.

Balloon	Stage	Inhale Time	Exhale Time	Circumference
1	1			
	2			
	3			
2	1			
	2			
	3			

	Stage	Inhale Time	Exhale Time	Circumference	Volume
Average Balloon	1				
	2				
	3				

Part II: Analysis

Graph the balloon volume (V, ordinate) versus time (t, time). A blank grid has been provided below and online; you may use one of these grids, or use graph paper as directed by your instructor. Allow the process to be continuous, although in reality it was stopped at various intervals for measurements. The resulting graph should contain only the time elapsed in the process of inhaling and exhaling, not the time required for recording the balloon size. For this procedure, assume that the air enters the balloon at a constant rate and the balloon is a perfect sphere.

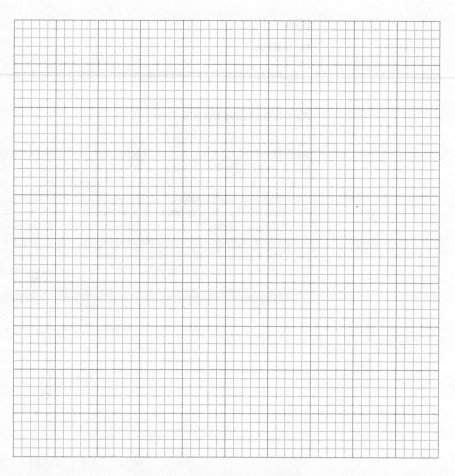

(a) What does the assumption of the air entering the balloon at a constant rate indicate about the slope?

(b) Calculate the following graphically.

- The rate at which the air enters the balloon in the first stage.
- The rate at which the air enters the balloon in the third stage.

(c) On the same graph, sketch the balloon volume (V, ordinate) versus time (t, time) if you were inflating a balloon that contained a pinhole leak.

(d) On the same graph, sketch the balloon volume (V, ordinate) versus time (t, time) if you were inflating a balloon from a helium tank.

Chapter 11 REVIEW QUESTIONS

For questions Review 11-1 to 11-10, your instructor will determine if you should complete this question by hand or using Excel. If you must complete this problem by hand, a blank graph has been provided online.

1. A computer engineer has measured the power dissipated as heat generated by a prototype microprocessor running at different clock speeds. Create a proper plot of the following experimental data set.

Speed (S) [GHz]	0.8	1.3	1.8	2.5	3.1
Power dissipated as heat (P) [W]	135	217	295	405	589

2. Due to increased demand, an industrial engineer is experimenting with increasing the speed (S) of a machine used in the production of widgets. The machine is normally rated to produce five widgets per second, and the engineer wants to know how many defective parts (D) are made at higher speeds, measured in defective parts per thousand. Create a proper plot of the following experimental data set.

Speed (S) [parts/min]	5.5	5.9	6.5	7.2	8.0
Defects in parts per thousand (D)	1	3	7	13	21

3. An engineer is conducting tests of two prototype toothbrush sanitizers that use ultraviolet radiation to kill pathogenic organisms while the toothbrush is stored. The engineer is trying to determine the minimum power needed to reliably kill pathogens on toothbrushes. Several toothbrushes are treated with a mix of bacteria, fungi, and viruses typically found in the human mouth, and then each is placed in one of the sanitizers for six hours at a specific power level (P). After six hours in the sanitizers, the viable pathogens remaining (R) on each toothbrush is assayed. Create a proper plot of the following experimental data set.

Power (P) [W]		10	18	25	40
Pathogens remaining (R) [%]	Sanitizer A	46	35	14	2
	Sanitizer B	58	41	21	7

4. Several reactions are carried out in a closed vessel. The following data are taken for the concentration (C) in units of grams per liter of solvent processed for compounds A and B as a function of time (t). Create a proper plot of the following experimental data set.

Time (t) [min]	Concentration [g/L]	
	A (C_A)	B (C_B)
36	0.145	0.160
65	0.120	0.155
100	0.100	0.150
160	0.080	0.140

5. The following experimental data are collected on the current (I, in units of milliamperes) in the positive direction and voltage (V, in units of volts) across the terminals of two different thermionic rectifiers. Create a proper plot of the following experimental data set.

| | Current (I) [mA] | |
Voltage (V) [V]	Rectifier A	Rectifier B
18	5	15
30	18	26
40	24	34
45	30	50

6. If an object is heated, the temperature of the body will increase. The energy (Q) associated with a change in temperature (ΔT) is a function of the mass of the object (m) and the specific heat (C_p). Specific heat is a material property, and values are available in literature. In an experiment, heat is applied to the end of an object, and the temperature change at the other end of the object is recorded. This leads to the theoretical relationship shown. An unknown material is tested in the lab, yielding the following results:

$$\Delta T = \frac{Q}{mC_p}$$

Heat applied (Q) [J]	12	17	25	40	50	58
Temp change (ΔT) [K]	1.50	2.00	3.25	5.00	6.25	7.00

Graph the experimental temperature change (ΔT, ordinate) versus the heat applied (Q).

7. Eutrophication is the result of excessive nutrients in a lake or other body of water, usually caused by runoff of nutrients (animal waste, fertilizers, and sewage) from the land, which causes a dense growth of plant life. The decomposition of the plants depletes the supply of oxygen, leading to the death of animal life. Sometimes, these excess nutrients cause an algae bloom— or rapid growth of algae, which normally occur in small concentrations in the water body.

The following table contains data to illustrate the relationship between pressure (depth of fluid), the temperature of the water, and the solubility of oxygen in the water. Create a proper plot of the data.

| Solubility of O_2 [mg/L] | Pressure (P) [mm Hg] | | |
Temperature (T) [°C]	760	1520	3040
10	11.3	22.6	45.1
20	9.1	18.2	36.4
30	7.6	15.2	30.3
40	6.5	12.9	25.9

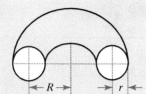

8. In the 1950s, a team at Los Alamos National Laboratories built several devices called "Perhapsatrons," thinking that PERHAPS they might be able to create controllable nuclear fusion. After several years of experiments, they were never able to maintain stable plasma and abandoned the project.

The perhapsatron used a toroidal (doughnut-shaped) plasma confinement chamber, similar to those used in more modern Tokamak fusion devices. You have taken a job at a fusion research lab, and your supervisor asks you to develop a simple spreadsheet to calculate the volume of a torus within which the plasma will be contained in a new experimental reactor.

(a) Create a table that calculates the volumes of various toruses with specific values for r and R. The tube radii (r) should range from 10 to 100 centimeters in increments of 10 centimeters. The torus radii (R) should range from 1.5 to 3 meters in increments of 0.5 meters. The volume of a torus can be determined using $V = 2\pi^2 R r^2$.

(b) Using the table of volumes, create a graph showing the relationship between volume (ordinate) and tube radius (r) for torus radii (R) of 2 and 3 meters.

(c) Using the table of volumes, create a graph showing the relationship between volume (ordinate) and torus radius (R) for tube radii (r) of 40, 70, and 100 centimeters.

9. Generally, when a car door is opened, the interior lights come on and turn off again when the door is closed. Some cars turn the interior lights on and off gradually. Suppose that you have a car with 25 watts of interior lights. When a door is opened, the power to the lights increases linearly from 0 to 25 watts over 2 seconds. When the door is closed, the power is reduced to zero in a linear fashion over 5 seconds.

(a) Create a proper plot of power (P, on the ordinate) and time (t).

(b) Using the graph, determine the total energy delivered to the interior lights if the door to the car is opened and then closed 10 seconds later.

10. One of the 22 named, derived units in the metric system is the volt, which can be expressed as 1 joule per coulomb ($V = J/C$). A coulomb is the total electric charge on approximately 6.24×10^{18} electrons. The voltage on a capacitor is given by $V = \Delta Q/C + V_0$ volts, where ΔQ is the change in charge [coulombs] stored, V_0 is the initial voltage on the capacitor, and C is the capacitance [farads].

(a) Create a proper plot of voltage (V, on the ordinate) and total charge (ΔQ) for a 5-farad capacitor with an initial voltage of 5 volts for $0 < \Delta Q < 20$.

(b) Using the graph, determine the total energy stored in the capacitor for an addition of 15 coulombs.

11. Below is a graph of the vertical position of a person bungee jumping, in meters. A copy of this graph has been provided online; you may use one of these graphs, or use graph paper as directed by your instructor.

(a) What is the closest this person gets to the ground?

(b) When this person stops bouncing, how high off the ground will the person be?

(c) If the person has a mass of 70 kilograms, how would the graph change for a jumper of 50 kilograms? Approximately sketch the results on the graph.

(d) If the person has a mass of 70 kilograms, how would the graph change for a jumper of 80 kilograms? Approximately sketch the results on the graph.

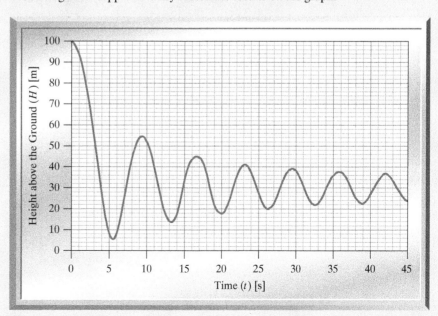

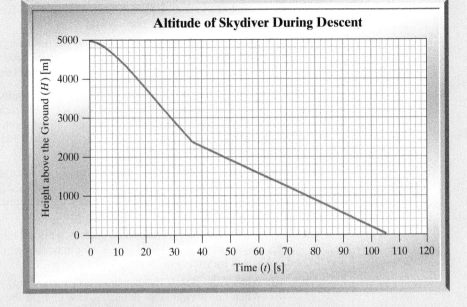

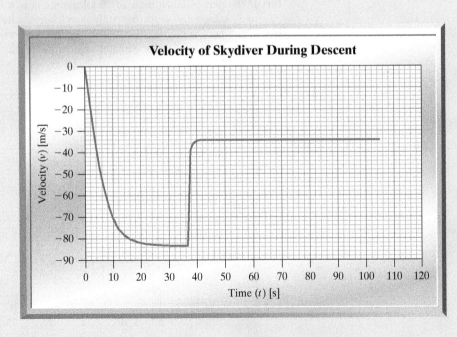

13. The graph below shows the current used to charge a capacitor over a period of 25 milliseconds [ms]. Choose from the following answers for (a)–(b).

1. Zero
2. Positive and constant
3. Positive and increasing
4. Positive and decreasing
5. Negative and constant
6. Negative with increasing magnitude
7. Negative with decreasing magnitude
8. Cannot be determined from information given

(a) At time $t = 10$ to 12 ms, classify the manner in which the **current** is changing.
(b) At time $t = 16$ to 18 ms, classify the manner in which the **charge** on the capacitor is changing.
(c) What is the total charge on the capacitor at time $t = 20$ ms?
(d) If the voltage on the capacitor at time 25 ms is 20 volts, what is the value of the capacitance? Express your answer using an appropriate prefix.

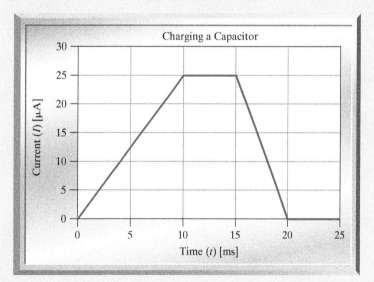

14. Answer the following questions using the graph. Choose from the following answers for (a)–(c):

1. Zero
2. Positive and constant
3. Positive and increasing
4. Positive and decreasing
5. Negative and constant
6. Negative with increasing magnitude
7. Negative with decreasing magnitude
8. Cannot be determined from information given

(a) Between points A and B, the total energy produced is:
(b) Between points A and B, the power generated is:
(c) Between points B and C, the power generated is:
(d) What is the power being generated at $t = 7$ minutes? State your answer in units of kilowatts.

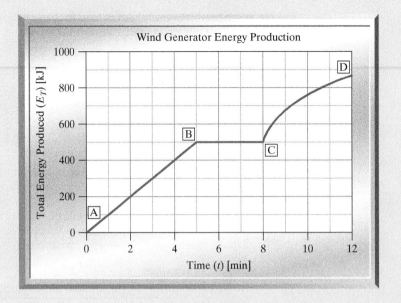

15. Answer the following questions using the graph. Choose from the following answers for (a)–(d):

1. Zero
2. Positive and constant
3. Positive and increasing
4. Positive and decreasing
5. Negative and constant
6. Negative with increasing magnitude
7. Negative with decreasing magnitude
8. Cannot be determined from information given

(a) For vehicle 2, between points A and D, the velocity is:
(b) For vehicle 2, between points D and E, the acceleration is:
(c) For vehicle 2, between points E and F, the distance is:
(d) What is the total distance traveled by vehicle 2 between points A and E? Give your answer in miles.
(e) Which vehicle travels the farthest distance between points A and F?

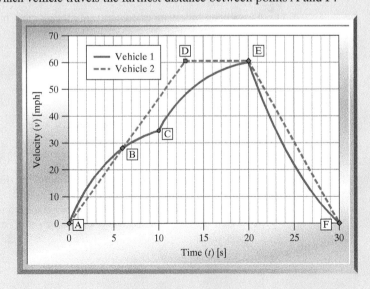

For questions Review 11-16 to 11-19, your instructor will determine if you should complete this question by hand or using Excel. If you must complete this problem by hand, a blank graph has been provided online.

---

16. In a simple electric circuit, the current (I) must remain below 40 milliamps ($I < 40$ mA), and must also satisfy the function $I > 10^{-6}\, e^{25V}$, where V is the voltage across a device called a diode.

  (a) Create a proper plot of these two inequalities with current on the ordinate. The values on the vertical axis should range from 0 to 50 milliamperes, and the values on the horizontal axis should range from 0 to 1 volt.

  (b) If graphing part **(a)** by hand, shade the region of the graph where *both* inequalities are satisfied.

  (c) Graphically determine the maximum allowable voltage across the diode. Indicate the location of this answer on your graph.

17. In a hard drive design, the faster the disk spins, the faster the information can be read from and written to the disk. In general, the more information to be stored on the disk, the larger the diameter of the disk must be. Unfortunately, the larger the disk, the lower the maximum rotational speed must be to avoid stress-related failures. Assume the minimum allowable rotational speed (S) of the hard drive is 6,000 revolutions per minute [rpm], and the rotational speed must meet the criterion $S < 12{,}000 - 150\, D^2$, where D is the diameter of the disk in inches.

  (a) Create a proper plot of these two inequalities with rotational speed on the ordinate and diameter on the abscissa. The values on the vertical axis should range from 0 to 12,000 rpm, and the values on the horizontal axis should range from 0 to 7 inches.

  (b) If graphing part **(a)** by hand, shade the region of the graph where both inequalities are satisfied.

  (c) Graphically determine the range of allowable rotational speeds for a 4-inch diameter disk. Indicate the location of this answer on your graph.

  (d) Graphically determine the largest diameter disk that meets the design criteria. Indicate the location of this answer on your graph.

18. We have decided to become entrepreneurs by raising turkeys for the Thanksgiving holiday. We already have purchased some land in the country with buildings on it, so that expense need not be a part of our analysis. A study of the way turkeys grow indicates that the mass of a turkey (m) from the time it hatches (at time zero) until it reaches maturity is:

$$m = K(1 - e^{-bt})$$

Here, we select values of K and b depending on the breed of turkey we decide to raise. The value (V) of our turkey is simply the mass of the turkey times the value per pound-mass (S) when we sell it, or:

$$V = Sm$$

Here, S is the value per pound-mass (in dollars). Finally, since we feed the turkey the same amount of food each day, the cumulative cost (C) to feed the bird is:

$$C = Nt$$

Here, N is the cost of one day's supply of food [$/day].

Create a graph of this situation, showing three lines: cumulative food cost, bird value, and profit on a particular day. For the graph, show the point after which you begin to lose money, and show the time when it is most profitable to sell the bird, indicating the day on which that occurs. Use values of $K = 21$ pound-mass, $b = 0.03$ per day, $S = \$1$ per pound-mass, and $N = \$0.12$ per day.

19. As an engineer, suppose you are directed to design a pumping system to safely discharge a toxic industrial waste into a municipal reservoir. The concentrated wastewater from the plant will be mixed with freshwater from the lake, and this mixture is to be pumped into the center of the lake. You realize that the more water you mix with the waste, the more dilute it will be and thus will have a smaller impact on the fish in the lake. On the other hand, the more water you use, the more it costs in electricity for pumping. Your objective is to determine the optimum amount of water to pump so the overall cost is a minimum.

■ Assume that the cost of pumping is given by the expression $C_{pump} = 10\ Q^2$. The cost C_{pump} [$/day] depends on the pumping rate Q [gallons per minute, or gpm] of the water used to dilute the industrial waste.

■ Now, suppose that some biologists have found that as more and more water dilutes the waste, the fish loss C_{fish} [$/day] can be expressed as $C_{fish} = 2{,}250 - 150\ Q$.

With this information, construct a graph, with pumping rate on the abscissa showing the pumping cost, the fish-loss cost, and total cost on the ordinate. For the scale, plot 0 to 15 gallons per minute for flow rate.

Determine both the minimum cost and the corresponding flow rate. Indicate the location of this answer on your graph.

20. We have obtained a contract to construct metal boxes (square bottom, rectangular sides, no top) for storing sand. Each box is to contain a specified volume and all edges are to be welded. Each box will require the following information: a volume (V, in units of cubic inches), the length of one side of the bottom (L, in units of inches), the box height (H, in units of inches), and the material cost (M, in units of dollars per square inch). To determine the total cost to manufacture a box, we must include not only the cost of the material, but also the cost of welding all the edges. Welding costs depend on the number of linear inches that are welded (W, in units of dollars per inch). The client does not care what the box looks like, but it should be constructed at the minimum cost possible.

(a) Construct a worksheet that will depict the cost of the material for one box, the welding cost for one box, and the total cost for the box. First, create at the top of your worksheet a section to allow the user to specify as absolute references the variables V, M, and W. Next, create a column for length ranging from 2 to 20 inches in increments of 2 inches. Finally, determine the material cost per box, welding cost per box, and total cost.

(b) Create a proper plot of the material cost, welding cost, and total cost (all shown as ordinate values) versus the box length.

For the following values, use the graph to determine the box shape for minimum cost: $V = 500$ cubic inches, $M = \$1.00$ per square inch, and $W = \$3.00$ per inch. Indicate the location of this answer on your graph.

(c) Below the table created in part (a), create a row to determine the minimum value for the material cost, the welding cost, and the total cost shown in the table. Use the information to create conditional formatting in the table to show the minimum values in the table as cells with a dark color background and white text. The highlighted cells should verify the solution found in part (b) using the graph.

21. Your company has developed a new high-mileage automobile. There are two options for manufacturing this new vehicle.

■ Process A: The factory can be completely retooled and workers trained to use the new equipment.

■ Process B: The old equipment can be modified.

A graph of the costs of each process and the revenues from sales of the vehicles is shown.

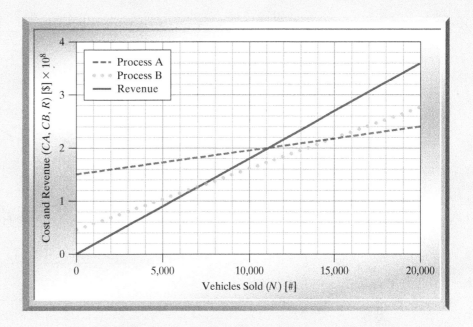

Use the chart to answer the following questions.

(a) What is the sales price per vehicle?

(b) What is the breakeven point (number of vehicles) for each of the two processes?

(c) Which process yields the most profit if 18,000 vehicles are sold? How much profit is made in this case?

(d) If the sales price per vehicle is reduced by $2,000 with a rebate offer, what is the new breakeven point (number of vehicles) for each of the two processes?

22. One of the fourteen Grand Challenges for Engineering as determined by the National Academy of Engineering committee is **Make Solar Energy Economical**. According to the NAE website: The solar "share of the total energy market remains rather small, well below 1 percent of total energy consumption, compared with roughly 85 percent from oil, natural gas, and coal." "... today's commercial solar cells ... typically convert sunlight into electricity with an efficiency of only 10 percent to 20 percent." "Given their manufacturing costs, modules of today's cells ... would produce electricity at a cost roughly 3 to 6 times higher than current prices." "To make solar economically competitive, engineers must find ways to improve the efficiency of the cells and to lower their manufacturing costs."

The following graph shows a breakeven analysis for a company planning to manufacture modular photoelectric panels. A copy of this graph has been provided online; you may use one of these graphs, or use graph paper as directed by your instructor.

(a) What is the fixed cost incurred in manufacturing the photoelectric panels?

(b) How much does it cost to manufacture each photoelectric panel?

(c) What is the sales price of one photoelectric panel?

(d) If the company makes and sells 30,000 panels, is there a net loss or profit, and how much?

While the company is still in the planning stages, the government starts a program to stimulate the economy and encourage green technologies. In this case, the government agrees to reimburse the company $250 for each of the first 10,000 units sold.

(e) Sketch a modified revenue curve for this situation.

(f) Using this new revenue curve, how many units must the company make to break even? Be sure to clearly indicate this point on the graph.

(g) Also using the new revenue curve, how many units must the company make and sell to make a profit of $1,500,000? Be sure to clearly indicate this point on the graph.

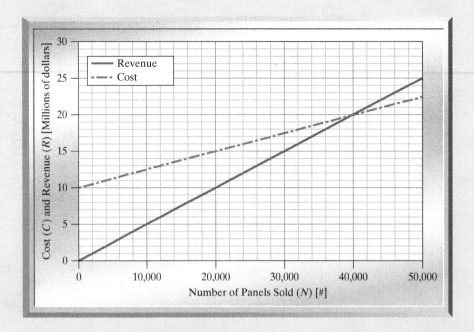

23. You are an engineer for a plastics manufacturing company. In examining cost-saving measures, your team has brainstormed the following ideas (labeled Idea A and Idea B). It is your responsibility to evaluate these ideas and recommend which one to pursue. You have been given a graph of the current process. A copy of this graph has been provided online; you may use one of these graphs, or use graph paper as directed by your instructor.

(a) What is the selling price of the product?

Current Cost: The current process has been running for a number of years, so there are no initial fixed costs to consider.

In the operating costs, the process requires the following:

- Material cost: $2.00/pound-mass of resin
- Energy cost: $0.15/pound-mass of resin
- Labor cost: $0.10/pound-mass of resin

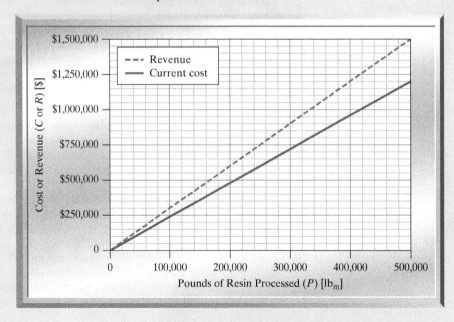

(b) There is also a cost associated with taking the scrap material to the landfill. Using the total cost determined from the graph, find the cost of landfill, in dollars per pounds-mass of resin.

Idea (A): Your customer will allow you to use regrind (reprocessed plastic) in the parts instead of 100% virgin plastic. Your process generates 10% scrap. Evaluate using all your scrap materials as regrind, with the regrind processed at your plant.

(c) You will need to purchase a regrind machine to process the plastic, estimated at a cost of $100,000. Using the regrind will alter the following costs, which account for using 10% scrap material:

- Material cost: $1.80/pound-mass of resin
- Energy cost: $0.16/pound-mass of resin
- Labor cost: $0.11/pound-mass of resin

This idea will eliminate the landfill charge required in the current process (see part **(b)**). Draw the total cost curve for Idea (A) on the graph or on a copy.

(d) How long (in pounds of resin processed) before the company reaches breakeven on Idea A?

(e) At what minimum level of production (in pound-mass of resin processed) will Idea (A) begin to generate more profit than the current process?

Idea (B): Your customer will allow you to use regrind (reprocessed plastic) in the parts instead of 100% virgin plastic. Evaluate using 25% regrind purchased from an outside vendor.

(f) Using the regrind from the other company will alter the following costs, which account for using 25% scrap material purchased from the outside vendor:

- Material cost: $1.85/pound-mass of resin
- Energy cost: $0.15/pound-mass of resin
- Labor cost: $0.11/pound-mass of resin

This idea will eliminate the landfill charge required in the current process (see part **(b)**) and will not require the purchase of a regrind machine as discussed in Idea (A). Draw the total cost curve for Idea (B) on the graph or on a copy.

(g) At what minimum level of production (in pound-mass of resin processed) will Idea (B) begin to generate more profit than the current process?

(h) At a production level of 500,000 pound-mass of resin, which Idea (A, B, or neither) gives the most profit over the current process?

(i) If the answer to part **(h)** is neither machine, list the amount of profit generated by the current process at 500,000 pound-mass of resin. If the answer to part **(h)** is Idea A or Idea B, list the amount of profit generated by that idea at 500,000 pound-mass of resin.

24. When a wind generator is installed there is a substantial initial cost, but daily operation requires no further cash payment. However, to keep the generator in proper operating condition, it must undergo maintenance once a year. Each maintenance cycle requires a cash payment of $5,000. The solid lines on the graph below show this situation. The stepped blue line shows the cost over time and the straight brown line shows the revenue derived from the generator.

As the second yearly maintenance approaches, you are informed by the manufacturer that a significant upgrade is available for additional cost. The upgrade will make the generator far more efficient, thus the revenue would increase substantially. The yearly maintenance cost after the upgrade would still be $5,000. The dashed lines show the cost and revenue projections if the upgrade is installed.

(a) What is the amount of revenue per year without the upgrade?

(b) What is the initial cost of the wind generator?

(c) How many years after the initial installation do you breakeven if the upgrade is installed? List your answer as number of years + number of months.

(d) What is the cost of the upgrade completed at the two-year maintenance cycle? Note that this figure includes the standard $5,000 maintenance fee.

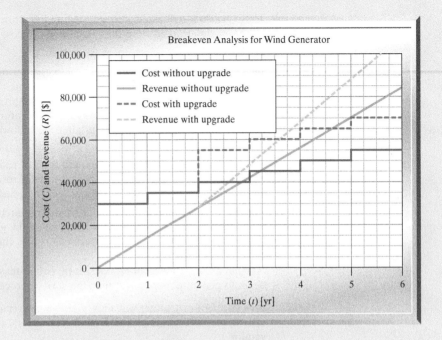

Breakeven Analysis for Wind Generator

Legend:
- Cost without upgrade
- Revenue without upgrade
- Cost with upgrade
- Revenue with upgrade

Y-axis: Cost (C) and Revenue (R) [$]
X-axis: Time (t) [yr]

(e) How many years after the initial installation would the profit be the same whether you upgrade or not? List your answer as number of years + number of months.

(f) How many years after the initial installation will you have made a profit of \$25,000 if the upgrade is NOT installed? List your answer as number of years + number of months.

(g) If the upgrade results in increased reliability thus increasing the maintenance interval to two years, though still at a cost of \$5,000 per maintenance, how many years after the initial installation will you breakeven after the upgrade? List your as number of years + number of months.

CHAPTER 12
MODELS AND SYSTEMS

A **model** is an abstract description of the relationship between variables in a system. A model allows the categorization of different types of mathematical phenomena so that general observations about the variables can be made for use in any number of applications.

For example, if we know that $t = v + 5$ and $M = z + 5$, any observations we make about v with respect to t also apply to z with respect to M. A specific model describes a *system* or *function* that has the same *trend* or *behavior* as a generalized model. In engineering, many specific models within different subdisciplines behave according to the same generalized model.

This section covers three general models of importance to engineers: **linear**, **power**, and **exponential**. It is worth noting that many applications of models within these three categories contain identical math but apply to significantly different disciplines.

Linear models occur when the dependent variable changes in direct relationship to changes in the independent variable. We discuss such systems, including springs, resistive circuits, fluid flow, and elastic materials, in this chapter by relating each model to Newton's generalized law of motion.

Power law systems occur when the independent variable has an exponent not equal to 1 or 0. We discuss these models by addressing integer and rational real exponents.

Exponential models are used in all engineering disciplines in a variety of applications. We discuss these models by examining the similarities between growth and decay models.

The following is an example of the level of knowledge of Excel needed to proceed. *If you are not able to quickly recreate the following exercise in Excel, including trendlines and formatting, please review trendline basics in appendix materials online before proceeding.*

Energy (E) stored in an **inductor** is related to its inductance (L) and the current (I) passing through it by the following equation:

$$E = \frac{1}{2}LI^2$$

The SI unit of inductance, **henry** [H], is named for Joseph Henry (1797–1878), credited with the discovery of self-inductance of electromagnets.

Three inductors were tested and the results are given here. Create a proper plot of the data and add a properly formatted power law trendline to each data set.

Current (*I*) [A]	2	6	10	14	16
Energy of Inductor 1 (*E*1) [J]	0.002	0.016	0.050	0.095	0.125
Energy of Inductor 2 (*E*2) [J]	0.010	0.085	0.250	0.510	0.675
Energy of Inductor 3 (*E*3) [J]	0.005	0.045	0.125	0.250	0.310

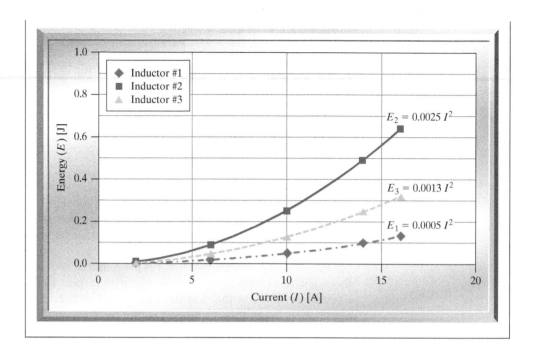

Figure 12-1 is an example of a properly formatted graph, showing an experimental data series with linear trendlines.

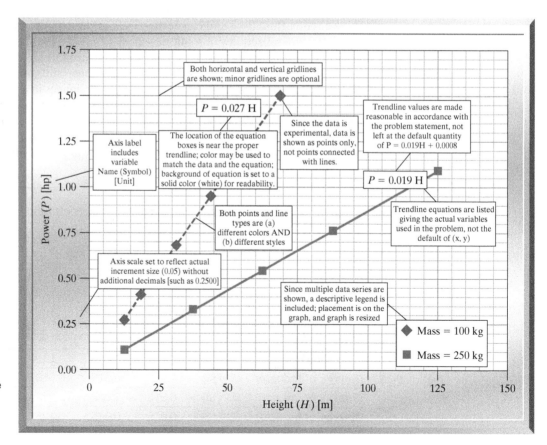

Figure 12-1

Example of a proper plot, showing multiple experimental data sets with linear trendlines.

12.1 LINEAR FUNCTIONS

Recognize the shape and boundaries of a linear function shown graphically
Recognize when an equation is a linear model
Determine the physical meaning and units of parameters of a linear function

Trend	Equation	Data Form	Graphical Example
Linear	$y = mx + c$	Defined value at $x = 0$ ($y = c$) <hr> Data appears as a linear (straight) line	

One of the most common models is **linear**, taking the form $y = mx + c$, where the ordinate value (y) is a function of the abscissa value (x) and a constant factor called the **slope** (m). At an initial value of the abscissa ($x = 0$), the ordinate value is equal to the **intercept** (c). Examples include

- Distance (d) traveled at constant velocity (v) over time (t) from initial position (d_0):

$$d = vt + d_0$$

- Total pressure (P_{total}), relating density (ρ), gravity (g), liquid height (H), and the pressure above the surface ($P_{surface}$):

$$P_{total} = \rho g H + P_{surface}$$

- Newton's second law, relating force (F), mass (m), and acceleration (a):

$$F = ma$$

Note that the intercept value (c) is zero in the last example.

General Model Rules

Given a linear system of the form $y = mx + c$ and assuming $x \geq 0$:

- When $m = 1$, the function is equal to $x + c$.
- When $m = 0$, $y = c$, regardless of the value of x (y never changes).
- When $m > 0$, as x increases, y increases, regardless of the value of c.
- When $m < 0$, as x increases, y decreases, regardless of the value of c.

● EXAMPLE 12-1

We want to determine the effect of depth of a fluid on the total pressure felt by a submerged object. Recall that the total pressure is

$$P_{total} = P_{surface} + P_{hydro} = P_{surface} + \rho g H$$

where P_{total} = total pressure [atm]; $P_{surface}$ = pressure at the surface [atm]; ρ = density [kg/m^3]; g = gravity [m/s^2]; H = depth [m]. We enter the lab, take data, and create the following chart.

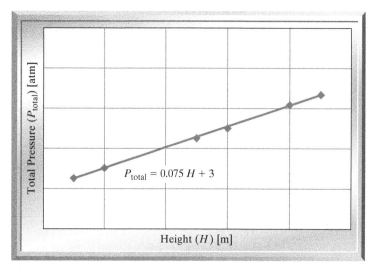

Determine the density of the fluid, in units of kilograms per cubic meter.

*We can determine the parameters by matching the trendline generated in Excel with the theoretical expression. In theory: total pressure = density * gravity * height of fluid + pressure on top of the fluid*
   *From graph: total pressure = 0.075 * height + 3*
   *By comparison: density * gravity = 0.075 [atm/m]*

$$\frac{0.075 \text{ atm}}{m} \left| \frac{101,325 \text{ Pa}}{1 \text{ atm}} \right| \frac{1 \frac{kg}{ms^2}}{1 \text{ Pa}} = \rho \left(\frac{9.8 \text{ m}}{s^2} \right)$$

$$\frac{7,600 \text{ kg}}{m^2 s^2} = \rho \left(\frac{9.8 \text{ m}}{s^2} \right)$$

$$\rho = \frac{7,600 \text{ kg}}{m^2 s^2} \left| \frac{s^2}{9.8 \text{ m}} \right. = \frac{775 \text{ kg}}{m^3}$$

Determine if the tank is open to the atmosphere or pressurized, and determine the pressure on the top of the fluid in units of atmospheres.

*Once again, we can compare the Excel trendline to the theoretical expression. In theory: total pressure = density * gravity * height of fluid + pressure on top of the fluid*
   *From graph: total pressure = 0.075 * height + 3*
   By comparison, the top of the tank is pressurized at 3 atm.

Increasingly, engineers are working at smaller and smaller scales. Tiny beads made of glass are on the order of 50 micrometers in diameter. They are manufactured so that they become hollow, allowing the wall thickness to be a few nanometers. The compositions of the glass were engineered, so when processed correctly, they would sustain a hollow structure and the glass walls would be infiltrated with hundreds of thousands of nanometer-sized pores. These beads can possibly revolutionize the way fluids and gases are stored for use. The pores are small enough that fluids and even gases could be contained under normal conditions. However, if activated properly, the pores would allow a path for a gas to exit the "container" when it is ready to be used.

S4800 5.0kV 10.2mm x2.20k SE(M)   20.0um

Photo courtesy of K. Richardson

COMPREHENSION CHECK 12-1

The graph shows the ideal gas law relationship ($PV = nRT$) between pressure (P) and temperature (T).

(a) What are the units of the slope (0.0087)?

(b) If the tank has a volume of 12 liters and is filled with nitrogen (formula, N_2; molecular weight, 28 grams per mole), what is the mass of gas in the tank in units of grams?

(c) If the tank is filled with 48 grams of oxygen (formula, O_2; molecular weight, 32 grams per mole), what is the volume of the tank in units of liters?

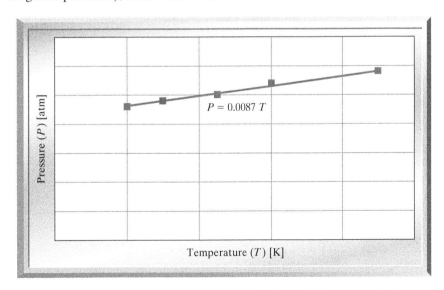

12.2 LINEAR RELATIONSHIPS

Most physics textbooks begin the study of motion ignoring how that object came to be moving in the first place. This is appropriate to the way physicists study the world, by observing the world as it is. Engineering is about changing the way things are. The fact that "engineer" is a verb as well as a noun is a reminder of this. As a result, engineers are concerned with forces and the changes those forces cause. While physicists study how far a car travels through the air when hit by a truck, engineers focus on stopping the truck before it hits the car or on designing an air-bag system or crush-proof doors. Engineering has many diverse branches because of the many different kinds of forces and ways to apply them.

Another Way of Looking at Newton's Laws

NOTE

Newton's First Law: A system keeps doing what it is doing unless the forces acting on the system change.

Newton's first law is given as "An object at rest remains at rest and an object in motion will continue in motion with a constant velocity unless it experiences a net external force." As we consider variables other than motion, we want to expand this definition: **A system keeps doing what it is doing unless the forces acting on the system change**.

NOTE

Newton's Second Law: When a force influences a change to a system parameter, the system opposes the change according to its internal resistance.

Newton's second law is given as "The acceleration of an object is directly proportional to the net force acting on it and inversely proportional to its mass." This can be interpreted as follows: When an external force acts on a system to cause acceleration, the system resists that acceleration according to its mass. Expanding Newton's second law, we can generalize it for use with variables other than motion: **When a force influences a change to a system parameter, the system opposes the change according to its internal resistance**.

In generalizing these relationships, we can start to establish a pattern observed in a wide variety of phenomena, summarized in Table 12-1.

Table 12-1 Generalized Newton's second law

When a "system"...	...is acted upon by a "force"...	...to change a "parameter"...	...the "system" opposes the change by a "resistance"	Equation
Physical object	External push or pull (F)	Acceleration (a)	Object mass (m)	$F = ma$

Springs

When an external force (F), such as a weight, is applied to a spring, it will cause the spring to stretch a distance (x), according to the following expression:

$$F = kx$$

This equation is called **Hooke's law**, named for Robert Hooke (1635–1703), an English scientist. Among other things, he is credited with creating the biological term "cell." The comparison of Hooke's Law and Newton's Second Law is shown in Table 12-2.

Table 12-2 Generalized second law . . . applied to springs

When a "system" . . .	. . . is acted upon by a "force" . . .	. . . to change a "parameter". . .	. . . the "system" opposes the change by a "resistance"	Equation
Physical object	External push or pull (F)	Acceleration (a)	Object mass (m)	$F = ma$
Spring	External push or pull (F)	Elongation (x)	Spring stiffness (k)	$F = kx$

The variable k is the **spring constant**, a measure of the stiffness of the spring. Stiff springs are hard to stretch and have high k values; springs with low k values are easy to stretch. The constant k is a material property of the spring, determined by how it is made and what material it is made from. The spring constant has units of force per distance, typically reported in newtons per meter.

● EXAMPLE 12-2

Two springs were tested; a weight was hung on one end and the resulting displacement measured. The results were graphed. Using the graph shown below, give the spring constant of each spring and determine which spring is stiffer.

Spring 1 has a linear trendline of $F = 66x$. The slope of the line is the spring constant:

$$k_1 = 66 \ N/m$$

Spring 2 has a linear trendline of $F = 8x$, which corresponds to:

$$k_2 = 8 \ N/m$$

Spring 1 is stiffer since it has a higher spring constant.

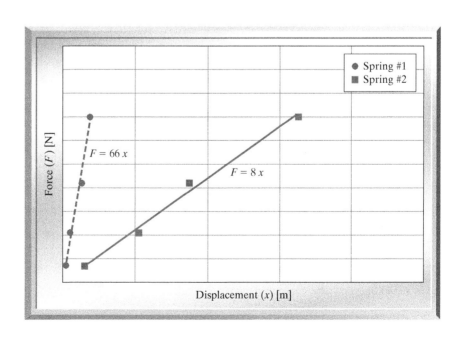

Electric Circuits

Electric current (I) is a measure of how many charges (normally electrons) flow through a wire or component in a given amount of time. This is analogous to measuring water flowing through a pipe as amount per time, whether the units are tons per hour, gallons per minute, or molecules per second.

Voltage (V) is the "force" that pushes the electrons around. Although its effects on charged particles are similar to those of a true force, voltage is quite different dimensionally. The unit of voltage is the **volt** [V], described as the potential difference (voltage) across a conductor when a current of one ampere dissipates one watt of power.

Resistance (R) is a measure of how difficult it is to push electrons through a substance or device. When a voltage is applied to a circuit, a current is generated. This current depends on the equivalent resistance of the circuit. Resistance has units of volts per ampere, which is given the special name **ohm** [Ω]. It is named for Georg Ohm (1789–1854), the German physicist who developed the theory, called **Ohm's Law**, to explain the relationship between voltage, current, and resistance. The similarities between Ohm's Law and Newton's Second Law are given in Table 12-3.

$$V = IR$$

> **NOTE**
>
> A now outdated term for voltage was actually "electromotive force" or EMF.

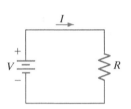

Table 12-3 Generalized second law . . . applied to circuits

When a "system" . . .	. . . is acted upon by a "force" . . .	. . . to change a "parameter" . . .	. . . the "system" opposes the change by a "resistance"	Equation
Physical object	External push or pull (F)	Acceleration (a)	Object mass (m)	$F = ma$
Electrical circuit	Circuit voltage (V) (electromotive force)	Circuit current (I)	Circuit resistance (R)	$V = IR$

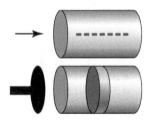

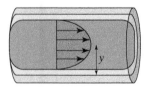

Fluid Flow

To create motion in a solid object, we can apply a force to that object by pushing on it. Imagine you have a small cube on the desk in front of you. If you take your pencil and push on that object at a single point, the entire object will move. For motion in a fluid to be created, a force must be applied over an area of the fluid. While both liquids and gases can be defined as fluids, we focus on liquids in this section. Imagine a section of fluid-filled pipe placed on the desk in front of you. If we apply a force at a single point in the fluid, only the particles at that point will move. To move the entire fluid uniformly, we must apply the force at all points at the pipe entrance simultaneously. Applying a force over the cross-sectional area of the pipe results in the application of a pressure to the fluid. The pressure that results in fluid flow has a special name: **shear stress** (τ, Greek letter tau).

As the fluid moves, we find that the fluid molecules in contact with the wall adhere to the wall and do not move. The motion of the fluid can be visualized as occurring in layers; as the distance from the wall increases, the fluid moves faster. The fluid moves fastest at the farthest point from the wall, which is the center of the pipe. Since the velocity changes depend on the location in the pipe from the wall, the parameter we are changing cannot be expressed as a simple velocity, but rather as a **velocity gradient**, given as ($\Delta v/\Delta y$ or $\dot{\gamma}$). This is sometimes called the **shear rate** or **strain rate**.

Not all fluids respond equally to an applied pressure. The fluid property that represents the resistance of a fluid against flow is called the **dynamic viscosity** (μ, Greek letter mu). The relationship between shear stress and the velocity profile of a fluid is called **Newton's law of viscosity**, named after Isaac Newton. Fluids that behave in this way are called **Newtonian fluids** (e.g., water and oil). The comparison between Newton's Law of Viscosity and Newton's Second Law is given in Table 12-4.

$$\tau = \mu \frac{\Delta v}{\Delta y}$$

Table 12-4 Generalized second law . . . applied to fluid flow

When a "system" . . .	. . . is acted upon by a "force" . . .	. . . to change a "parameter" . . .	. . . the "system" opposes the change by a "resistance"	Equation
Physical object	External push or pull (F)	Acceleration (a)	Object mass (m)	$F = ma$
Fluid	Shear stress (τ)	Shear rate ($\Delta v/\Delta y$)	Dynamic viscosity (μ)	$\tau = \mu \dfrac{\Delta v}{\Delta y}$

Sometimes, a fluid must have a certain amount of stress (called the **yield stress**, τ_0) applied before it will begin to move like a Newtonian fluid. These fluids are called **Bingham plastics**, named after Eugene Bingham, a chemist who made many contributions to the field of **rheology** (the science of deformation and flow of matter, a term he, along with Markus Reiner, is credited in creating). Examples of Bingham plastics include toothpaste and slurries.

$$\tau = \mu \frac{\Delta v}{\Delta y} + \tau_0$$

Common units of dynamic viscosity are **centipoise** [cP], named after the French physician Jean Louis Poiseuille (1799–1869) who studied the flow of blood in tubes. Dynamic viscosity is a function of temperature. In most instances, viscosity decreases with increasing temperature; as the fluid heats up, it becomes easier to move.

Property	Symbol	Typical Units	Equivalent Units
Dynamic viscosity	μ	cP	1P = 1g/(cm s)
Kinematic viscosity	ν	St	1St = 1cm²/s

Another useful term in describing a fluid is **kinematic viscosity** (ν, Greek letter nu). The kinematic viscosity is the ratio of dynamic viscosity to density and is given the unit of **stokes** [St], named after George Stokes (1819–1903), the Irish mathematician and physicist who made important contributions to science, including Stokes' law, optics, and physics. Several values of dynamic and kinematic viscosity are given in Table 12-5.

$$\nu = \frac{\mu}{\rho}$$

Table 12-5 Summary of material properaties for several liquids

Liquid	Specific Gravity	Dynamic Viscosity (μ) [cP]	Kinematic Viscosity (ν) [cSt]
Acetone	0.791	0.331	0.419
Corn syrup	1.36	1,380	1,015
Ethanol	0.789	1.194	1.513
Glycerin	1.260	1,490	1,183
Honey	1.36	5,000	3,676
Mercury	13.600	1.547	0.114
Molasses	1.400	8,000	5,714
Olive oil	0.703	101	143
SAE 30W oil	0.891	290	325
Water	1.000	1.000	1.000

COMPREHENSION CHECK 12-2

Fluid A has a dynamic viscosity of 0.5 centipoise and a specific gravity of 1.1. What is the density of Fluid A in units of pound-mass per cubic foot?

COMPREHENSION CHECK 12-3

Fluid A has a dynamic viscosity of 0.5 centipoise and a specific gravity of 1.1. What is the dynamic viscosity of Fluid A in units of pound-mass per foot second?

COMPREHENSION CHECK 12-4

Fluid A has a dynamic viscosity of 0.5 centipoise and a specific gravity of 1.1. What is the kinematic viscosity of Fluid A in units of stokes?

Elastic Materials

Elasticity is the property of an object or material that causes it to be restored to its original shape after distortion. A rubber band is easy to stretch and snaps back to near its original length when released, but it is not as elastic as a piece of piano wire. The piano wire is harder to stretch, but would be said to be more elastic than the rubber band because of the precision of its return to its original length. The term elasticity is quantified by **Young's modulus** or **modulus of elasticity** (E), the amount of deformation resulting from an applied force. Young's modulus is named for Thomas Young (1773–1829), a British scientist, who contributed to several fields: material elongation theory; optics, with his "double slit" optical experiment that led to the deduction that light travels in waves; and fluids, with the theory of surface tension and capillary action.

Like fluids, elastic materials accept a force applied over a unit area rather than a point force. **Stress** (σ, Greek letter sigma) is the amount of force applied over a unit area of the material, which has units of pressure [Pa]. The **strain** (ε, Greek letter epsilon) is the ratio of the elongation to the original length, yielding a dimensionless number. Since the modulus values tend to be large, they are usually expressed in units of Gigapascals [GPa]. The generalized second law as applied to an elastic material is shown in Table 12-6.

$$\sigma = E\varepsilon$$

Table 12-6 Generalized second law . . . applied to elastic materials

When a "system" . . .	. . . is acted upon by a "force" . . .	. . . to change a "parameter" . . .	. . . the "system" opposes the change by a "resistance"	Equation
Physical object	External push or pull (F)	Acceleration (a)	Object mass (m)	$F = ma$
Elastic object	Stress (σ)	Strain (ε)	Modulus of elasticity (E)	$\sigma = E\varepsilon$

From this discussion, you can see examples from many areas of engineering that are similar to Newton's second law. We often want to change something and find that it resists this change; this relationship is often linear. In all of these situations, we discover a coefficient that depends on the material encountered in the particular situation (mass, spring stiffness, circuit resistance, fluid viscosity, or modulus of elasticity).

Many other examples are not discussed here, such as Fourier's law of heat transfer, Fick's law of diffusion, and Darcy's law of permeability. You can enhance your understanding of your coursework by attempting to generalize the knowledge presented in a single theory to other theories that may be presented in other courses. Many different disciplines of engineering are linked by common themes, and the more you can connect these theories across disciplines, the more meaningful your classes will become.

Combinations of Springs and Circuits

When connected, both springs and circuits form a resulting system that behaves like a single spring or single resistor. In a combination of springs, the system stiffness depends on the stiffness of each individual spring and on the configuration, referred to as the effective spring constant (k_{eff}). In a network of circuits, the system resistance depends on the value of the individual resistors and on the configuration, referred to as the effective resistance (R_{eff}).

Springs in Parallel

When springs are attached in *parallel*, they must *displace the same distance* even though they may have different spring constants. The derivation below shows how this leads to an effective spring constant that is the sum of the individual spring constants in the system. Each spring is responsible for supporting a proportional amount of the force.

Writing Hooke's law for two springs each displacing the same distance (x):

$$F_1 = k_1 x \qquad\qquad (a)$$
$$F_2 = k_2 x \qquad\qquad (b)$$

Solve for F_1 in terms of F_2 since the displacement is the same:

$$F_1 = k_1 \frac{F_2}{k_2} = F_2 \frac{k_1}{k_2} \tag{c}$$

Writing Hooke's law as applied to the overall system:

$$F = k_{eff} x \tag{d}$$

The total force applied to the configuration (F) is the sum of the force supported by each spring:

$$F = F_1 + F_2 \tag{e}$$

Eliminating force (F) from Equation (e) with Equation (d):

$$k_{eff} x = F_1 + F_2 \tag{f}$$

Eliminating displacement (x) with Equation (b):

$$k_{eff} \frac{F_2}{k_2} = F_1 + F_2 \tag{g}$$

Substituting for F_1 with Equation (c):

$$k_{eff} \frac{F_2}{k_2} = F_2 \frac{k_1}{k_2} + F_2 \tag{h}$$

Dividing Equation (h) by F_2:

$$\frac{k_{eff}}{k_2} = \frac{k_1}{k_2} + 1 \tag{i}$$

Multiplying Equation (i) by k_2 gives:

$$\boldsymbol{k_{eff} = k_1 + k_2} \tag{j}$$

Springs in Series

When two springs are attached in *series*, the *force is the same for both springs*. The effective spring constant is derived below. The applied force affects each spring as though the other spring did not exist, and each spring can stretch a different amount.

Writing Hooke's law for two springs each under the same applied force (F):

$$F = k_1 x_1 \tag{k}$$
$$F = k_2 x_2 \tag{l}$$

Solve for x_1 in terms of x_2 since the force is the same:

$$x_1 = \frac{k_2}{k_1} x_2 \tag{m}$$

Writing Hooke's law as applied to the overall system:

$$F = k_{eff} x \tag{n}$$

NOTE

Springs in series are acted on by the same force for both springs.

The total distance stretched by the configuration (x) is the sum of the distance stretched by each spring:

$$x = x_1 + x_2 \tag{o}$$

Eliminating force (F) from Equation (n) with Equation (l):

$$k_2 x_2 = k_{eff} x \tag{p}$$

Eliminating displacement (x) with Equation (o):

$$k_2 x_2 = k_{eff}(x_1 + x_2) \tag{q}$$

Substituting for x_1 with Equation (m):

$$k_2 x_2 = k_{eff}\left(\frac{k_2}{k_1} x_2 + x_2\right) \tag{r}$$

Dividing Equation (r) by x_2:

$$k_2 = k_{eff}\left(\frac{k_2}{k_1} + 1\right) \tag{s}$$

Dividing Equation (s) by k_2 gives:

$$1 = k_{eff}\left(\frac{1}{k_1} + \frac{1}{k_2}\right) \tag{t}$$

NOTE

A system of two springs in series will always be less stiff than either spring individually.

Thus,

$$k_{eff} = \frac{1}{\left(\frac{1}{k_1} + \frac{1}{k_2}\right)} = \left(\frac{1}{k_1} + \frac{1}{k_2}\right)^{-1} \tag{u}$$

These equations for two springs connected in parallel and series generalize to any number of springs. For N springs in parallel, the effective spring constant is

$$k_{eff} = k_1 + k_2 + \cdots + k_{N-1} + k_N \tag{v}$$

For N springs in series, the effective spring constant is

$$k_{eff} = \left(\frac{1}{k_1} + \frac{1}{k_2} + \cdots + \frac{1}{k_{N-1}} + \frac{1}{k_N}\right)^{-1} \tag{w}$$

● EXAMPLE 12-3

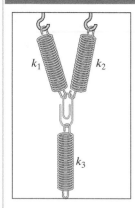

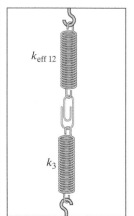

Find the displacement (x) in the spring combination shown, where Spring 1 (with a stiffness k_1) and Spring 2 (with a stiffness k_2) are connected in parallel, and the combination is then connected to Spring 3 (with a stiffness k_3) in series. Use the following values:

$$F = 0.2 \text{ N}$$
$$k_1 = 10 \text{ N/m}$$
$$k_2 = 5 \text{ N/m}$$
$$k_3 = 8 \text{ N/m}$$

First, we recognize that k_1 and k_2 are in parallel, so we can solve for an effective spring constant, using Equation (j).

$$k_{eff12} = k_1 + k_2 = 10 \text{ N/m} + 5 \text{ N/m} = 15 \text{ N/m}$$

The combination can then be redrawn to show k_{eff12} and k_3 in series.
Next, we solve for the effective spring constant using Equation (u).

$$k_{eff} = \left(\frac{1}{k_{eff12}} + \frac{1}{k_3} \right)^{-1} = \left(\frac{1}{15 \text{ N/m}} + \frac{1}{8 \text{ N/m}} \right)^{-1} = 5.2 \text{ N/m}$$

We can now solve for the displacement, using Hooke's law:

$$F = k_{eff} x$$

$$x = \frac{F}{k_{eff}} = \frac{0.2 \text{ N}}{5.2 \text{ N/m}} = 0.04 \text{ m} = 4 \text{ cm}$$

COMPREHENSION CHECK 12-5

You have three springs, with stiffness 1, 2, and 3 newtons per meter [N/m], respectively. How many unique spring stiffnesses can be formed with these springs? Consider each spring alone, pairs of springs in both parallel and series, and all springs used at once.

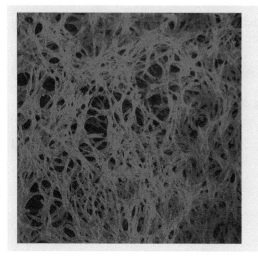

Human fibroblasts are connective tissue cells present in organs throughout the body. In this image, these cells can be seen spreading within a semi-interpenetrating network made of a polymer called polyethylene glycol diacrylate-hyaluronic acid (Pegda-HA). This material can be injected in a minimally invasive manner and cross-linked inside the body to form an insoluble gel with mechanical properties similar to many soft tissues in the human body. Such materials are being widely studied as "scaffolds" for cell transplantation in tissue engineering and regenerative medicine. The material degrades within 4–6 weeks, yielding physiological metabolites and water soluble polymers that are readily excreted through the kidneys.

Photo courtesy of K. Webb and J. Kutty

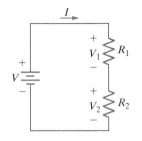

Resistors in Series

When two resistors are connected in *series*, the *current through both of the resistors is the same*, even though the value of each resistor may be different. The derivation below shows the effective resistance of two resistors connected in series. Note that the voltage is applied to the entire system.

Writing Ohm's law for two resistors each with the same current:

$$V_1 = IR_1 \tag{A}$$
$$V_2 = IR_2 \tag{B}$$

Solving for V_1 in terms of V_2 since the current is the same:

$$V_1 = R_1 \frac{V_2}{R_2} = V_2 \frac{R_1}{R_2} \tag{C}$$

Writing Ohm's law as applied to the overall system:

$$V = IR_{\text{eff}} \tag{D}$$

The total voltage applied to the configuration (V) is the sum of the voltage applied to each resistor:

$$V = V_1 + V_2 \tag{E}$$

Eliminating voltage (V) from Equation (E) with Equation (D):

$$IR_{\text{eff}} = V_1 + V_2 \tag{F}$$

Eliminating current (I) from Equation (F) with Equation (B):

$$R_{\text{eff}} \frac{V_2}{R_2} = V_1 + V_2 \tag{G}$$

Substitution for V_1 with Equation (C):

$$R_{\text{eff}} \frac{V_2}{R_2} = V_2 \frac{R_1}{R_2} + V_2 \tag{H}$$

Dividing Equation (H) by V_2:

$$R_{\text{eff}} \frac{1}{R_2} = \frac{R_1}{R_2} + 1 \tag{I}$$

Multiplying Equation (I) by R_2:

$$\boldsymbol{R_{eff} = R_1 + R_2} \tag{J}$$

NOTE

Resistors in series have the same current through both of the resistors.

NOTE

A system of two resistors in series will always provide more resistance than either resistor individually.

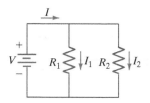

Resistors in Parallel

When two resistors are connected in *parallel*, the *voltage across both of the resistors is the same.* The current through each resistor may be different. The voltage is applied to the entire system.

Writing Ohm's law for two resistors each with the same voltage:

$$V = I_1 R_1 \tag{K}$$
$$V = I_2 R_2 \tag{L}$$

NOTE

Resistors in parallel have the same voltage through both of the resistors.

Solving for I_1 in terms of I_2 since the current is the same:

$$I_1 = \frac{R_2}{R_1} I_2 \tag{M}$$

Writing Ohm's law as applied to the overall system:

$$V = I R_{\text{eff}} \tag{N}$$

The total current (I) is the sum of the current flowing through each resistor:

$$I = I_1 + I_2 \tag{O}$$

Eliminating voltage (V) from Equation (N) using Equation (L):

$$I_2 R_2 = I R_{\text{eff}} \tag{P}$$

Eliminating current (I) using Equation (O):

$$I_2 R_2 = (I_1 + I_2) R_{\text{eff}} \tag{Q}$$

Substituting for I_1 using Equation (M):

$$I_2 R_2 = \left(\frac{R_2}{R_1} I_2 + I_2 \right) R_{\text{eff}} \tag{R}$$

Dividing Equation (R) by I_2:

$$R_2 = R_{\text{eff}} \left(\frac{R_2}{R_1} + 1 \right) \tag{S}$$

Dividing Equation (S) by R_2 gives:

$$1 = R_{\text{eff}} \left(\frac{1}{R_1} + \frac{1}{R_2} \right) \tag{T}$$

NOTE

A system of two resistors in parallel will always have less resistance than either resistor individually.

Thus,

$$\boldsymbol{R_{\text{eff}}} = \frac{1}{\frac{1}{R_1} + \frac{1}{R_2}} = \left(\frac{1}{R_1} + \frac{1}{R_2} \right)^{-1} \tag{U}$$

These equations for two resistors connected in parallel and series generalize to any number of resistors. For N resistors in parallel, the effective resistance is

$$R_{\text{eff}} = \left(\frac{1}{R_1} + \frac{1}{R_2} + \cdots + \frac{1}{R_{N-1}} + \frac{1}{R_N} \right)^{-1} \tag{V}$$

This form, along with spring equation (w) shown earlier, is sometimes referred to as the "reciprocal of the sum of the reciprocals."

For N resistors in series, the effective resistance is

$$R_{\text{eff}} = R_1 + R_2 + \cdots + R_{N-1} + R_N \tag{W}$$

WARNING!

Some of you may have seen a "simpler" form of the equation for two springs in series or two resistors in parallel.

For two springs in series: $k_{eff} = \dfrac{k_1 k_2}{k_1 + k_2}$

For two resistors in parallel: $R_{eff} = \dfrac{R_1 R_2}{R_1 + R_2}$

These forms are sometimes referred to as "the product over the sum."

THESE FORMS *DO NOT GENERALIZE* TO MORE THAN TWO ELEMENTS.

If you have three or more elements, then you must use the "reciprocal of the sum of the reciprocals" form given earlier.

● **EXAMPLE 12-4**

Find the current (I) in the circuit shown. Resistor 1 (with resistance R_1) and Resistor 2 (with resistance R_2) are connected in series, and the combination is then connected to Resistor 3 (with resistance R_3) in parallel. Use the following values:

$V = 12$ V
$R_1 = 7.5$ kΩ
$R_2 = 2.5$ kΩ
$R_3 = 40$ kΩ

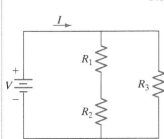

First, we recognize that R_1 and R_2 are in series, so we reduce R_1 and R_2 to a single effective resistor by using Equation (J).

$$R_{eff12} = R_1 + R_2 = 7.5 \text{ k}\Omega + 2.5 \text{ k}\Omega = 10 \text{ k}\Omega$$

Next, we can redraw the circuit so R_{eff12} and R_3 are in parallel. We solve for the effective resistance by using Equation (U).

$$R_{eff} = \left(\frac{1}{R_{eff12}} + \frac{1}{R_3} \right)^{-1} = \left(\frac{1}{10 \text{ k}\Omega} + \frac{1}{40 \text{ k}\Omega} \right)^{-1} = 8 \text{ k}\Omega$$

We can now solve the problem with Ohm's law:

$$V = IR_{eff}$$

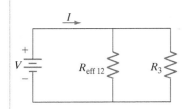

$$I = \frac{V}{R_{eff}} = \frac{12 \text{ V}}{8 \text{ k}\Omega} = 0.0015 \text{ A} = 1.5 \text{ mA}$$

COMPREHENSION CHECK 12-6

You have three resistors with resistance 2, 2, and 3 ohms [Ω], respectively. How many unique resistances can be created with these resistors? Consider each resistor alone, pairs of resistors both in parallel and in series, and all resistors used at once.

When Are Components Connected in Series, Parallel, or Neither?

Note that in each diagram, the lines with one end loose indicate where the circuit or spring configuration is connected to other things.

Series

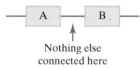

When one end (but not both) of each of two components is connected together with NOTHING ELSE CONNECTED AT THAT POINT, they are in series.

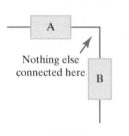

Note that they do not necessarily have to be in a straight line as shown. Electrical components can be physically mounted in any position relative to one another, and as long as a wire connects one end of each together (with nothing else connected there), they would be in series. Two springs can be connected by a string, so that the string makes a right angle direction change over a pulley, and the two springs would be in series.

Parallel

When each end of one component is connected to each of the two ends of another component, they are in parallel.

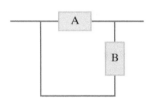

Similar to the series connection, the components do not have to be physically mounted parallel to each other or side by side, as long both ends are connected directly together with no intervening components. This is simple to do with electrical components since wire can be easily connected between any two points. Can you determine a method to physically connect two springs in parallel so that one is vertical and the other horizontal?

Sample Combinations

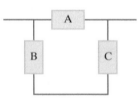

In the figure at left, B and C are in series. A is neither in series nor parallel with B or C since the lines extending to the left and right indicate connection to other stuff. A is, however, in parallel with the series combination of B and C.

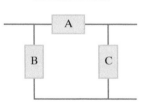

In the figure at left, no components are in series or parallel with anything since the lines extending to the left and right indicate connection to other stuff. Note the extra line at lower right.

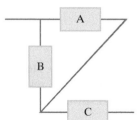

In the figure at left, A and B are in parallel. C is neither in series nor parallel with A or B. C is, however, in series with the parallel combination of A and B.

Capacitors and Inductors

In a capacitor, the **voltage** depends not only on the total charge stored, but also on the physical construction of the device, particularly the surface area of the plates. The charge (Q) stored in a capacitor is proportional to the voltage (V) across it, where C is the proportionality constant.

$$Q = CV$$

Note that C must have units of coulombs per volt, and is called **capacitance**. Capacitance is measured in units of **farads** [F], where one farad equals one coulomb per volt, or $1\,\text{F} = 1\,\text{C/V}$.

In its simplest form, an **inductor** is just a coil of wire. **Inductance** (L) is measured in units of **henrys** [H]. The voltage across an inductor is equal to the inductance of the device times the instantaneous rate of change of current through the inductor

$$V = L\frac{dI}{dt}$$

Dimensionally, the henry is one volt second per ampere [V s/A]. This can be shown to be dimensionally equal to resistance times time [Ω s] or energy per current squared [J/A^2].

For both systems, we can write a generalized form of Newton's second law, shown in Table 12-7.

Table 12-7 Generalized second law . . . applied to capacitors and inductors

When a "system" . . .	. . . is acted upon by a "force" . . .	. . . to change a "parameter" . . .	. . . the "system" opposes the change by a "resistance"	Equation
Physical object	External push or pull (F)	Acceleration (a)	Object mass (m)	$F = ma$
Capacitor	Charge (Q)	Voltage (V)	Capacitance (C)	$Q = CV$
Inductor	Voltage (V)	Rate of change of current (dI/dt)	Inductance (L)	$V = L\dfrac{dI}{dt}$

Combining Capacitors and Inductors

Mathematically, capacitors in series or parallel combine like springs, and inductors combine like resistors.

For two capacitors, C_1 and C_2 in **parallel**, the equivalent capacitance is given by

$$C_{eq} = C_1 + C_2$$

In general, for any number of capacitors in parallel, the equivalent capacitance is

$$C_{eq} = \sum_{i=1}^{N} C_i$$

On the other hand, two capacitors in **series** combine as the reciprocal of the sum of the reciprocals, given by

$$C_{eq} = \frac{1}{\dfrac{1}{C_1} + \dfrac{1}{C_2}}$$

or in general for any number of series capacitors

$$C_{eq} = \frac{1}{\sum\limits_{i=1}^{N} \dfrac{1}{C_i}}$$

To help you remember which configuration matches which mathematical form, consider that the larger the area of the plates of the capacitor, the larger the capacitance. If capacitors are connected in parallel, the total plate area connected to each terminal is greater, thus the capacitance increases. This is represented by the sum, not the reciprocal of the sum of the reciprocals.

COMPREHENSION CHECK 12-7

You have four 60 nanofarad [nF] capacitors. Using two or more of these capacitors in parallel or series, how many different equivalent capacitances can you form that are greater than 110 nF? Show the circuits for each such connection and list the resulting capacitances.

For two inductors, L_1 and L_2 in **series**, the equivalent inductance is given by

$$L_{eq} = L_1 + L_2$$

In general, for any number of inductors in series, the equivalent inductance is

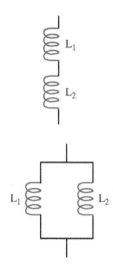

$$L_{eq} = \sum\limits_{i=1}^{N} L_i$$

On the other hand, two inductors in **parallel** combine as the reciprocal of the sum of the reciprocals, given by

$$L_{eq} = \frac{1}{\dfrac{1}{L_1} + \dfrac{1}{L_2}}$$

or in general for any number of parallel inductors

$$L_{eq} = \frac{1}{\sum\limits_{i=1}^{N} \dfrac{1}{L_i}}$$

To help you remember which configuration matches which mathematical form, consider that the more turns of wire the current has to go through in an inductor, the larger the inductance. If inductors are connected in series, the total number of turns of wire the current must go through is larger, thus the inductance is larger, so this must be the sum, not the reciprocal of the sum of the reciprocals.

12.3 POWER FUNCTIONS

LEARN TO: Recognize the shape and boundaries of a power function shown graphically
Recognize when an equation is a power model
Determine the physical meaning and units of parameters of a power function

Trend	Equation	Data Form	Graphical Example
Power	$y = bx^m$	Positive m Value of zero at $x = 0$ ————————— Negative m Value of infinity at $x = 0$	

Generalized power models take the form $y = bx^m + c$. One example:

- One expression for the volume (V) of a conical frustrum with base radius (r) is

$$V = \frac{\pi (H + h)}{3} r^2 - V_T$$

where H is the height of the frustrum, h is the height of the missing conical top, and V_T is the volume of the top part of the cone that is missing. In this case, $b = \dfrac{\pi (H + h)}{3}$ and $c = -V_T$.

In this chapter, we will only consider power law models, where c is zero. In the next chapter we will discuss ways of dealing with data when the value of c is non-zero. Examples of a power model where $c = 0$:

- Many geometric formulae involving areas, volumes, etc., such as the volume of a sphere (V) as a function of radius (r):

$$V = 4/3\pi r^3$$

- Distance (d) traveled by a body undergoing constant acceleration (a) over time (t), starting from rest:

$$d = at^2$$

- Energy calculations in a variety of contexts, both mechanical and electrical, such as the kinetic energy (KE) of an object as a function of the object's velocity (v), where the constant (k) depends upon the object shape and type of motion:

$$KE = kmv^2$$

- Ideal gas law relationships, such as Boyle's law, relating volume (V) and pressure (P) of an ideal gas, holding temperature (T) and quantity of gas (n) constant:

$$V = (nRT)P^{-1}$$

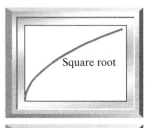

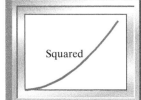

General Model Rules

Given a power system of the form $y = bx^m + c$, assuming $x \geq 0$:

- When $m = 1$, the model is a linear function.

- When $m = 0$, $y = b + c$, regardless of the value of x (y never changes).

- When m is rational, the function will contain a rational exponent or may be described with a radical symbol ($\sqrt{}$). Certain rational exponents have special names ($\frac{1}{2}$ is "square root," $\frac{1}{3}$ is "cube root").

- When m is an integer, the function will contain an integer exponent on the independent variable. Certain exponents have special names (2 is "squared," 3 is "cubed").

- When $0 < |m| < 1$ and $x < 0$, the function may contain complex values.

● EXAMPLE 12-5

NOTE

With a positive integer exponent, the dependent variable (volume) increases as the independent variable (radius) increases. This observation is true with any power model with a positive integer exponent.

The volume (V) of a cone is calculated in terms of the radius (r) and height (H) of the cone. The relationship is described by the following equation:

$$V = \frac{\pi r^2 H}{3}$$

Given a height of 10 centimeters, calculate the volume of the cone when the radius is 3 centimeters.

$$V = \frac{\pi (3 \text{ cm})^2 (10 \text{ cm})}{3} \approx 94.2 \text{ cm}^3$$

What is the volume of the cone when the radius is 8 centimeters?

$$V = \frac{\pi (8 \text{ cm})^2 (10 \text{ cm})}{3} \approx 670 \text{ cm}^3$$

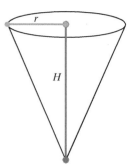

● EXAMPLE 12-6

The resistance (R [g/(cm^{4}s)]) of blood flow in an artery or vein depends upon the radius (r [cm]), as described by **Poiseuille's equation**:

$$R = \frac{8\mu L}{\pi} r^{-4}$$

The dynamic viscosity of blood (μ [g/(cm s)]) and length of the artery or vein (L [cm]) are constants in the system. In studying the effects of a cholesterol-lowering drug, you mimic the constricting of an artery being clogged with cholesterol, shown in the illustration. You use the data you collect to create the following graph.

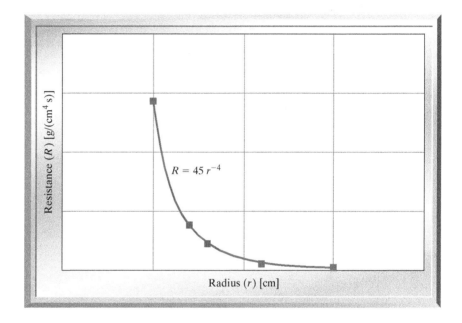

NOTE

With a negative integer exponent, the dependent variable (resistance) decreases as the independent variable (radius) increases. This trend is true for any power model with a negative integer exponent.

If the length of the artificial artery tested was 505 centimeters, what is the dynamic viscosity of the sample used to mimic blood, in units of grams per centimeter second [g/(cm s)]?

The constant "45" has physical meaning, found by comparison to the theoretical expression.

In theory: $R = \dfrac{8\,\mu L}{\pi} r^{-4}$ and from graph: $R = 45 r^{-4}$

By comparison:

$$45\,\frac{g}{s} = \frac{8\,\mu L}{\pi} = \frac{8\,\mu\,(505\text{ cm})}{\pi}$$

$$\mu = 0.035\text{ g/(cm s)}$$

COMPREHENSION CHECK 12-9

The graph shows the ideal gas law relationship ($PV = nRT$) between pressure (P) and volume (V). If the tank is at a temperature of 300 kelvins and is filled with nitrogen (formula, N_2; molecular weight, 28 grams per mole), what is the mass of gas in the tank in units of grams?

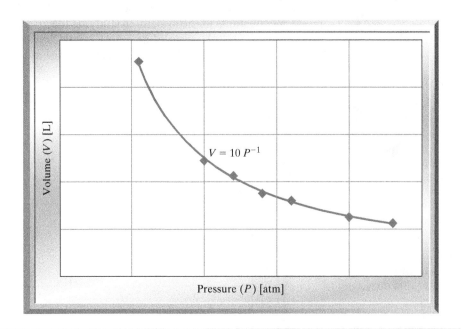

$V = 10\,P^{-1}$

Volume (V) [L]

Pressure (P) [atm]

COMPREHENSION CHECK 12-10

The graph above shows the ideal gas law relationship ($PV = nRT$) between pressure (P) and volume (V). If the tank is filled with 10 grams of oxygen (formula, O_2; molecular weight, 32 grams per mole), what is the temperature of the tank in units of degrees Celsius?

12.4 EXPONENTIAL FUNCTIONS

LEARN TO: Recognize the shape and boundaries of an exponential function shown graphically
Recognize when an equation is an exponential model
Determine the physical meaning and units of parameters of an experimental function

Trend	Equation	Data Form	Graphical Example
Exponential	$y = be^{mx} + c$	Defined value at $x = 0$ ($y = b + c$)	
		Positive m: asymptotic to c for large negative values of x	
		Negative m: asymptotic to c at large positive values of x	

Exponential models take the form $y = be^{mx} + c$. Examples include

- A newly forged ingot has an initial temperature (T_0) and is left to cool at room temperature (T_R). The temperature (T) of the ingot as it cools over time (t) is given by

$$T = (T_0 - T_R) e^{mt} + T_R$$

where m will be a negative value and $c = T_R$. Note that $b = T_0 - T_R$, so that at $t = 0$, $T = T_0$ as expected.

- The voltage (V) across a capacitor (C) as a function of time (t), with initial voltage (V_0) discharging its stored charge through resistance (R):

$$V = V_0 e^{-t/(RC)}$$

- The number (N) of people infected with a virus such as smallpox or H1N1 flu as a function of time (t), given the following: an initial number of infected individuals (N_0), no artificial immunization available and dependence on contact conditions between species (C):

$$N = N_0 e^{Ct}$$

- The transmissivity (T) of light through a gas as a function of path length (L), given an absorption cross-section (s) and density of absorbers (N):

$$T = e^{-sNL}$$

- The growth of bacteria (C) as a function of time (t), given an initial concentration of bacteria (C_0) and depending on growth conditions (g):

$$C = C_0 e^{gt}$$

Note that all exponents must be dimensionless, and thus unitless. For example, in the first equation, the quantity m *must have units of inverse time so that the quantity of* mt *will be unitless.*

Note that the intercept value (c) is zero in all of the above examples except the first one.

General Model Rules

Given an exponential system of the form $y = be^{mx} + c$:

- When $m = 0$, $y = b + c$ regardless of the value of x (y never changes).
- When $m > 0$, the model is a **growth function**. The minimum value of the growth model for $x \geq 0$ is $b + c$. As x approaches infinity, y approaches infinity.
- When $m < 0$, the model is a **decay function**. The value of the decay model approaches c as x approaches infinity. When $x = 0$, $y = b + c$.

What Is "e"?

The **exponential constant** "e" is a transcendental number, thus also an irrational number, that can be rounded to 2.71828. It is defined as the base of the natural logarithm function. Sometimes, e is referred to as **Euler's number** or the **Napier constant**. The reference to Euler comes from the Swiss mathematician Leonhard Euler (pronounced "oiler," 1707–1783), who made vast contributions to calculus, including the notation and terminology used today. John Napier (1550–1617) was a Scottish mathematician credited with inventing logarithms and popularizing the use of the decimal point.

Growth Functions

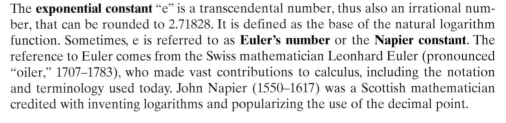

Growth function

An exponential **growth function** is a type of function that increases without bound as the independent variable increases. For a system to be considered an exponential growth function, the exponential growth model ($y = be^{mx} + c$) with m is a positive value that represents the **growth rate**.

A more general exponential growth function can be formed by replacing the Napier constant with an arbitrary constant, or $y = ba^{mx} + c$. In general, a must be greater than 1 for the system to be a growth function. The value of a is referred to as the *base*, m is the *growth rate*, b is the *initial value*, and c is a *vertical shift*. Note that when $a = 1$ or $m = 0$, the system is reduced to $y = b + c$, which is a constant.

● EXAMPLE 12-7

In 1965, Gordon E. Moore, co-founder of Intel Corporation, claimed in a paper that the number of transistors on an integrated circuit will double every 2 years. This idea by Moore was later referred to as **Moore's law**. The Intel 4004 CPU was released in 1971 as the first commercially available microprocessor. The Intel 4004 CPU contained 2,300 transistors. This system can be modeled with the following growth function:

$$T = T_0 2^{t/2}$$

In the equation, T_0 represents the initial number of transistors, and t is the number of years since T_0 transistors were observed on an integrated circuit. Predict the number of transistors on an integrated circuit in 1974 using the Intel 4004 CPU as the initial condition.

$$t = 1974 - 1971 = 3 \text{ years}$$

$$T = T_0 2^{t/2} = 2{,}300\left(2^{3/2}\right) = 2{,}300\left(2^{1.5}\right) \approx 6{,}505 \text{ transistors}$$

In 1974, the Intel 8080 processor came out with 4,500 transistors on the circuit.

Predict the number of transistors on integrated circuits in 1982 using the Intel 4004 CPU as the initial condition.

$$t = 1982 - 1971 = 11 \text{ years}$$

$$T = T_0 2^{t/2} = 2{,}300\left(2^{11/2}\right) = 2{,}300\left(2^{5.5}\right) \approx 104{,}087 \text{ transistors}$$

In 1982, the Intel 286 microprocessor came out with 134,000 transistors in the CPU.

Predict the number of transistors on integrated circuits in 2007 using the Intel 4004 CPU as the initial condition.

$$t = 2007 - 1971 = 36 \; years$$

$$T = T_0 2^{t/2} = 2{,}300 \left(2^{36/2} \right) = 2{,}300 \left(2^{18} \right) \approx 603{,}000{,}000 \; transistors$$

In 2007, the NVIDIA G80 came out with 681,000,000 transistors in the CPU.

No one really knows how long Moore's law will hold up. It is perhaps interesting to note that claims have consistently been made for the past 30 years that Moore's law will only hold up for another 10 years. Although many prognosticators are still saying this, some are not. There is, however, a limit to how small a transistor can be made. Any structure has to be at least one atom wide, for example, and as they become ever smaller, quantum effects will probably wreak havoc. Of course, chips can be made larger, multilayer structures can be built, new technologies may be developed (the first functional memristor was demonstrated in 2008), and so forth.

● **EXAMPLE 12-8**   An environmental engineer has obtained a bacteria culture from a municipal water sample and allowed the bacteria to grow. After several hours of data collection, the following graph is created. The growth of bacteria is modeled by the following equation, where B_0 is the initial concentration of bacteria at time zero, and g is the growth constant.

$$B = B_0 \, e^{gt}$$

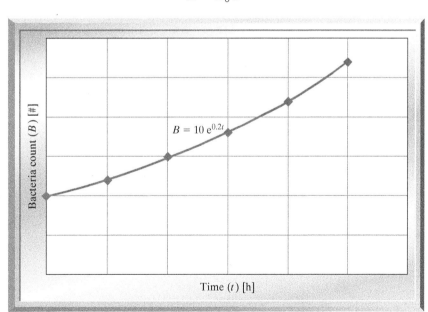

What was the initial concentration of bacteria?

In theory: $B = B_0 e^{gt}$ and from graph: $B = 10e^{0.2t}$

By comparison: $B_0 = 10$ bacteria

What was the growth constant (g) of this bacteria strain?

In theory: $B = B_0 e^{gt}$ and from graph: $B = 10e^{0.2t}$

By comparison: $g = 0.2$ per hour. Recall that exponents must be unitless, so the quantity of ($g \, t$) must be a unitless group. To be unitless, g must have units of inverse time.

The engineer wants to know how long it will take for the bacteria culture population to grow to 30,000.

To calculate the amount of time, plug in 30,000 for B and solve for t:

$$30{,}000 = 10e^{0.2t}$$

$$3{,}000 = e^{0.2t}$$

$$\ln(3{,}000) = \ln(e^{0.2t}) = 0.2t$$

$$t = \frac{\ln(3{,}000)}{0.2\left[\frac{1}{h}\right]} = 40 \text{ h}$$

Decay Functions

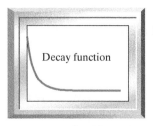

Decay function

A **decay function** is a type of function that decreases and asymptotically approaches a value as the independent variable increases. In the exponential decay model $(y = be^{-mx} + c)$, m is a positive value that represents the **decay rate**.

An electrical engineer wants to determine how long it will take for a particular capacitor in a circuit to discharge. The engineer wired a voltage source across a capacitor (C, farads) and a resistor (R, ohms) connected in series. After the capacitor is fully charged, the circuit is completed between the capacitor and resistor, and the voltage source is removed from the circuit. The product of R and C in a circuit like this is called the "time constant" and is usually denoted by the Greek letter tau ($\tau = RC$).

The following equation can be used to calculate the voltage across a discharging capacitor at a particular time:

NOTE

Exponential models are often given in the form $y = be^{-t/\tau} + c$, where t is time; thus τ also has units of time. In this case, the constant τ is often called the **time constant**. Basically, the time constant is a measure of the time required for the response of the system to go approximately two-thirds of the way from its initial value to its final value, as t approaches infinity. The exact value is not $2/3$, but $1 - e^{-1} \approx 0.632$ or 63.2%.

$$V = V_0 e^{-\frac{t}{\tau}} = V_0 e^{-\frac{t}{RC}}$$

Assuming a resistance of 100 kiloohms [kΩ], a capacitance of 100 microfarads [μF], and an initial voltage (V_0) of 20 volts [V], determine the voltage across the capacitor after 10 seconds.

$$V = 20 \text{ [V] } e^{-\frac{10 \text{ s}}{(100 \text{ k}\Omega)(100 \text{ } \mu\text{F})}}$$

$$= 20 \text{ [V] } e^{-\frac{10 \text{ s}}{(100 \times 10^3 \Omega)(100 \times 10^{-6} \text{F})}} \approx 7.36 \text{ V}$$

Assuming a resistance of 200 kiloohms [kΩ], a capacitance of 100 microfarads [μF], and an initial voltage (V_0) of 20 volts [V], determine the voltage across the capacitor after 20 seconds.

$$V = 20[V]e^{-\frac{20 \text{ s}}{(200 \text{ k}\Omega)(100 \text{ } \mu\text{F})}} \approx 7.36 \text{ V}$$

Note that doubling the resistance in the circuit doubles the amount of time required to discharge the capacitor. In RC circuits, it is easy to increase the discharge time of a capacitor by increasing the resistance in the circuit.

The decay of a radioactive isotope was tracked over a number of hours, resulting in the following data. The decay of a radioactive element is modeled by the following equation, where C_0 is the initial amount of the element at time zero, and k is the decay constant of the isotope.

$$C = C_0 e^{-kt}$$

Determine the initial concentration and decay constant of the isotope, including value and units.

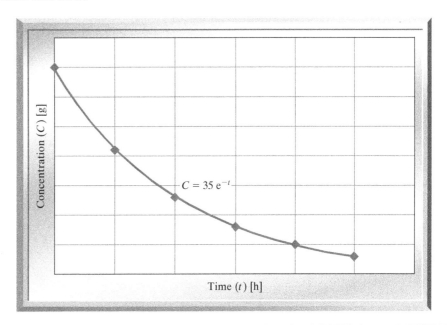

$$C = 35\, e^{-t}$$

Picture of a single mortar shot. The creation of fireworks involves knowledge of chemistry (what materials to include to get the desired colors), physics and dynamics (what amounts of combustible charge should be included to launch the object properly), and artistry (what colors, shapes, patterns, and sounds the firework should emit such that it is enjoyable to watch). This picture is a close-up of the instant when a firework is detonating.

Photo courtesy of E. Fenimore

In-Class Activities

ICA 12-1

The graph shows the ideal gas law relationship ($PV = nRT$) between volume (V) and temperature (T).

(a) What are the units of the slope (0.0175)?

(b) If the tank has a pressure of 1.2 atmospheres and is filled with nitrogen (formula, N_2; molecular weight, 28 grams per mole), what is the mass of gas in the tank in units of grams?

(c) If the tank is filled with 10 grams of oxygen (formula, O_2; molecular weight, 32 grams per mole), what is the pressure of the tank (P) in units of atmospheres?

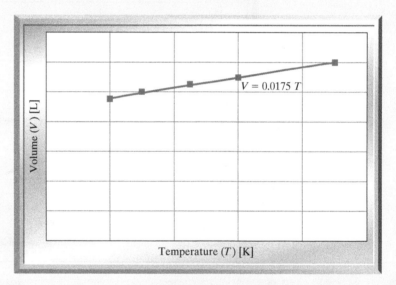

ICA 12-2

An inductor is an electrical device that can store energy in the form of a magnetic field. In the simplest form, an inductor is a cylindrical coil of wire, and its inductance (L), measured in henrys [H], can be calculated by

$$L = \frac{\mu_0 n^2 A}{\ell}$$

where

μ_0 = permeability of free space = $4\pi \times 10^{-7}$ [newtons per ampere squared, N/A^2]
n = number of turns of wire [dimensionless]
A = cross-sectional area of coil [square meters, m^2]
ℓ = length of coil [meters, m]
L = inductance [henrys, H] = [J/A^2]

Several inductors were fabricated with the same number of turns of wire (n) and the same length (ℓ), but with different diameters, thus different cross-sectional areas (A). The inductances were measured and plotted as a function of cross-sectional area, and a mathematical model was developed to describe the relationship, as shown on the graph below.

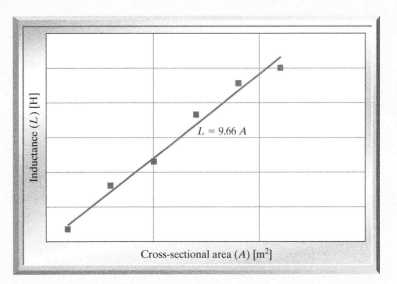

$$L = 9.66\,A$$

Cross-sectional area (A) [m^2]

(a) What are the units of the slope (9.66)?
(b) For an inductor fabricated as described above, what is its diameter if its inductance is 0.2 henrys? Give your answer in centimeters.
(c) If the length of the coil (ℓ) equals 0.1 meter, how many turns of wire (n) are in the inductor?

ICA 12-3

Solid objects, such as your desk or a rod of aluminum, can conduct heat. The magnitude of the thermal diffusivity of the material determines how quickly the heat moves through a given amount of material. The equation for thermal diffusivity (α) is given by:

$$\alpha = \frac{k}{\rho\, C_\mathrm{p}}$$

Experiments are conducted to change the thermal conductivity (k) of the material while holding the specific heat (C_p) and the density (ρ) constant. The results are shown graphically.

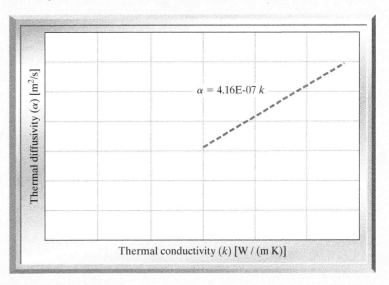

$$\alpha = 4.16\mathrm{E}\text{-}07\,k$$

Thermal conductivity (k) [W / (m K)]

(a) What are the units of the constant 4.16×10^{-7}? Simplify your answer.

(b) If the specific heat of the material is 890 joules per kilogram kelvin, what is the density of the material?

(c) If the material has a density of 4,500 kilograms per cubic meter, what is the specific heat of the material in units of joules per kilogram kelvin?

ICA 12-4

Mercury has a dynamic viscosity of 1.55 centipoises and a specific gravity of 13.6.

(a) What is the density of mercury in units of kilograms per cubic meter?

(b) What is the dynamic viscosity of mercury in units of pound-mass per foot second?

(c) What is the dynamic viscosity of mercury in units of pascal seconds?

(d) What is the kinematic viscosity of mercury in units of stokes?

ICA 12-5

SAE 10W30 motor oil has a dynamic viscosity of 0.17 kilograms per meter second and a specific gravity of 0.876.

(a) What is the density of the motor oil in units of kilograms per cubic meter?

(b) What is the dynamic viscosity of the motor oil in units of pound-mass per foot second?

(c) What is the dynamic viscosity of the motor oil in units of centipoise?

(d) What is the kinematic viscosity of the motor oil in units of stokes?

ICA 12-6

You have two springs each of stiffness 1 newton per meter [N/m] and one spring of stiffness 2 newtons per meter [N/m].

(a) There are ___ configurations possible, with ___ unique combinations, resulting in ___ different stiffness values.

A "configuration" is a way of combining the springs. For example, two springs in parallel is one configuration; two springs in series is a second configuration.

A "combination" is the specific way of combining given springs to form an effective spring constant. For example, combining Spring #1 and #2 in parallel is one combination; combining Spring #1 and #3 in parallel is a second combination. These combinations may or may not result in a unique effective spring constant.

(b) What is the stiffest combination, and what is the spring constant of this combination?

(c) What is the least stiff combination, and what is the spring constant of this combination?

ICA 12-7

You have three resistors of resistance 30 ohm [Ω].

(a) There are ___ configurations possible, with ___ unique combinations, resulting in ___ different resistance values.

A "configuration" is a way of combining the resistors. For example, two resistors in parallel is one configuration; two resistors in series is a second configuration.

A "combination" is the specific way of combining given resistors to form an effective resistance. For example, combining Resistor #1 and #2 in parallel is one combination; combining Resistor #1 and #3 in parallel is a second combination. These combinations may or may not result in a unique effective resistance.

(b) What is the greatest resistance that can be made from a combination of resistors, and what is the effective resistance of this combination?

(c) What is the least resistance that can be made from a combination of resistors, and what is the effective resistance of this combination?

ICA 12-8

Four springs were tested, with the results shown graphically below. Use the graph to answer the following questions.

(a) Which spring is the stiffest?
(b) Which spring, if placed in parallel with Spring C, would yield the stiffest combination?
(c) Which spring, if placed in series with Spring C, would yield the stiffest combination?
(d) Rank the following combinations in order of stiffness:

Spring A and Spring D are hooked in parallel
Spring B and Spring C are hooked in series, then connected with Spring D in parallel
Spring A
Spring D

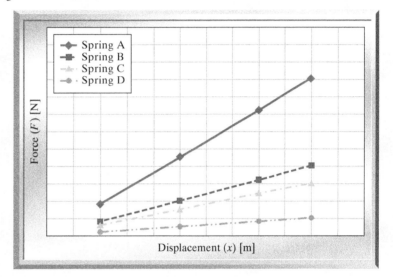

ICA 12-9

Four circuits were tested, with the results shown graphically below. Use the graph to answer the following questions.

(a) Which resistor gives the most resistance?
(b) What is the resistance of Resistor A?
(c) Which resistor, if placed in parallel with Resistor C, would yield the highest resistance?
(d) Which resistor, if placed in series with Resistor C, would yield the highest resistance?

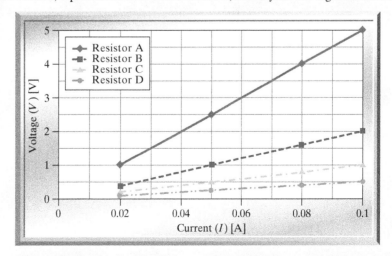

ICA 12-10

Assume you have an unlimited number of inductors all with the same inductance L.

(a) How would you connect 4 of these inductors so that the equivalent inductance equals L?

(b) How would you connect N^2 of these inductors so that the equivalent inductance equals L?

ICA 12-11

(a) The equivalent capacitance of the circuit shown is 6 nF. Determine the value of C.

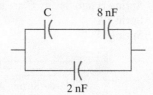

C   8 nF

2 nF

(b) The equivalent capacitance of the circuit shown is 5 nF. Determine the value of C.

1 nF

4 nF

C

3 nF

ICA 12-12

A standard guitar, whether acoustic or electric, has six strings, all with essentially the same total length between the bridge and the nut at the tuning head. Each string vibrates at a different frequency determined by the tension on the string and the mass per unit length of the string. In order to create pitches (notes) other than these six, the guitarist presses the strings down against the fretboard, thus shortening the length of the strings and changing their frequencies. In other words, the vibrating frequency of a string depends on tension, length, and mass per unit length of the string.

The equation for the fundamental frequency of a vibrating string is given by

$$f = \frac{\sqrt{T/\mu}}{2L}$$

where

f = frequency [Hz]
T = string tension [N]
μ = mass per unit length [kg/m]
L = string length [m]

Many electric guitars have a device often called a "whammy" bar or a "tremolo" bar that allows the guitarist to change the tension on the strings quickly and easily, thus changing the frequency of the strings. (Think of Jimi Hendrix simulating "the rockets' red glare, the bombs bursting in air" in his rendition of *The Star Spangled Banner* – a true *tour de force*.) In designing a new whammy bar, we test our design by collecting data using a single string on the guitar and creating a graph of the observed frequency at different string tensions as shown.

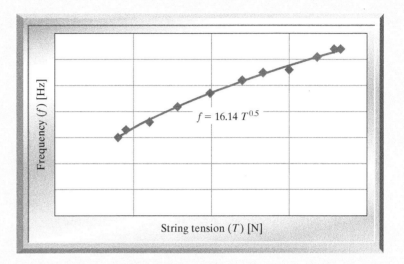

(a) What are the units of the coefficient (16.14)?
(b) If the observed frequency is 150 hertz, what is the string tension in newtons?
(c) If mass per unit length is 2.3 grams per meter, what is the length of the string in meters?
(d) If the length of the string is 0.67 meters, what is the mass per unit length in kilograms per meter?

ICA 12-13

A standard guitar, whether acoustic or electric, has six strings, all with essentially the same total length between the bridge and the nut at the tuning head. Each string vibrates at a different frequency determined by the tension on the string and the mass per unit length of the string. In order to create pitches (notes) other than these six, the guitarist presses the strings down against the fretboard, thus shortening the length of the strings and changing their frequencies. In other words, the vibrating frequency of a string depends on tension, length, and mass per unit length of the string.

The equation for the fundamental frequency of a vibrating string is given by

$$f = \frac{\sqrt{T/\mu}}{2L}$$

where

f = frequency [Hz]
T = string tension [N]
μ = mass per unit length [kg/m]
L = string length [m]

Many electric guitars have a device often called a "whammy" bar or a "tremolo" bar that allows the guitarist to change the tension on the strings quickly and easily, thus changing the frequency of the strings. (Think of Jimi Hendrix simulating "the rockets red glare, the bombs bursting in air" in his rendition of *The Star Spangled Banner* – a true *tour de force*.) In designing a new whammy bar, we test our design by collecting data using a single string on the guitar and creating a graph of the observed frequency at different string lengths as shown.

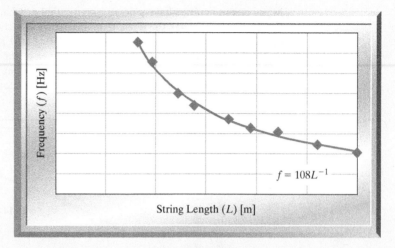

(a) Is the relationship between frequency and length linear, power, or exponential?
(b) What are the units of the coefficient (108)?
(c) If the tension on the string is 135 newtons, what is the mass per unit length in grams per meter?
(d) If the mass per length of the string is 3.5 grams per meter, what is the tension in newtons?

ICA 12-14

Solid objects, such as your desk or a rod of aluminum, can conduct heat. The magnitude of the thermal diffusivity of the material determines how quickly the heat moves through a given amount of material. The equation for thermal diffusivity (α) is given by:

$$\alpha = \frac{k}{\rho \, C_p}$$

Experiments are conducted to change the specific heat (C_p) of the material while holding the thermal conductivity (k) and the density (ρ) constant. The results are shown graphically.

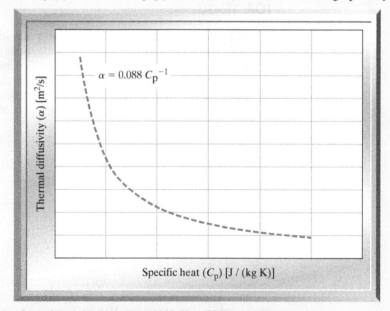

(a) What are the units of the constant 0.088? Simplify your answer.
(b) If the thermal conductivity of the material is 237 watts per meter kelvin, what is the density of the material?
(c) If the material has a density of 4,500 kilograms per cubic meter, what is the thermal conductivity of the material in units of watts per meter kelvin?

ICA 12-15

Eutrophication is a process whereby lakes, estuaries, or slow-moving streams receive excess nutrients that stimulate excessive plant growth. This enhanced plant growth, often called an algal bloom, reduces dissolved oxygen in the water when dead plant material decomposes and can cause other organisms to die. Nutrients can come from many sources, such as fertilizers; deposition of nitrogen from the atmosphere; erosion of soil containing nutrients; and sewage treatment plant discharges. Water with a low concentration of dissolved oxygen is called hypoxic. A biosystems engineering models the algae growth in a lake. The concentration of algae (C), measured in grams per milliliter [g/mL], can be calculated by

$$C = C_0 e^{\left(\frac{kt}{r}\right)}$$

where

C_0 = initial concentration of algae [?]

k = multiplication rate of the algae [?]

r = estimated nutrient supply amount [mg of nutrient per mL of sample water]

t = time [days]

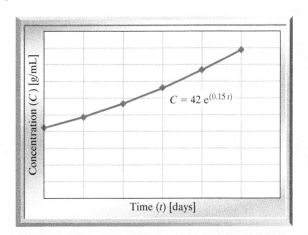

(a) For the exponential model shown, list the value and units of the parameters m and b. You do not need to simplify any units. Recall that an exponential model has the form: $y = be^{mx}$.
(b) What are the units on the multiplication rate of the algae (k)?
(c) If the algae are allowed to grow for 10 days with an estimated nutrient supply of 3 milligrams of nutrient per milliliter of water sample, what is the multiplication rate of the algae (k)?

ICA 12-16

The graph below shows the relationship between current and voltage in a 1N4148 small signal diode (a semiconductor device that allows current to flow in one direction but not the other).

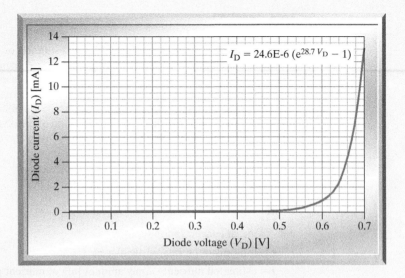

Semiconductor diodes can be characterized by the Shockley Equation:

$$I_D = I_0\left(e^{\frac{qV_D}{nkT}} - 1\right)$$

where

I_D is the diode current [amperes]

I_0 is the reverse saturation current, constant for any specific diode

q is the charge on a single electron, 1.602×10^{-19} coulombs

V_D is the voltage across the diode [volts]

n is the emission coefficient, having a numerical value typically between 1 and 2, and constant for any specific device.

k is Boltzmann's Constant, 1.381×10^{-23} joules per kelvin

T is the temperature of the device [kelvin]

(a) What are the units of the -1 following the exponential term? Justify your answer.

(b) If the device temperature is 100 degrees Fahrenheit, what are the units of the emission coefficient, n, and what is its numerical value? (*Hint: Electrical power [W] equals a volt times an ampere: $P = VI$. One ampere equals one coulomb per second.*)

(c) What is the numerical value and units of the reverse saturation current, I_0? Use an appropriate metric prefix in your final answer.

ICA 12-17

The total quantity (mass) of a radioactive substance decreases (decays) with time as

$$m = m_0 e^{-\frac{t}{\tau}}$$

where

t = time [days]

τ = time constant

m_0 = initial mass (at $t = 0$)

m = mass at time t [mg]

A few milligrams each of three different isotopes of uranium were assayed for isotopic composition over a period of several days to determine the decay rate of each. The data was graphed and a mathematical model derived to describe the decay of each isotope.

(a) What are the units of τ if time is measured in days?

(b) What is the initial amount of each isotope at $t = 0$?

Isotope	Half-life [days]
230U	20.8
231U	4.2
237U	6.75
240U	0.59

(c) When will 1 milligram of the original isotope to remain in each sample?

(d) Four isotopes of uranium are shown in the table with their half-lives. Which isotope most likely matches each of the three samples? Note that one isotope does not have a match on the graph.

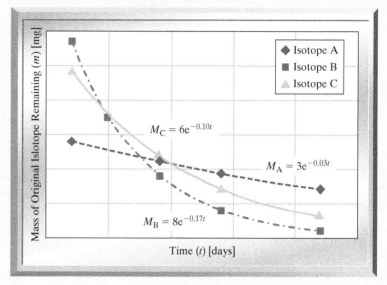

ICA 12-18

Match the data series from the options shown on the graph to the following model types. You may assume that power and exponential models do not have a constant offset. You may also assume that only positive values are shown on the two axes. For each match, write "Series X," where X is the appropriate letter, A through F. If no curve matches the specified criterion, write "No Match." If more than one curve matches a given specification, list both series.

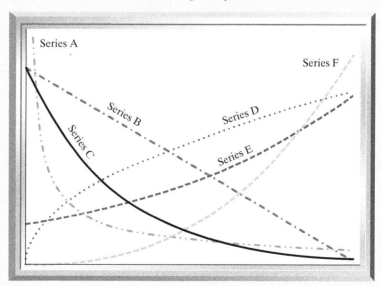

(a) Exponential, negative numeric value in exponent

(b) Power, negative numeric value in exponent

(c) Linear, negative slope

(d) Exponential, positive numeric value in exponent

(e) Power, positive numeric value in exponent

Chapter 12 REVIEW QUESTIONS

1. For a simple capacitor with two flat plates, the capacitance (C) [F] can be calculated by

$$C = \frac{\varepsilon_r \varepsilon_0 A}{d}$$

where

$\varepsilon_0 = 8.854 \times 10^{-12}$ [F/m] (the permittivity of free space in farads per meter)
ε_r = relative static permittivity, a property of the insulator [dimensionless]
A = area of overlap of the plates [m²]
d = distance between the plates [m]

Several experimental capacitors were fabricated with different plate areas (A), but with the same inter-plate distance ($d = 1.2$ mm) and the same insulating material, and thus the same relative static permittivity (ε_r). The capacitance of each device was measured and plotted versus the plate area. The graph and trendline are shown below. The numeric scales were deliberately omitted.

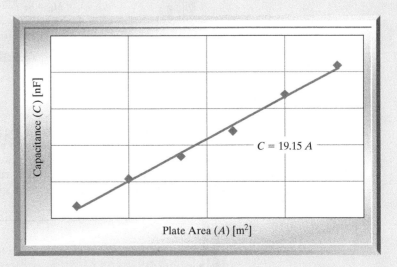

(a) What are the units of the slope (19.15)?
(b) If the capacitance is 2 nanofarads [nF], what is the area (A) of the plates?
(c) What is the relative static permittivity of the insulating layer?
(d) If the distance between the plates were doubled, how would the capacitance be affected?

2. When we wish to generate hydroelectric power, we build a dam to back up the water in a river. If the water has a height (H, in units of feet) above the downstream discharge, and we can discharge water through the turbines at a rate (Q, in units of cubic feet per second [cfs]), the maximum power (P, in units of kilowatts) we can expect to generate is:

$$P = CHQ$$

For a small "run of the river" hydroelectric facility, we have obtained the following data.

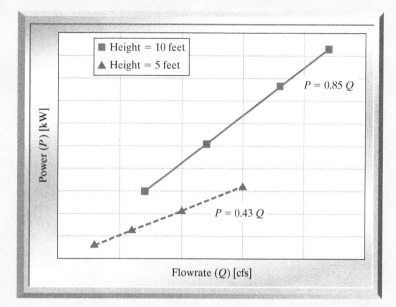

Flowrate (Q) [cfs]

(a) Using the trendline results, and examining the general equation above, determine the value and units of the coefficient C for a height of 10 feet.

(b) If the flow rate was 15 cubic feet per second and the height is 3 meters, what would the power output be in units of horsepower?

(c) If the flow rate was 10 cubic feet per second and the height is 8 meters, what would the power output be in units of horsepower?

3. When rain falls over an area for a sufficiently long time, it will run off and collect at the bottom of hills and eventually find its way into creeks and rivers. A simple way to estimate the maximum discharge flow rate (Q, in units of cubic feet per second [cfs]) from a watershed of area (A, in units of acres) with a rainfall intensity (i, in units of inches per hour) is given by an expression commonly called the Rational Method, as

$$Q = CiA$$

Values of C vary between about 0 (for flat rural areas) to almost 1 (in urban areas with a large amount of paved area).

A survey of a number of rainfall events was made over a 10-year period for three different watersheds. The data that resulted is given in the table below. Watershed A is 120 acres, B is 316 acres, and C is 574 acres.

Storm event	Watershed	Rainfall Intensity (i) [in/h]	Maximum Runoff (Q) [cfs]
1	A	0.5	30
2	A	1.1	66
3	A	1.6	96
4	A	2.1	126
5	B	0.3	47
6	B	0.7	110
7	B	1.2	188
8	B	1.8	283
9	C	0.4	115
10	C	1	287
11	C	1.5	430
12	C	2.4	690

(a) Create a graph containing all three watersheds, with flowrate on the ordinate and fit linear trendlines to obtain a simple model for each watershed.
From the information given and the trendline model obtained, answer the following:

(b) What is the value and units of the coefficient C?

(c) What would the maximum flow rate be from a watershed of 400 acres if the rainfall intensity was 0.6 inches per hour?

(d) How long would it take at this flowrate to fill an Olympic sized swimming pool that is 50 meters long, 20 meters wide, and 2 meters deep?

4. You are experimenting with several liquid metal alloys to find a suitable replacement for the mercury used in thermometers. You have attached capillary tubes with a circular cross-section and an inside diameter of 0.3 millimeters to reservoirs containing 5 cubic centimeters of each alloy. You mark the position of the liquid in each capillary tube when the temperature is 20 degrees Celsius, systematically change the temperature, and measure the distance the liquid moves in the tube as it expands or contracts with changes in temperature. Note that negative values correspond to contraction of the material due to lower temperatures. The data you collected for four different alloys is shown in the table below.

Alloy G1		Alloy G2		Alloy G3		Alloy G4	
Temperature (T) [°C]	Distance (d) [cm]	Temperature (T) [°C]	Distance (d) [cm]	Temperature (T) [°C]	Distance (d) [cm]	Temperature (T) [°C]	Distance (d) [cm]
22	1.05	21	0.95	24	2.9	25	5.1
27	3.05	29	7.65	30	7.2	33	13.8
34	6.95	33	10.6	34	9.8	16	−4.3
14	−3.5	17	−2.6	19	−0.6	13	−7.05
9	−5.1	3	−14.8	12	−6.15	6	−14.65
2	−8.7	−2	−19.8	4	−11.5	−2	−22.15
−5	−11.7	−8	−25.4	−5	−18.55	−6	−26.3
−11	−15.5					−12	−32.4

(a) In Excel, create two new columns for each compound to calculate the change in temperature (ΔT) relative to 20°C (for example, 25°C gives $\Delta T = 5$°C) and the corresponding change in volume (ΔV).
Plot the change in volume versus the change in temperature; fit a linear trendline to each data set.

(b) From the trendline equations, determine the value and units of the coefficient of thermal expansion, β, for each alloy. Note that $\Delta V = \beta V \Delta T$, where V is the initial volume.

(c) There is a small constant offset (C) in each trendline equation $(\Delta V = \beta V \Delta T + C)$. What is the physical origin of this constant term? Can it be safely ignored? In other words, is its effect on the determination of β negligible?

5. The resistance of a wire (R [ohm]) is a function of the wire dimensions (A = cross-sectional area, L = length) and material (ρ = resistivity) according to the relationship

$$R = \frac{\rho L}{A}$$

The resistance of three wires was tested. All wires had the same cross-sectional area.

Length (L) [m]	0.01	0.1	0.25	0.4	0.5	0.6
Resistance Wire 1 (R1) [Ω]	8.00E-05	8.00E-04	2.00E-03	3.50E-03	4.00E-03	4.75E-03
Resistance Wire 2 (R2) [Ω]	4.75E-05	4.80E-04	1.00E-03	2.00E-03	2.50E-03	3.00E-03
Resistance Wire 3 (R3) [Ω]	1.50E-04	1.70E-03	4.25E-03	7.00E-03	8.50E-03	1.00E-02

(a) Plot the data and fit a linear trendline model to each wire.
(b) From the following chart, match each wire (1, 2, and 3) with the correct material according to the results of the resistivity determined from the trendlines, assuming a 0.2-centimeter diameter wire was used.

Material	Resistivity (ρ) [Ωm] $\times 10^{-8}$
Aluminum	2.65
Copper	1.68
Iron	9.71
Silver	1.59
Tungsten	5.60

6. Use the figure shown to answer the following questions.

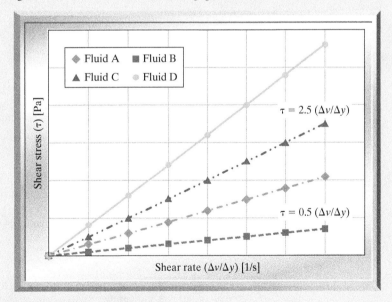

(a) Which fluid has the lowest dynamic viscosity?
(b) What is the dynamic viscosity of Fluid B in units of centipoise?
(c) If the specific gravity of Fluid C is 0.8, what is the kinematic viscosity of Fluid C in units of stokes?

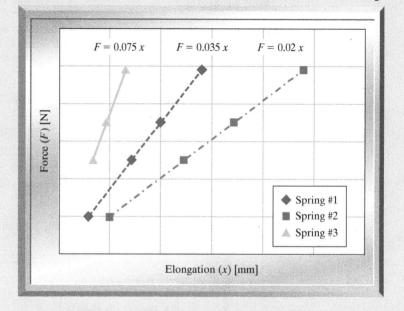

Choose one correct spring or spring combination that will meet the following criteria as closely as possible. Assume you have one of each spring available for use. List the spring or spring combination and the resulting spring constant.

(a) You want the spring or spring system to hold 95 grams and displace approximately 1 centimeter.

(b) You want the spring or spring system to displace approximately 4 centimeter when holding 50 grams.

10. You have three resistors. You conduct several tests and determine the following data.

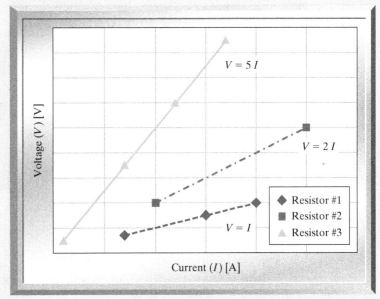

Choose one correct resistor or resistor combination that will meet the following criteria as closely as possible. Assume you have one of each resistor available for use. List the resistor or resistor combination and the resulting resistor constant.

(a) You want the resistor or resistor system to provide approximately 20 amperes when met with 120 volts.

(b) You want the resistor or resistor system to provide approximately 46 amperes when met with 30 volts.

(c) You want the resistor or resistor system to provide approximately 15 amperes when met with 120 volts.

(d) You want the resistor or resistor system to provide approximately 33 amperes when met with 45 volts.

11. Use the diagrams shown to answer the following questions.

(a) Determine the equivalent stiffness of four springs connected as shown.

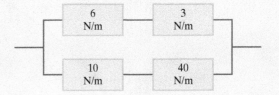

(b) Determine the equivalent stiffness of four springs connected as shown.

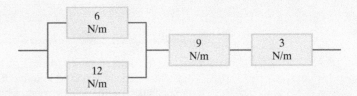

(c) Determine the equivalent resistance of four resistors connected as shown.

(d) Determine the equivalent resistance of four resistors connected as shown.

12. When a buoyant cylinder of height H, such as a fishing cork, is placed in a liquid and the top is depressed and released, it will bob up and down with a period T. We can conduct a series of tests and see that as the height of the cylinder increases, the period of oscillation also increases. A less dense cylinder will have a shorter period than a denser cylinder, assuming of course all the cylinders will float. A simple expression for the period is:

$$T = 2\pi\sqrt{\frac{\rho_{cylinder}}{\rho_{liquid}}\frac{H}{g}}$$

where g is the acceleration due to gravity, $\rho_{cylinder}$ is the density of the material, and ρ_{liquid} is the density of the fluid. By testing cylinders of differing heights, we wish to develop a model for the oscillation period, shown in the graph below.

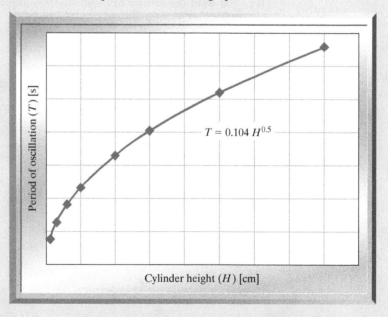

(a) What are the units of the coefficient (0.104) shown in the model?
(b) What is the oscillation period in units of seconds of a cylinder that is 4-inches tall?
(c) If the oscillation period is 0.2 seconds, what is the height of the cylinder in units of inches?
(d) We will conduct a series of tests with a new plastic (polystretchypropylene) that has a specific gravity of 0.6. What is the specific gravity of the fluid?

13. It is extremely difficult to bring the internet to some remote parts of the world. This can be inexpensively facilitated by installing antennas tethered to large helium balloons. To help analyze the situation, assume we have inflated a large spherical balloon. The pressure on the inside of the balloon is balanced by the elastic force exerted by the rubberized material. Since we are dealing with a gas in an enclosed space, the Ideal Gas Law will be applicable.

$$PV = nRT$$

where

P = pressure [atm]
V = volume [L]
n = quantity of gas [moles]
R = ideal gas constant [0.08206 (atm L)/(mol K)]
T = temperature [K]

If the temperature increases, the balloon will expand and/or the pressure will increase to maintain the equality. As it turns out, the increase in volume is the dominant effect, so we will treat the change in pressure as negligible.

The circumference of an inflated spherical balloon is measured at various temperatures; the resulting data are shown in the graph below.

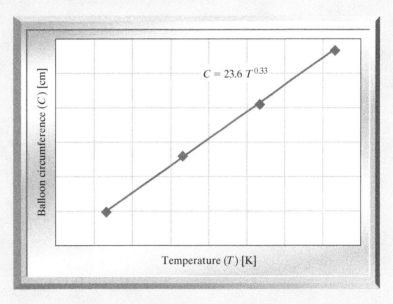

(a) What are the units of the constant 0.33?
(b) What are the units of the constant 23.6?
(c) What would the temperature of the balloon be if the circumference was 162 centimeters?
(d) If a circle with an area of 100 square centimeters is drawn on the balloon at 20 degrees Celsius, what would the area be at a temperature of 100 degrees Celsius?
(e) If the pressure inside the balloon is 1.2 atmospheres, how many moles of gas does it contain?

14. The data shown graphically below was collected during testing of an electromagnetic mass driver. The energy to energize the electromagnets was obtained from a bank of capacitors. The capacitor bank was charged to various voltages, and for each voltage, the exit velocity of the projectile was measured when the mass driver was activated.

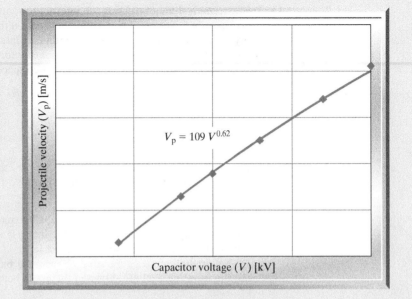

$V_p = 109\ V^{0.62}$

Projectile velocity (V_p) [m/s]

Capacitor voltage (V) [kV]

(a) What would the velocity be if the capacitors were charged to 100,000 volts?
(b) What voltage would be necessary to accelerate the projectile to 1,000 meters per second?
(c) Assume that the total capacitance is 5 farads. If the capacitors are initially charged to 10,000 volts and are discharged to 2,000 volts during the launch of a projectile, what is the mass of the projectile if the overall conversion of energy stored in the capacitors to kinetic energy in the projectile has an efficiency of 20%? Recall that the energy stored in a capacitor is given by $E = 0.5\ CV^2$, where C is capacitance in farads and V is voltage in volts.

EXCEL

15. A standard guitar, whether acoustic or electric, has six strings, all with essentially the same total length between the bridge and the nut at the tuning head. Each string vibrates at a different frequency determined by the tension on the string and the mass per unit length of the string. In order to create pitches (notes) other than these six, the guitarist presses the strings down against the fretboard, thus shortening the length of the strings and changing their frequencies. In other words, the vibrating frequency of a string depends on tension, length, and mass per unit length of the string.

The equation for the fundamental frequency of a vibrating string is given by

$$f = \frac{\sqrt{T/\mu}}{2L}$$

(a) Create a graph of the observed frequency data, including the power trendline and equation generated by Excel.

(b) If the tension was reduced to half of its original value, would the frequency increase or decrease and by what percentage of the original values?

(c) If the tension on the string is 125 newtons, what is the mass per unit length in grams per meter?

(d) If the mass per length of the string is 3 grams per meter, what is the tension in newtons?

16. Your supervisor has assigned you the task of designing a set of measuring spoons with a "futuristic" shape. After considerable effort, you have come up with two geometric shapes that you believe are really interesting.

    You make prototypes of five spoons for each shape with different depths and measure the volume each will hold. The table below shows the data you collected.

Depth (d) [cm]	Volume (V_A) [mL] Shape A	Volume (V_B) [mL] Shape B
0.5	1	1.2
0.9	2.5	3.3
1.3	4	6.4
1.4	5	7.7
1.7	7	11

Use Excel to plot and determine appropriate power models for this data. Use the resulting models to determine the depths of a set of measuring spoons comprising the following volumes for each of the two designs:

Volume Needed (V) [tsp or tbsp]	Depth of Design A (d_A) [cm]	Depth of Design B (d_B) [cm]
1/4 tsp		
1/2 tsp		
3/4 tsp		
1 tsp		
1 tbsp		

17. One of the NAE Grand Challenges for Engineering is **Engineering the Tools of Scientific Discovery**. According to the NAE website: "Grand experiments and missions of exploration always need engineering expertise to design the tools, instruments, and systems that make it possible to acquire new knowledge about the physical and biological worlds."

    Solar sails are a means of interplanetary propulsion using the radiation pressure of the sun to accelerate a spacecraft. The table below shows the radiation pressure at the orbits of several planets.

Planet	Distance from Sun (d) [AU]	Radiation Pressure (P) [µPa]
Mercury	0.46	43.3
Venus	0.72	17.7
Earth	1	9.15
Mars	1.5	3.96
Jupiter	5.2	0.34

NOTE

The astronomical unit (AU) is the average distance from the Earth to the Sun.

(a) Plot this data and determine the power law model for radiation pressure as a func of distance from the sun.
(b) What are the units of the exponent in the trendline?
(c) What are the units of the other constant in the trendline?
(d) What is the radiation pressure at Uranus (19.2 AU from sun)?
(e) At what distance from the sun is the radiation pressure 5 μPa?

18. When volunteers build a Habitat for Humanity house, it is found that the more houses are completed, the faster each one can be finished since the volunteers become be trained and more efficient. A model that relates the building time and the number of ho completed can generally be given by

$$t = t_0\, e^{-N/\nu} + t_M$$

where

t = time required to construct one house [days]
t_0 = a constant related to (but not equal) the time required to build the first house
N = the number of houses completed [dimensionless]
ν = a constant related to the decrease in construction time as N increases
t_M = another constant related to construction time

A team of volunteers has built several houses, and their construction time was recorde four of those houses. The construction time was then plotted as a function of numbe previously built houses and a mathematical model derived as shown below. Using this i mation, answer the following questions:

(a) What are the units of the constants 8.2, 3, and 2.8?
(b) If the same group continues building houses, what is the minimum time to cons one house that they can expect to achieve?
(c) How long did it take for them to construct the first house?
(d) How many days (total) were required to build the first five houses?

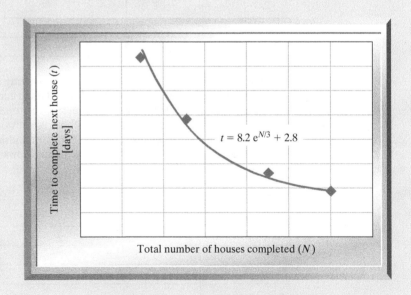

$t = 8.2\, e^{N/3} + 2.8$

Time to complete next house (t) [days] vs. Total number of houses completed (N)

19. As part of an electronic music synthesizer, you need to build a gizmo to convert a linear voltage to an exponentially related current. You build three prototype circuits, make several measurements of voltage and current in each, and graph the results as shown below.

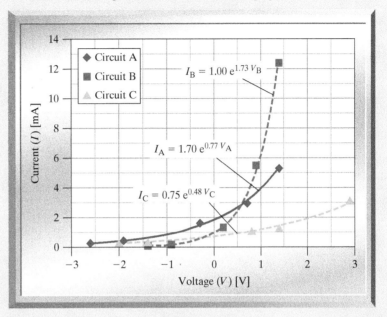

Assume that each circuit is modeled by the equation

$$I_X = A_X e^{(R_M/(R_X V_T))V_X}$$

where

I_X is the current in circuit X [milliamperers, mA]
A_X is a scaling factor associated with circuit X
R_M is a master resistor, and has the same value in all circuits [ohms, Ω]
R_X is a resistor in circuit X whose value is different in each circuit [ohms, Ω]
V_T is the thermal voltage, and has a value of 25.7 volts
V_X is the voltage in circuit X [volts, V]

(a) What are the units of A_X?
(b) If you wish $I_X = 1$ mA when $V_X = 0$, what should the value of A_X be?
(c) Using the trendline models, if $R_M = 10$ kΩ, what is the value of R_A?

20. Essentially all manufactured items are made to some "tolerance," or how close the actual product is to the nominal specifications. For example, if a company manufactures hammers, one customer might specify that the hammers should weigh 16 ounces. With rounding, this means that the actual weight of each hammer meets the specification if it weighs between 15.5 and 16.5 ounces. Such a hammer might cost 10 dollars. However, if the U.S. military, in its quest for perfection, specifies that an essentially identical hammer should have a weight of 16.000 ounces, then in order to meet specifications, the hammer must weigh between 15.9995 and 16.0005 ounces. In other words, the weight must fall within a range of one-thousandth of an ounce. Such a hammer might cost $1,000.

You have purchased a "grab bag" of 100 supposedly identical capacitors. You got a really good price, but there are no markings on the capacitors. All you know is that they are all the same nominal value. You wish to discover not only the nominal value, but the tolerance: are they within 5% of the nominal value, or within 20%? You set up a simple circuit with a known resistor and each of the unknown capacitors. You charge each capacitor to

10 volts, and then use an oscilloscope to time how long it takes for each capacitor to discharge to 2 volts. In a simple RC (resistor–capacitor) circuit, the voltage (V_C) across a capacitor (C) discharging through a resistor (R) is given by:

$$V_C = V_0 e^{-t/(RC)}$$

where t is time in seconds and V_0 is the initial voltage across the capacitor.

After measuring the time for each capacitor to discharge to from 10 to 2 V, you scan the list of times, and find the fastest and slowest. Since the resistor is the same in all cases, the fastest time corresponds to the smallest capacitor in the lot, and the slowest time to the largest. The fastest time was 3.3 microseconds and the slowest was 3.7 microseconds. For the two capacitors, you have the two pairs of data points.

(a) Enter these points into a worksheet, then plot these points in Excel, the pair for C_1 and the pair for C_2, on the same graph, using time as the independent variable. Fit exponential trendines to the data.

Time for C_1 (s)	Voltage of C_1	Time for C_2 (s)	Voltage of C_2
0	10	0	10
3.3×10^{-6}	2	3.7×10^{-6}	2

(b) Assuming you chose a precision resistor for these measurements that had a value of $R = 1,000.0$ ohms, determine the capacitance of the largest and smallest capacitors.

(c) You selected the fastest and slowest discharge times from a set of 100 samples. Since you had a fairly large sample set, it is not a bad assumption, according to the Laws of Large Numbers, that these two selected data sets represent capacitors near the lower and higher end of the range of values within the tolerance of the devices. Assuming the nominal value is the average of the minimum and maximum allowable values, what is the nominal value of the set of capacitors?

(d) What is the tolerance, in percent, of these devices? As an example, if a nominal 1 μF (microfarad) capacitor had an allowable range of 0.95 μF $< C <$ 1.05 μF, the tolerance would be 5%.

If standard tolerances of capacitors are 5%, 10%, and 20%, to which of the standard tolerances do you think these capacitors were manufactured? If you pick a smaller tolerance than you calculated, justify your selection. If you picked a higher tolerance, explain why the tolerance is so much larger than the measured value.

CHAPTER 13
MATHEMATICAL MODELS

As we have already seen, a large number of phenomena in the physical world obey one of the three basic mathematical models.

- Linear: $y = mx + b$
- Power: $y = bx^m + c$
- Exponential: $y = be^{mx} + c$

As we have mentioned previously, Excel can determine a mathematical model (trendline equation) for data conforming to all three of these model types, with the restriction that the constant c in the power and exponential forms must be 0.

Here, we consider how to determine the best model type for a specific data set, as well as learning methods of dealing with data that fit a power or exponential model best but have a nonzero value of c.

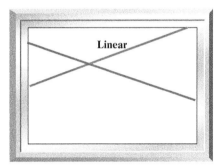

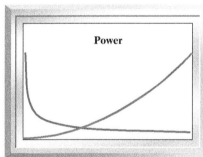

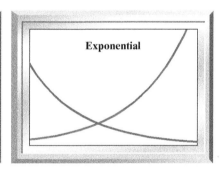

Except as otherwise noted, the entire discussion in this chapter assumes that the data fits one of the three trendlines models: linear, power, or exponential. You should always keep this in mind when using the techniques discussed here.

13.1 SELECTING A TRENDLINE TYPE

LEARN TO: Evaluate the functional relationship between paired data sets using Excel trendlines
Utilize boundary limits to determine whether a chosen model is appropriate
Utilize linearization of data and/or of graph axes to determine whether a model is
appropriate

When you determine a trendline to fit a set of data, in general you want the line, which may be straight or curved, to be as close as is reasonable to most of the data points.

The objective is **not** *to ensure that the curve passes through every point.*

To determine an appropriate model for a given situation, we use five guidelines, presented in general order of importance:

1. Do we already know the model type that the data will fit?

2. What do we know about the behavior of the process under consideration, including initial and final conditions?

3. What do the data look like when plotted on graphs with logarithmic scales?

4. How well does the model fit the data?

5. Can we consider other model types?

Guideline 1: Determine if the Model Type Is Known

If you are investigating a phenomenon that has already been studied by others, you may already know which model is correct or perhaps you can learn how the system behaves by looking in appropriate technical literature. In this case, all you need are the specific values for the model parameters since you already know the form of the equation. As we have seen, Excel is quite adept at churning out the numerical values for trendline equations.

If you are certain you know the proper model type, you can probably skip Guidelines 2 and 3, although it might be a good idea to quantify how well the model fits the data as discussed in Guideline 4. For example, at this point you should know that the extension of simple springs has a linear relationship to the force applied.

At other times, you may be investigating situations for which the correct model type is unknown. If you cannot determine the model type from experience or references, continue to Guideline 2.

Guideline 2: Evaluate What Is Known About the System Behavior

The most important thing to consider when selecting a model type is whether the model makes sense in light of your understanding of the physical system being investigated. Since there may still be innumerable things with which you are unfamiliar, this may seem like an unreasonable expectation. However, by applying what you *do* know to the problem at hand, you can often make an appropriate choice without difficulty.

When investigating an unknown phenomenon, we typically know the answer to at least one of three questions:

1. How does the process behave in the initial state?
2. How does the process behave in the final state?

3. What happens to the process between the initial and the final states—if we sketch the process, what does it look like? Does the parameter of interest increase or decrease? Is the parameter asymptotic to some value horizontally or vertically?

● EXAMPLE 13-1

Suppose we do not know Hooke's law and would like to study the behavior of a spring. We hang the spring from a hook, pull downward on the bottom of the spring with varying forces, and observe its behavior. We know initially the spring will stretch a little under its own weight even before we start pulling on it, although in most cases this is small or negligible. As an extreme case, however, consider what would happen if you hang one end of a Slinky® from the ceiling, letting the other end fall as it will.

As we pull on the spring, we realize the harder we pull, the more the spring stretches. In fact, we might assume that in a simple world, if we pull twice as hard, the spring will stretch twice as far, although that might not be as obvious. In words we might say,

* **The distance the spring stretches (x) is directly proportional to the pulling force (F)**, or we might express the behavior as an equation:*

$$x = kF + b$$

where b is the amount of stretch when the spring is hanging under its own weight. This is what we mean by using an "expected" form. Always remember, however, that what you "expect" to happen may be in error.

*   In addition, suppose we had tested this spring by hanging five different weights on it and measuring the stretch each time. After plotting the data, we realize there is a general trend that as the weight (force) increases, the stretch increases, but the data points do not lie exactly on a straight line. We have two options:*

- *If we think our assumption of linear behavior may be in error, we can try nonlinear models.*
- *Or we can use a linear model, although the fit may not be as good as one or more of the nonlinear models.*

To bring order to these questions, we should ask the following sequence of questions:

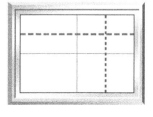

Is the system linear?

Linear systems have the following characteristics. If any of these is not true, then the system is not linear.

1. As the independent variable gets larger, the dependent variable continues to increase (positive slope) or decrease (negative slope) without limit. (See item 4 below.)

2. If the independent variable becomes negative, as it continues negative, the dependent variable continues to decrease (positive slope) or increase (negative slope) without limit unless one of the variables is constant. (See item 4 below.)

3. The rate of increase or decrease is constant; in other words, it will not curve upward or downward, but is a straight line.

4. There are no horizontal or vertical asymptotes unless the dependent variable is defined for only *one* value of the independent variable *or* if the dependent variable is the same value for *all* values of the independent variable.

Examples illustrating if a system is or is not linear:

- You are driving your car at a constant speed of 45 miles per hour [mph]. The longer you drive, the farther you go, without limit. In addition, your distance increases by the same amount each hour, regardless of total time elapsed. This is a linear system.

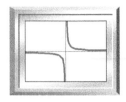

- You observe the temperature of the brake disks on your car to be slowly decreasing. If it continued to decrease without limit, the temperature would eventually be less than absolute zero; thus, it is not linear. The temperature will eventually approach the surrounding air temperature; thus, there is a horizontal asymptote.

If the system is not linear, is there a vertical asymptote?

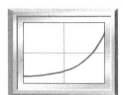

If there *is* a vertical asymptote, it will also have a horizontal asymptote. This is a power law model with a negative exponent. REMEMBER: We are assuming that our data fit one of the three models being considered here, and the previous statement is certainly not true for all other models. For example, $y = \tan x$ has multiple vertical asymptotes, but no horizontal asymptote.

If there is not a vertical asymptote, is there a horizontal asymptote?

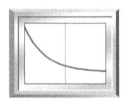

If there is a horizontal asymptote (but not a vertical one), then the model is exponential. If the horizontal asymptote occurs for positive values of the independent variable, then the exponent is negative. If the horizontal asymptote occurs for negative values of the independent variable, then the exponent is positive.

What if there is not a horizontal asymptote or a vertical asymptote?

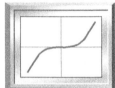

It is a power law model with a positive exponent. Such models can have a variety of shapes.

This sequence of questions can be represented pictorially as shown below. Remember, this is only valid if we assume the data fits one of the three models being discussed.

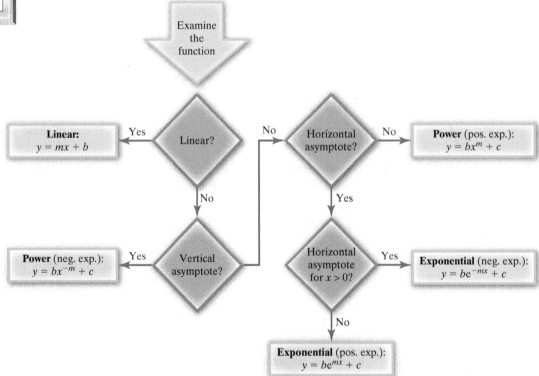

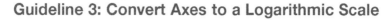

Guideline 3: Convert Axes to a Logarithmic Scale

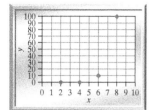

If the logarithm of the dependent or independent variable is plotted instead of the variable itself, do the modified data points appear to lie on a straight line?

To see how logarithmic axes are constructed, let us consider a simple case. Plotting the data points below gives the graph shown to the left.

x	2	4	6	8
y	0.1	1	10	100

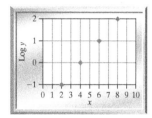

One way to linearize the data is to take the logarithm (base 10) of the independent variable and plot the results of log (y).

x	2	4	6	8
y	0.1	1	10	100
log y	−1	0	1	2

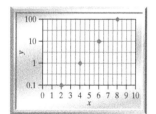

Another method of linearization is to take the logarithm (base 10) of the axis values, and plot the original y values on this altered axis.

A note about the use of logarithmic scales:

- The original data would fit an exponential model ($y = 0.01e^{1.15x}$), and when plotted on a logarithmic vertical axis, the data points appear in a straight line.
- The logarithmic axis allows us to more easily distinguish between the values of the two lowest data points, even though the data range covers three orders of magnitude. On the original graph, 0.1 and 1 were almost in the same vertical position.
- Note that you *do not* have to calculate the logarithms of the data points. You simply plot the actual values on a logarithmic scale.

Logarithm graphs are discussed in more detail in the next section. We can use logarithmic axes to help us determine an appropriate model type using the following process:

1. Plot the data using normal (linear) scales for both axes. If the data appear to lie more or less in a straight line, a linear model is likely to be a good choice.

2. Plot the data on a logarithmic vertical scale and a normal (linear) horizontal scale. If the data then appear to lie more or less in a straight line, an exponential model is likely to be a good choice.

3. Plot the data with logarithmic scales for *both* axes. If the data then appear to lie more or less in a straight line, a power law model is likely to be a good choice.

4. Although not covered in this course, you could plot the data on a logarithmic horizontal scale and a normal (linear) vertical scale. If the data then appear to lie more or less in a straight line, a logarithmic model is likely to be a good choice.

REMEMBER, this is only valid if we assume the data fits one of the three models being discussed. This process is summarized in the chart below.

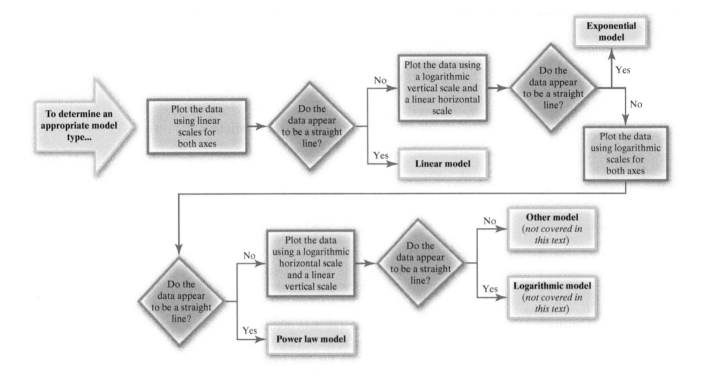

Guideline 4: Consider the R^2 Value

When a trendline is generated in Excel, the program can automatically calculate an R^2 **value**, sometimes called the **coefficient of determination**. The R^2 value is an indication of the variation of the actual data from the equation generated—in other words, it is a measure of how well the trendline fits the data. The value of R^2 varies between 0 and 1. If the value of R^2 is exactly equal to 1, a perfect correlation exists between the data and the trendline, meaning that the curve passes exactly through all data points. The farther R^2 is from 1, the less confidence we have in the accuracy of the model generated. When fitting a trendline to a data set, we always report the R^2 value to indicate how well the fit correlates with the data.

In reality, a fit of $R^2 = 1$ is rare, since experimental data are imprecise in nature. Human error, imprecision in instrumentation, fluctuations in testing conditions, and natural specimen variation are among the factors that contribute to a less-than-perfect fit. **The best R^2 value is not necessarily associated with the best model and should be used as a guide only**. Once again, making such decisions becomes easier with experience.

When displaying the equation corresponding to a trendline, you may have already noticed how to display the R^2 value.

✍ *To display an R^2 value:*

- Right-click or double-click on the trendline, or select the trendline then choose **Design > Add Chart Element > Trendline > More Trendline Options ...**
- In the **Format Trendline** palette that opens, from the **Trendline** Options tab, check the box for **Display R-squared value on chart**. Click the "X" to close.

⌘ **Mac OS:** To show the R^2 value on a Mac, double-click the trendline. In the window that opens, click **Options** and select **Display *R*-squared value**. Click **OK**.

Try different models and compare the R^2 values.

- If one of the R^2 values is considerably smaller than the others, say, more than 0.2 less, then that model very likely can be eliminated.
- If one of the R^2 values is considerably larger than the others, say, more than 0.2 greater, then that model very likely is the correct one.
  In any case, you should always consider Guidelines 1 through 3 above to minimize the likelihood of error.

WARNING!

While practicing with trendlines in the preceding chapters, you may have noticed a choice for polynomial models. Only rarely would this be the proper choice, but we mention it here for one specific reason—a polynomial model can always be found that will perfectly fit any data set. In general, if there are N data points, a polynomial of order $N - 1$ can be found that goes exactly through all N points. Excel can only calculate polynomials up to sixth order. For example, a data set with five data points is plotted below. A fourth-order polynomial can be found that perfectly fits the data. Let us consider a simple spring stretching example to illustrate why a perfect fit to the data is not necessarily the correct model.

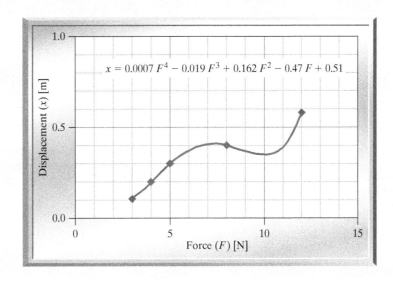

$$x = 0.0007\,F^4 - 0.019\,F^3 + 0.162\,F^2 - 0.47\,F + 0.51$$

The graph shows the five data points for spring displacement as a function of force. As force increases, displacement increases, but the points are certainly not in a straight line. Also shown is a fourth-order polynomial model that goes through every point—a perfect fit. This, however, is a terrible model.

Presumably you agree that as force increases, displacement *must* increase as well. The polynomial trendline, however, suggests that as force increases from about 7 to 10 newtons, the displacement *decreases*.

Always ask yourself if the model you have chosen is obviously incorrect, as in this case. We do not use polynomial models in this book, and so discuss them no further.

THE THEORY OF OCCAM'S RAZOR

It is vain to do with more what can be done with less.
or
Entities are not to be multiplied beyond necessity.

—William of Occam

It is probably appropriate to mention Occam's Razor at this point. Those who choose to pursue scientific and technical disciplines should keep the concept of Occam's Razor firmly in mind. **Occam's Razor refers to the concept that the simplest explanation or model to describe a given situation is usually the correct one.** It is named for William of Occam, who lived in the first half of the fourteenth century and was a theologian and philosopher.

● **EXAMPLE 13-2**

The velocity of a ball was recorded as it rolled across a floor after being released from a ramp at various heights. The velocities were then plotted versus the release heights. We want to fit a trendline to the data.

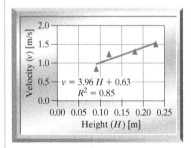

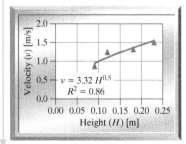

We start with the simplest form, a linear fit, shown on the left. We know that if the ramp is at a height of zero, the ball will not roll down the ramp without any external forces. The linear fit yields an intercept value of 0.6, indicating that the ball will have an initial velocity of 0.6 meter per second when the ramp is horizontal, which we know to be untrue. It seems unlikely experimental variation alone would generate an error this large, so we try another model.

We choose a power fit, shown in the center. With an R^2 value of 0.86, the equation fits the data selection well, but is there a better fit? Using the same data, we try a third-order polynomial to describe the data. The polynomial model, which gives a perfect fit, is shown on the bottom with an R^2 value of 1.

While the polynomial trendline gave the best fit, is this really the correct way to describe the data? Recall that in theory the potential energy of the ball is transformed into kinetic energy according to the conservation of energy law, written in general terms

$$PE_{initial} = KE_{final} \quad \text{or} \quad mgH = \frac{1}{2}mv^2$$

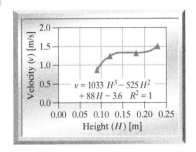

Therefore, the relationship between velocity and height is a relationship of the form

$$v = (2gH)^{1/2} = (2g)^{1/2}H^{1/2}$$

The relation between velocity and height is a power relationship; velocity varies as the square root of the height. The experimental error is responsible for the inaccurate trendline fit. In most instances, the polynomial trendline will give a precise fit but an inaccurate description of the phenomenon. **It is better to have an accurate interpretation of the experimental behavior than a perfect trendline fit!**

Guideline 5: Should We Consider Model Types Not Covered Here?

Many phenomena may be accurately characterized by a linear model, power law model, or exponential model. However, there are innumerable systems for which a different model type must be chosen. Many of these are relatively simple, but some are mind-bogglingly complicated. For example, modeling electromagnetic waves (used for television, cell phones, etc.) or a mass oscillating up and down while hanging from a spring requires the use of trigonometric functions.

You should always keep in mind that the system or phenomenon you are studying may not fit the three common models we have covered in this book.

NOTE ON ADVANCED MATH

Actually, sinusoids (sine or cosine) can be represented by exponential models through a mathematical trick first concocted by Leonhard Euler, so we now refer to it as Euler's identity. The problem is that the exponents are imaginary (some number times the square root of -1).

Euler's identity comes up in the study of calculus, and frequently in the study of electrical or computer engineering, early in the study of electric circuits. Euler's identity can be expressed in several different forms. The basic identity can be stated as the following equation, where i is the square root of -1:

$$e^{i\pi} = -1$$

Another form often used in electrical engineering is

$$\cos\theta = 0.5(e^{i\theta} + e^{-i\theta})$$

13.2   INTERPRETING LOGARITHMIC GRAPHS

LEARN TO: Plot data using logarithmic axis to linearize the data
Interpret a graph using logarithmic scales to develop a mathematical model

A "regular" plot, shown on a graph with both axes at constant-spaced intervals, is called **rectilinear**. When a linear function is graphed on rectilinear axis, it will appear as a straight line. Often, it is convenient to use a scale on one or both axes that is not linear, where values are not equally spaced but instead "logarithmic," meaning that powers of 10 are equally spaced. Each set of 10 is called a **decade** or **cycle**. A logarithmic scale that ranges either from 10 to 1,000 would be two cycles, 10–100 and 100–1,000. Excel allows you to select a logarithmic scale for the abscissa, the ordinate, or both.

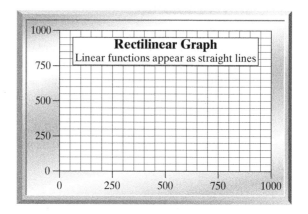

If one scale is logarithmic and the other linear, the plot is called **semilogarithmic** or **semilog**. Note in the figure below on the left that the abscissa has its values equally spaced and so is a linear scale. However, the ordinate has powers of 10 equally spaced and thus is a logarithmic scale.

If both scales are logarithmic, the plot is called **full logarithmic** or **log–log**. Note in the figure below on the right that both axes have powers of 10 equally spaced.

There are four different combinations of linear and logarithmic axes, each corresponding to one of four specific trendline types that will appear linear on that particular graph type. If the plotted data points are more or less in a straight line when plotted with a specific axis type, the corresponding trendline type is a likely candidate, as discussed earlier.

Once the data are plotted as logarithmic, how do you read data from this graph? This is perhaps best shown through examples.

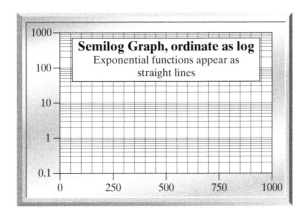

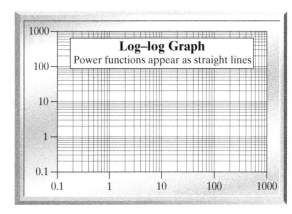

Derivation of Power Law Model

Consider a power law model:

$$y = bx^m$$

Now take the logarithm of both sides of the equation.

$$\log y = \log (bx^m) = \log b + \log x^m = \log b + m \log x$$

Using the commutative property of addition, you can write:

$$\log y = m \log x + \log b$$

Since b is a constant, $\log b$ is also a constant. Rename $\log b$ and call it b'. Since x and y are both variables, $\log x$ and $\log y$ are also variables. Call them x' and y', respectively.

Using the new names for the transformed variables and the constant b:

$$y' = mx' + b'$$

This is a linear model! Thus, if the data set can be described by a power law model and you plot the logarithms of both variables (instead of the variables themselves), the transformed data points will lie on a straight line. The slope of this line is m, although "slope" has a somewhat different meaning than in a linear model. The "intercept" value, b, occurs when $x = 1$, since $\log(1) = 0$.

NOTE

For a refresher on logarithm rules, please see Appendix A online.

● **EXAMPLE 13-3**

When a body falls, it undergoes a constant acceleration. Using the figure, determine the mathematical equation for distance (d), in units of meters, of a falling object as a function of time (t), in units of seconds.

Since the graph appears linear on log–log paper, we can assume a power law relationship exists of the form:

$$d = bt^m$$

For illustration, a line has been sketched between the points for further clarification of function values.

To establish the power of the function (m), we estimate the number of decades of "rise" (shown as vertical arrows) divided by the decades of "run" (horizontal arrow):

$$\text{Slope} = \frac{\text{Change in decades of distance}}{\text{Change in decades of time}} = \frac{2 \text{ decade}}{1 \text{ decade}} = 2$$

To establish the constant value (b), we estimate it as the ordinate value when the abscissa value is 1, shown in the shaded circle. When the time is 1 second, the distance is 5 meters.

The resulting function:

$$d = 5t^2$$

This matches well with the established theory, which states

$$d = \frac{1}{2}gt^2$$

The value of ½ g is approximately 5 m/s².

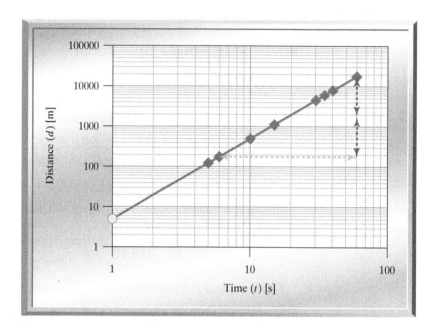

Derivation of Exponential Law Model

NOTE

For a refresher on logarithm rules, please see Appendix A online.

Consider an exponential model:

$$y = be^{mx}$$

Now take the logarithm of both sides of the equation.

$$\log y = \log(be^{mx}) = \log b + \log e^{mx} = \log b + (mx)\log e$$

Using the commutative property of addition, you can write:

$$\log y = m(\log e)x + \log b$$

Since b is a constant, $\log b$ is also a constant. Rename $\log b$ and call it b'. Since y is a variable, $\log y$ is also a variable; call it y'.

Using the new names for the transformed variable y and the constant b:

$$y' = m(\log e)x + b'$$

This is a linear model! Thus, if the data set can be described by an exponential law model, and you plot the logarithm of y (instead of y itself) versus x, the transformed data points will lie on a straight line. The slope of this line is $m(\log e)$, but again, "slope" has a somewhat different interpretation. The term ($\log e$) is a number, approximately equal to 0.4343; the slope is 0.4343 m.

● EXAMPLE 13-4   A chemical reaction is being carried out in a reactor; the results are shown graphically in the figure. Determine the mathematical equation that describes the reactor concentration (C), in units of moles per liter, as a function of time spent in the reactor (t), in units of seconds.

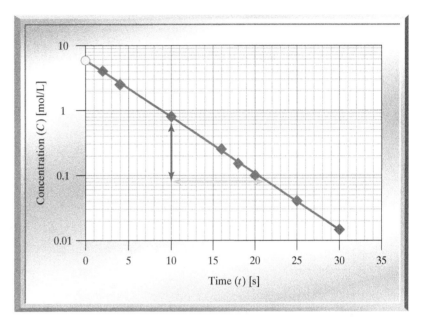

Since the graph appears linear on semilog paper where the ordinate is logarithmic, we can assume an exponential law relationship exists of the form:

$$C = be^{mt}$$

For illustration, a line has been sketched between the points for further clarification of function values.

Since this is an exponential function, to determine the value of m, we must first determine the slope:

$$\text{Slope} = \frac{\text{Change in decades of concentration}}{\text{Change in time}}$$

$$= \frac{-1 \text{ decade}}{21.5 \text{ s} - 10 \text{ s}} = -0.087 \text{ s}^{-1}$$

The value of m is then found from the relationship: slope = m(log e).

$$m = \frac{\text{slope}}{\log e} = \frac{-0.087 \text{ s}^{-1}}{0.4343} = -0.2 \text{ s}^{-1}$$

When time = 0 seconds, the constant (b) can be read directly and has a value of 6 [mol/L]. The resulting function:

$$C = 6e^{-0.2t}$$

COMPREHENSION CHECK 13-1

An unknown amount of oxygen, kept in a piston type container at a constant temperature, was subjected to increasing pressure (P), in units of atmospheres; as the pressure (P) was increased, the resulting volume (V) was recorded in units of liters. We have found that a log–log plot aligns the data in a straight line. Using the figure, determine the mathematical equation for volume (V) in units of liters, and of a piston filled with an ideal gas subjected to increasing pressure (P) in units of atmospheres.

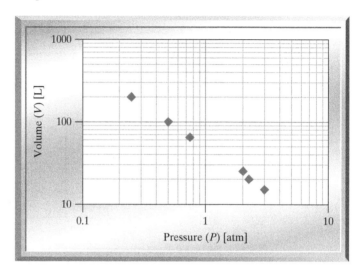

COMPREHENSION CHECK 13-2

The data shown graphically in the figure describe the discharge of a capacitor through a resistor. Determine the mathematical equation that describes the voltage (V), in units of volts, as a function of time (t), in units of seconds.

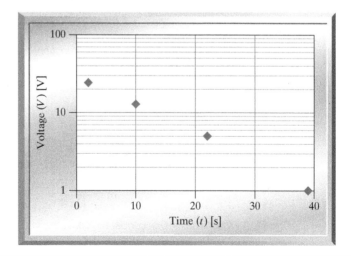

13.3 CONVERTING SCALES TO LOG IN EXCEL

LEARN TO: Use Excel to convert a graph into logarithmic axis to make a data series appear linear

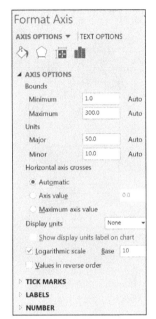

✎ *To convert axis to logarithmic:*

- Right-click the axis > Format Axis or double-click on the axis. The **Format Axis** palette will appear.
- Click **Axis Options**, then check the box for **Logarithmic scale**. The Base should automatically appear as 10; this default value is correct.

Alternatively:

- Click the chart. In the toolbar, select **Design > Add Chart Element > Axis > More Axis Options**.
- In the corresponding palette, select **Axis Options > Bar Graph Symbol**.
- Click **Axis Options**, then check the box for **Logarithmic scale**.

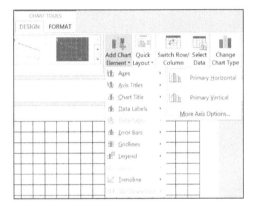

⌘ **Mac OS:** Double-click on the axis you want to convert to logarithmic. The Format Axis window will appear. Click **Scale** in the list on the left side of the window, and then click the checkbox near the bottom that says "Logarithmic scale."

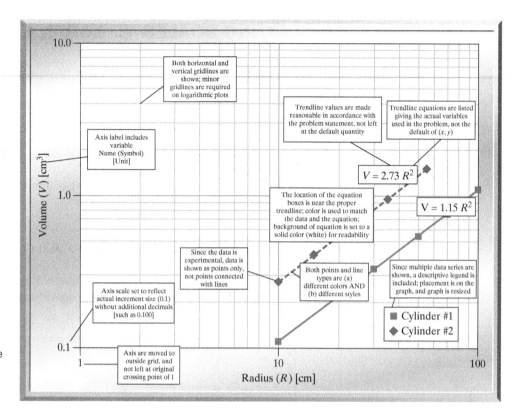

Figure 13-1 Example of a proper plot, showing multiple experimental data sets with trendlines and logarithmic axes.

Above is an example of a properly formatted graph, showing an experimental data series with power trendlines. The axes have been made logarithmic to allow the data series to appear linear.

13.4 DEALING WITH LIMITATIONS OF EXCEL

LEARN TO: Understand the limitations in using Excel to model power or exponential data containing an offset

Determine appropriate steps to alter data using Excel if an offset is present

As we have mentioned earlier, Excel will not correctly calculate a trendline for a power or exponential model containing a vertical offset. In other words, it can calculate appropriate values for b and m in the forms

$$y = bx^m + c \quad \text{or} \quad y = be^{mx} + c$$

only if $c = 0$. Note that if the data inherently has a vertical offset, Excel may actually calculate a trendline equation, but the values of b and m will not be accurate.

In addition, if any data value, dependent or independent, is less than or equal to zero, Excel cannot calculate a power law model. If one or more dependent variable data points are less than or equal to zero, exponential models are unavailable.

In the real world, there are numerous systems best modeled by either a power or an exponential model with a nonzero value of c or with negative values, so we need a method for handling such situations.

Case 1: Vertical Asymptote

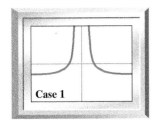

Since a vertical asymptote implies a power model with a negative exponent, there will be a horizontal asymptote as well. If the horizontal asymptote is not the horizontal axis (implying a vertical offset), Excel will calculate the model incorrectly or not at all. The object here is to artificially move the asymptote to the horizontal axis by subtracting the offset value from every data point. If you have a sufficient range of data, you may be able to extract the offset from the data.

For example, if the three data points with the largest values of x (or smallest if the asymptote goes to the left) have corresponding y values of 5.1, 5.03, and 5.01, the offset is likely to be about 5. (This assumes there are other values in the data set with considerably different y values.) You can also try to determine from the physical situation being modeled at what nonzero value the asymptote occurs. In either case, simply subtract the offset value from the vertical component of *every* data point, plot this modified data, and determine a power trendline. Once the trendline equation is displayed, edit it by adding the offset to the power term. Note that you subtract the value from the data points but add it to the final equation.

Case 2: No Horizontal Asymptote

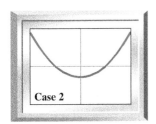

Assuming it has been established that the model should not be linear, Case 2 implies a power model with a positive exponent. If you have a data point for $x = 0$, the corresponding y value should be very close to the vertical offset. Also, you may be able to determine the offset value by considering the physical situation. In either case, proceed as in Case 1, subtracting the offset from every data point, etc.

Case 3: Horizontal Asymptote, No Vertical Asymptote

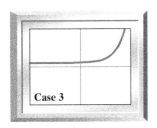

Case 3 implies an exponential model. The object, as in Case 1, is to artificially move the asymptote to the horizontal axis. Also as in Case 1, you may be able to determine the offset by considering the physical system or by looking at the data points with the largest or smallest values. Again, subtract the determined value from every data point, etc.

Case 4: A Few Values with Small Negative Value, Most Positive

In Case 4, the negative values may be a result of measurement inaccuracy. Either delete these points from the data set or change the negative values to a very small positive value.

Case 5: Many or All Data Points Negative

If the independent values are negative, try multiplying every independent value by -1. If this works, then make the calculated value of b negative after the trendline equation is calculated. You may have to apply some of the procedures in the previous cases after negating each data value.

Negative dependent values may simply be a negative offset to the data. If you can determine the asymptote value, ask if essentially all values are greater than the asymptote value. If so, it is probably just an offset. If not, then multiply every dependent data value by -1, and proceed in a manner similar to that described in the preceding paragraph.

NOTE

Sometimes, due to inaccuracy of measurement, one or more of the data points near the asymptote may be negative after the offset value is subtracted, and Excel will be unable to process the data. You can circumvent this either by deleting such data points or by making the vertical component a very small positive value.

● **EXAMPLE 13-5**

The following data were collected in an experiment. We wish to determine an appropriate model for the data.

As the independent variable gets larger, the dependent variable appears to be approaching 10. This is even more apparent when graphed. Subtracting this assumed offset from every data point gives a new column of modified dependent data.
Since we subtracted 10 from every data point, we need to correct the equation by adding 10, giving $y = 14.3e^{-0.5x} + 10$.

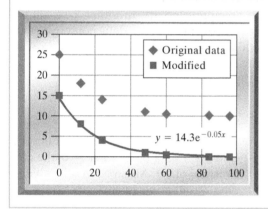

Independent	Dependent	Modified Dependent
0	25.0	15.0
12	18.0	8.0
24	14.0	4.0
48	11.0	1.0
60	10.5	0.5
84	10.2	0.2
96	10.1	0.1

If All Else Fails

If you are convinced that the model is exponential or power with an offset but you cannot determine its value, consider making further measurements for larger or smaller values of the independent variable. Particularly in data that has a horizontal asymptote, further measurements may make the value of the asymptote more obvious. In the first chart below, the value of the asymptote is not clear. By extending the measurements in the direction of the asymptote (positive in this case), it is clear that the asymptote has a value of 2. Note also that it becomes much clearer that the data are not linear.

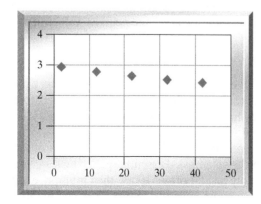

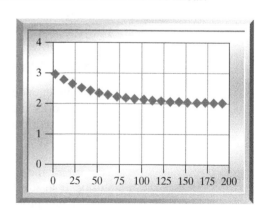

● EXAMPLE 13-6   The data shown describe the discharge of a capacitor through a resistor. Before the advent of microprocessors, intermittent windshield wipers in automobiles often used such circuits to create the desired time delay. We wish to determine an appropriate model for the data.

Time (t) [s]	2	10	22	39
Voltage (V) [V]	24	13	5	1

- *Select the data series and create a linear trendline, being sure to display the equation and the R^2 value.*
- *Without deleting the first trendline, click one of the data points again—be sure you select the points and not the trendline—and again add a trendline, but this time choose a power trend.*
- *Repeat this process for an exponential trend.*

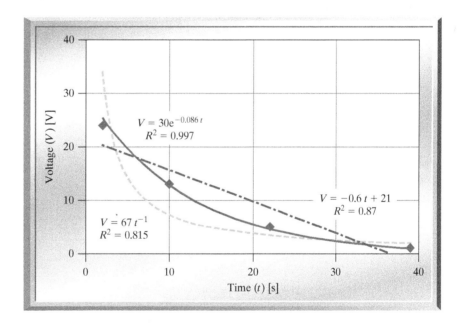

You should now have a chart with three trendlines. Things to note:

- *Neither the linear nor power trendlines are very good compared to the exponential line, and both have an R^2 value less than 0.9. These are probably not the best choice.*
- *The exponential model fits the data very closely and has an R^2 value greater than 0.95; thus, it is probably the best choice.*

As a model check, compare the graph by using logarithmic scales. If the model is exponential, the data should appear linear on a semilogarithmic plot with the ordinate shown as logarithmic.

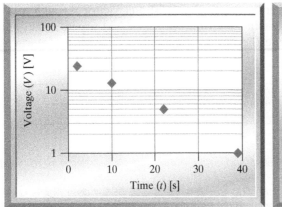 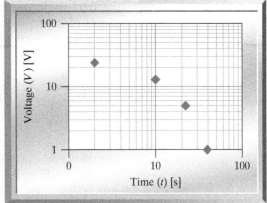

Based on this analysis, you would choose the exponential model. As it turns out, the exponential model is indeed the correct one, being the solution to a differential equation describing the capacitor's behavior. Most students learn about this in second semester physics, and some study it in much more depth in electrical and computer engineering courses.

● **EXAMPLE 13-7**

These data describe the temperature of antifreeze (ethylene glycol) in the radiator of a parked car. The temperature of the surrounding environment is −20 degrees Fahrenheit. The initial temperature (at $t = 0$) is unknown.

Time (t) [min]	10	18	25	33	41
Temperature (T) [°F]	4.5	1.0	−2.1	−4.6	−6.4

- Determine an appropriate model type for these data.
- Determine the vertical offset of the data.
- Plot the modified data and generate the correct trendline equation to describe this data.

It seems reasonable that the temperature will be asymptotic to the surrounding temperature (−20 degrees Fahrenheit) as time goes on. Also, there is no known mechanism whereby the temperature could possibly go to infinity for any finite value of time, so there is no vertical asymptote. This indicates an exponential model with a negative exponent. Since the asymptote is at −20 degrees Fahrenheit, subtract −20 (i.e., add 20) from every data point before plotting.

Time (t) [min]	10	18	25	33	41
Temperature (T) [°F]	4.5	1.0	2.1	4.6	−6.4
Offset temperature (T_O) [°F]	24.5	21.0	17.9	15.4	13.6

Since you subtracted −20 from every data point, you should add −20 to the trendline equation, giving

$$T = 29.5e^{-0.019t} - 20$$

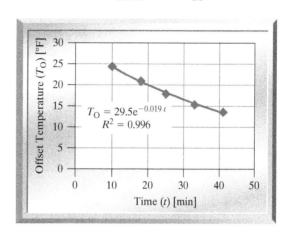

COMPREHENSION CHECK 13-3

The following data were collected during an experiment. We wish to determine an appropriate model for the data.

Independent	Dependent
0	−25
10	−45
20	−85
25	−106
30	−154

COMPREHENSION CHECK 13-4

Assume the car in Example 13-7 is cranked up and driven 50 feet into a garage. The temperature inside the garage is 5 degrees Fahrenheit. These data describe the temperature of antifreeze in the radiator after it is driven into the garage and the motor turned off.
- Determine an appropriate model type for these data.
- Determine the vertical offset of the data.
- Plot the modified data and generate the correct trendline equation to describe this data.

Time (t) [min]	5	13	25	34	51
Temperature (T) [°F]	−13.0	−10.0	−6.8	−4.5	−1.5

In-Class Activities

ICA 13-1

Capillary action draws liquid up a narrow tube against the force of gravity as a result of surface tension. The height the liquid will move up the tube depends on the radius of the tube. The following data were collected for water in a glass tube in air at sea level. Show the resulting data and trendline, with equation and R^2 value, on the appropriate graph type (rectilinear, semilog, or log–log) to make the data appear linear.

Radius (r) [cm]	0.01	0.05	0.10	0.20	0.40	0.50
Height (H) [cm]	14.0	3.0	1.5	0.8	0.4	0.2

ICA 13-2

Several reactions are carried out in a closed vessel. The following data are taken for the concentration (C) of compounds A, B, and C [grams per liter] as a function of time (t) [minutes], from the start of the reaction. Show the resulting data and trendlines, with equation and R^2 value, on the appropriate graph type (rectilinear, semilog, or log–log) to make the data appear linear.

Time (t) [min]	2	5	8	15	20
Concentration of A (C_A) [g/L]	0.021	0.125	0.330	1.120	2.050
Concentration of B (C_B) [g/L]	0.032	0.202	0.550	1.806	3.405
Concentration of C (C_C) [g/L]	0.012	0.080	0.200	0.650	1.305

ICA 13-3

An environmental engineer has obtained a bacteria culture from a municipal water sample and allowed the bacteria to grow. The data are shown below. Show the resulting data and trendline, with equation and R^2 value, on the appropriate graph type (rectilinear, semilog, or log–log) to make the data appear linear.

Time (t) [h]	2	3	5	6	7	9	10
Concentration (C) [ppm]	21	44	111	153	203	318	385

ICA 13-4

In a turbine, a device used for mixing, the power requirement depends on the size and shape of impeller. In the lab, you have collected the following data. Show the resulting data and trendline, with equation and R^2 value, on the appropriate graph type (xy scatter, semilog, or log–log) to make the data appear linear.

Diameter (D) [ft]	0.5	0.75	1	1.5	2	2.25	2.5	2.75
Power (P) [hp]	0.004	0.04	0.13	0.65	3	8	18	22

ICA 13-5

Being quite interested in obsolete electronics, Angus has purchased several electronic music synthesis modules dating from the early 1970s and is testing them to find out how they work. One module is a voltage-controlled amplifier (VCA) that changes the amplitude (loudness) of an audio signal by changing a control voltage into the VCA. All Angus knows is that the magnitude of the control voltage should be less than 5 volts. He sets the audio input signal to an amplitude of 1 volt, then measures the audio output amplitude for different control voltage values. The table below shows these data. Show the resulting data and trendline, with equation and R^2 value, on the appropriate graph type (xy scatter, semilog, or log–log) to make the data appear linear.

Control voltage (V) [V]	−4.0	−2.5	−1.0	0.0	1.0	2.5	4.0
Output amplitude (A) [V]	0.116	0.324	0.567	0.962	1.690	3.320	7.270

ICA 13-6

Referring to the previous ICA, Angus is also testing a voltage-controlled oscillator. In this case, a control voltage (also between −5 and +5 volts) changes the frequency of oscillation in order to generate different notes. The table below shows these measurements. Show the resulting data and trendline, with equation and R^2 value, on the appropriate graph type (xy scatter, semilog, or log–log) to make the data appear linear.

Control voltage (V) [V]	−4.0	−2.5	−1.0	0.0	1.0	2.5	4.0
Output frequency (f) [Hz]	28	99	227	539	989	3,110	8,130

The following instructions apply to ICA 13-7 to ICA 13-9. Examine the following models. Determine if the graph will appear linear on:

(A) Rectilinear axes
(B) Semi log, abscissa as logarithmic, axes
(C) Semi log, ordinate as logarithmic, axes
(D) Logarithmic (both) axes
(E) None of the above

ICA 13-7

Q	Model	Abscissa	Ordinate	Will appear linear on ...				
				A	B	C	D	E
(a)		F	L					
(b)	$L = BF^{0.5}$	L	B					
(c)		F	B					

ICA 13-8

Q	Model	Abscissa	Ordinate	Will appear linear on ...				
				A	B	C	D	E
(a)		V	R					
(b)	$R = H^{0.5}V^{-2}L$	L	R					
(c)		V	L					
(d)		V	H					

ICA 13-9

Q	Model	Abscissa	Ordinate	Will appear linear on ...				
				A	B	C	D	E
(a)		S	M					
(b)	$M = \dfrac{W}{T}S^2 e^{-\frac{R}{L}}$	W	T					
(c)		1/L	M					
(d)		R	T					

The following instructions apply to ICA 13-10 to ICA 13-21. Examine the following graph of a fictitious function. Determine the model type shown:

(A) Exponential
(B) Linear
(C) Power
(D) None of the above

Determine the value and units of m and b for the model.

ICA 13-10

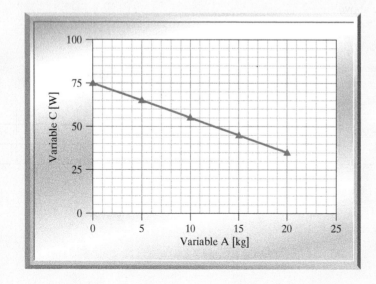

Model type ...			
A	B	C	D

Determine parameter value & units			
m		b	
value	units	value	units

ICA 13-11

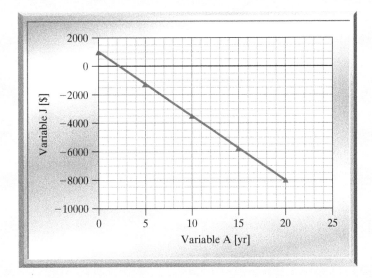

Model type …			
A	B	C	D

Determine parameter value & units			
m		b	
value	units	value	units

ICA 13-12

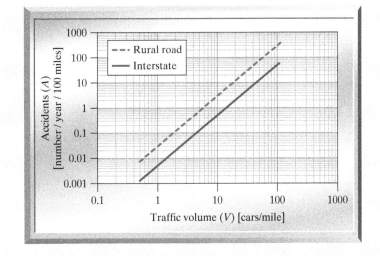

Model type …			
A	B	C	D

Determine parameter value & units			
m		b	
value	units	value	units

ICA 13-13

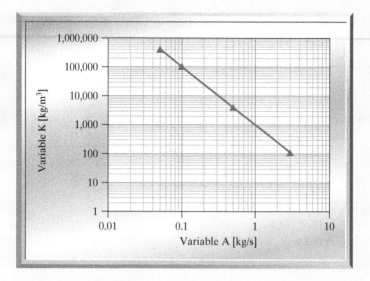

Model type ...			
A	B	C	D

Determine parameter value & units			
m		b	
value	units	value	units

ICA 13-14

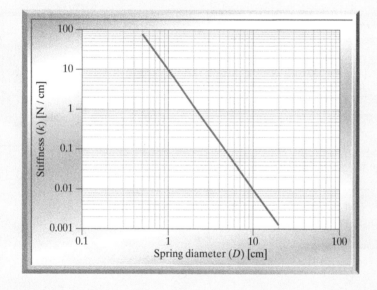

Model type ...			
A	B	C	D

Determine parameter value & units			
m		b	
value	units	value	units

ICA 13-15

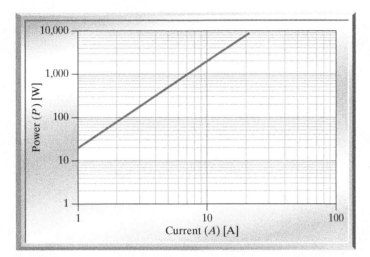

Model Type ...			
A	B	C	D

Determine parameter value & units			
m		b	
value	units	value	units

ICA 13-16

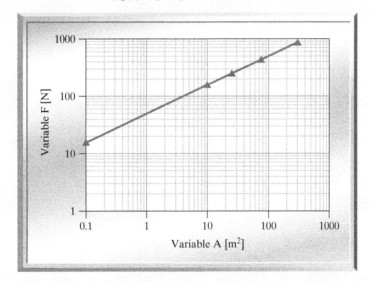

Model Type ...			
A	B	C	D

Determine parameter value & units			
m		b	
value	units	value	units

ICA 13-17

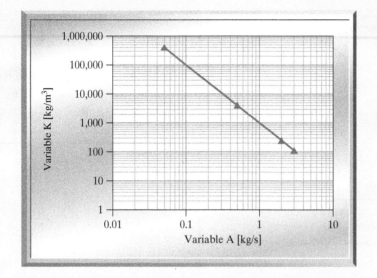

Model Type ...			
A	B	C	D

Determine parameter value & units			
m		b	
value	units	value	units

ICA 13-18

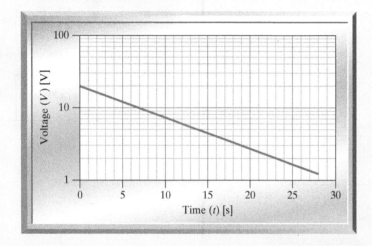

Model Type ...			
A	B	C	D

Determine parameter value & units			
m		b	
value	units	value	units

ICA 13-19

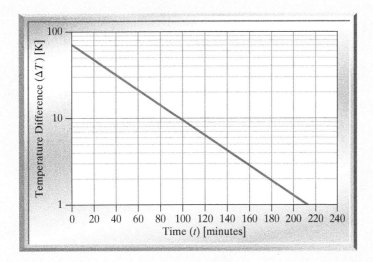

Model Type ...			
A	B	C	D

Determine parameter value & units			
m		b	
value	units	value	units

ICA 13-20

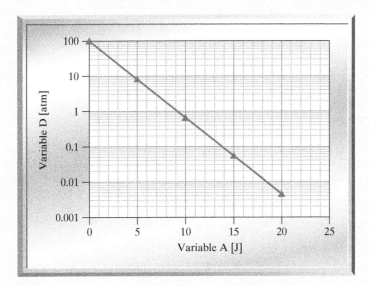

Model Type ...			
A	B	C	D

Determine parameter value & units			
m		b	
value	units	value	units

ICA 13-21

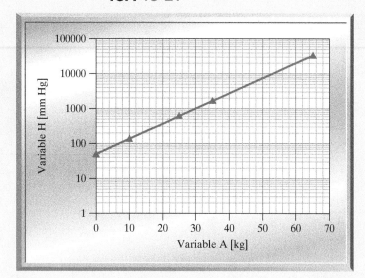

Model Type ...			
A	B	C	D

Determine parameter value & units			
m		b	
value	units	value	units

ICA 13-22

As a reminder, Reynolds Number is discussed in the chapter on Dimensionless Numbers.

When discussing the flow of a fluid through a piping system, we say that friction occurs between the fluid and the pipe wall due to viscous drag. The loss of energy due to the friction of fluid against the pipe wall is described by the friction factor. The **Darcy friction factor** (f) was developed by Henry Darcy (1803–1858), a French scientist who made several important contributions to the field of hydraulics. The friction factor depends on several other factors, including flow regime, Reynolds number, and pipe roughness. The friction factor can be determined in several ways, including from the Moody diagram (shown below).

Olive oil having a specific gravity of 0.914 and a viscosity of 100.8 centipoise is draining by gravity from the bottom of a tank. The drain line from the tank is a 4-inch diameter pipe made of commercial steel (pipe roughness, $\varepsilon = 0.045$ millimeters). The velocity is 11 meters per second. Determine the friction factor for this system, using the following process:

Step 1: Determine the Reynolds number: $Re = \dfrac{\rho v \mathrm{D}}{\mu}$.

Step 2: Determine flow regime.

- If the flow is laminar ($Re \leq 2{,}000$), proceed to Step 4.
- If the flow is turbulent or transitional ($Re > 2{,}000$), continue with Step 3.

Step 3: Determine the relative roughness ratio: (ε/D).
Step 4: Determine the *Darcy friction factor* (f) from the diagram.

ICA 13-23

Repeat ICA 13-22 with the following conditions:

Lactic acid, with a specific gravity of 1.249 and dynamic viscosity of 40.33 centipoise, is flowing in a 1½-inch diameter galvanized iron pipe at a velocity of 1.5 meters per second. Assume the pipe roughness (ε) of galvanized iron is 0.006 inches. Determine the friction factor for this system.

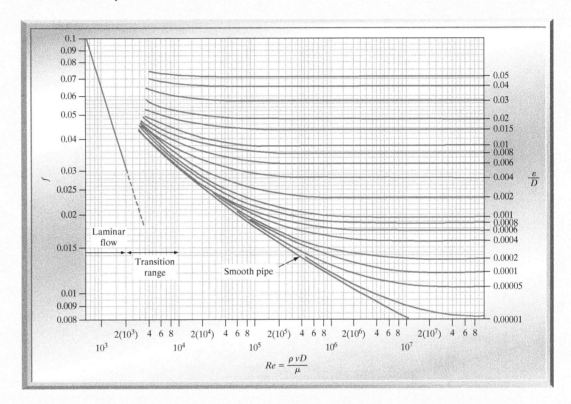

ICA 13-24

This activity requires data from ICA 8-41; the procedure is shown here for reference.

Materials

Bag of cylinders   Scale   Calipers   Ruler

Procedure

For each cylinder, record the mass, length, and diameter and / or width in an Excel workbook.

Analysis

- Using formulas in Excel, determine the volume and density for each cylinder.
- Use data from constant mass set, graph density (ordinate) versus length.
- Use data from constant volume set, graph density (ordinate) versus mass.
- Both graphs should be proper plots, with appropriate trendlines and logarithmic axes to prove your trendline choices by making the data appear linear.

Chapter 13 REVIEW QUESTIONS

1. An environmental engineer has obtained a bacteria culture from a municipal water sample and has allowed the bacteria to grow.

Time (t) [min]	1	2	4	6	7	9	10
Concentration (C) [ppm]	9	15	32	63	102	220	328

(a) Show the resulting data and trendline, with equation and R^2 value, on the appropriate graph type (xy scatter, semilog, or log–log) to make the data appear linear.

(b) Assume the value of "m" in the resulting model is the growth constant. Use the trendline determined to find the value and units of the growth constant for this bacteria.

2. An environmental engineer has obtained a bacteria culture from a municipal water sample and allowed the bacteria to grow.

Time (t) [min]	1	2	4	6	7	9	10
Concentration (C) [ppm]	11.9	17.1	27.0	37.3	42.0	52.3	56.9

(a) Show the resulting data and trendline, with equation and R^2 value, on the appropriate graph type (xy scatter, semilog, or log–log) to make the data appear linear.

(b) Assume the value of "m" in the resulting model is the growth constant. Use the trendline determined to find the value and units of the growth constant for this bacteria.

3. An environmental engineer has obtained a bacteria culture from a municipal water sample and allowed the bacteria to grow.

Time (t) [min]	1	2	4	6	7	9	10
Concentration (C) [ppm]	0.5	4.2	32.5	107.5	170.6	346.0	489.8

(a) Show the resulting data and trendline, with equation and R^2 value, on the appropriate graph type (xy scatter, semilog, or log–log) to make the data appear linear.

(b) Assume the value of "m" in the resulting model is the growth constant. Use the trendline determined to find the value and units of the growth constant for this bacteria.

4. A growing field of inquiry that poses both great promise and great risk for humans is nanotechnology, the construction of extremely small machines. Over the past couple of decades, the size that a working gear can be made has consistently gotten smaller. The table shows milestones along this path.

Years from 1967	0	5	7	16	25	31	37
Minimum gear size [mm]	0.8	0.4	0.2	0.09	0.007	2E-04	8E-06

(a) Show the resulting data and trendline, with equation and R^2 value, on the appropriate graph type (xy scatter, semilog, or log–log) to make the data appear linear.

(b) According to this model, how many years does it take (from any point in time) for the minimum size to be cut in half?

(c) According to the model, during what year will the smallest gear be one-tenth the size of the smallest gear in 2009?

5. If an object is heated, the temperature of the object will increase. The thermal energy (Q) associated with a change in temperature (ΔT) is a function of the mass of the object (m) and the specific heat (C_p). Specific heat is a material property, and values are available in literature. In an experiment, heat is applied to the end of an object, and the temperature change at the other end of the object is recorded. An unknown material is tested in the lab, yielding the following results.

Heat applied (Q) [J]	2	8	10	13	18	27
Temp change (ΔT) [K]	1.5	6.0	7.0	9.0	14.0	22.0

(a) Show the resulting data and trendline, with equation and R^2 value, on the appropriate graph type (xy scatter, semilog, or log–log) to make the data appear linear.

(b) If the material was titanium, what mass of sample was tested?

(c) If a 4-gram sample was used, which of the following materials was tested?

Material	Specific Heat Capacity (C_p) [J/(g K)]
Aluminum	0.91
Copper	0.39
Iron	0.44
Lead	0.13
Molybdenum	0.30
Titanium	0.54

6. The Volcanic Explosivity Index (*VEI*) is based primarily on the amount of material ejected from a volcano, although other factors play a role as well, such as height of plume in the atmosphere. The table below shows the number of volcanic eruptions (N) over the past 10,000 years having a VEI of between 2 and 7.

There are also VEI values of 0, 1, and 8. There is a level 0 volcano erupting somewhere on the Earth essentially all the time. There are one or more level 1 volcanoes essentially every day. The last known level 8 volcano was about 26,000 years ago.

Volcanic Explosivity Index (*VEI*) [–]	Number of Eruptions (*N*) [–]
2	3,477
3	868
4	421
5	168
6	51
7	5

(a) Show the resulting data and trendline, with equation and R^2 value, on the appropriate graph type (xy scatter, semilog, or log–log) to make the data appear linear.

(b) How many level 1 volcanoes does the model predict should have occurred in the last 10,000 years?

(c) How many level 8 volcanoes does the model predict should have occurred in the last 10,000 years?

7. Biosystems engineers often need to understand how plant diseases spread in order to formulate effective control strategies. The rate of spread of some diseases is more or less linear, some increase exponentially, and some do not really fit any standard mathematical model.

Grey leaf spot of corn is a disease (caused by a fungus with the rather imposing name of *Cercospora zeae-maydis*) that causes chlorotic (lacking chlorophyll) lesions and eventually necrotic (dead) lesions on corn leaves, thus reducing total photosynthesis and yield. In extremely severe cases, loss of the entire crop can result.

During a study of this disease, the number of lesions per corn leaf was counted every 10 days following the initial observation of the disease, which we call day 0. At this time, there was an average of one lesion on every 20 leaves, or 0.05 lesions per leaf. The data collected during the growing season are tabulated.

(a) Show the resulting data and trendline, with equation and R^2 value, on the appropriate graph type (*xy* scatter, semilog, or log–log) to make the data appear linear.

(b) According to the model, how many lesions were there per leaf at the start of the survey?

(c) How many lesions are there per leaf after 97 days?

(d) If the model continued to be accurate, how many days would be required to reach 250 lesions per leaf?

Day	Lesions per Leaf	Day	Lesions per Leaf
0	0.05	110	4
20	0.10	120	6
30	0.20	140	17
40	0.26	150	20
60	0.60	170	40
80	1.30	190	112
90	2	200	151

8. A **pitot tube** is a device used to measure the velocity of a fluid, typically, the airspeed of an aircraft. The failure of a pitot tube is credited as the cause of Austral Líneas Aéreas flight 2553 crash in October 1997. The pitot tube had frozen, causing the instrument to give a false reading of slowing speed. As a result, the pilots thought the plane was slowing down, so they increased the speed and attempted to maintain their altitude by lowering the wing slats. Actually, they were flying at such a high speed that one of the slats ripped off, causing the plane to nosedive; the plane crashed at a speed of 745 miles per hour.

In the pitot tube, as the fluid moves, the velocity creates a pressure difference between the ends of a small tube. The tubes are calibrated to relate the pressure measured to a specific velocity. This velocity is a function of the pressure difference (P, in units of pascals) and the density of the fluid (ρ in units of kilogram per cubic meter).

$$v = \left(\frac{2}{\rho}\right)^{0.5} P^m$$

Pressure (P) [Pa]	50,000	101,325	202,650	250,000	304,000	350,000	405,000	505,000
Velocity fluid A (v_A) [m/s]	11.25	16.00	23.00	25.00	28.00	30.00	32.00	35.75
Velocity fluid B (v_B) [m/s]	7.50	11.00	15.50	17.00	19.00	20.00	22.00	24.50

Fluid	Specific Gravity
Acetone	0.79
Citric acid	1.67
Glycerin	1.26
Mineral Oil	0.90

(a) Show the resulting data and trendline, with equation and R^2 value, on the appropriate graph type (*xy* scatter, semilog, or log–log) to make the data appear linear.

(b) Determine the value and units of the density for each data set using the trendline equations.

(c) From the chart at left, match each data set (A, B) with the correct fluid name according to the results of the density determined from the trendlines.

9. As part of an electronic music synthesizer, you need to build a gizmo to convert a linear voltage to an exponentially related current. You build three prototype circuits and make several measurements of voltage and current in each. The collected data is given in the table below.

Circuit A		Circuit B		Circuit C	
Voltage (V_A) [V]	Current (I_A) [mA]	Voltage (V_B)[V]	Current (I_B) [mA]	Voltage (V_C) [V]	Current (I_C) [mA]
−2.7	0.28	−2.7	0.11	0	0.79
−0.4	1.05	−1.5	0.36	0.5	1.59
0	1.74	0	1.34	1.4	5.41
1.2	3.17	0.8	2.37	2.3	20.28
2.9	7.74	2.6	14.53	2.9	41.44

(a) Show the resulting data and trendline, with equation and R^2 value, on the appropriate graph type (*xy* scatter, semilog, or log–log) to make the data appear linear.

(b) Which of the three circuits comes the closest to doubling the current for an increase of one volt? Note that this doubling is independent of the actual values of voltage. Example: If the current was 0.3 mA at 2.7 volts, it should be 0.6 mA at 3.7 volts, 1.2 mA at 4.7 volts, 2.4 mA at 5.7 volts, etc.

(c) Calculate the value that should appear in the exponent if the current is to double with each increase of 1 volt. Note that you should perform this calculation without referring to the data, the plots, or the trendline equations. This is a purely theoretical calculation.

10. The data below was collected during testing of an electromagnetic mass driver. The energy to energize the electromagnets was obtained from a bank of capacitors. The capacitor bank was charged to various voltages, and for each voltage, the exit velocity of the projectile was measured when the mass driver was activated.

Voltage (V) [kV]	9	13	15	18	22	25
Velocity (v_p) [m/s]	430	530	580	650	740	810

(a) Show the resulting data and trendline, with equation and R^2 value, on the appropriate graph type (*xy* scatter, semilog, or log-log) to make the data appear linear.

(b) What would the velocity be if the capacitors were charged to 1,000 volts?

(c) What voltage would be necessary to accelerate the projectile to 1,000 meters per second?

(d) Assume that the total capacitance is 5 farads. If the capacitors are initially charged to 10,000 volts and are discharged to 2,000 volts during the launch of a projectile, what is the mass of the projectile if the overall conversion of energy stored in the capacitors to kinetic energy in the projectile has an efficiency of 0.2? Recall that the energy stored in a capacitor is given by $E = 0.5\ CV^2$, where C is capacitance in farads and V is voltage in volts.

NOTE

Due to several complicated nonlinear losses in the system that are far beyond the scope of this course, this is a case of a model in which the exponent does not come out to be an integer or simple fraction, so rounding to two significant figures is appropriate. In fact, this model is only a first approximation— a really accurate model would be considerably more complicated.

11. The relationship of the power required by a propeller (shown as the power number, on the ordinate) and the Reynolds number (abscissa) is shown in the graph below. For a propeller, the Reynolds number (Re) is written slightly differently, as

$$Re = \frac{D^2 n \rho}{\mu}$$

where D is the blade diameter [meters] and n is the shaft speed [hertz]. The power number (N_p) is given by the following, where P is the power required [watts].

$$N_p = \frac{P}{\rho n^3 D^5}$$

Use the chart below to answer the following questions:

(a) If the Reynolds number is 500, what is the power number for a system described by Curve A?

(b) If the power number (N_p) is 30, what is the Reynolds number for a system described by Curve A?

(c) If the Reynolds number is 4,000, what is the power (P) required in units of watts at a shaft speed (n) of 0.03 hertz? Assume the system contains acetone, with a kinematic viscosity of 0.419 stokes. The density of acetone is 0.785 grams per cubic centimeter. Use Curve B in the graph to determine your answer. (*Hint:* Use the Reynolds number of the system to first calculate the diameter, then find the power number, and then calculate the power.)

(d) If the power number (N_p) is 5, what is the diameter (D) of the blade in units of centimeters at a shaft speed (n) of 0.02 hertz? Assume the system contains brine, with a kinematic viscosity of 0.0102 stokes. Use Curve A in the graph to determine your answer. (*Hint:* Find the Reynolds number of the system first, and then calculate the diameter.)

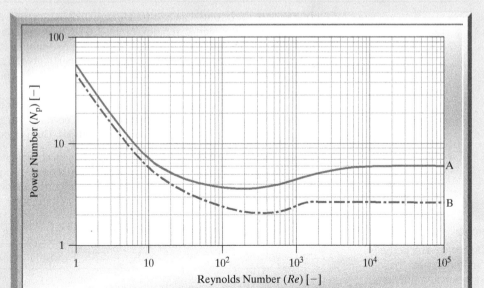

Ethylene glycol has a dynamic viscosity of 9.13 centipoise and a specific gravity of 1.109.

(c) If the fluid flows around a sphere of diameter 1 centimeter travelling at a velocity of 2.45 centimeters per second, determine the drag force on the particle in units of newtons. (*Hint:* First determine the Reynolds number.)

(d) If a coefficient of drag of 10 is produced, what is the diameter of the particle? Assume the fluid is moving at 1 centimeter per second. (*Hint:* First determine the Reynolds number.)

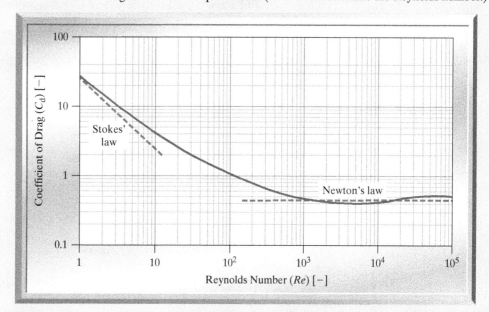

13. When discussing the flow of a fluid through a piping system, we say that friction occurs between the fluid and the pipe wall due to viscous drag. The loss of energy due to the friction of fluid against the pipe wall is described by the friction factor. The Darcy friction factor (f) was developed by Henry Darcy (1803–1858), a French scientist who made several important contributions to the field of hydraulics. The friction factor depends upon several other factors, including flow regime, Reynolds number, and pipe roughness. The friction factor can be determined in several ways, including the Moody diagram (discussed in ICA 13-22) and several mathematical approximations presented here.

In the laminar flow range, the *Darcy friction factor* can be determined by the following formula, shown as the linear line on the Moody diagram: (see ICA 13-22 for the Moody diagram)

$$f = \frac{64}{Re}$$

In the turbulent range, the friction factor is a function of the Reynolds number and the roughness of the pipe (ε). For turbulent flow smooth pipes (where the relative roughness ratio (ε/D) is very small), the *Blasius formula* can be used to calculate an approximate value for the Darcy friction factor.

$$f = 0.316\,(Re)^{-1/4}$$

This simple formula was developed by Paul Richard Heinrich Blasius (1883–1970), a German fluid dynamics engineer. Later, a more accurate but more complex formula was developed in 1939 by C. F. Colebrook. Unlike the Blasius formula, the Colebrook formula directly takes into account the pipe roughness.

The *Colebrook formula* is shown below. Notice that both sides of the equation contain the friction factor, requiring an iterative solution.

$$\frac{1}{\sqrt{f}} = -2\log\left(\frac{\varepsilon/D}{3.7} + \frac{2.51}{Re\sqrt{f}}\right)$$

To begin the iteration, the Colebrook calculation must have an initial value. Use the Blasius approximation as the first value for f, and determine the first iterative value of the Colebrook equation to use as your friction factor.

While this will only give us an approximation of the correct friction factor, a true solution requires using iteration. If you have covered iteration in Excel (see Appendix Materials), your instructor may provide other instructions on how to determine f.

Prepare an Excel worksheet to compute the friction factor.

Sample Data						
Fluid	Water		Pipe Type	Commercial Steel		
Density (ρ) [g/cm^3]	Viscosity (μ) [cP]	Volumetric Flowrate (Q) [gpm]	Diameter (D) [in]	Roughness (ε) [mm]	Reynolds Number (Re) [-]	Flow Regime
1	1.002	500	6	0.045	263,020	Turbulent

Darcy Friction Factor (f) [-]			Initial f Value			
Laminar	Colebrook		Blasius		Moody Value	
	0.0174		0.0140		0.0185	

Input Parameters:

- Fluid: should be chosen from a drop-down list using the material properties listed below. Used with the lookup function to determine:
  - Density   (ε) [grams per cubic centimeter]
  - Viscosity   (μ) [centipoises]
  - Volumetric flow rate   (Q) [gallons per minute]
  - Diameter   (D) [inches]
- Type of pipe: should be chosen from a drop-down list using the properties listed below. Used with the lookup function to determine:
  - Pipe roughness   (ε) [millimeters]

Output Parameters:

Be sure to include the appropriate unit conversions. You may add cells to the worksheet template to complete the necessary unit conversions.

- Reynolds number.
- Flow regime (laminar, transitional, or turbulent).
- Only the correct Darcy friction factor (one of these two values) should be displayed based on the flow regime.
  - For laminar flow, use the equation: $f = 64/Re$.
  - For turbulent flow determined with the Colebrook formula, use the Blasius equation as the initial f value.
- Determine the friction factor by hand from the Moody diagram (see ICA 13-22) and list the value found from the graph in the worksheet, as a comparison to your determined value.

Use the following parameters as a test case:

- Fluid = Acetone
- Pipe Type = Cast Iron
- Volumetric Flowrate = 50 gpm
- Pipe Diameter = 2 in

COMPREHENSION CHECK ANSWERS

CHAPTER 7

CC 7-1

Standard	Scientific	Engineering	With Prefix
(a) 3,100 J	3.1×10^3 J	3.1×10^3 J	3.1 kJ
(b) 26,510,000 W	2.651×10^7 W	26.51×10^6 W	26.51 MW
(c) 459,000 s	4.59×10^5 s	459×10^3 s	459 ks
(d) 0.00000032 g	3.2×10^{-7} g	320×10^{-9} g	320 ng

CC 7-2

(a) Incorrect: 5 s
(b) Incorrect: 60 mm
(c) Incorrect: 3,800 mL OR 3.8 L

CC 7-3

5.5 mi

CC 7-4

1,800 min

CC 7-5

5×10^{-9} pL

CC 7-6

2 km/min

CC 7-7

26 flushes

CC 7-8

84 ft^3

CC 7-9

14 cubits

CC 7-10

10.3 m/s

CC 7-11

	Common	Dimensions						
Quantity	Units	M	L	T	Θ	N	J	I
Density	lb$_m$/ft^3	1	−3	0	0	0	0	0
Evaporation	slug/h	1	0	−1	0	0	0	0
Flowrate	gal/min	0	3	−1	0	0	0	0

CC 7-12

	Common	Dimensions						
Quantity	Units	M	L	T	Θ	N	J	I
Energy	calories	1	2	−2	0	0	0	0
Power	horsepower	1	2	−3	0	0	0	0
Pressure	atmospheres	1	−1	−2	0	0	0	0
Voltage	volts	1	2	−3	0	0	0	1

CC 7-13

B. Energy

CC 7-14

M	L	T	Θ	N	J	I
1	2	−3	0	0	0	−2

CC 7-15

No; the quantity on the left hand side $\{=\}$L/T and the quantity on the right hand side $\{=\}$L^2/T

CC 7-16

(a) 210 Tm
(b) 0.022 light years

CC 7-17

2.72 gal

CHAPTER 8

CC 8-1

161,000 $\dfrac{\text{mi}}{\text{h}^2}$

CC 8-2

13.3 N

CC 8-3

2.2 N

CC 8-4

3120 $\dfrac{\text{lb}_m}{\text{ft}^3}$

CC 8-5

1.53

CC 8-6

4.85 g

CC 8-7

0.03 moles

CC 8-8

194.5 K

CC 8-9

$0.000357 \dfrac{\text{BTU}}{\text{gK}}$

CC 8-10

221 in Hg

CC 8-11

1.22 atm

CC 8-12

220 kPa

CC 8-13

2.4 L

CC 8-14

16.9 m

CC 8-15

20 K

CC 8-16

0.83 h

CC 8-17

1.04 h

CC 8-18

61.3 W

CC 8-19

0.3 V

CC 8-20

14.4 W

CC 8-21

−1.07 μA

CC 8-22

$\dfrac{1}{\text{S}}$

CHAPTER 9

CC 9-1

B. $MT^{-3}\Theta$

CC 9-2

D. Dimensionless

CC 9-3

$M^{-1}L^3$

CC 9-4

$\dfrac{\Delta P}{\rho v^2}$

CHAPTER 10

CC 10-1

Relative addressing; cell F23 displays 13

CC 10-2

Absolute addressing; cell H26 displays 30

CC 10-3

Mixed addressing
Cell G30 displays 30
Cell F28 displays 5

CC 10-4

Mixed addressing
Cell G30 displays 5
Cell J28 displays 30

CC 10-5

A1.	12
A2.	11
A3.	10
A4.	32
A5.	3.14159265
A6.	#NAME? (Excel doesn't understand "PI" without the function parenthesis)
A7.	110
A8.	48
A9.	1.570796
A10.	1
A11.	0.893997
A12.	0.785408
A13.	45.00055
A14.	#NAME? (Excel does not have a function named "cubrt")
Correct expression:	or =27^(1/3) =POWER(27,1/3)

CC 10-6

B

CC 10-7

The cell will be blank
32
B9

CC 10-8

A
C
B

CC 10-9

No
YES
No
YES
No

CC 10-10

** See video in online materials

CC 10-11

** See video in online materials

CC 10-12

City ascending: Fountain Inn

City descending first, Site Name descending second: Rochester Property

Contaminant ascending first, Site Name ascending second: Sangamo Weston

CHAPTER 11

CC 11-1

- No axis labels
- Is year 1 1993 or 2000 or . . .?
- Need different line types
- Missing vertical gridlines

CC 11-2

- No units or description of axis quantities (what is T?)
- Need different symbols
- No legend shown
- Need gridlines if wish to read data

CC 11-3

- Missing units on both axis
- Should be line only, no points
- No legend needed
- Poor choice of increment on abscissa (count by 27)
- Too many decimals displayed on ordinate

CC 11-4

- No variable names given
- Abscissa labels do not show enough decimals to distinguish between gridlines (0.25, 0.5, 0.75, 1 . . .)
- Poor choice of increment on ordinate (major grid count by 8, minor grid counts by 1.6)
- Need legend
- Different line types needed

CC 11-5

18 meters

32 meters

CC 11-6

(a) 2. Positive and constant
(b) 1. Zero
(c) 5. Negative and constant
(d) 3. Positive and increasing
(e) 3. Positive and increasing
(f) 3. Positive and increasing

CC 11-7

(a) Machine 2
(b) Machine 2
(c) 1×10^6 feet
(d) Machine 2
(e) Machine 1

CC 11-8

(a) Fixed: $2500; Variable: $50/year
(b) Approximately $750/year
(c) 2.5 years
(d) 4 years

CHAPTER 12

CC 12-1

(a) atm/K   **(b)** 35.6 g   **(c)** 14.1 L

CC 12-2

63.1 lb_m/ft^3

CC 12-3

3.36×10^{-4} lb$_m$/(ft s)

CC 12-4

4.55×10^{-3} St

CC 12-5

There are 17 unique spring stiffnesses.
Each spring can be used alone. There are three unique stiffnesses: 1 N/m, 2 N/m, 3 N/m
The following parallel combinations are possible:

Parallel Combination	Effective Spring Constant
Spring 1 (1 N/m) + Spring 2 (2 N/m)	3 N/m
Spring 1 (1 N/m) + Spring 2 (2 N/m)	4 N/m
Spring 2 (2 N/m) + Spring 3 (3 N/m)	5 N/m
Spring 1 (1 N/m) + Spring 2 (2 N/m) + Spring 3 (3 N/m)	6 N/m

The following series combinations are possible:

Series Combination	Effective Spring Constant
Spring 1 (1 N/m) + Spring 2 (2 N/m)	0.67 N/m
Spring 1 (1 N/m) + Spring 3 (3 N/m)	0.75 N/m
Spring 2 (2 N/m) + Spring 3 (3 N/m)	1.2 N/m
Spring 1 (1 N/m) + Spring 2 (2 N/m) + Spring 3 (3 N/m)	0.54 N/m

Another combination is to place two in series, and connect that combination to a third in parallel.

Combination in Series...	Connected in Parallel to...	Effective Spring Constant
Spring 1 (1 N/m) + Spring 2 (2 N/m)	Spring 3 (3 N/m)	3.67 N/m
Spring 1 (1 N/m) + Spring 3 (3 N/m)	Spring 2 (2 N/m)	2.75 N/m
Spring 2 (2 N/m) + Spring 3 (3 N/m)	Spring 1 (1 N/m)	2.2 N/m

The final combination is to place two in parallel, and connect that combination to a third in series.

Combination in Parallel...	Connected in Series to...	Effective Spring Constant
Spring 1 (1 N/m) + Spring 2 (2 N/m)	Spring 3 (3 N/m)	1.5 N/m
Spring 1 (1 N/m) + Spring 3 (3 N/m)	Spring 2 (2 N/m)	1.3 N/m
Spring 2 (2 N/m) + Spring 3 (3 N/m)	Spring 1 (1 N/m)	0.83 N/m

CC 12-6

There are 12 unique combinations.

The following combinations are possible: NOTE: Units on all values are ohms [Ω].

Singles: 2, 3

2 in series: 4, 5

2 in parallel: 1, 1.2

3 in series: 7

3 in parallel: 0.75

Series combination of 2 in parallel with third: 1.72, 1.43

Parallel combination of 2 in series with third: 4, 3.2

CC 12-7

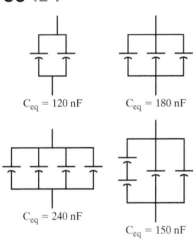

$C_{eq} = 120$ nF $C_{eq} = 180$ nF

$C_{eq} = 240$ nF

$C_{eq} = 150$ nF

CC 12-8

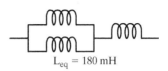

$L_{eq} = 180$ mH

CC 12-9

11.4 g

CC 12-10

117 °C

CC 12-11

$C_0 = 35$ g; $k = 1$ h^{-1}

CHAPTER 13

CC 13-1

$V = 50\,P^{-1}$

CC 13-2

$V = 30\,e^{-0.89t}$

CC 13-3

$y = -25.6\,e^{0.06\,x}$

CC 13-4

Data is exponential. The vertical offset is 5°F

$T = 5 - 20\,e^{-0.022\,t}$